How Do We Relationship?

4

STORY AND ART BY

Tamifull

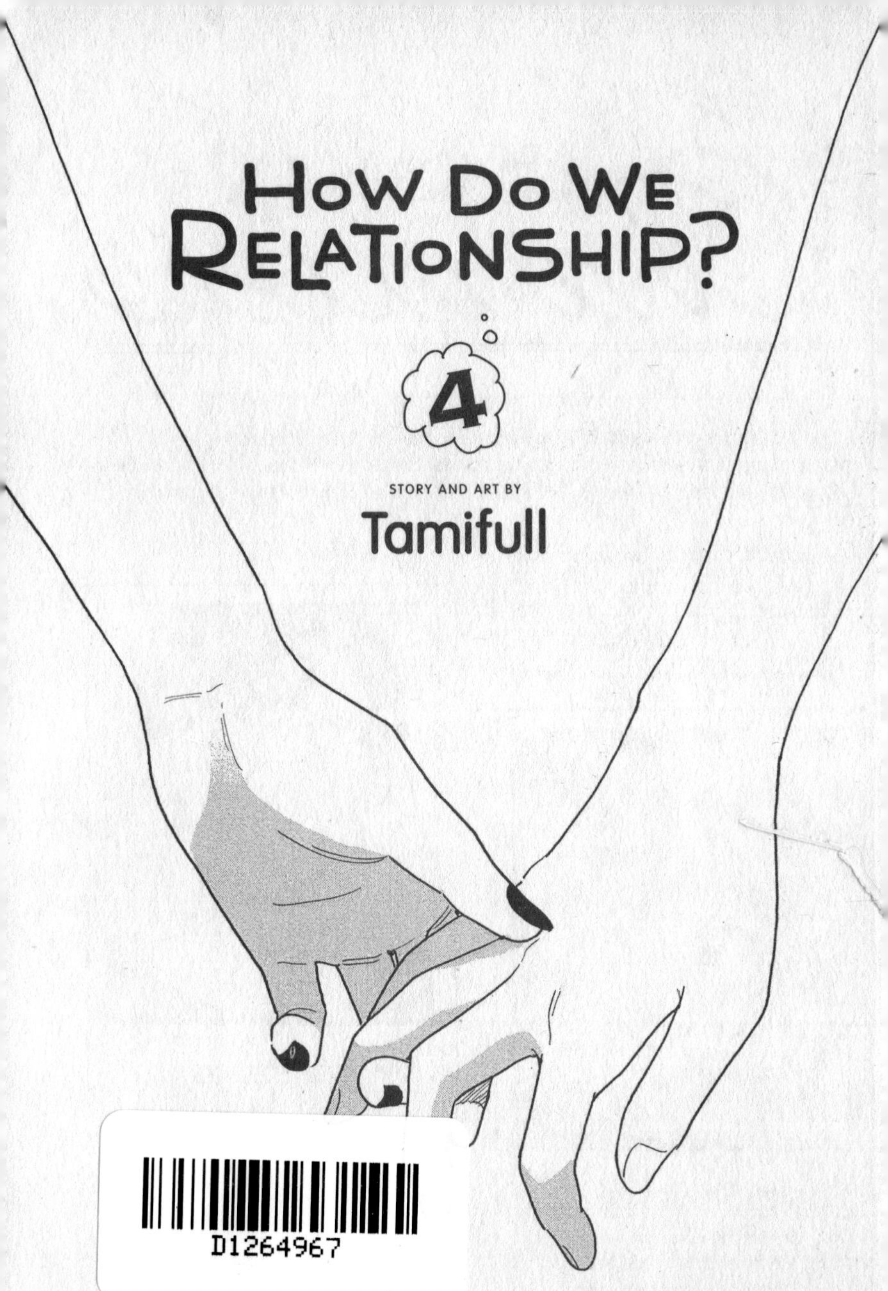

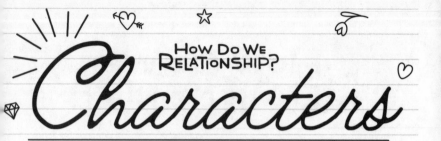

HOW DO WE RELATIONSHIP?
Characters

S U M M A R Y

Saeko and Miwa open up to each other and say "I like girls!" on the night of their band club's welcome party for new students, then ride that wave right into dating. It's a total romance, interwoven with the tales of the lives of their light music club friends!

Band Club 1ST-YEARS

Miwa Inuzuka (Bass)

She's really popular, but she's never fallen in love with someone who likes her back. Saeko is her first girlfriend.

Saeko Sawatari (Guitar)

She has an assertive presence in the club and a bad habit of getting jealous over Miwa.

They're dating ♡

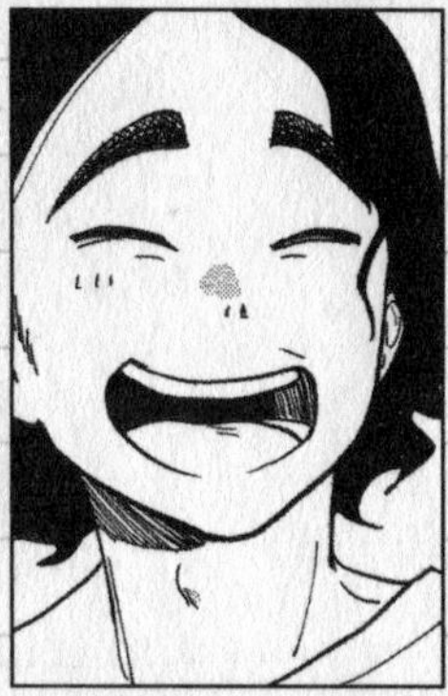

Mikkun (Vocals)

A pessimist to the bone. He's cheerful, though, and good at singing.

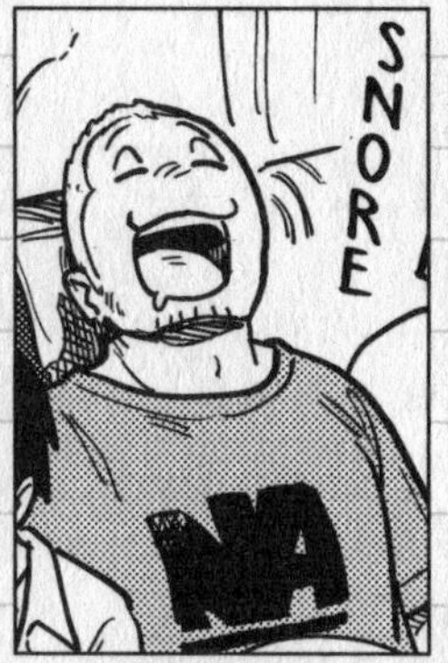
SNORE

Lucha (Guitar)

A refreshing and lovable character with an outsized body. Came from an all-boys' high school.

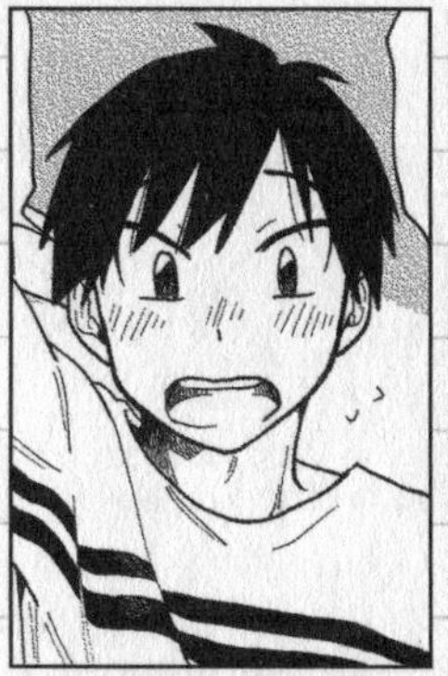

Tsuruta (Drums)

Fell in love with Miwa at first sight, and immediately confessed. He's got no chill when it comes to girls.

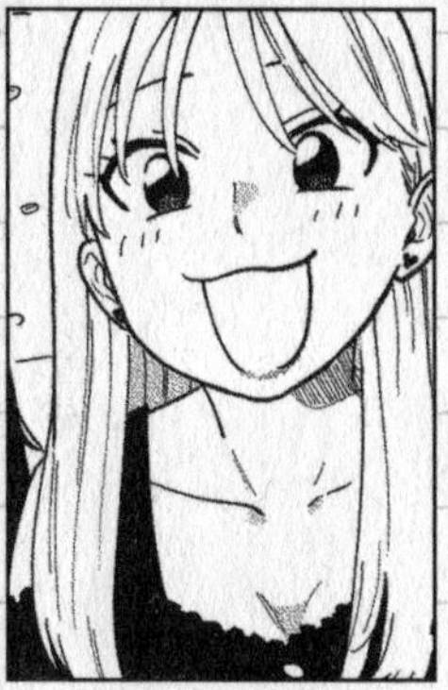

Rika (Vocals)

The crazy girl of the club. She's uninhibited when it comes to sex and is occasionally an airhead.

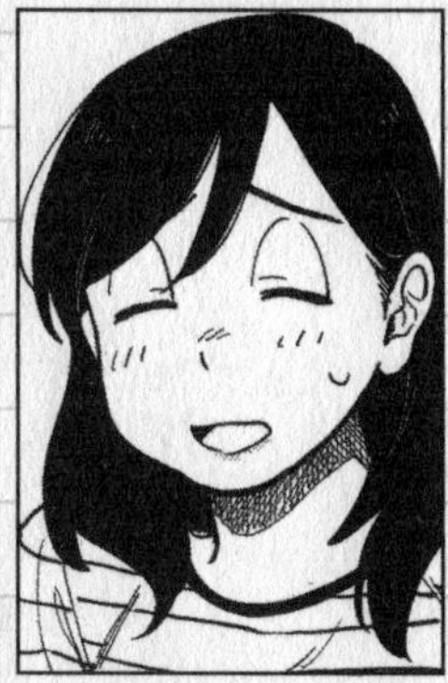

Usshi (Guitar)

The one with the most common sense. She has anxieties about her lack of romantic experience.

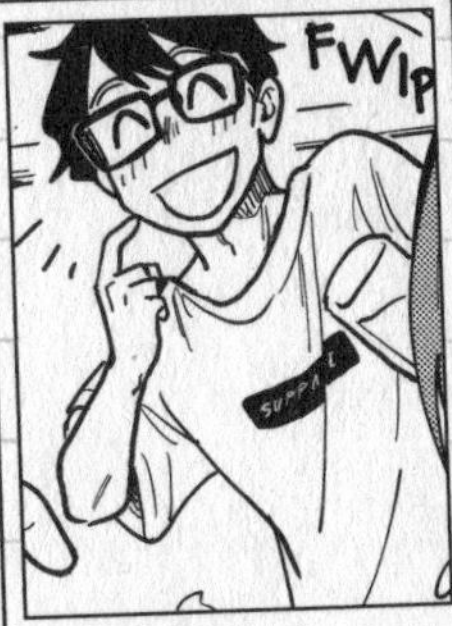
FWIP

Inoken (Drums)

Just a little bit annoying. He's interested in Miwa.

THE LOVELY UPPERCLASSMEN

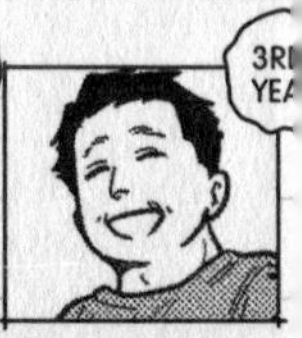

The President

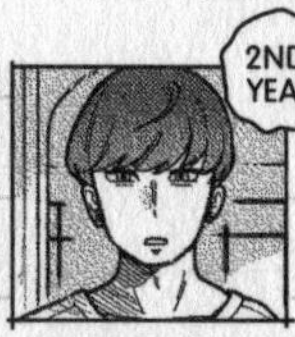
2ND-YEAR

Kan

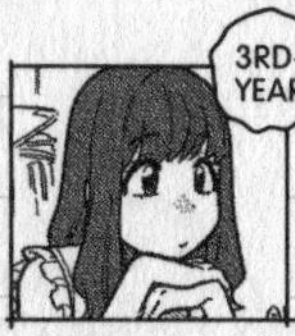
3RD-YEAR

Arisa

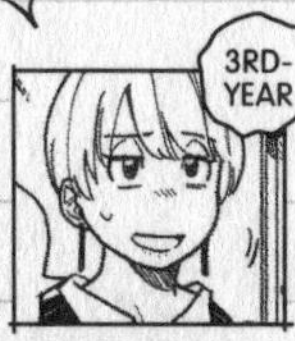
3RD-YEAR

Mozu

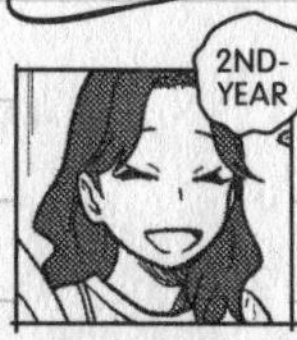
2ND-YEAR

Miho

Contents.

Chapter 28: A Lie for You

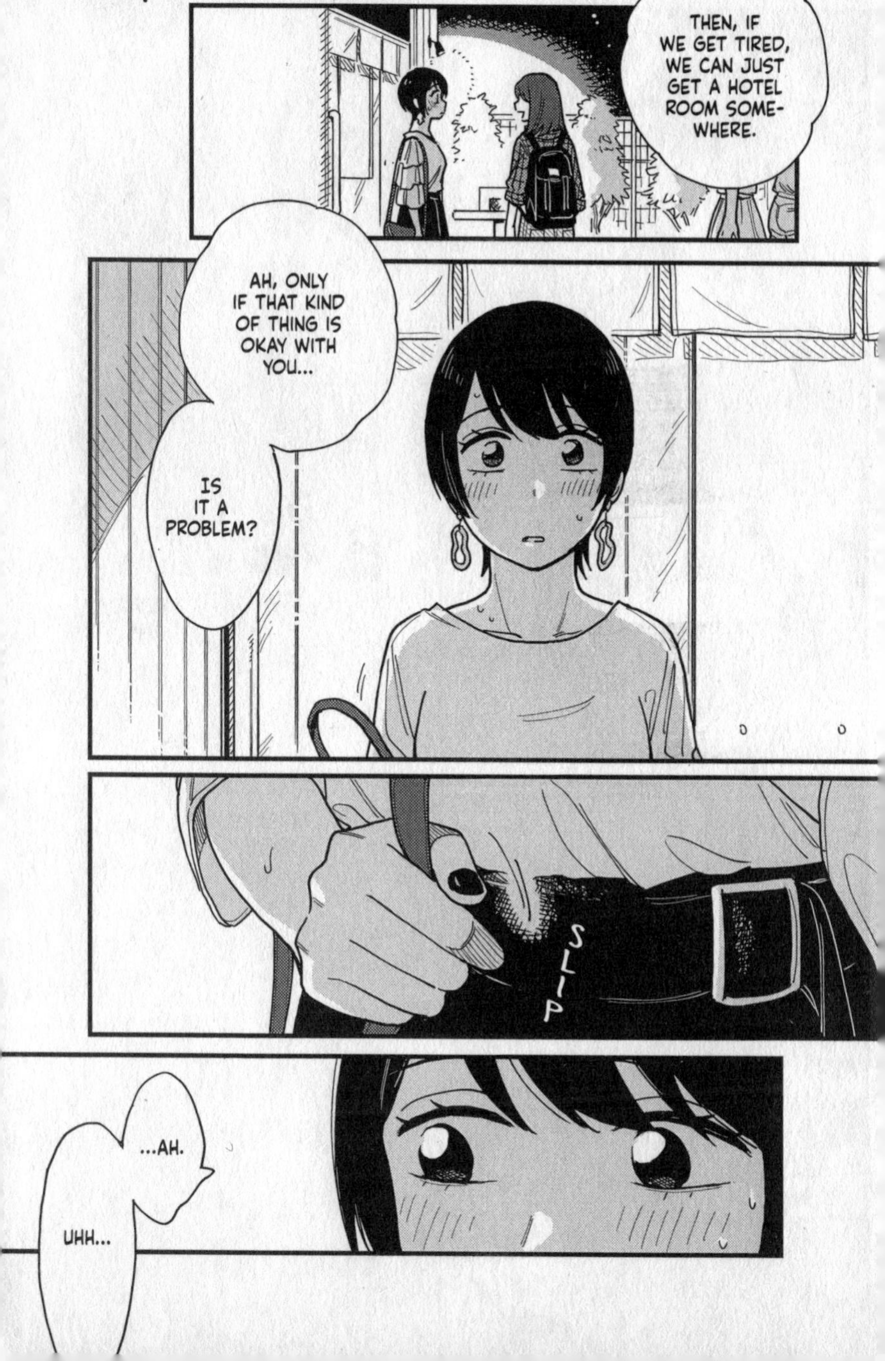
THEN, IF WE GET TIRED, WE CAN JUST GET A HOTEL ROOM SOMEWHERE.
AH, ONLY IF THAT KIND OF THING IS OKAY WITH YOU...
IS IT A PROBLEM?
SLIP
...AH.
UHH...

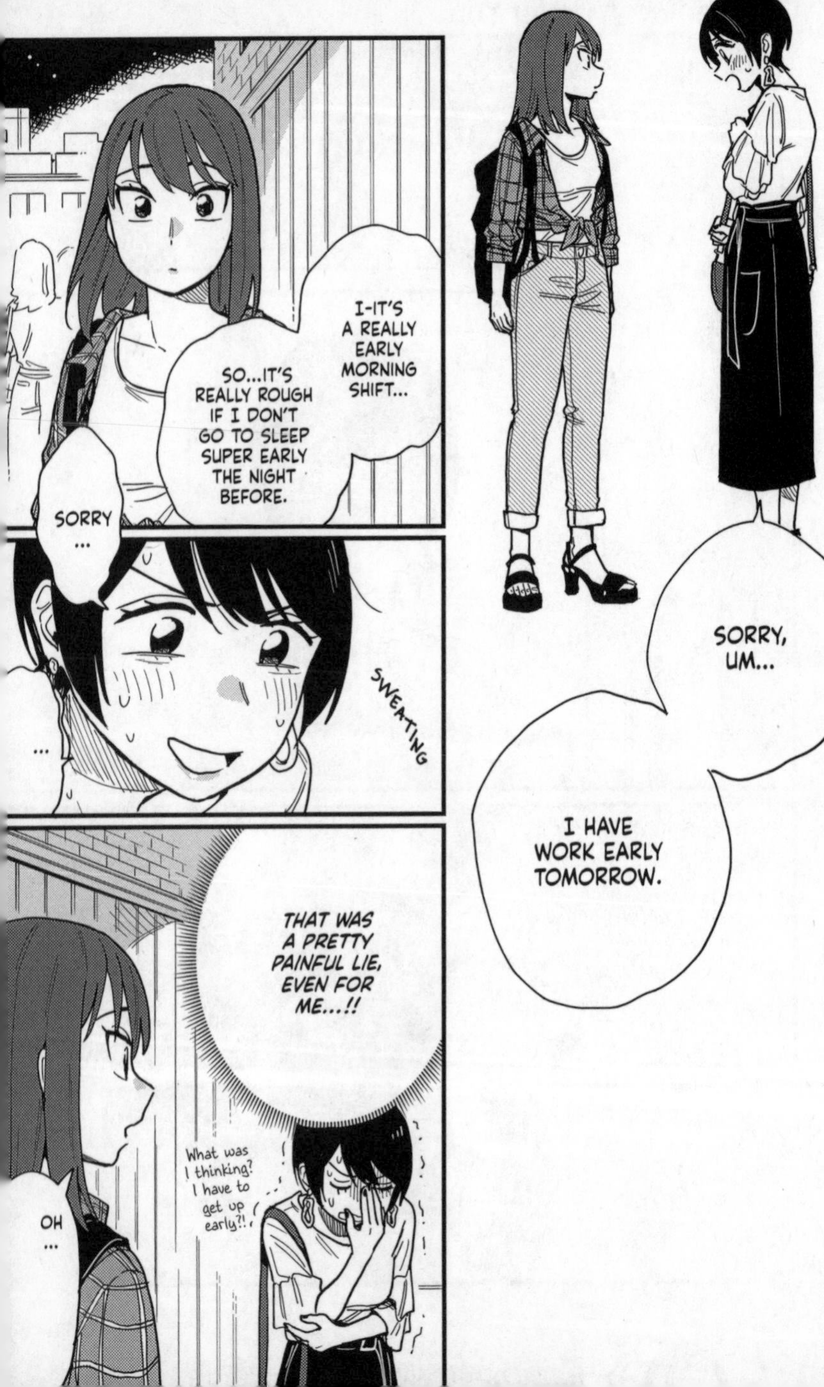

SORRY, UM...
I HAVE WORK EARLY TOMORROW.
I-IT'S A REALLY EARLY MORNING SHIFT...
SO...IT'S REALLY ROUGH IF I DON'T GO TO SLEEP SUPER EARLY THE NIGHT BEFORE.
SORRY ...
SWEATING
...
THAT WAS A PRETTY PAINFUL LIE, EVEN FOR ME...!!
What was I thinking? I have to get up early?!
OH ...

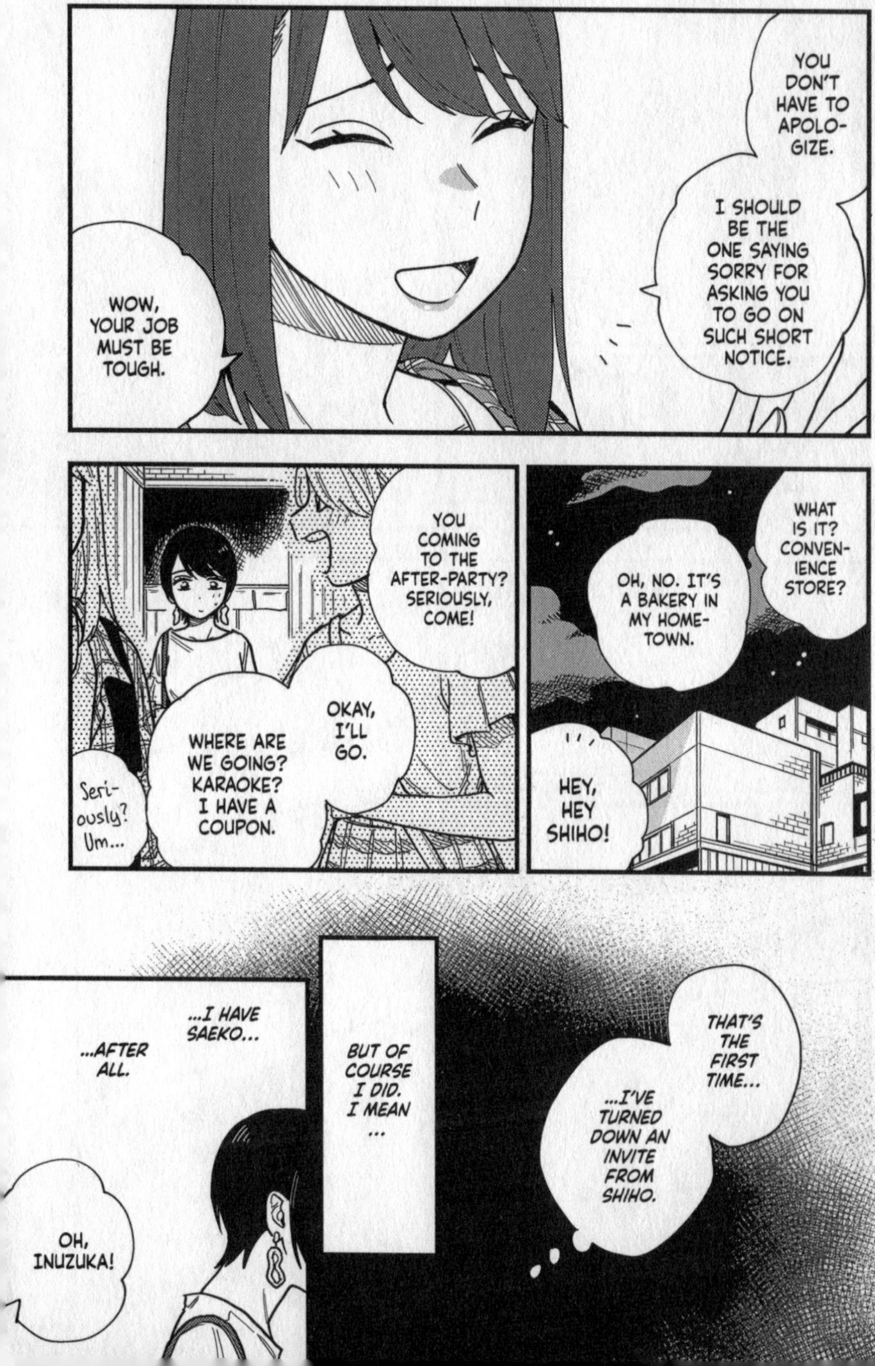
YOU DON'T HAVE TO APOLOGIZE.
I SHOULD BE THE ONE SAYING SORRY FOR ASKING YOU TO GO ON SUCH SHORT NOTICE.
WOW, YOUR JOB MUST BE TOUGH.
WHAT IS IT? CONVENIENCE STORE?
OH, NO. IT'S A BAKERY IN MY HOMETOWN.
HEY, HEY SHIHO!
YOU COMING TO THE AFTER-PARTY? SERIOUSLY, COME!
OKAY, I'LL GO.
WHERE ARE WE GOING? KARAOKE? I HAVE A COUPON.
Seriously? Um...
THAT'S THE FIRST TIME...
...I'VE TURNED DOWN AN INVITE FROM SHIHO.
BUT OF COURSE I DID. I MEAN...
...I HAVE SAEKO...
...AFTER ALL.
OH, INUZUKA!

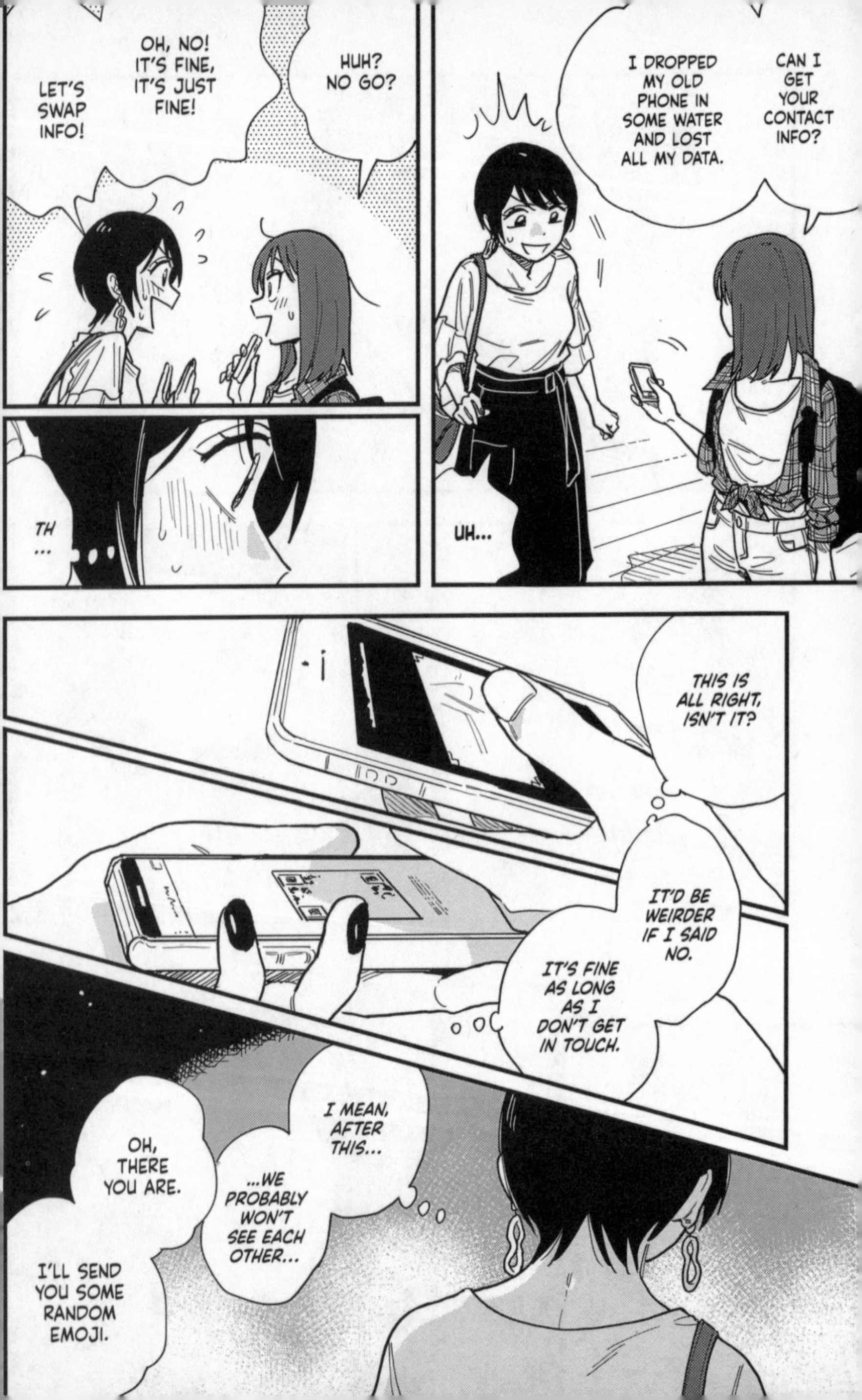
CAN I GET YOUR CONTACT INFO?
I DROPPED MY OLD PHONE IN SOME WATER AND LOST ALL MY DATA.
UH...
HUH? NO GO?
OH, NO! IT'S FINE, IT'S JUST FINE!
LET'S SWAP INFO!
TH...
THIS IS ALL RIGHT, ISN'T IT?
IT'D BE WEIRDER IF I SAID NO.
IT'S FINE AS LONG AS I DON'T GET IN TOUCH.
I MEAN, AFTER THIS...
...WE PROBABLY WON'T SEE EACH OTHER...
OH, THERE YOU ARE.
I'LL SEND YOU SOME RANDOM EMOJI.

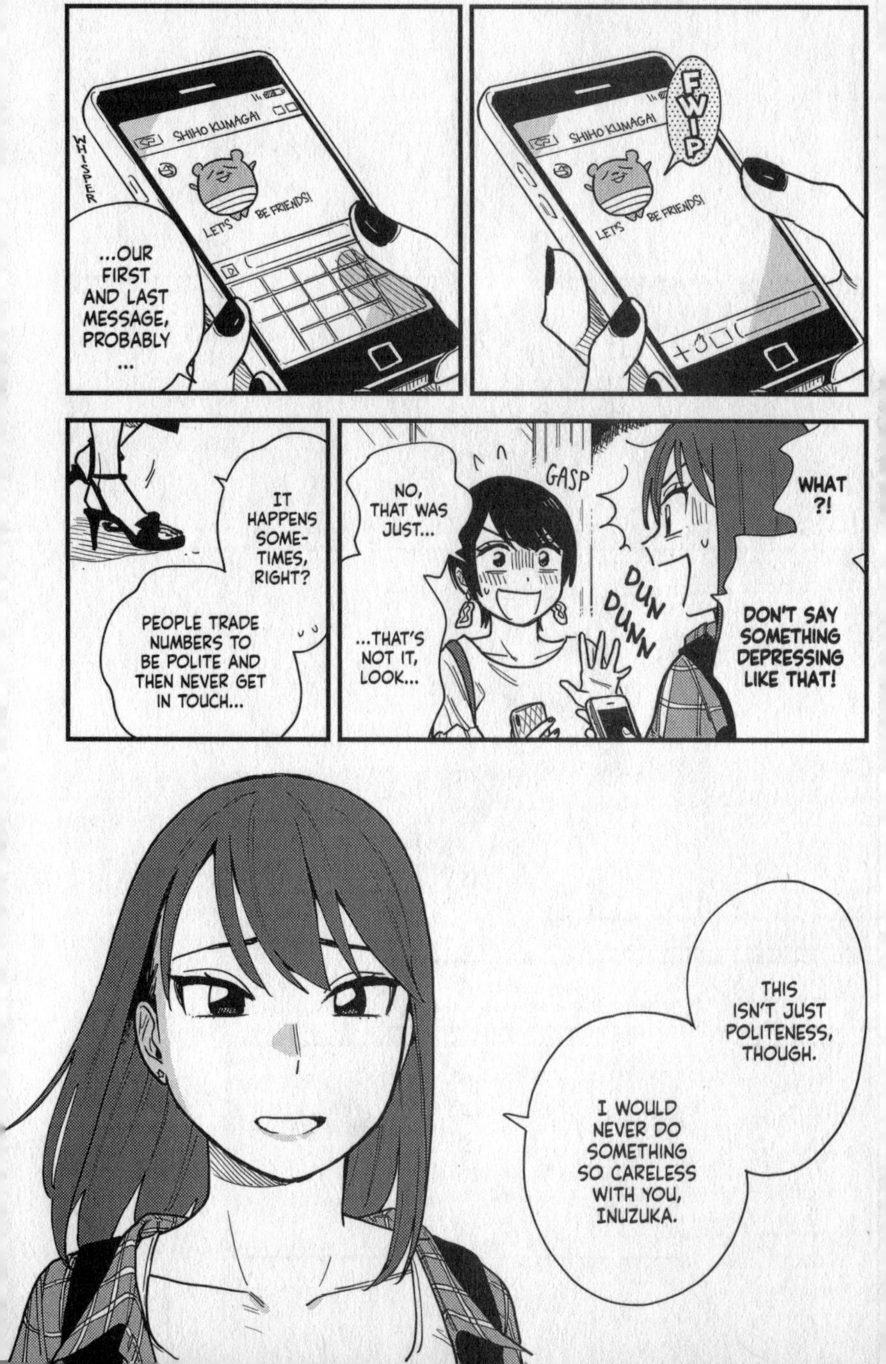
FWIP
SHIHO KUMAGAI
LET'S BE FRIENDS!
WHISPER
SHIHO KUMAGAI
LET'S BE FRIENDS!
...OUR FIRST AND LAST MESSAGE, PROBABLY...
WHAT?!
DON'T SAY SOMETHING DEPRESSING LIKE THAT!
DUN DUNN
GASP
NO, THAT WAS JUST...
...THAT'S NOT IT, LOOK...
IT HAPPENS SOME-TIMES, RIGHT?
PEOPLE TRADE NUMBERS TO BE POLITE AND THEN NEVER GET IN TOUCH...
THIS ISN'T JUST POLITENESS, THOUGH.
I WOULD NEVER DO SOMETHING SO CARELESS WITH YOU, INUZUKA.

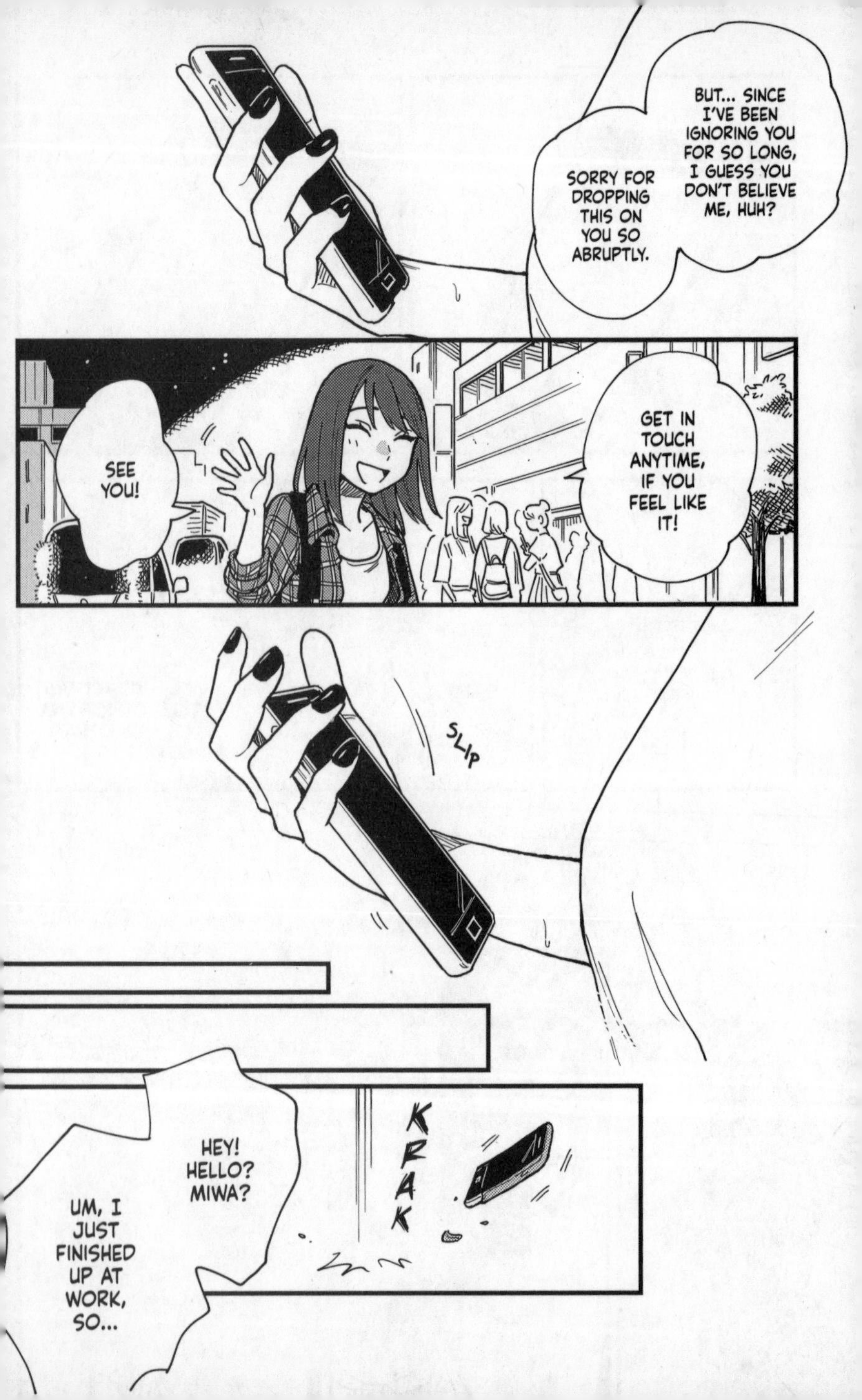
BUT... SINCE I'VE BEEN IGNORING YOU FOR SO LONG, I GUESS YOU DON'T BELIEVE ME, HUH?
SORRY FOR DROPPING THIS ON YOU SO ABRUPTLY.
GET IN TOUCH ANYTIME, IF YOU FEEL LIKE IT!
SEE YOU!
SLIP
KRAK
HEY! HELLO? MIWA?
UM, I JUST FINISHED UP AT WORK, SO...

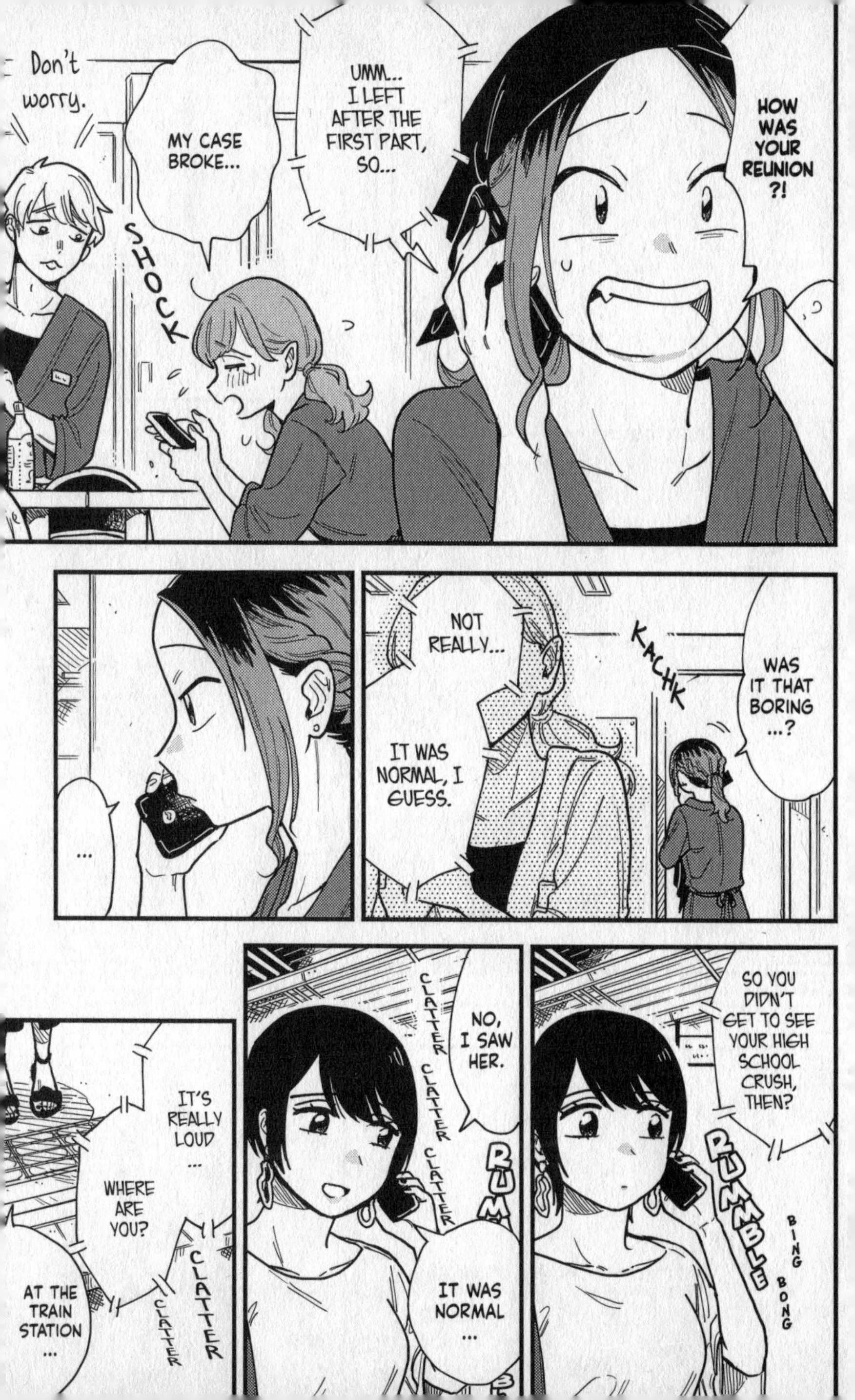
HOW WAS YOUR REUNION?!
UMM... I LEFT AFTER THE FIRST PART, SO...
MY CASE BROKE...
SHOCK
Don't worry.
WAS IT THAT BORING...?
KACHK
NOT REALLY...
IT WAS NORMAL, I GUESS.
...
SO YOU DIDN'T GET TO SEE YOUR HIGH SCHOOL CRUSH, THEN?
RUMBLE
BING BONG
NO, I SAW HER.
CLATTER CLATTER CLATTER
RUM
IT WAS NORMAL...
IT'S REALLY LOUD...
WHERE ARE YOU?
CLATTER
CLATTER
AT THE TRAIN STATION...

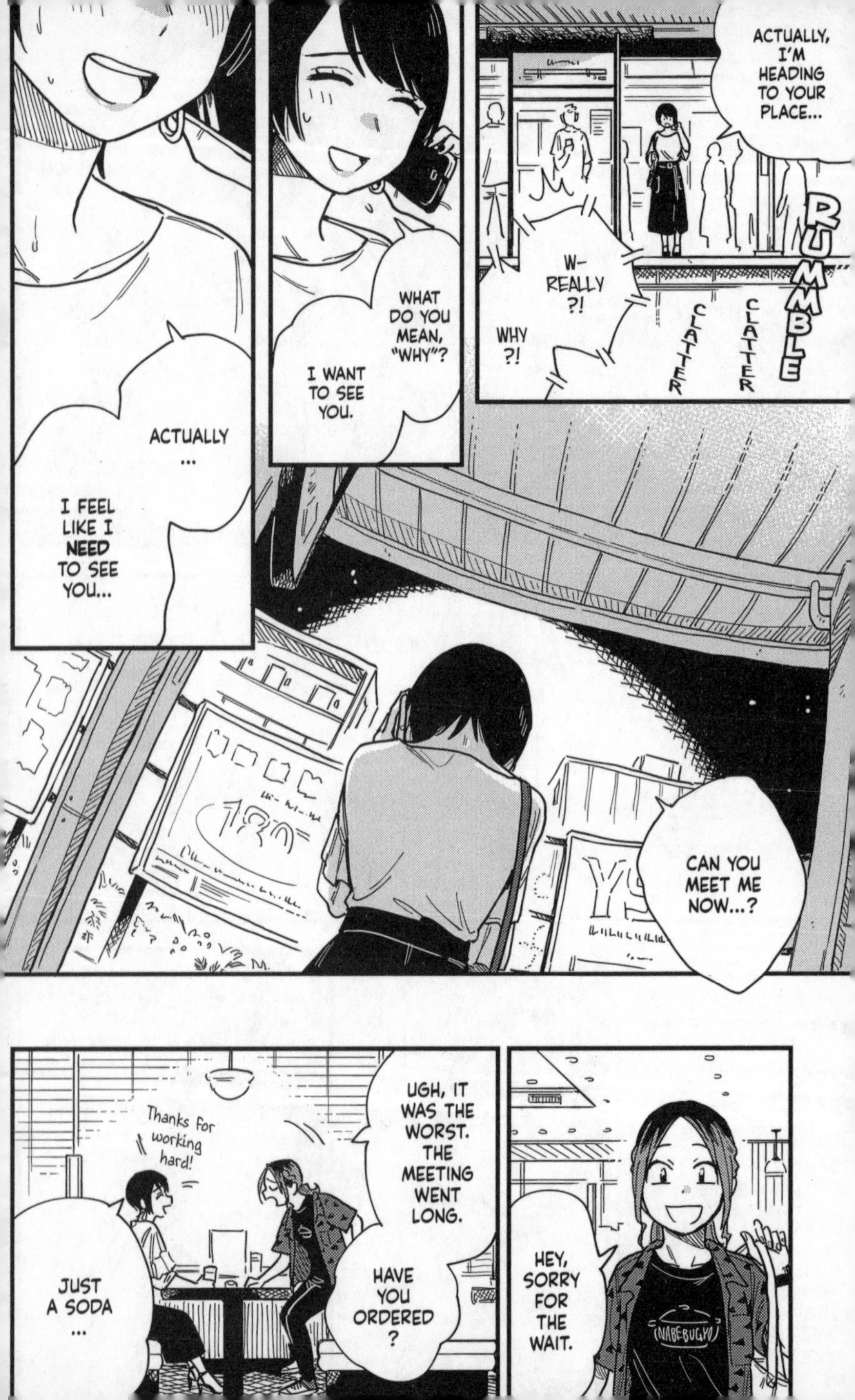
ACTUALLY, I'M HEADING TO YOUR PLACE...
RUMBLE
CLATTER
CLATTER
W- REALLY ?!
WHY ?!
WHAT DO YOU MEAN, "WHY"?
I WANT TO SEE YOU.
ACTUALLY ...
I FEEL LIKE I NEED TO SEE YOU...
CAN YOU MEET ME NOW...?
HEY, SORRY FOR THE WAIT.
NABEBUGYO
UGH, IT WAS THE WORST. THE MEETING WENT LONG.
HAVE YOU ORDERED?
Thanks for working hard!
JUST A SODA ...

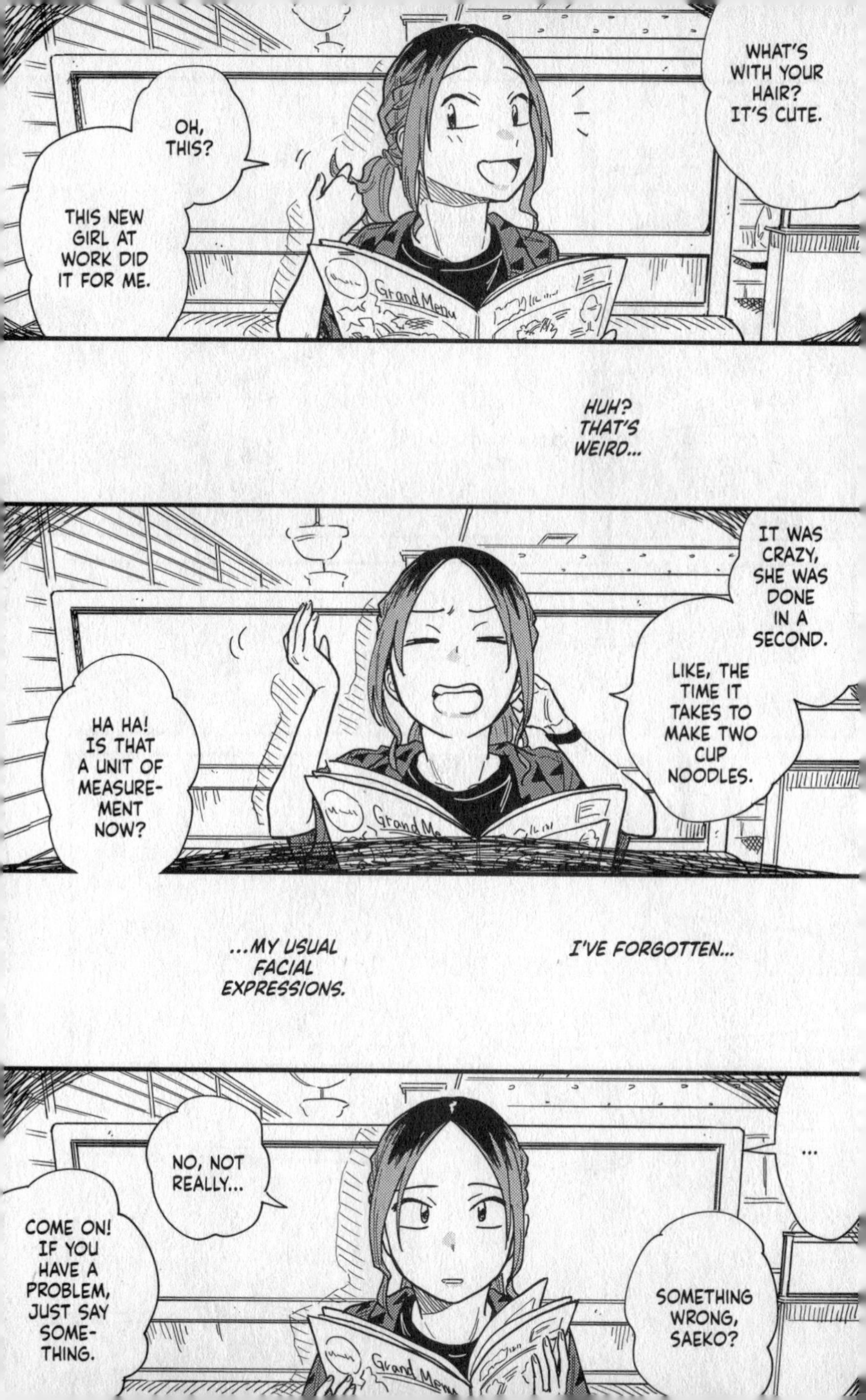
WHAT'S WITH YOUR HAIR? IT'S CUTE.
OH, THIS?
THIS NEW GIRL AT WORK DID IT FOR ME.
HUH? THAT'S WEIRD...
IT WAS CRAZY, SHE WAS DONE IN A SECOND.
LIKE, THE TIME IT TAKES TO MAKE TWO CUP NOODLES.
HA HA! IS THAT A UNIT OF MEASUREMENT NOW?
I'VE FORGOTTEN...
...MY USUAL FACIAL EXPRESSIONS.
...
SOMETHING WRONG, SAEKO?
NO, NOT REALLY...
COME ON! IF YOU HAVE A PROBLEM, JUST SAY SOMETHING.

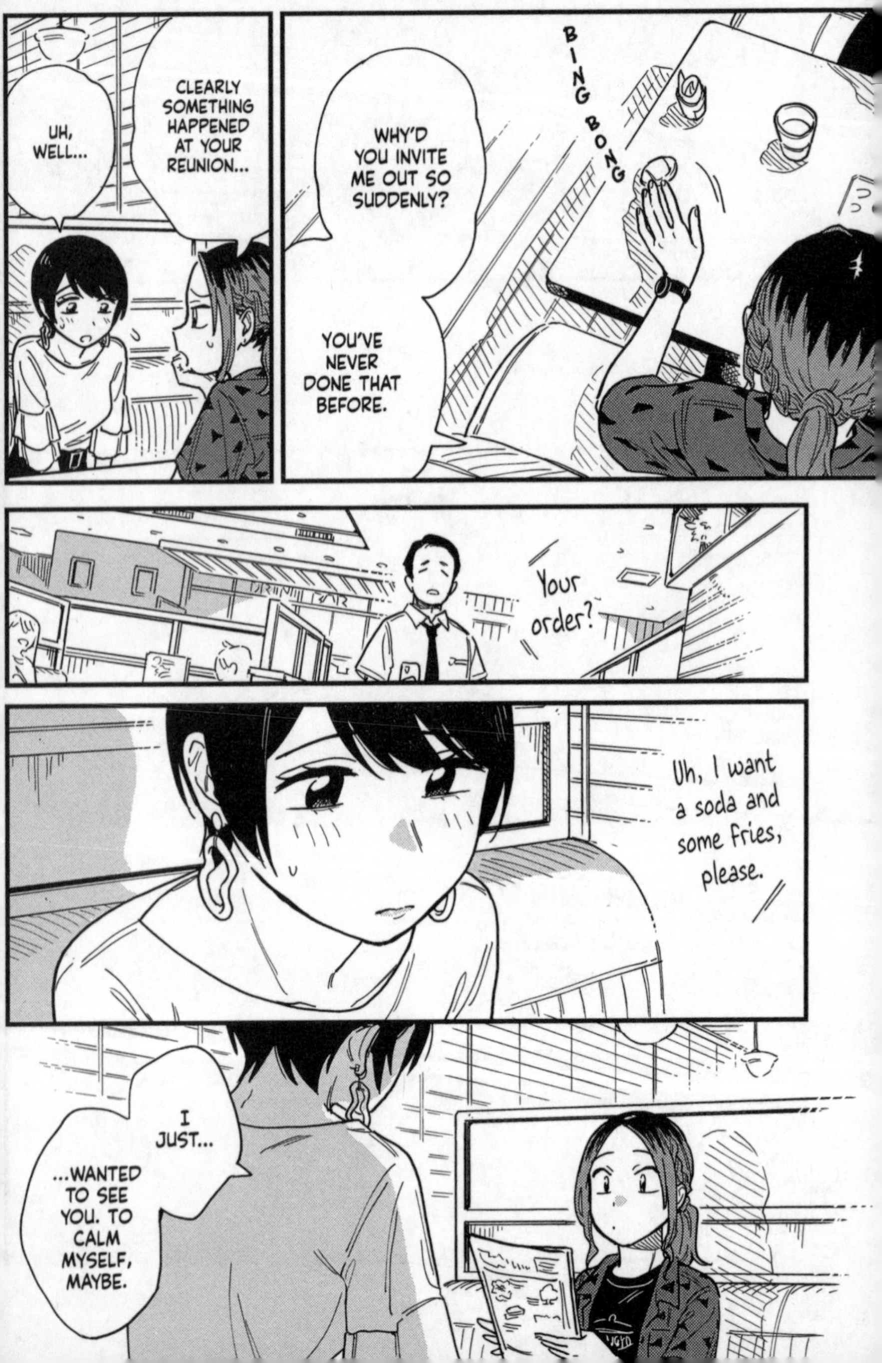
BING BONG
WHY'D YOU INVITE ME OUT SO SUDDENLY?
YOU'VE NEVER DONE THAT BEFORE.
CLEARLY SOMETHING HAPPENED AT YOUR REUNION...
UH, WELL...
Your order?
Uh, I want a soda and some fries, please.
I JUST...
...WANTED TO SEE YOU. TO CALM MYSELF, MAYBE.

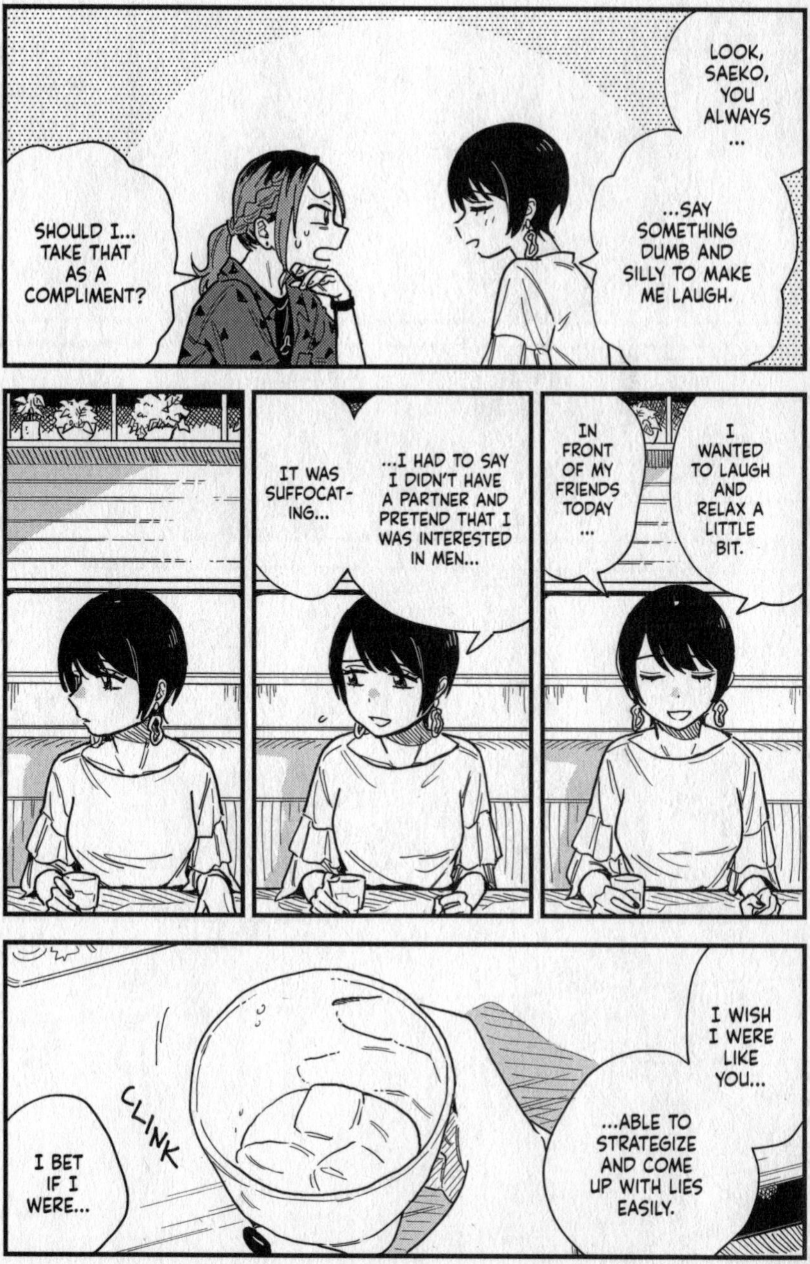
LOOK, SAEKO, YOU ALWAYS ...
...SAY SOMETHING DUMB AND SILLY TO MAKE ME LAUGH.
SHOULD I... TAKE THAT AS A COMPLIMENT?
I WANTED TO LAUGH AND RELAX A LITTLE BIT.
IN FRONT OF MY FRIENDS TODAY ...
...I HAD TO SAY I DIDN'T HAVE A PARTNER AND PRETEND THAT I WAS INTERESTED IN MEN...
IT WAS SUFFOCAT-ING...
I WISH I WERE LIKE YOU...
...ABLE TO STRATEGIZE AND COME UP WITH LIES EASILY.
CLINK
I BET IF I WERE...

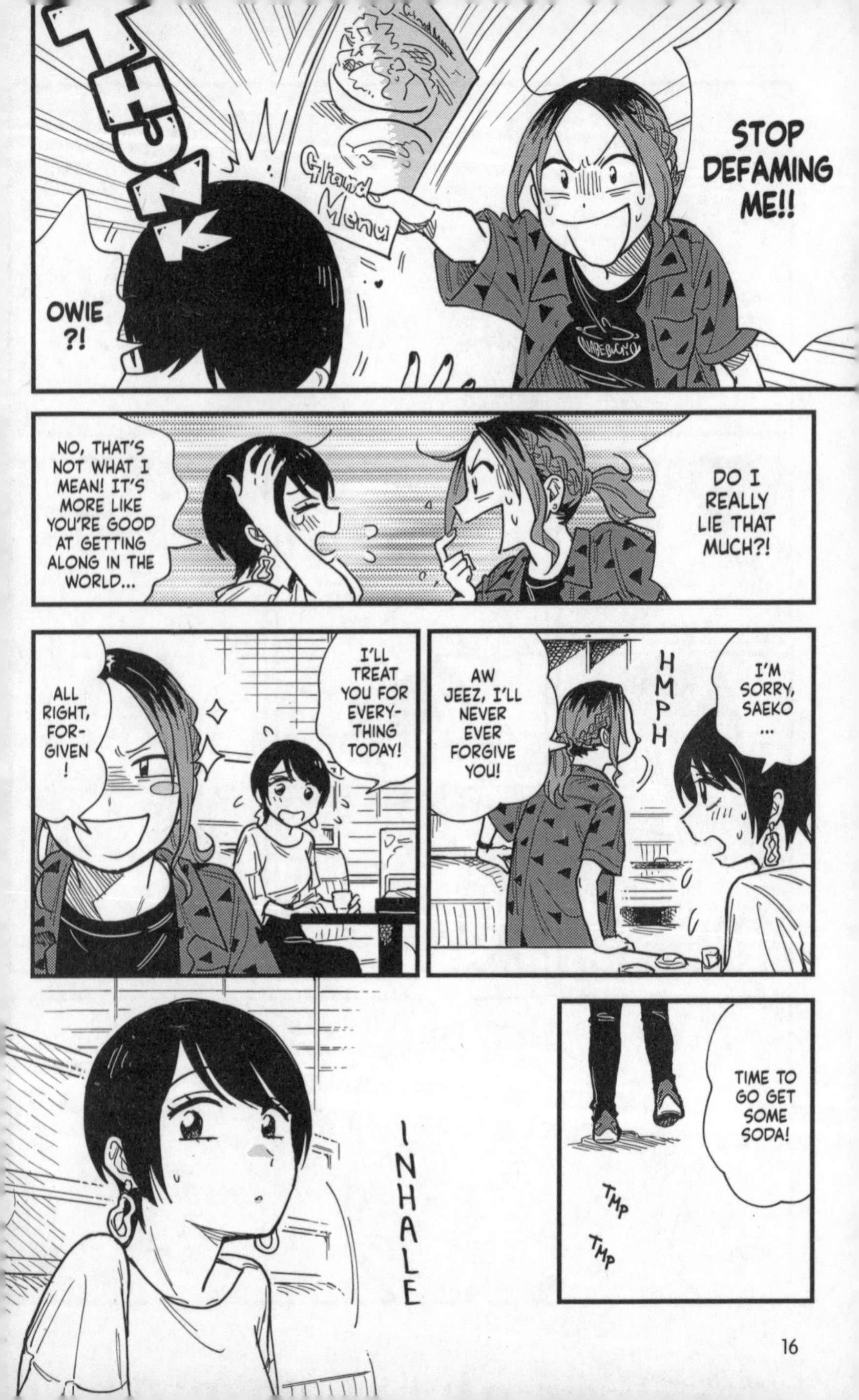
STOP DEFAMING ME!!
THUNK
OWIE ?!
DO I REALLY LIE THAT MUCH?!
NO, THAT'S NOT WHAT I MEAN! IT'S MORE LIKE YOU'RE GOOD AT GETTING ALONG IN THE WORLD...
I'M SORRY, SAEKO ...
HMPH
AW JEEZ, I'LL NEVER EVER FORGIVE YOU!
I'LL TREAT YOU FOR EVERY-THING TODAY!
ALL RIGHT, FOR-GIVEN!
TIME TO GO GET SOME SODA!
TMP
TMP
INHALE

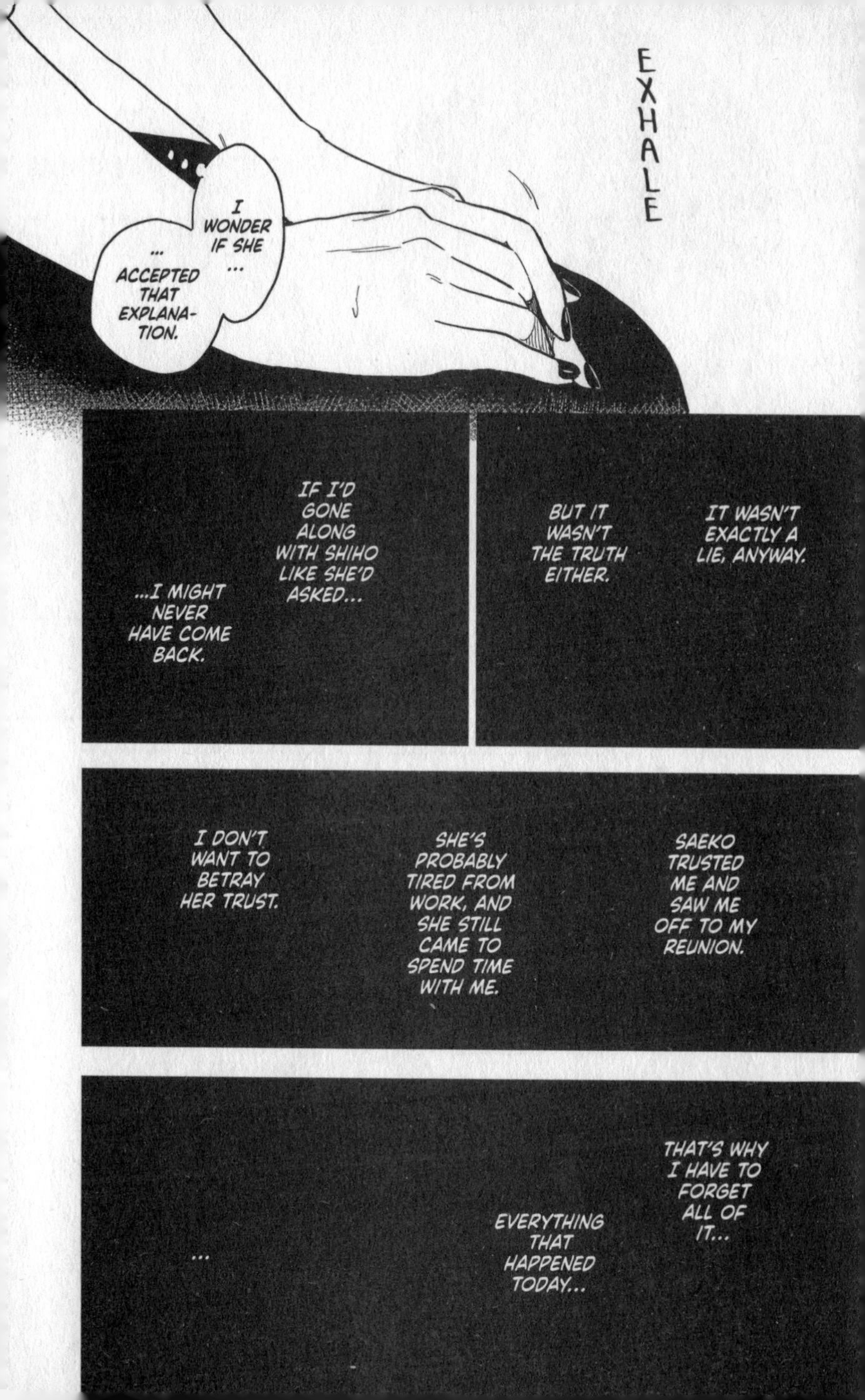
EXHALE
I WONDER IF SHE ...
... ACCEPTED THAT EXPLANATION.
IT WASN'T EXACTLY A LIE, ANYWAY.
BUT IT WASN'T THE TRUTH EITHER.
IF I'D GONE ALONG WITH SHIHO LIKE SHE'D ASKED...
...I MIGHT NEVER HAVE COME BACK.
SAEKO TRUSTED ME AND SAW ME OFF TO MY REUNION.
SHE'S PROBABLY TIRED FROM WORK, AND SHE STILL CAME TO SPEND TIME WITH ME.
I DON'T WANT TO BETRAY HER TRUST.
THAT'S WHY I HAVE TO FORGET ALL OF IT...
EVERYTHING THAT HAPPENED TODAY...
...

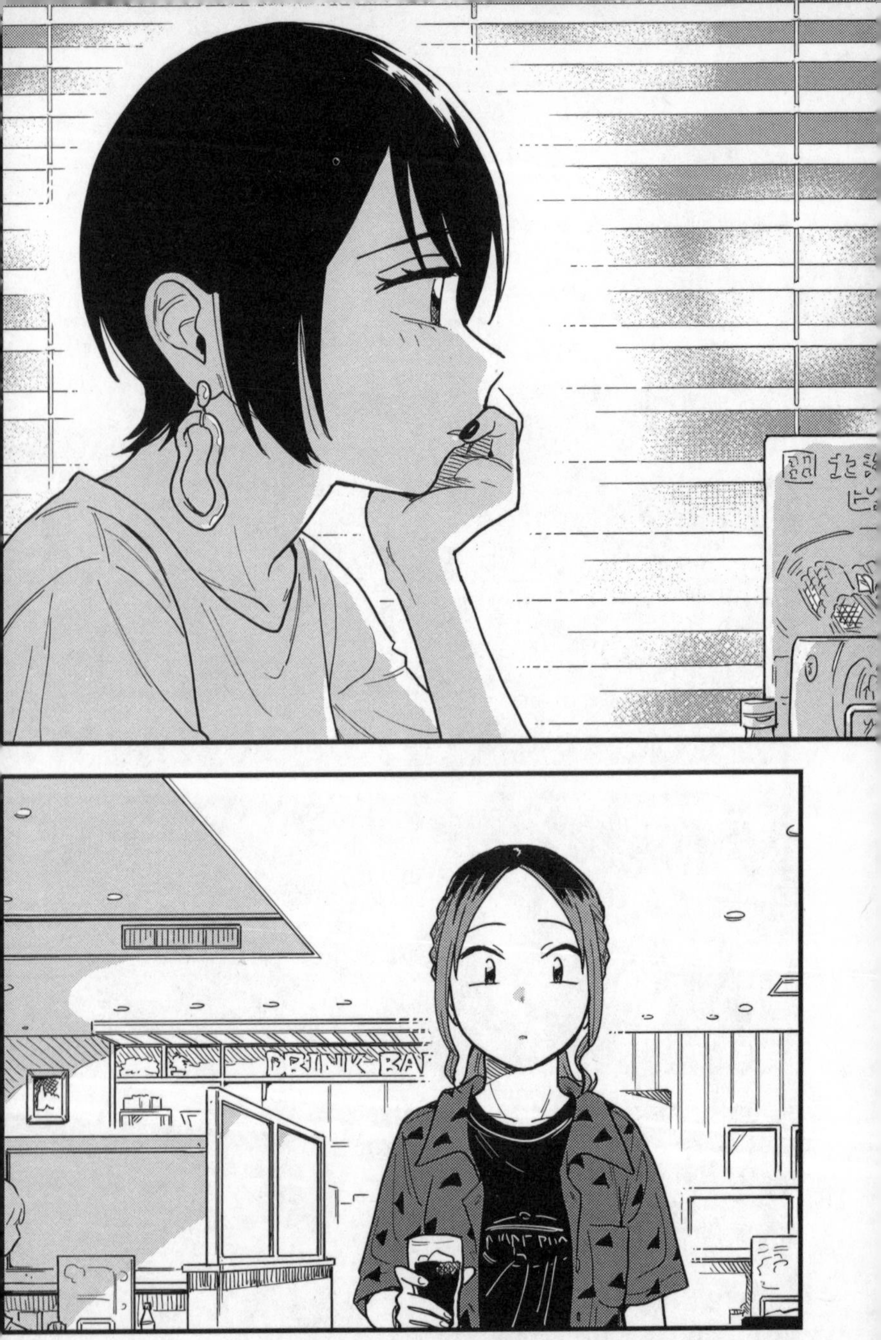
DRINK BA

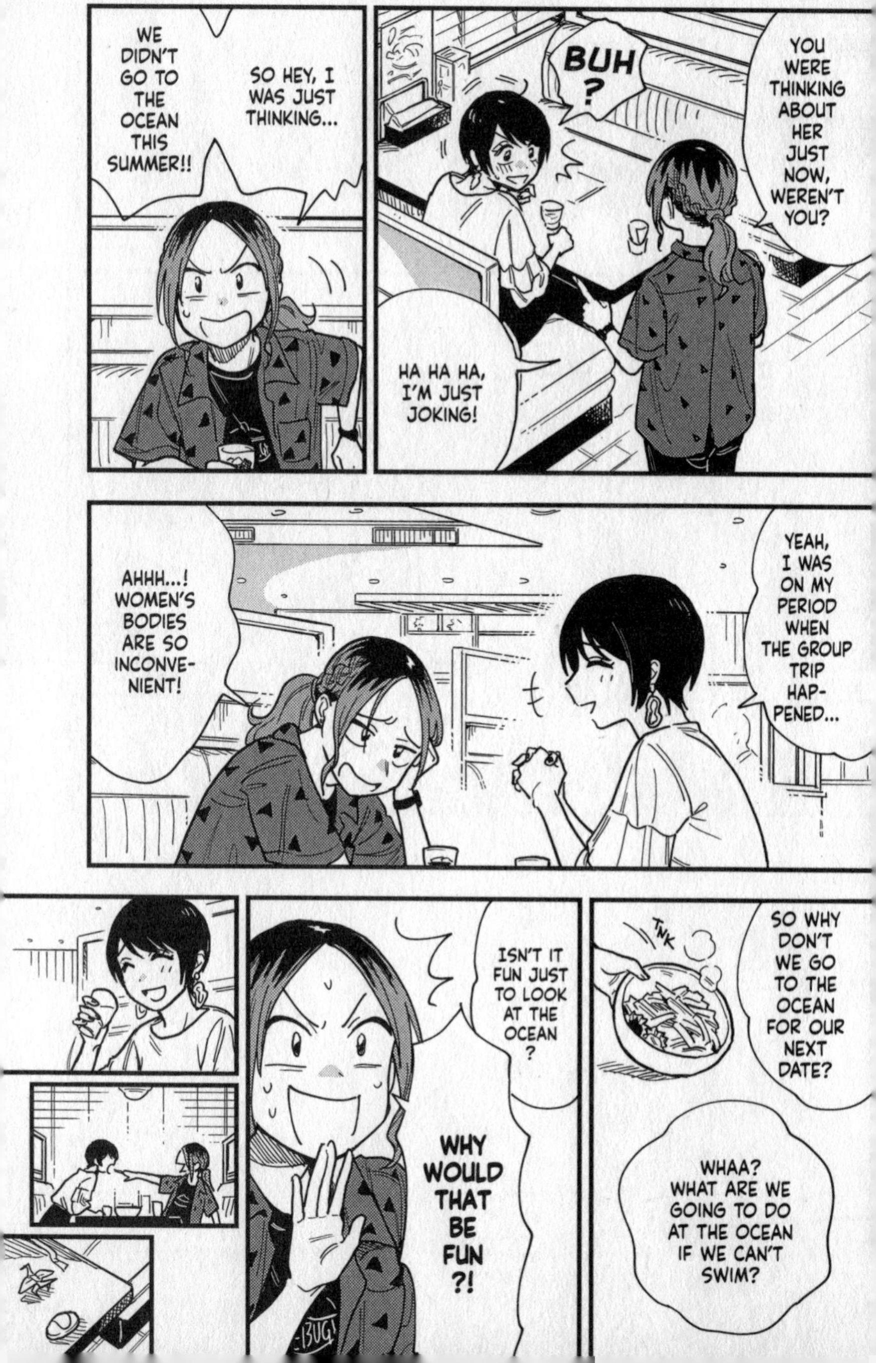
YOU WERE THINKING ABOUT HER JUST NOW, WEREN'T YOU?
BUH?
HA HA HA, I'M JUST JOKING!
SO HEY, I WAS JUST THINKING...
WE DIDN'T GO TO THE OCEAN THIS SUMMER!!
YEAH, I WAS ON MY PERIOD WHEN THE GROUP TRIP HAPPENED...
AHHH...! WOMEN'S BODIES ARE SO INCONVENIENT!
TNK
SO WHY DON'T WE GO TO THE OCEAN FOR OUR NEXT DATE?
WHAA? WHAT ARE WE GOING TO DO AT THE OCEAN IF WE CAN'T SWIM?
ISN'T IT FUN JUST TO LOOK AT THE OCEAN?
WHY WOULD THAT BE FUN?!

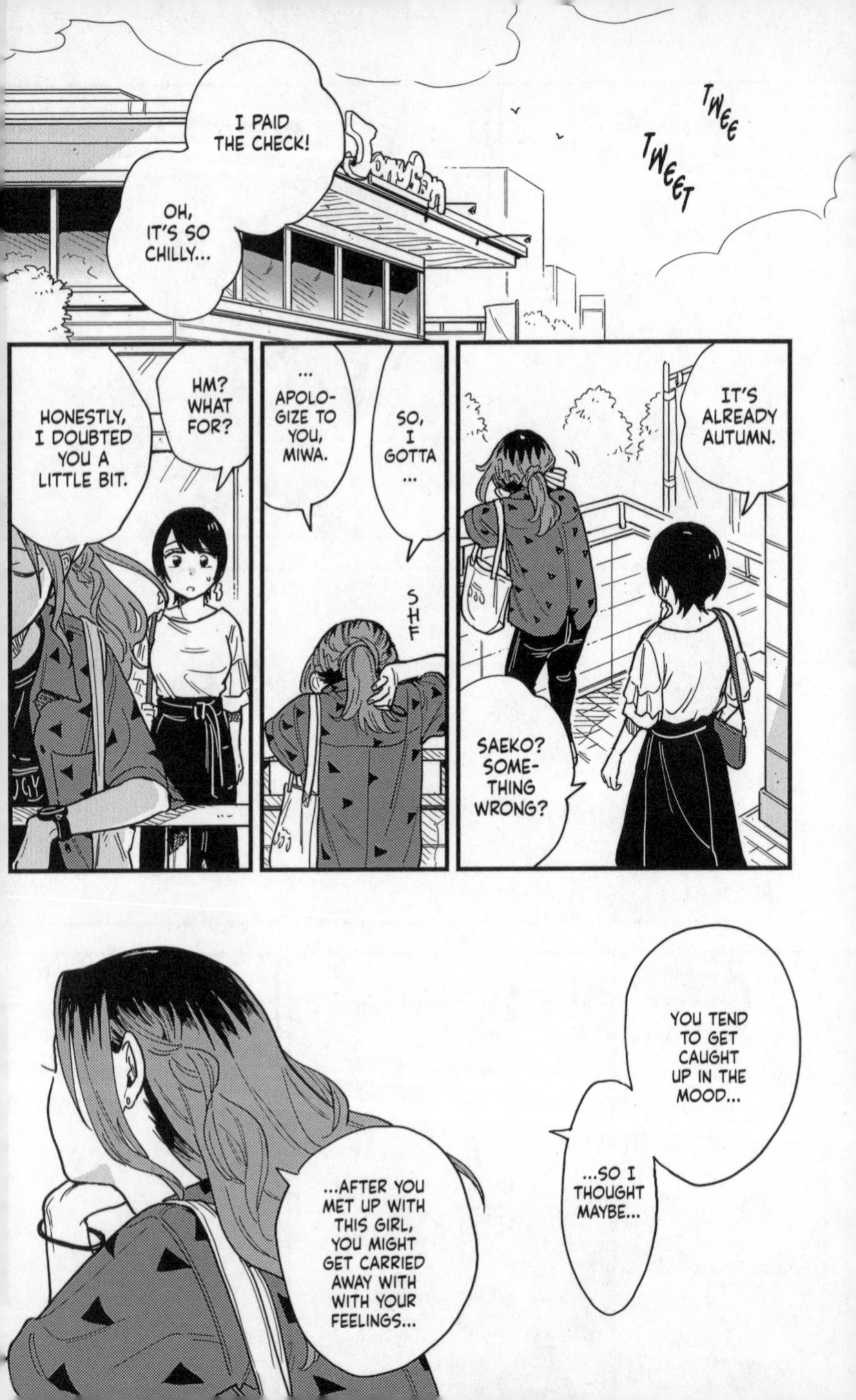
TWEE
TWEET
I PAID THE CHECK!
OH, IT'S SO CHILLY...
IT'S ALREADY AUTUMN.
SAEKO? SOMETHING WRONG?
SO, I GOTTA...
... APOLOGIZE TO YOU, MIWA.
SHF
HM? WHAT FOR?
HONESTLY, I DOUBTED YOU A LITTLE BIT.
YOU TEND TO GET CAUGHT UP IN THE MOOD...
...SO I THOUGHT MAYBE...
...AFTER YOU MET UP WITH THIS GIRL, YOU MIGHT GET CARRIED AWAY WITH WITH YOUR FEELINGS...

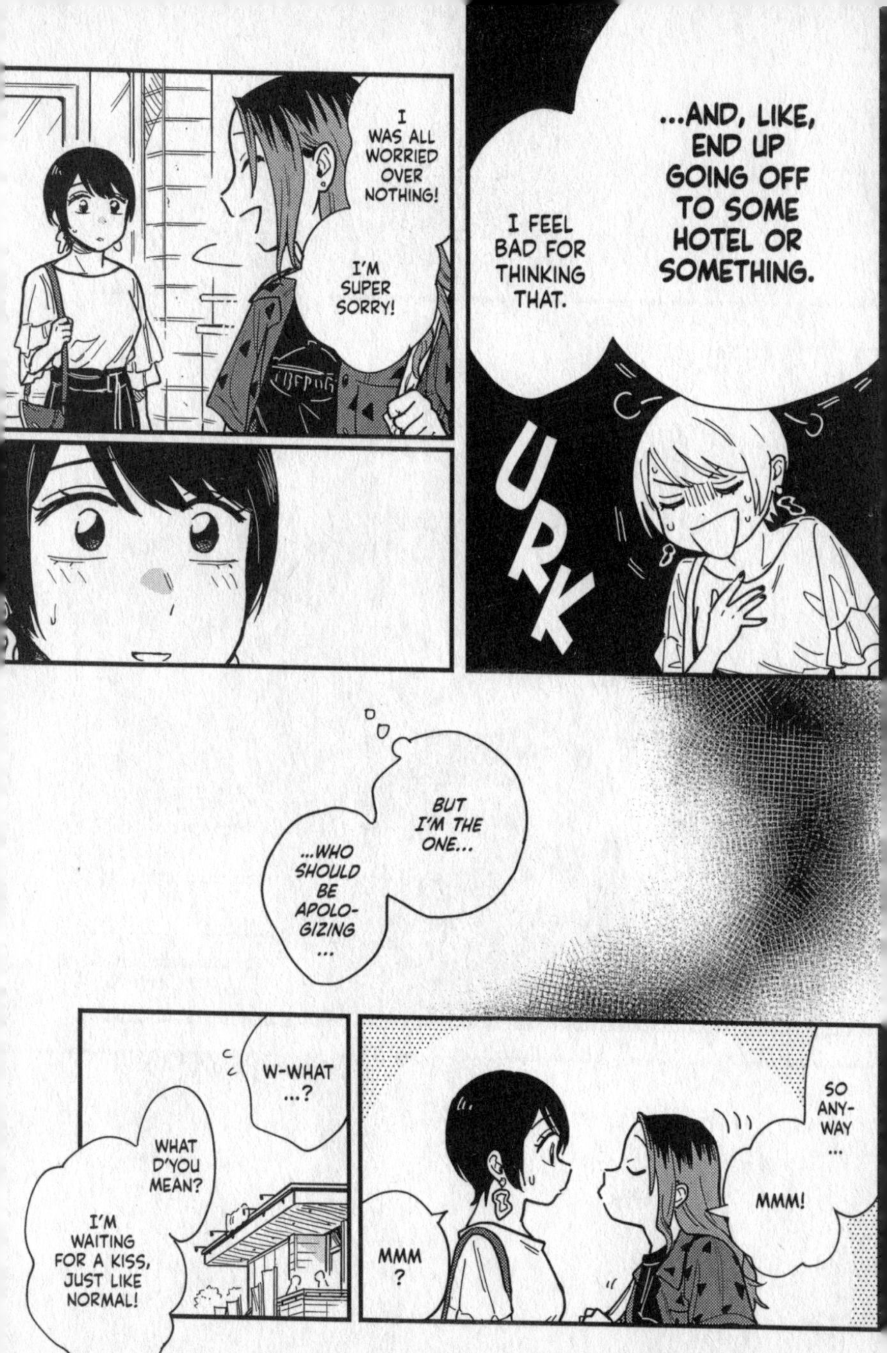
...AND, LIKE, END UP GOING OFF TO SOME HOTEL OR SOMETHING.
I FEEL BAD FOR THINKING THAT.
URK
I WAS ALL WORRIED OVER NOTHING!
I'M SUPER SORRY!
BUT I'M THE ONE...
...WHO SHOULD BE APOLOGIZING ...
SO ANYWAY ...
MMM!
MMM ?
W-WHAT ...?
WHAT D'YOU MEAN?
I'M WAITING FOR A KISS, JUST LIKE NORMAL!

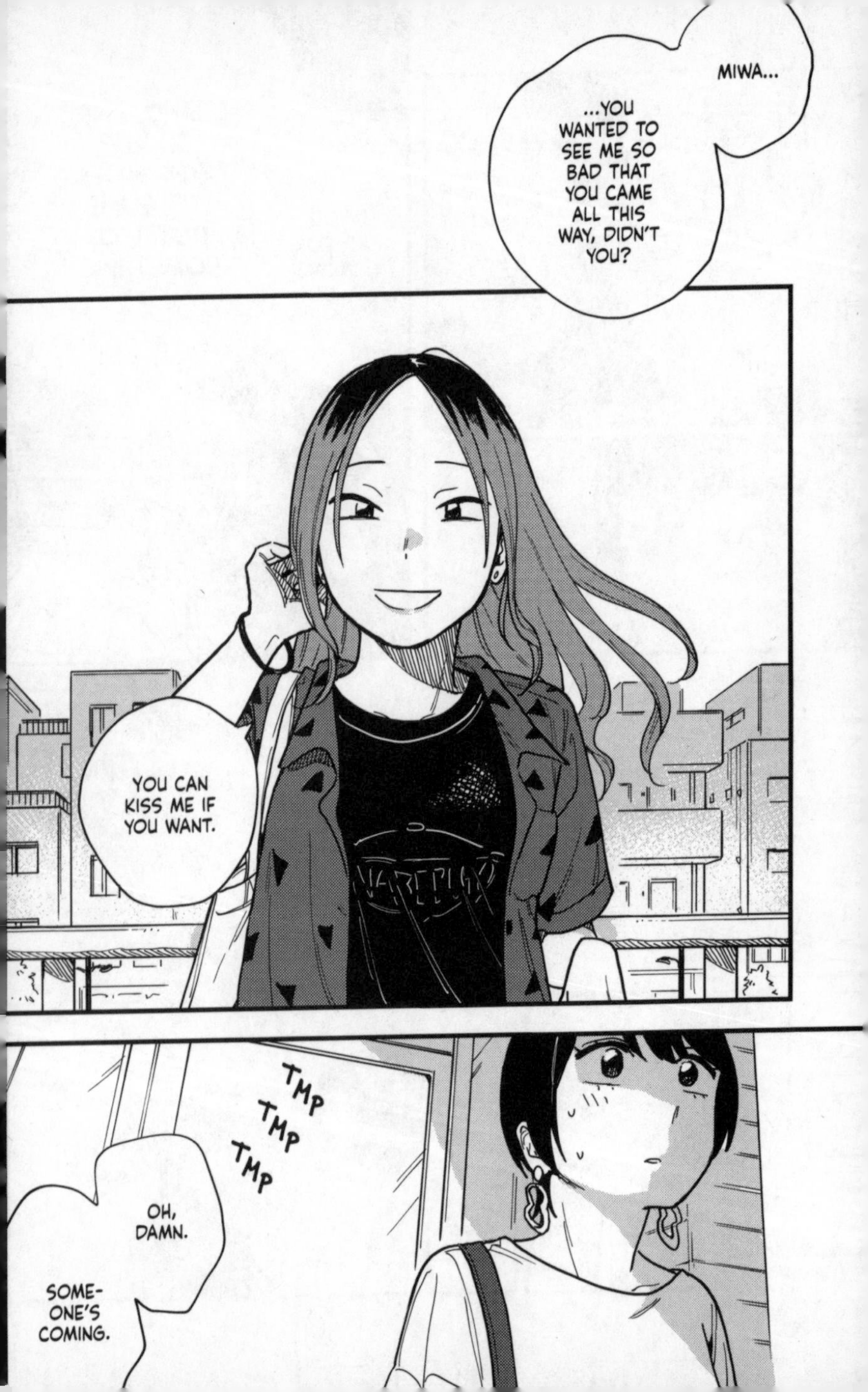
MIWA...
...YOU WANTED TO SEE ME SO BAD THAT YOU CAME ALL THIS WAY, DIDN'T YOU?
YOU CAN KISS ME IF YOU WANT.
TMP TMP TMP
OH, DAMN.
SOME-ONE'S COMING.

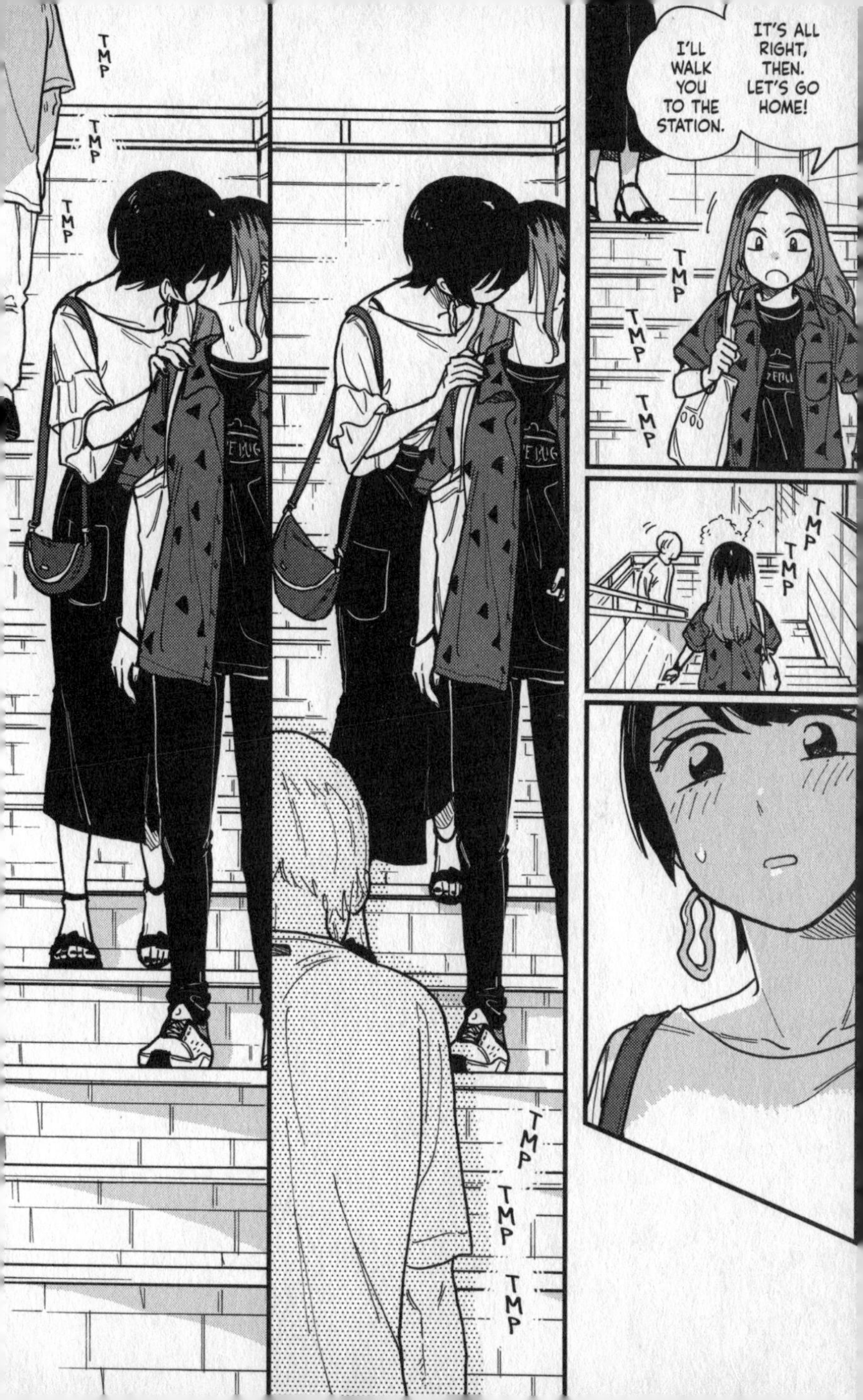
IT'S ALL RIGHT, THEN. LET'S GO HOME!
I'LL WALK YOU TO THE STATION.
TMP
TMP
TMP
TMP
TMP
TMP
TMP
TMP
TMP
TMP
TMP

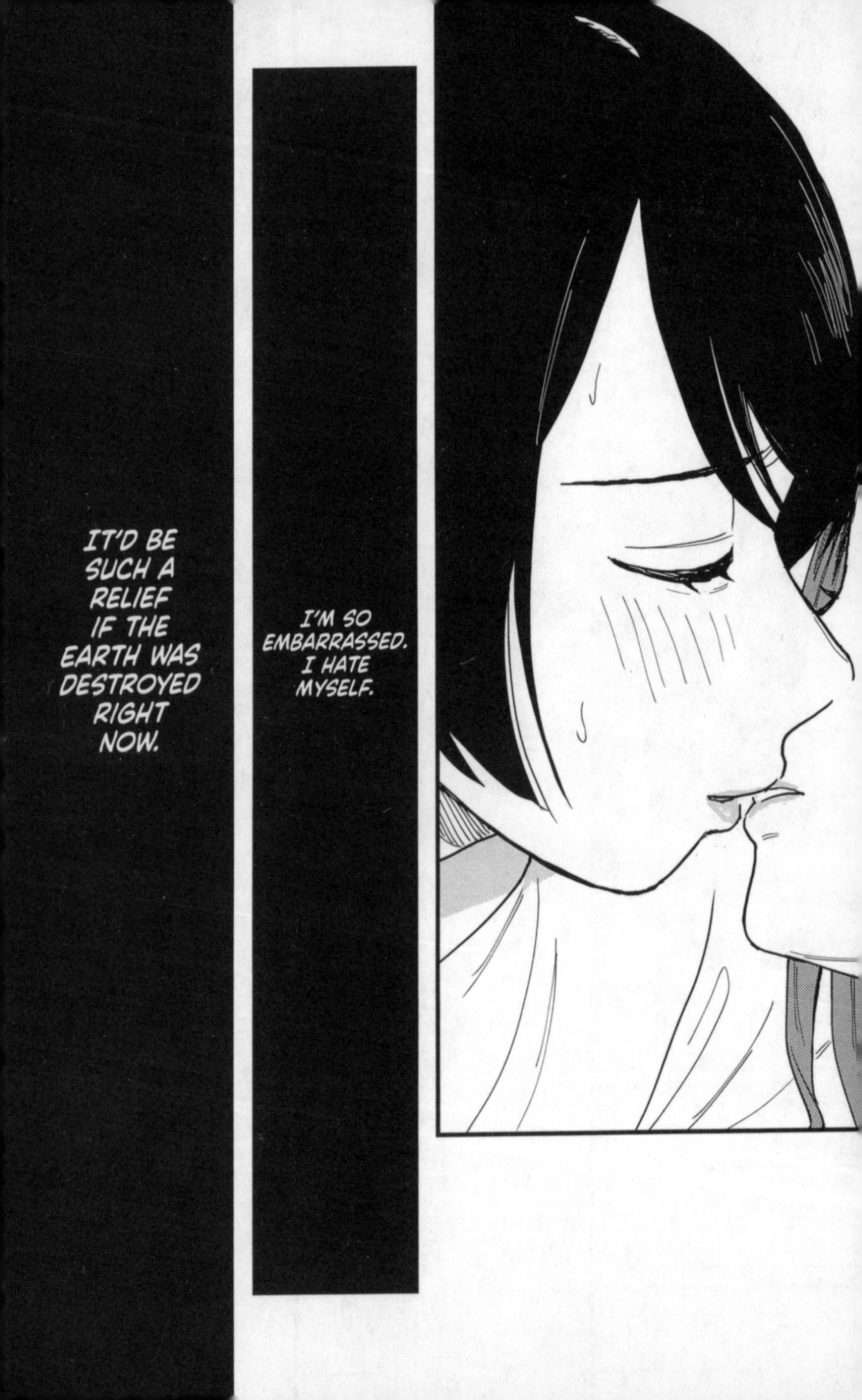
I'M SO EMBARRASSED. I HATE MYSELF.
IT'D BE SUCH A RELIEF IF THE EARTH WAS DESTROYED RIGHT NOW.

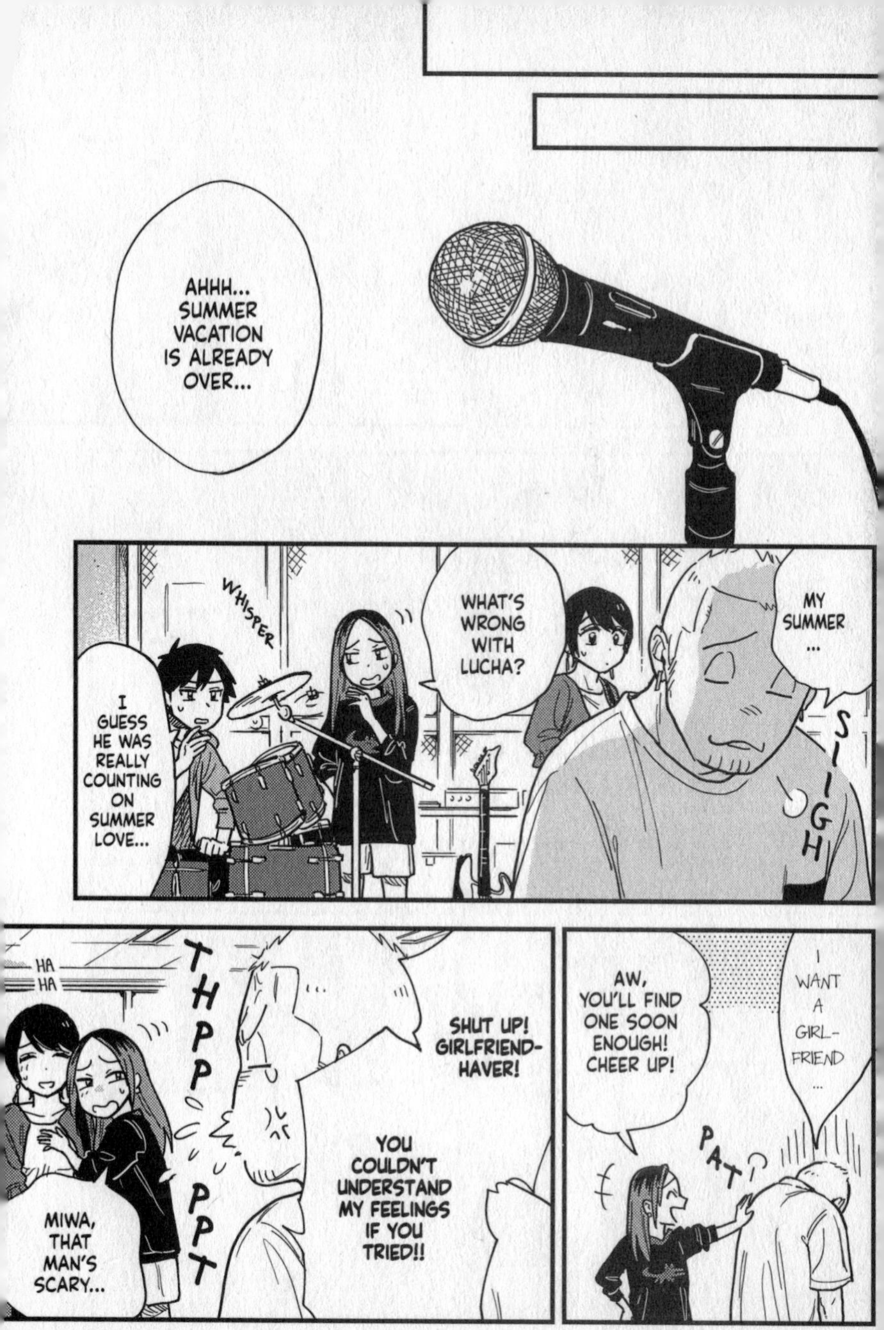

AHHH... SUMMER VACATION IS ALREADY OVER...
MY SUMMER ...
SIIIGH
WHAT'S WRONG WITH LUCHA?
WHISPER
I GUESS HE WAS REALLY COUNTING ON SUMMER LOVE...
I WANT A GIRL-FRIEND ...
AW, YOU'LL FIND ONE SOON ENOUGH! CHEER UP!
PAT
...
SHUT UP! GIRLFRIEND-HAVER!
YOU COULDN'T UNDERSTAND MY FEELINGS IF YOU TRIED!!
THPPPPPT
HA HA
MIWA, THAT MAN'S SCARY...

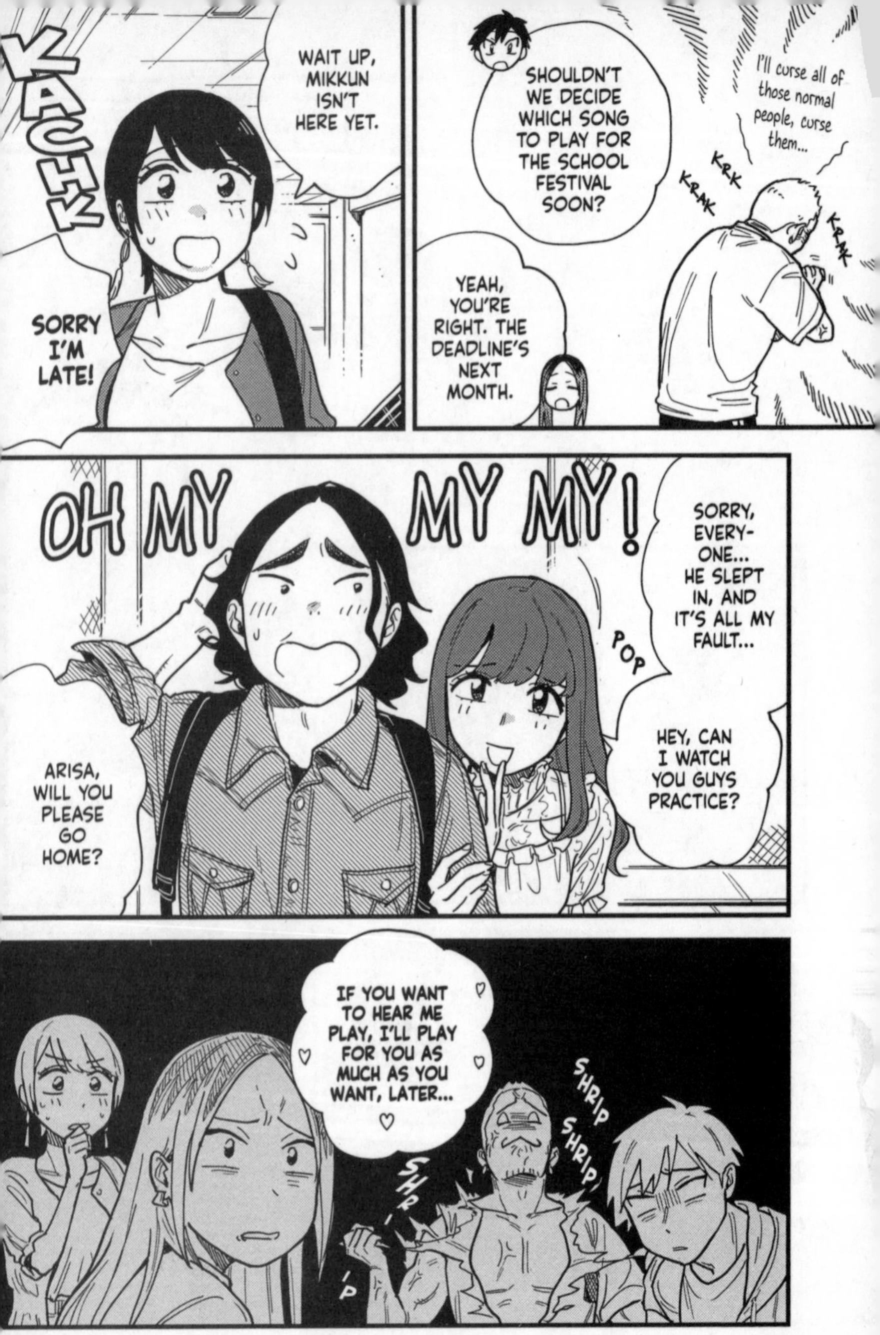
I'll curse all of those normal people, curse them...
KRK
KRAK
KRNK
SHOULDN'T WE DECIDE WHICH SONG TO PLAY FOR THE SCHOOL FESTIVAL SOON?
YEAH, YOU'RE RIGHT. THE DEADLINE'S NEXT MONTH.
WAIT UP, MIKKUN ISN'T HERE YET.
KACHK
SORRY I'M LATE!
SORRY, EVERY-ONE... HE SLEPT IN, AND IT'S ALL MY FAULT...
POP
HEY, CAN I WATCH YOU GUYS PRACTICE?
OH MY MY MY!
ARISA, WILL YOU PLEASE GO HOME?
IF YOU WANT TO HEAR ME PLAY, I'LL PLAY FOR YOU AS MUCH AS YOU WANT, LATER...
SHRIP
SHRIP
SHRIP

HOW DO WE RELATIONSHIP?

How Do We
RELATIONSHIP?

Chapter 29: The Bud of Friendship

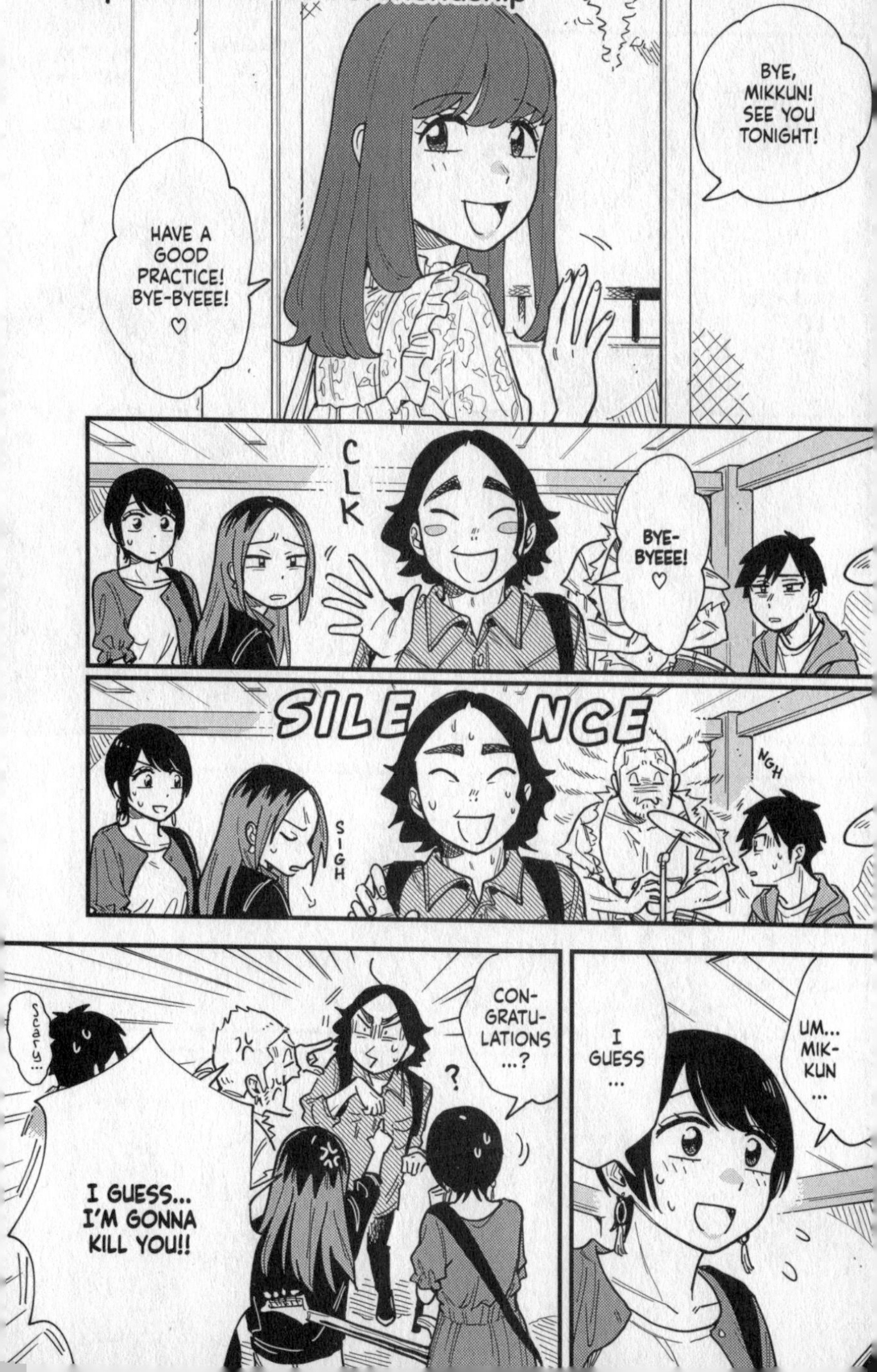
BYE, MIKKUN! SEE YOU TONIGHT!
HAVE A GOOD PRACTICE! BYE-BYEEE! ♡
CLK
BYE-BYEEE! ♡
SILENCE
NGH
SIGH
UM... MIK-KUN...
I GUESS...
CON-GRATU-LATIONS...?
?
scary...
I GUESS... I'M GONNA KILL YOU!!

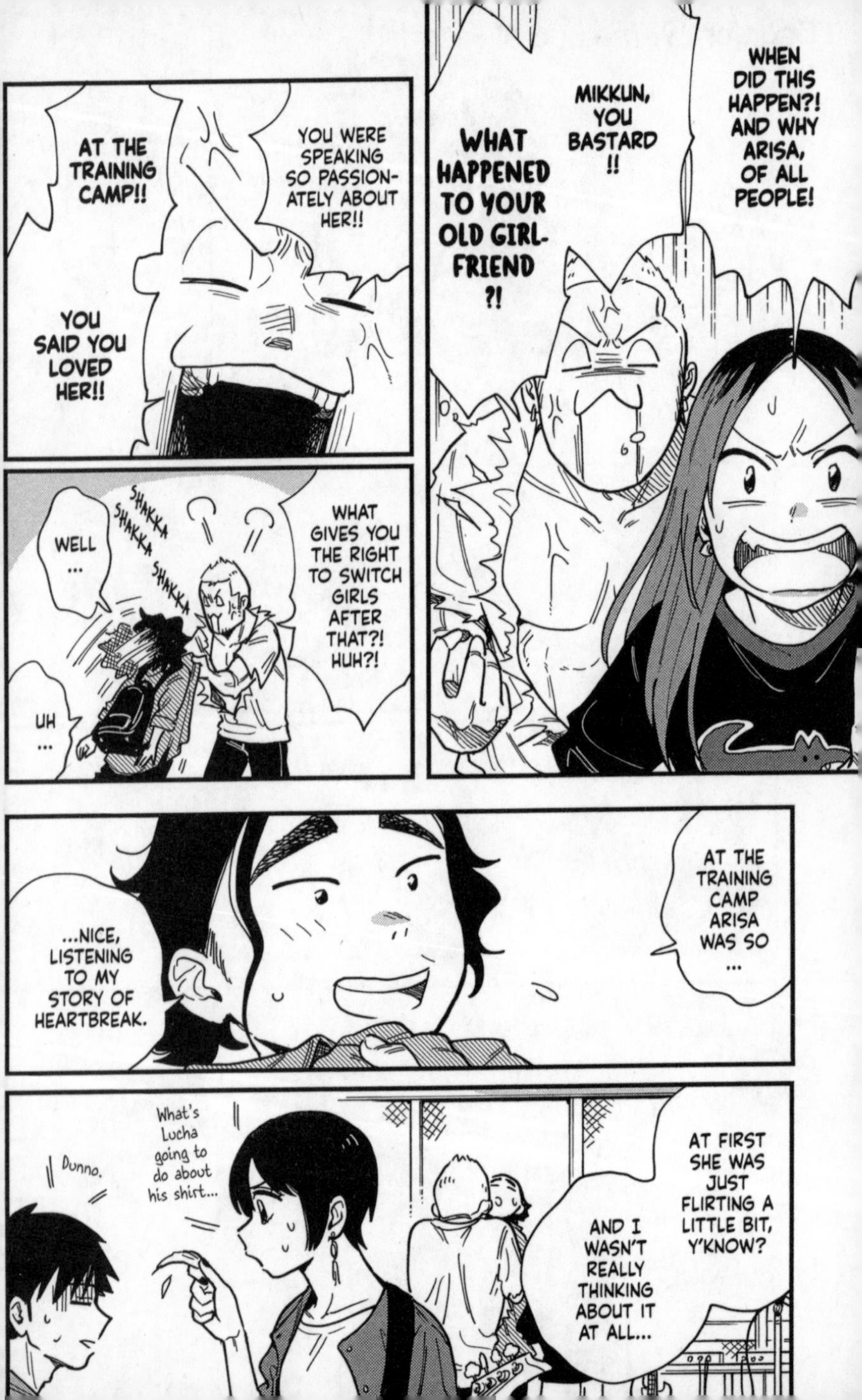
WHEN DID THIS HAPPEN?! AND WHY ARISA, OF ALL PEOPLE!
MIKKUN, YOU BASTARD !!
WHAT HAPPENED TO YOUR OLD GIRL-FRIEND ?!
YOU WERE SPEAKING SO PASSION-ATELY ABOUT HER!!
AT THE TRAINING CAMP!!
YOU SAID YOU LOVED HER!!
WHAT GIVES YOU THE RIGHT TO SWITCH GIRLS AFTER THAT?! HUH?!
SHAKKA SHAKKA SHAKKA
WELL ...
UH ...
AT THE TRAINING CAMP ARISA WAS SO ...
...NICE, LISTENING TO MY STORY OF HEARTBREAK.
AT FIRST SHE WAS JUST FLIRTING A LITTLE BIT, Y'KNOW?
AND I WASN'T REALLY THINKING ABOUT IT AT ALL...
What's Lucha going to do about his shirt...
Dunno.

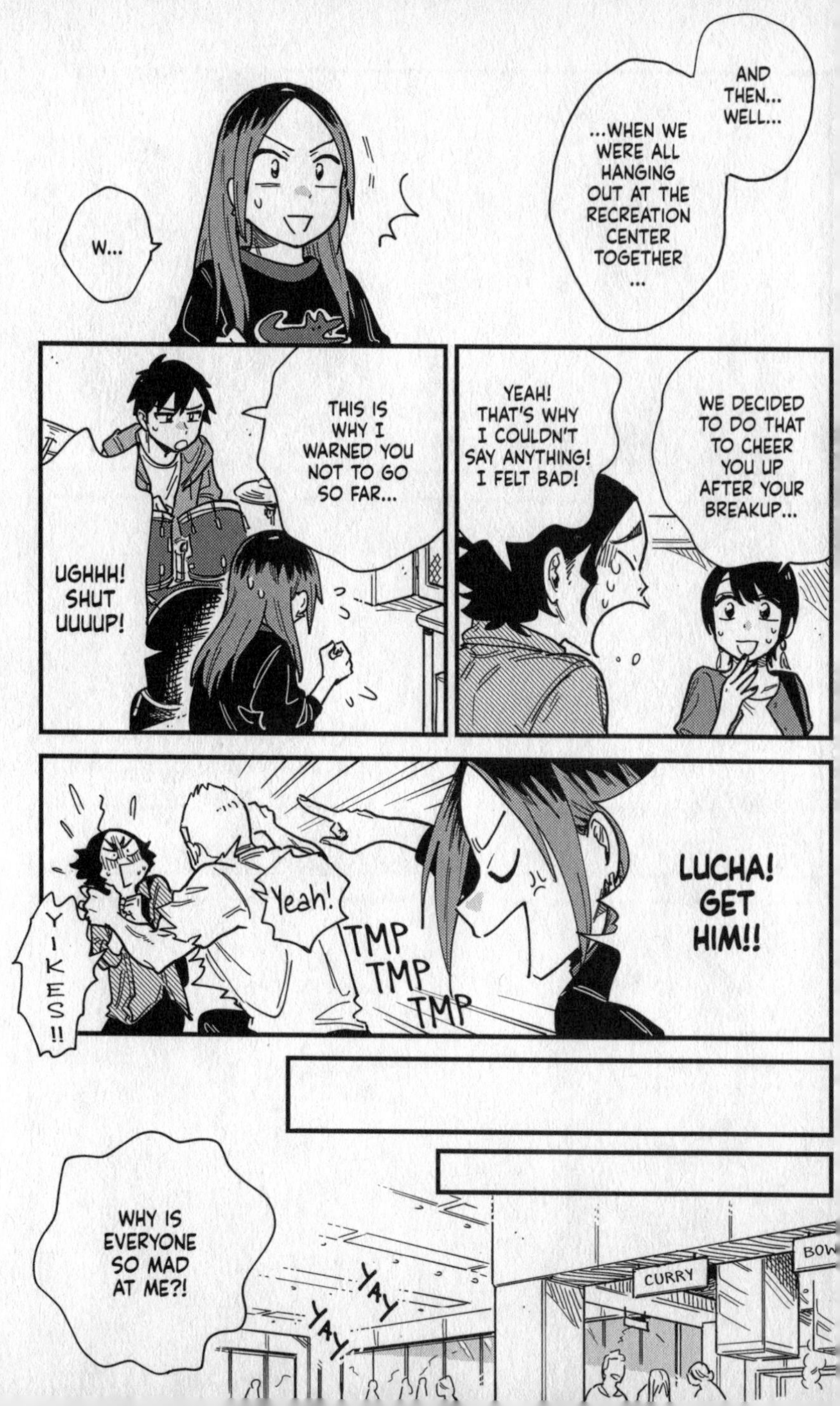
AND THEN... WELL...
...WHEN WE WERE ALL HANGING OUT AT THE RECREATION CENTER TOGETHER ...
W...
WE DECIDED TO DO THAT TO CHEER YOU UP AFTER YOUR BREAKUP...
YEAH! THAT'S WHY I COULDN'T SAY ANYTHING! I FELT BAD!
THIS IS WHY I WARNED YOU NOT TO GO SO FAR...
UGHHH! SHUT UUUUP!
LUCHA! GET HIM!!
TMP TMP TMP
Yeah!
YIKES!!
CURRY
YAY YAY
WHY IS EVERYONE SO MAD AT ME?!

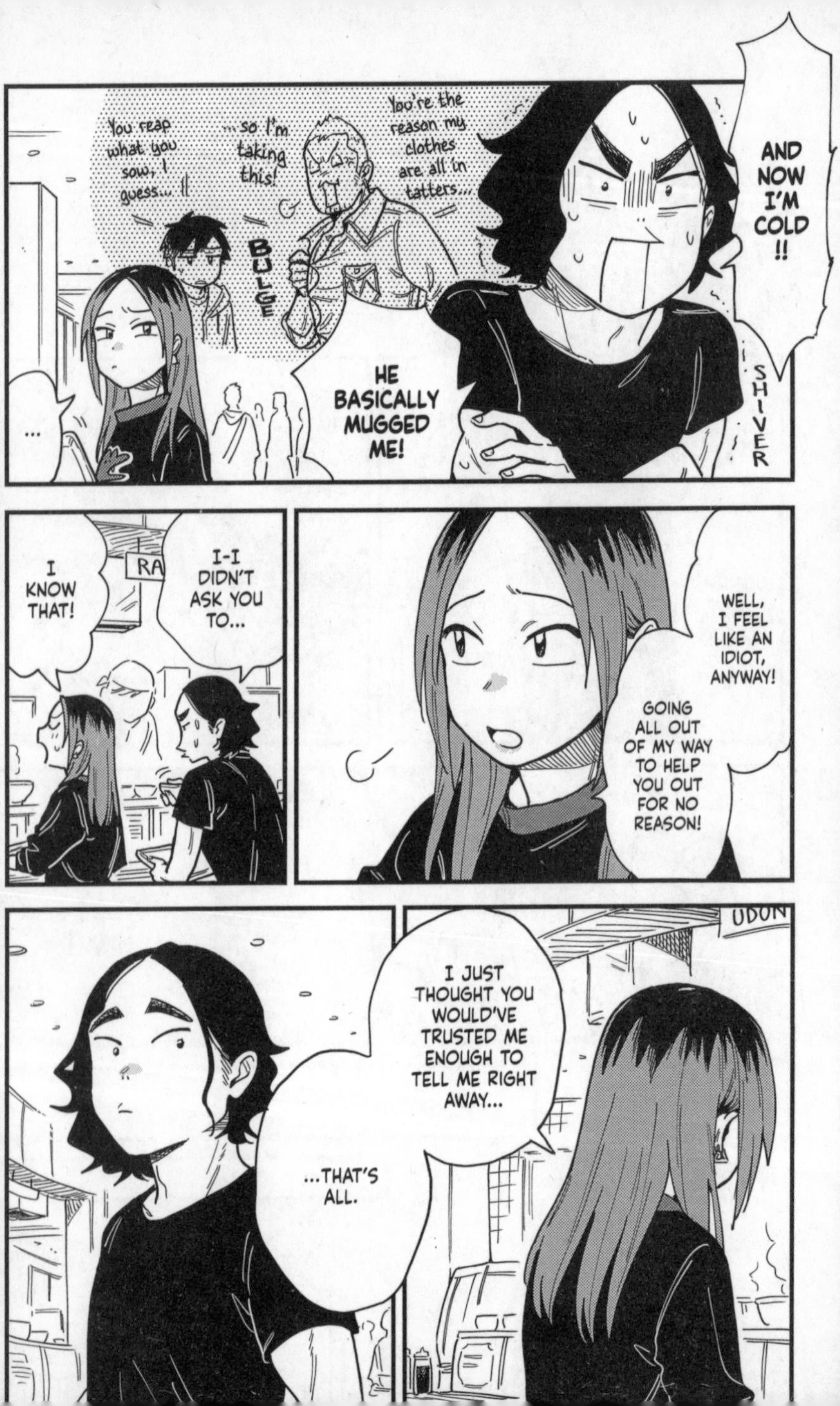
AND NOW I'M COLD!!
SHIVER
You're the reason my clothes are all in tatters...
...so I'm taking this!
You reap what you sow, I guess...
BULGE
HE BASICALLY MUGGED ME!
...
WELL, I FEEL LIKE AN IDIOT, ANYWAY!
GOING ALL OUT OF MY WAY TO HELP YOU OUT FOR NO REASON!
I-I DIDN'T ASK YOU TO...
RA
I KNOW THAT!
UDON
I JUST THOUGHT YOU WOULD'VE TRUSTED ME ENOUGH TO TELL ME RIGHT AWAY...
...THAT'S ALL.

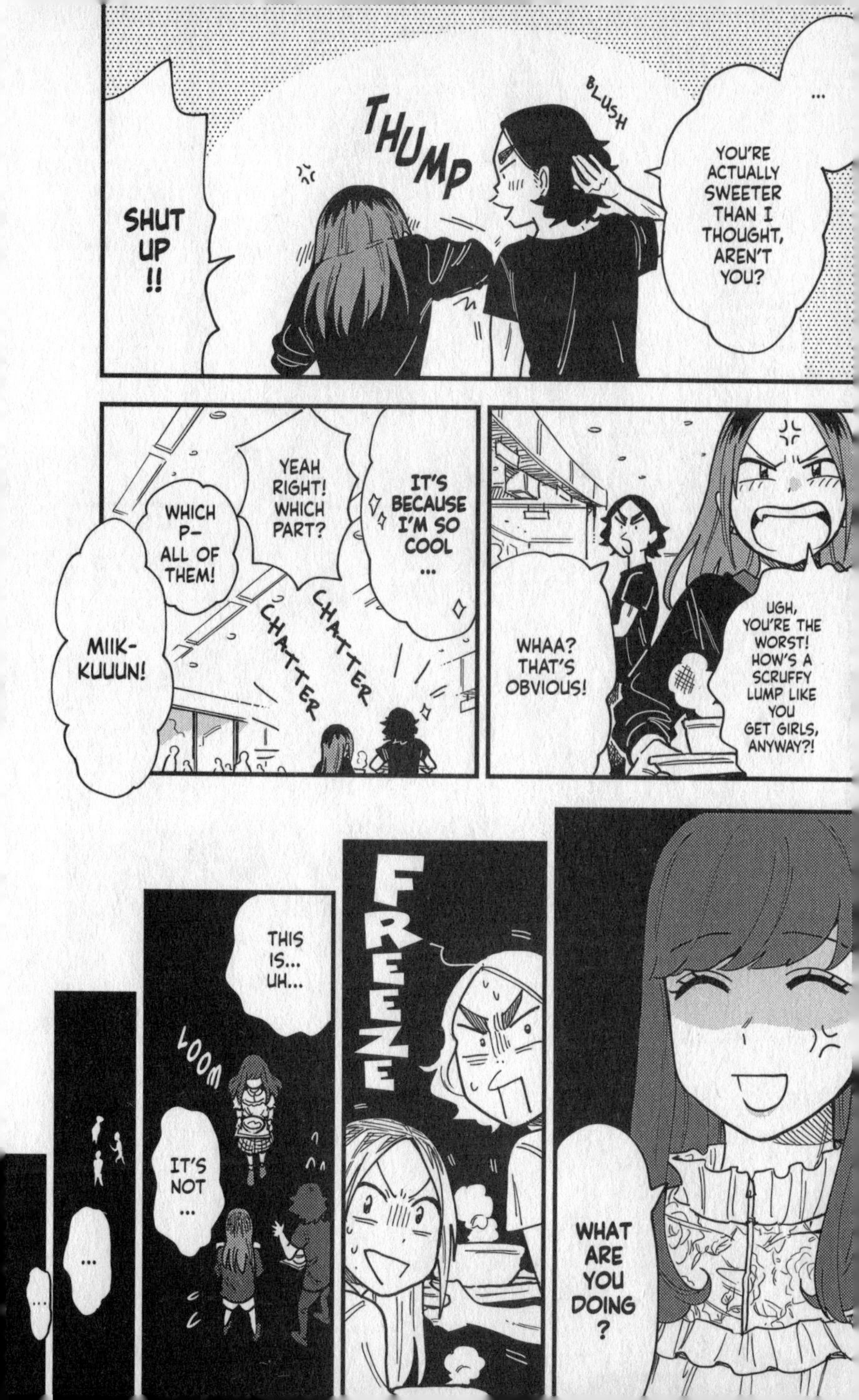
...
YOU'RE ACTUALLY SWEETER THAN I THOUGHT, AREN'T YOU?
BLUSH
THUMP
SHUT UP !!
UGH, YOU'RE THE WORST! HOW'S A SCRUFFY LUMP LIKE YOU GET GIRLS, ANYWAY?!
WHAA? THAT'S OBVIOUS!
IT'S BECAUSE I'M SO COOL ...
YEAH RIGHT! WHICH PART?
WHICH P— ALL OF THEM!
CHATTER CHATTER
MIIK-KUUUN!
WHAT ARE YOU DOING ?
FREEZE
THIS IS... UH...
LOOM
IT'S NOT ...
...
...

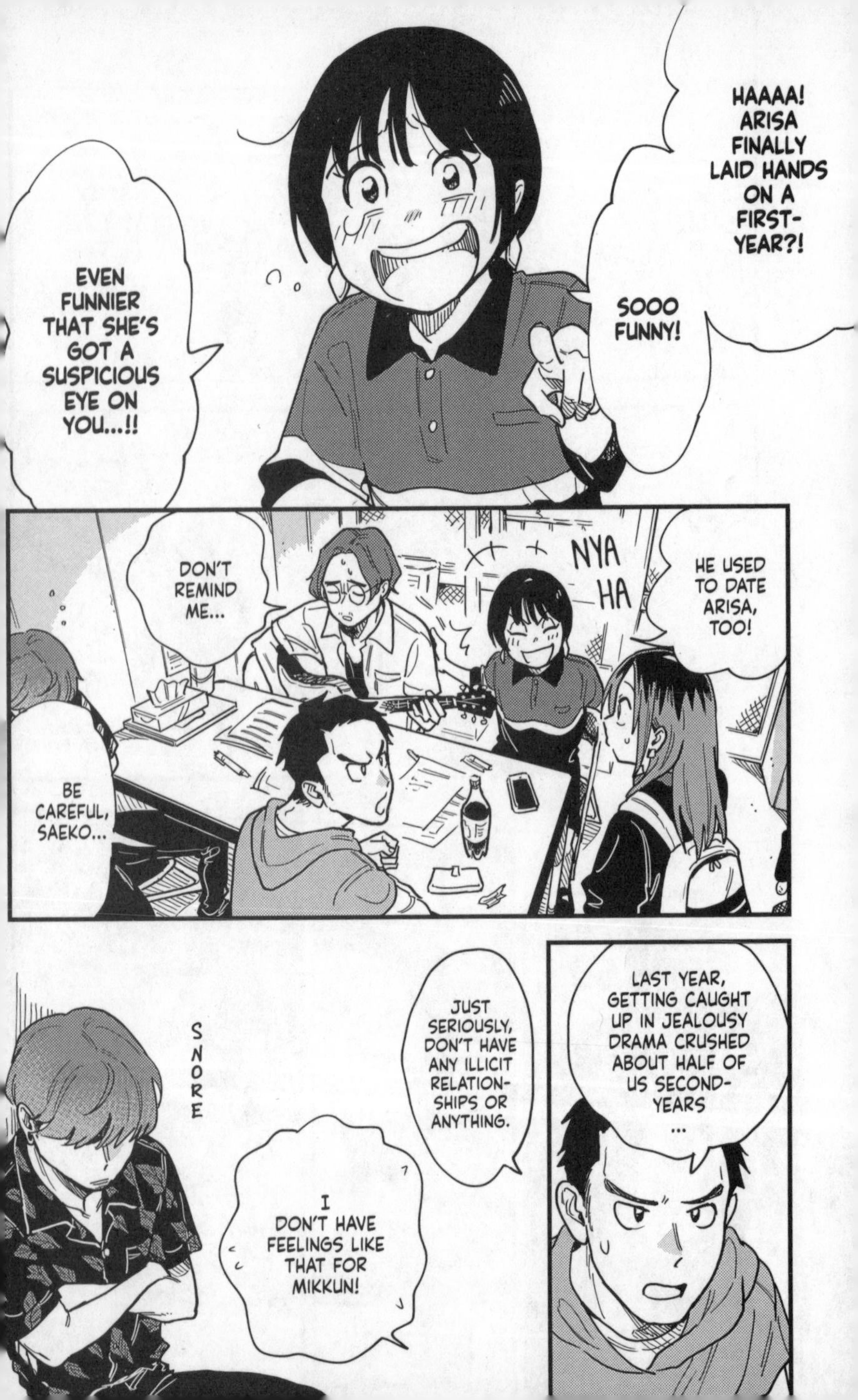
HAAAA! ARISA FINALLY LAID HANDS ON A FIRST-YEAR?!
SOOO FUNNY!
EVEN FUNNIER THAT SHE'S GOT A SUSPICIOUS EYE ON YOU...!!
HE USED TO DATE ARISA, TOO!
NYA HA
DON'T REMIND ME...
BE CAREFUL, SAEKO...
LAST YEAR, GETTING CAUGHT UP IN JEALOUSY DRAMA CRUSHED ABOUT HALF OF US SECOND-YEARS ...
JUST SERIOUSLY, DON'T HAVE ANY ILLICIT RELATION-SHIPS OR ANYTHING.
SNORE
I DON'T HAVE FEELINGS LIKE THAT FOR MIKKUN!

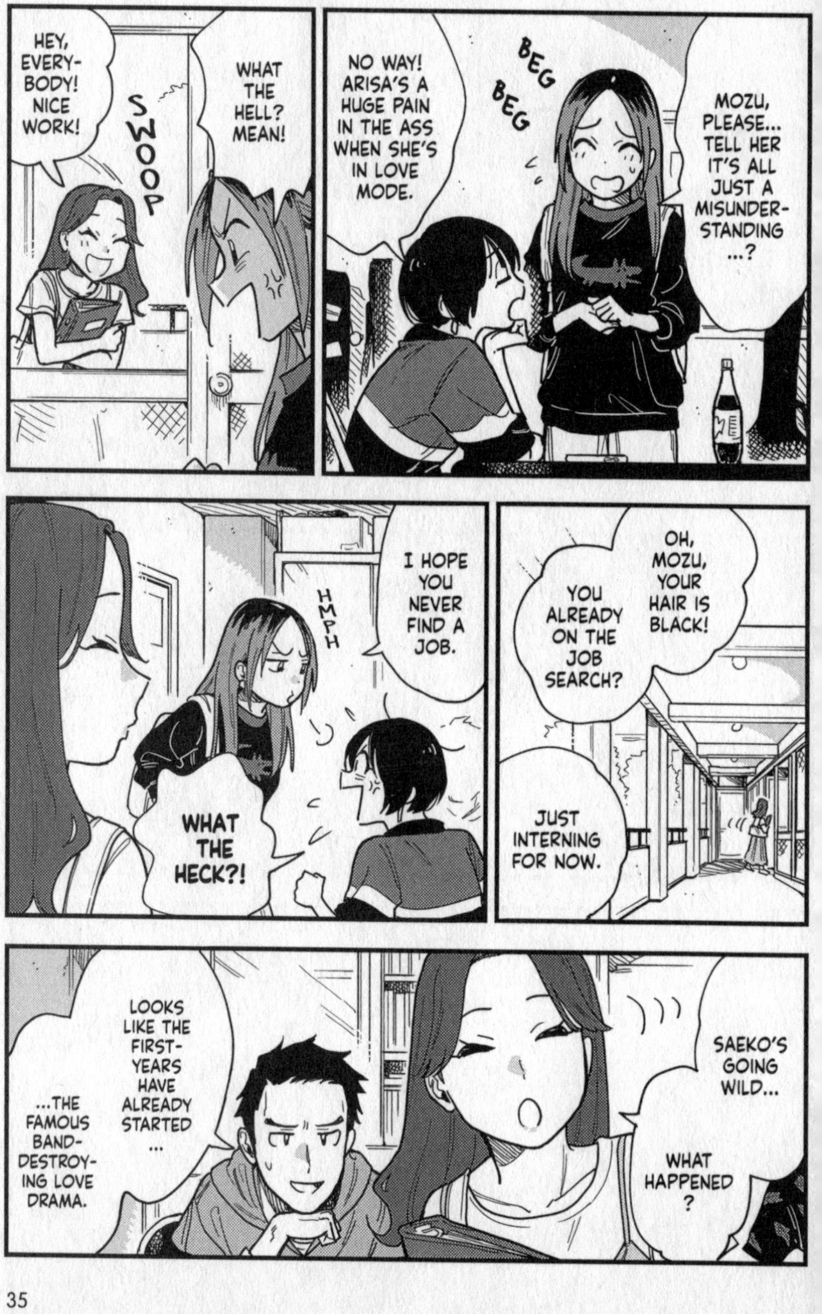
MOZU, PLEASE... TELL HER IT'S ALL JUST A MISUNDER-STANDING ...?
BEG BEG
NO WAY! ARISA'S A HUGE PAIN IN THE ASS WHEN SHE'S IN LOVE MODE.
WHAT THE HELL? MEAN!
SWOOP
HEY, EVERY-BODY! NICE WORK!
OH, MOZU, YOUR HAIR IS BLACK!
YOU ALREADY ON THE JOB SEARCH?
JUST INTERNING FOR NOW.
I HOPE YOU NEVER FIND A JOB.
HMPH
WHAT THE HECK?!
SAEKO'S GOING WILD...
WHAT HAPPENED ?
LOOKS LIKE THE FIRST-YEARS HAVE ALREADY STARTED ...
...THE FAMOUS BAND-DESTROY-ING LOVE DRAMA.

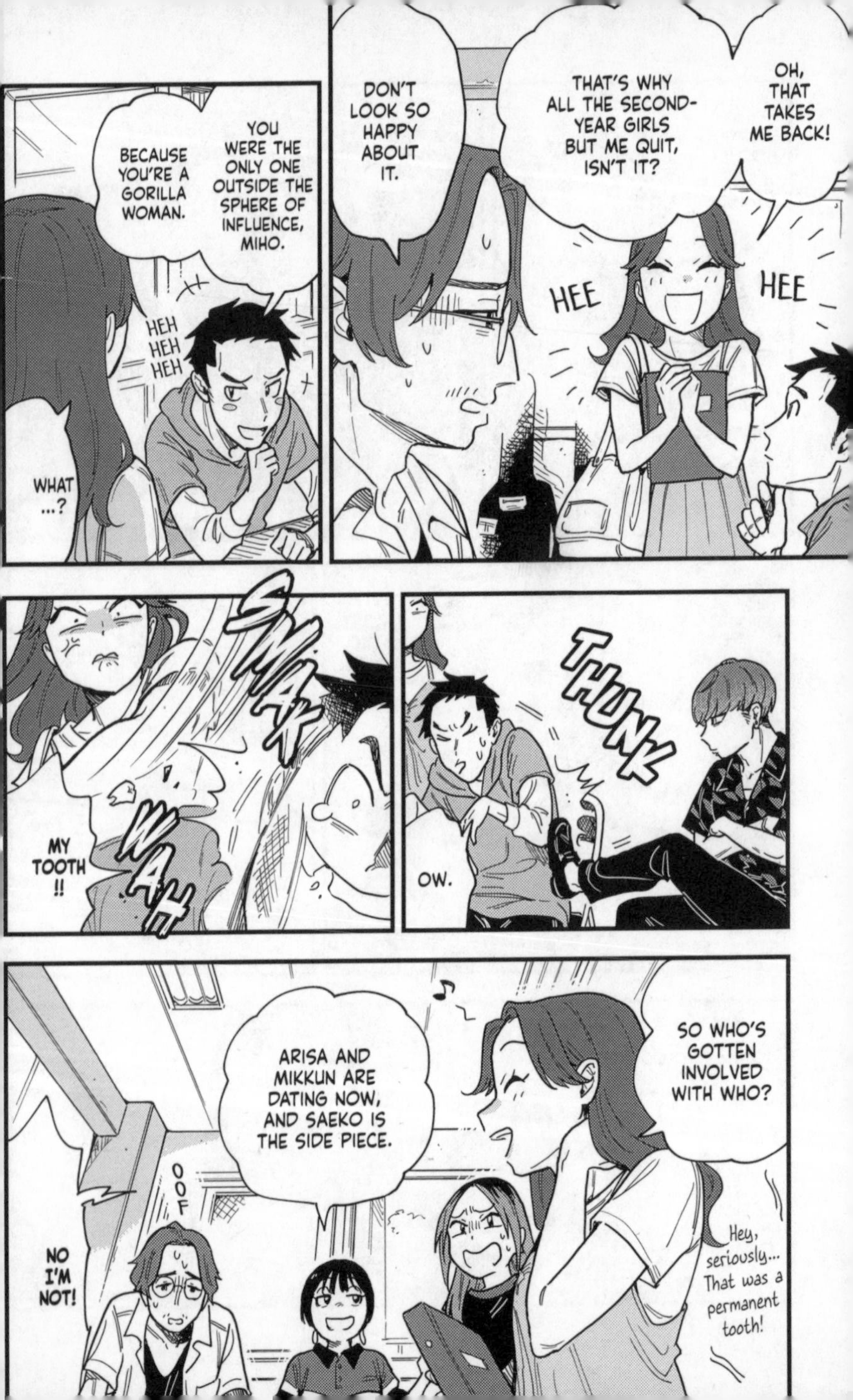
OH, THAT TAKES ME BACK!
THAT'S WHY ALL THE SECOND-YEAR GIRLS BUT ME QUIT, ISN'T IT?
HEE
HEE
DON'T LOOK SO HAPPY ABOUT IT.
YOU WERE THE ONLY ONE OUTSIDE THE SPHERE OF INFLUENCE, MIHO.
BECAUSE YOU'RE A GORILLA WOMAN.
HEH HEH HEH
WHAT ...?
THUNK
OW.
SMAK
WAH
MY TOOTH !!
SO WHO'S GOTTEN INVOLVED WITH WHO?
ARISA AND MIKKUN ARE DATING NOW, AND SAEKO IS THE SIDE PIECE.
OOF
NO I'M NOT!
Hey, seriously... That was a permanent tooth!

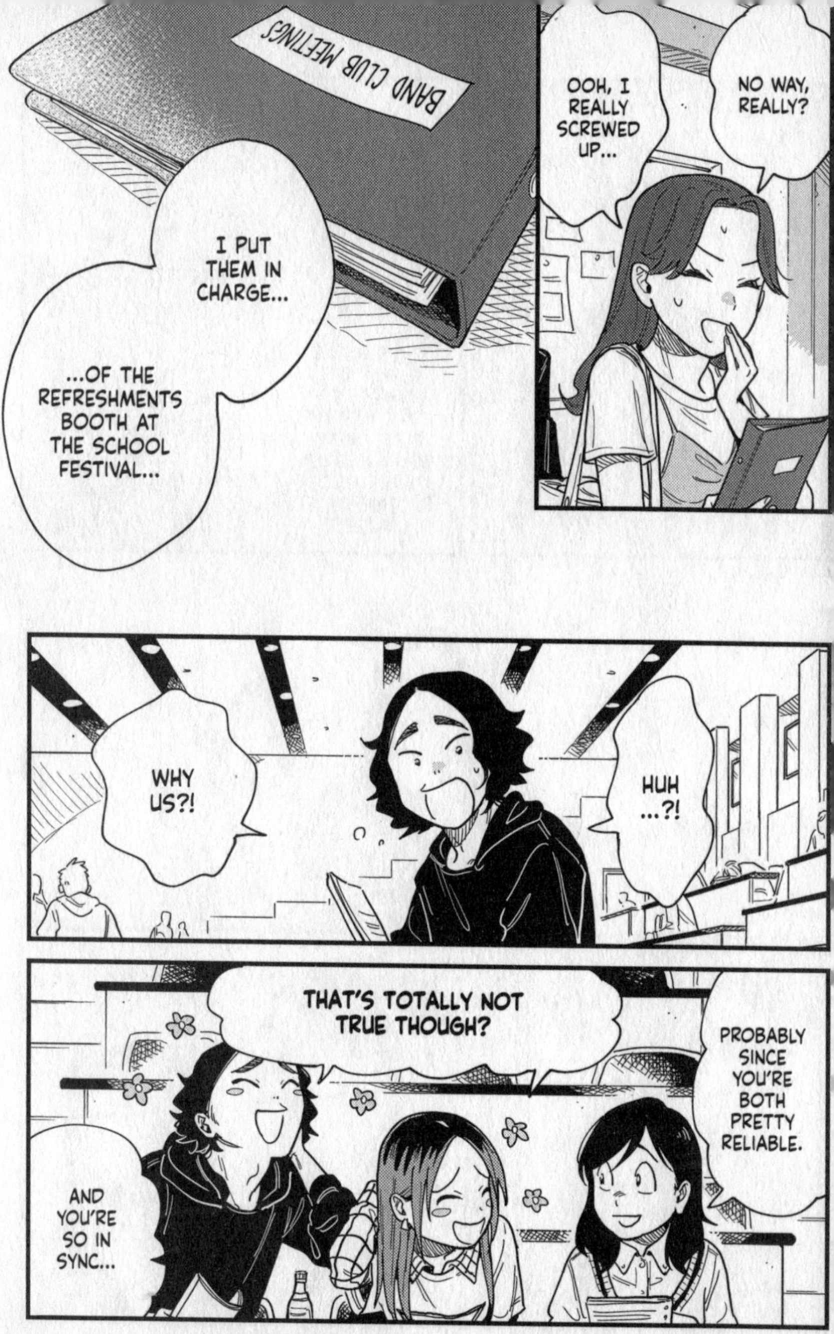
NO WAY, REALLY?
OOH, I REALLY SCREWED UP...
BAND CLUB MEETINGS
I PUT THEM IN CHARGE...
...OF THE REFRESHMENTS BOOTH AT THE SCHOOL FESTIVAL...
HUH ...?!
WHY US?!
PROBABLY SINCE YOU'RE BOTH PRETTY RELIABLE.
THAT'S TOTALLY NOT TRUE THOUGH?
AND YOU'RE SO IN SYNC...

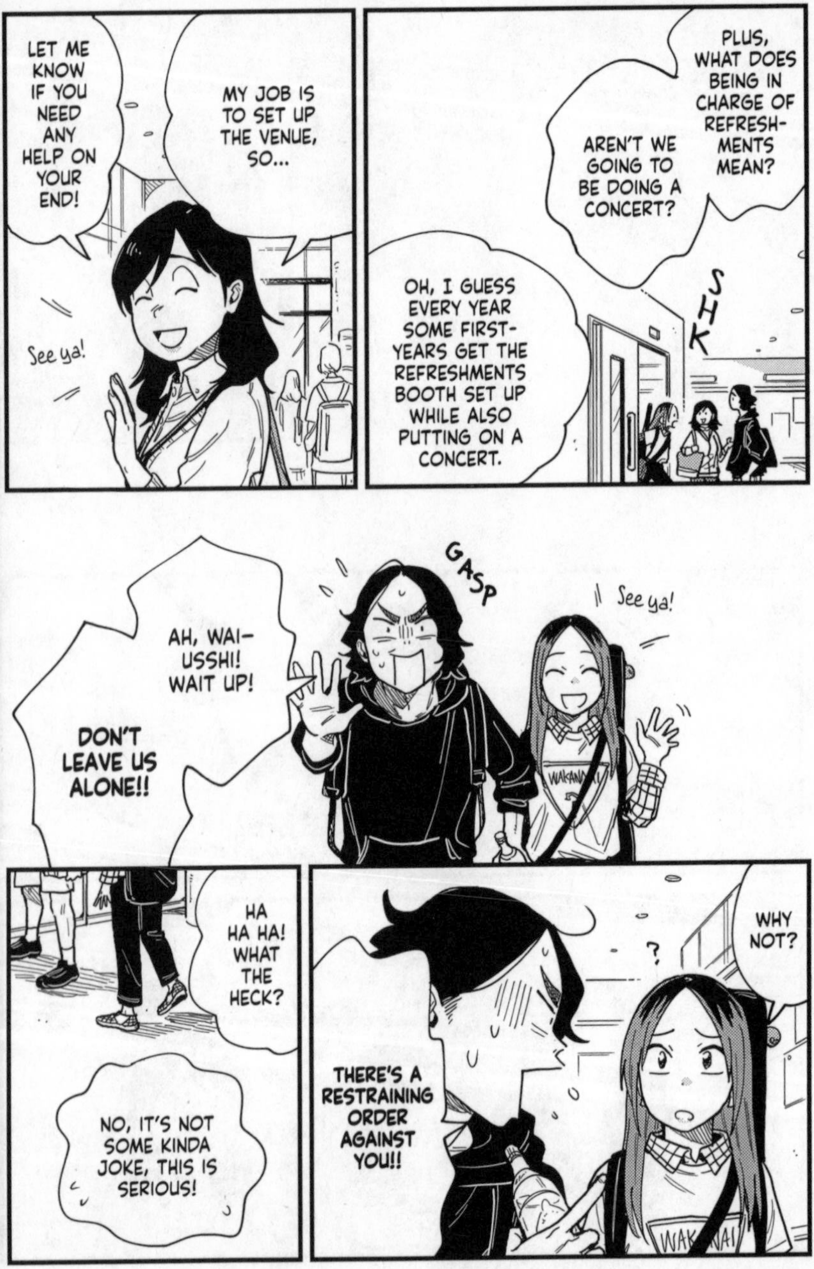
PLUS, WHAT DOES BEING IN CHARGE OF REFRESH-MENTS MEAN?
AREN'T WE GOING TO BE DOING A CONCERT?
SHK
OH, I GUESS EVERY YEAR SOME FIRST-YEARS GET THE REFRESHMENTS BOOTH SET UP WHILE ALSO PUTTING ON A CONCERT.
MY JOB IS TO SET UP THE VENUE, SO...
LET ME KNOW IF YOU NEED ANY HELP ON YOUR END!
See ya!
See ya!
GASP
AH, WAI-USSHI! WAIT UP!
DON'T LEAVE US ALONE!!
WHY NOT?
?
THERE'S A RESTRAINING ORDER AGAINST YOU!!
HA HA HA! WHAT THE HECK?
NO, IT'S NOT SOME KINDA JOKE, THIS IS SERIOUS!

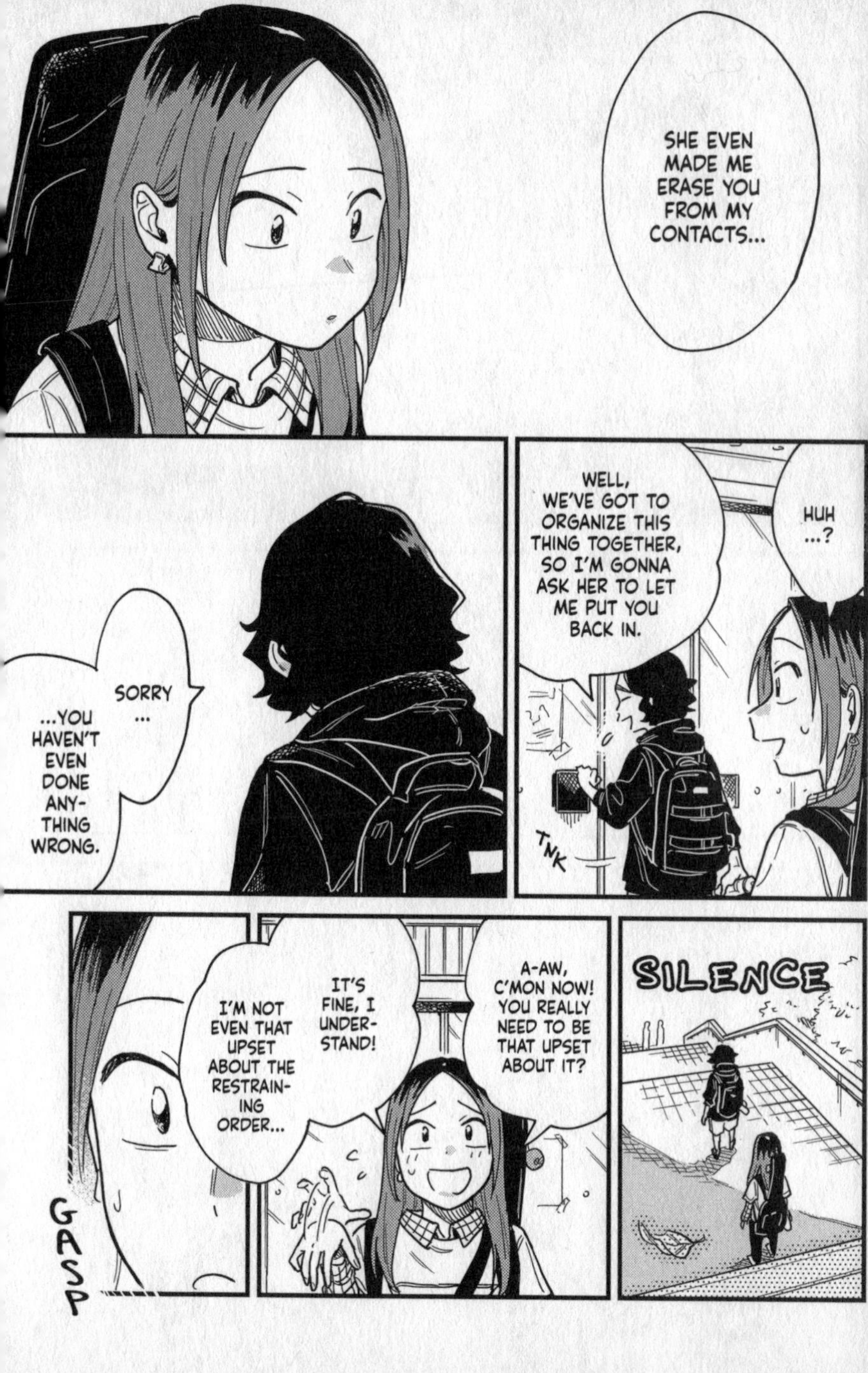
SHE EVEN MADE ME ERASE YOU FROM MY CONTACTS...
HUH ...?
WELL, WE'VE GOT TO ORGANIZE THIS THING TOGETHER, SO I'M GONNA ASK HER TO LET ME PUT YOU BACK IN.
TNK
SORRY ...
...YOU HAVEN'T EVEN DONE ANY-THING WRONG.
SILENCE
A-AW, C'MON NOW! YOU REALLY NEED TO BE THAT UPSET ABOUT IT?
IT'S FINE, I UNDER-STAND!
I'M NOT EVEN THAT UPSET ABOUT THE RESTRAIN-ING ORDER...
GASP

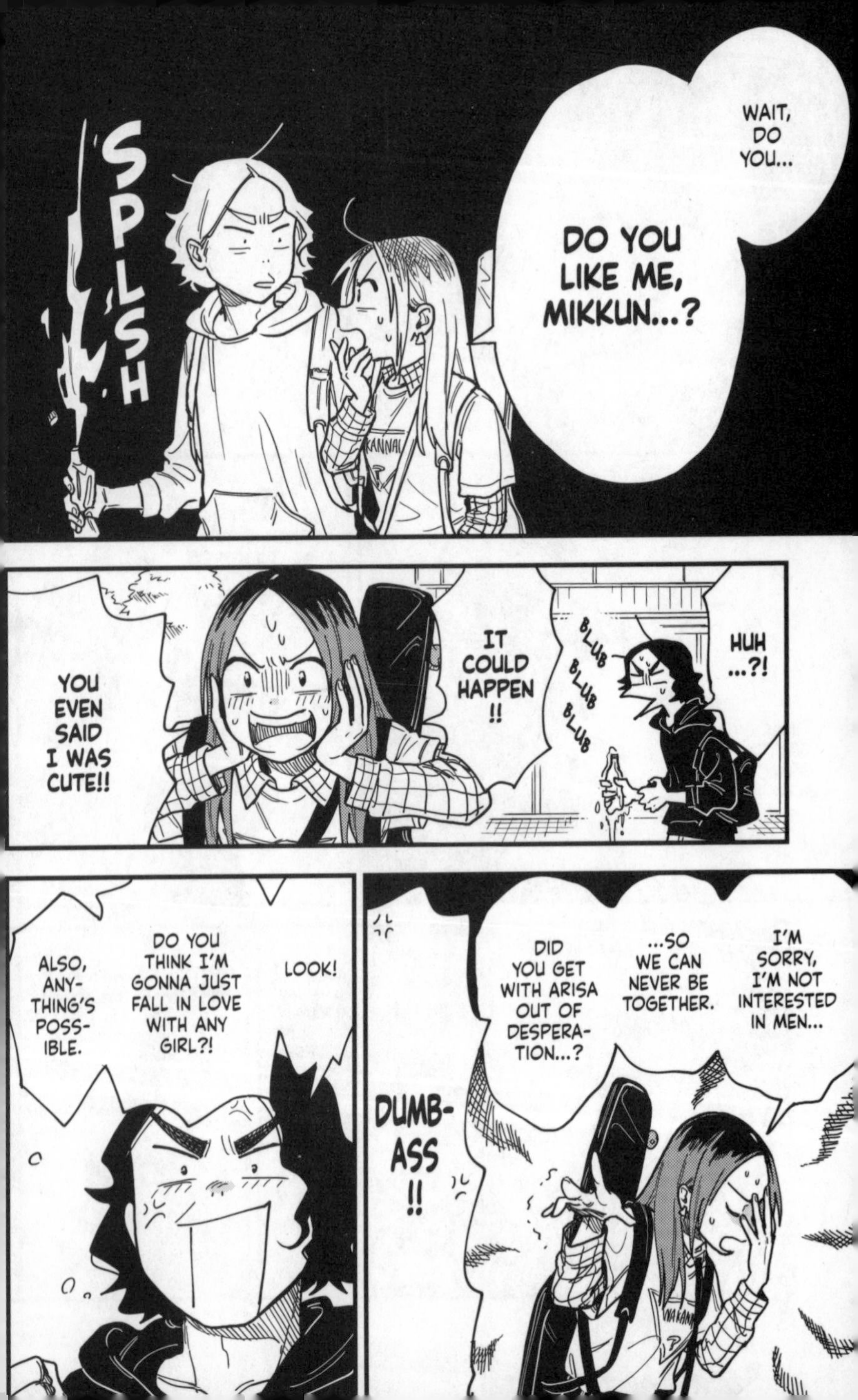
WAIT, DO YOU...
DO YOU LIKE ME, MIKKUN...?
SPLSH
HUH...?!
BLUB BLUB BLUB
IT COULD HAPPEN!!
YOU EVEN SAID I WAS CUTE!!
I'M SORRY, I'M NOT INTERESTED IN MEN...
...SO WE CAN NEVER BE TOGETHER.
DID YOU GET WITH ARISA OUT OF DESPERA-TION...?
DUMB-ASS!!
LOOK!
DO YOU THINK I'M GONNA JUST FALL IN LOVE WITH ANY GIRL?!
ALSO, ANY-THING'S POSS-IBLE.

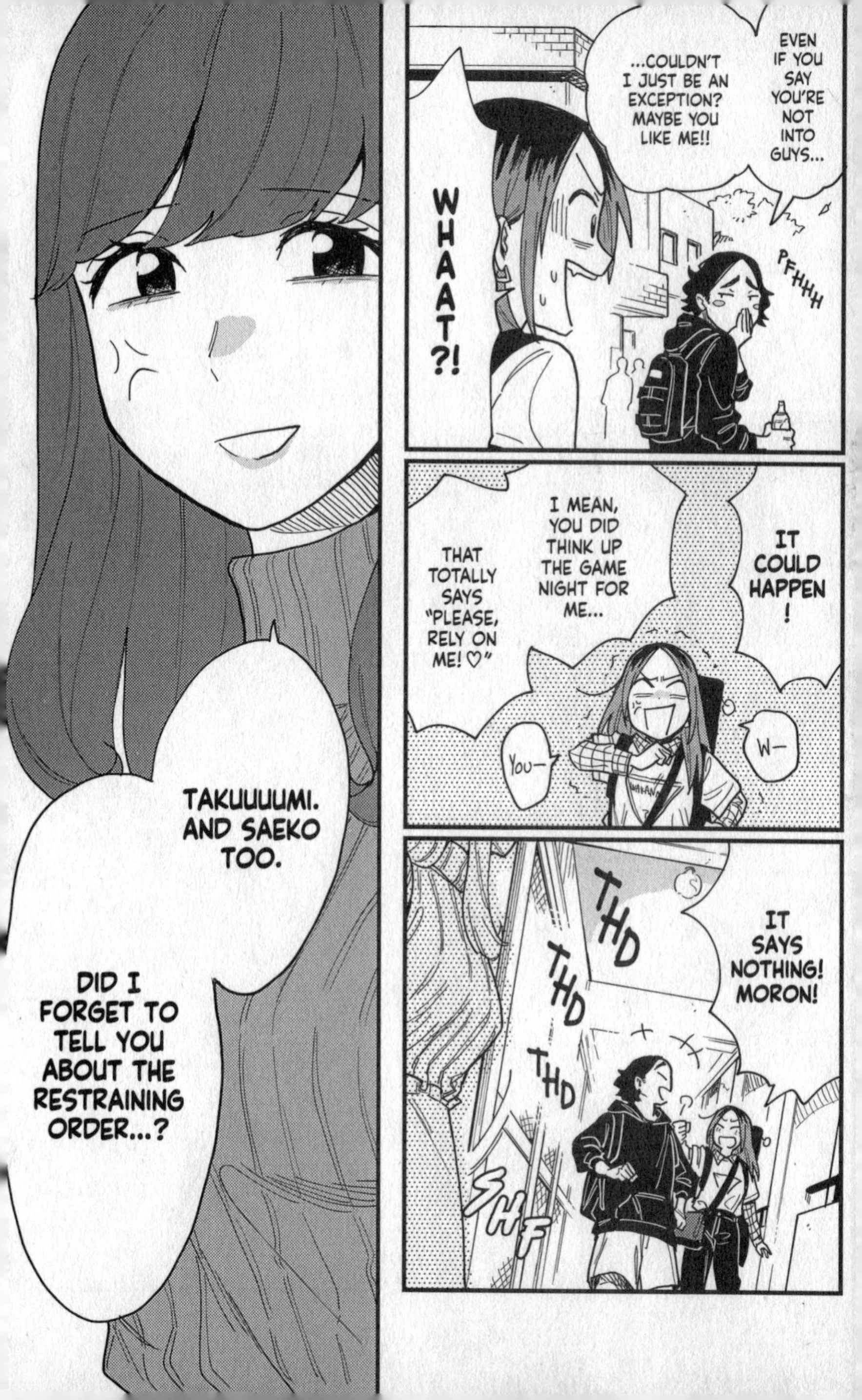
EVEN IF YOU SAY YOU'RE NOT INTO GUYS...
...COULDN'T I JUST BE AN EXCEPTION? MAYBE YOU LIKE ME!!
PFHHHH
WHAAAT?!
IT COULD HAPPEN!
I MEAN, YOU DID THINK UP THE GAME NIGHT FOR ME...
THAT TOTALLY SAYS "PLEASE, RELY ON ME! ♡"
W—
You—
IT SAYS NOTHING! MORON!
THD
THD
THD
SHF
TAKUUUUMI. AND SAEKO TOO.
DID I FORGET TO TELL YOU ABOUT THE RESTRAINING ORDER...?

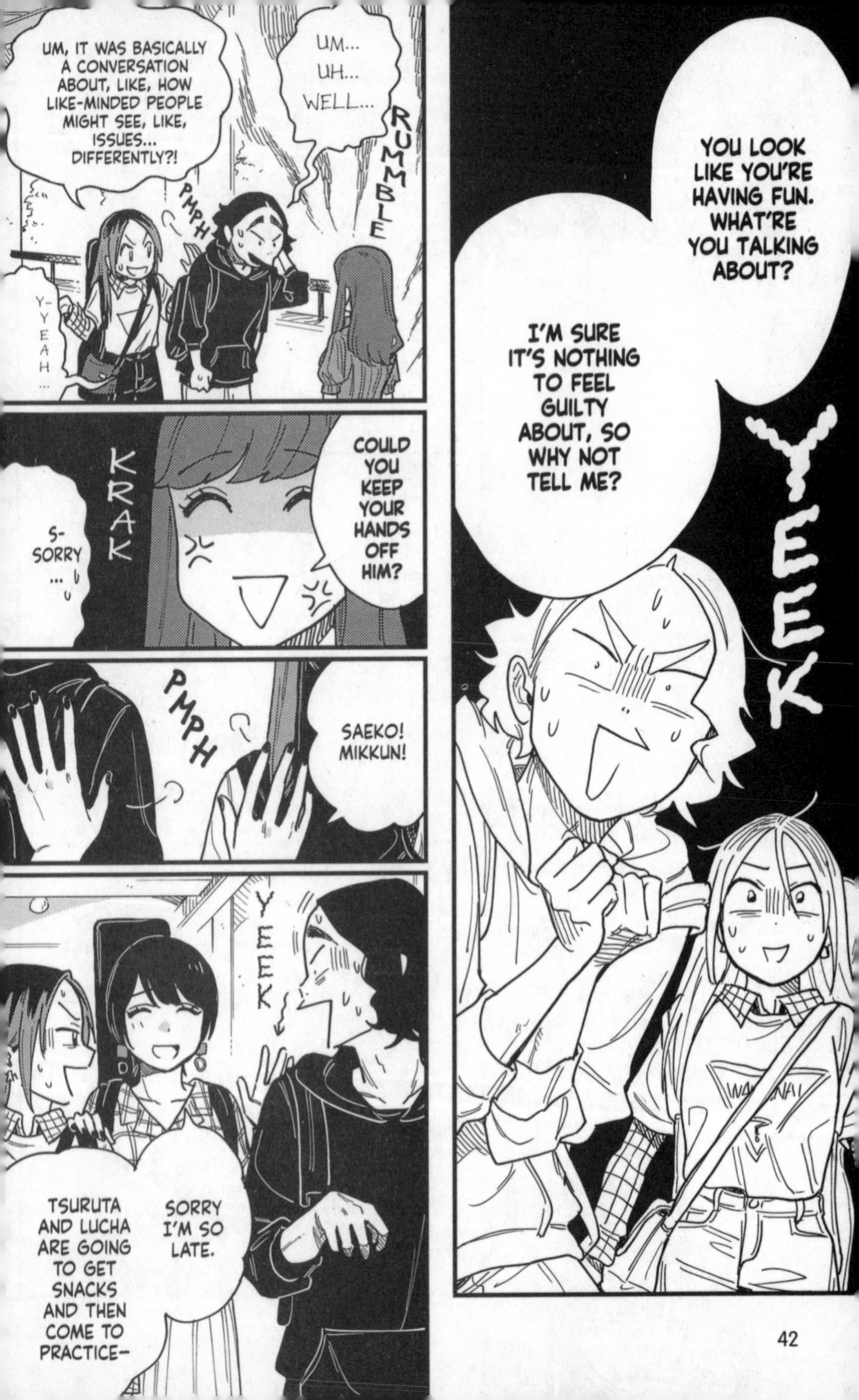
YOU LOOK LIKE YOU'RE HAVING FUN. WHAT'RE YOU TALKING ABOUT?
I'M SURE IT'S NOTHING TO FEEL GUILTY ABOUT, SO WHY NOT TELL ME?
YEEK
RUMBLE
UM... UH... WELL...
PMPH
UM, IT WAS BASICALLY A CONVERSATION ABOUT, LIKE, HOW LIKE-MINDED PEOPLE MIGHT SEE, LIKE, ISSUES... DIFFERENTLY?!
Y-YEAH...
COULD YOU KEEP YOUR HANDS OFF HIM?
KRAK
S-SORRY...
SAEKO! MIKKUN!
PMPH
YEEK
SORRY I'M SO LATE.
TSURUTA AND LUCHA ARE GOING TO GET SNACKS AND THEN COME TO PRACTICE-

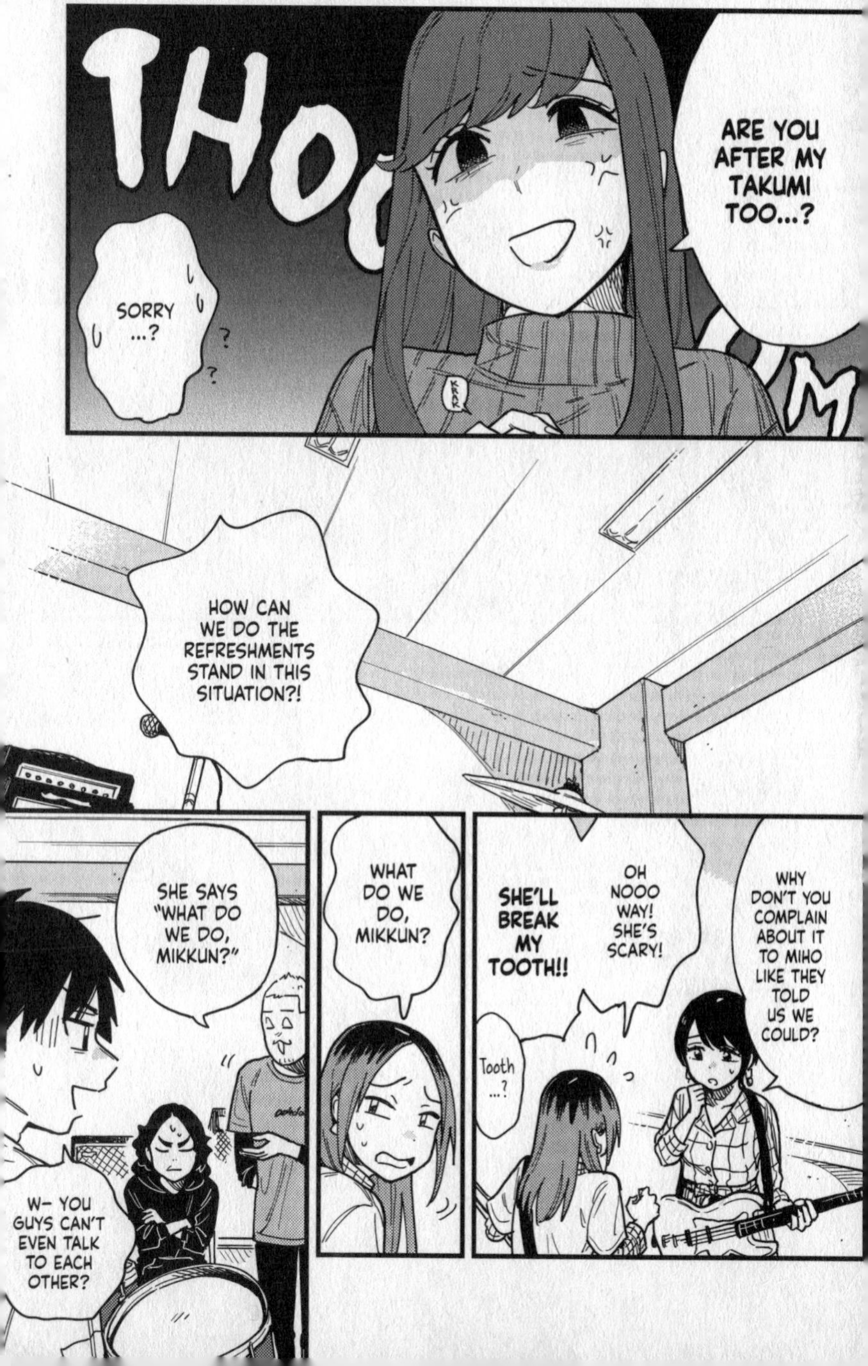
ARE YOU AFTER MY TAKUMI TOO...?
THO
M
KRAK
SORRY ...?
?
?
HOW CAN WE DO THE REFRESHMENTS STAND IN THIS SITUATION?!
WHY DON'T YOU COMPLAIN ABOUT IT TO MIHO LIKE THEY TOLD US WE COULD?
OH NOOO WAY! SHE'S SCARY!
SHE'LL BREAK MY TOOTH!!
Tooth ...?
WHAT DO WE DO, MIKKUN?
SHE SAYS "WHAT DO WE DO, MIKKUN?"
W- YOU GUYS CAN'T EVEN TALK TO EACH OTHER?

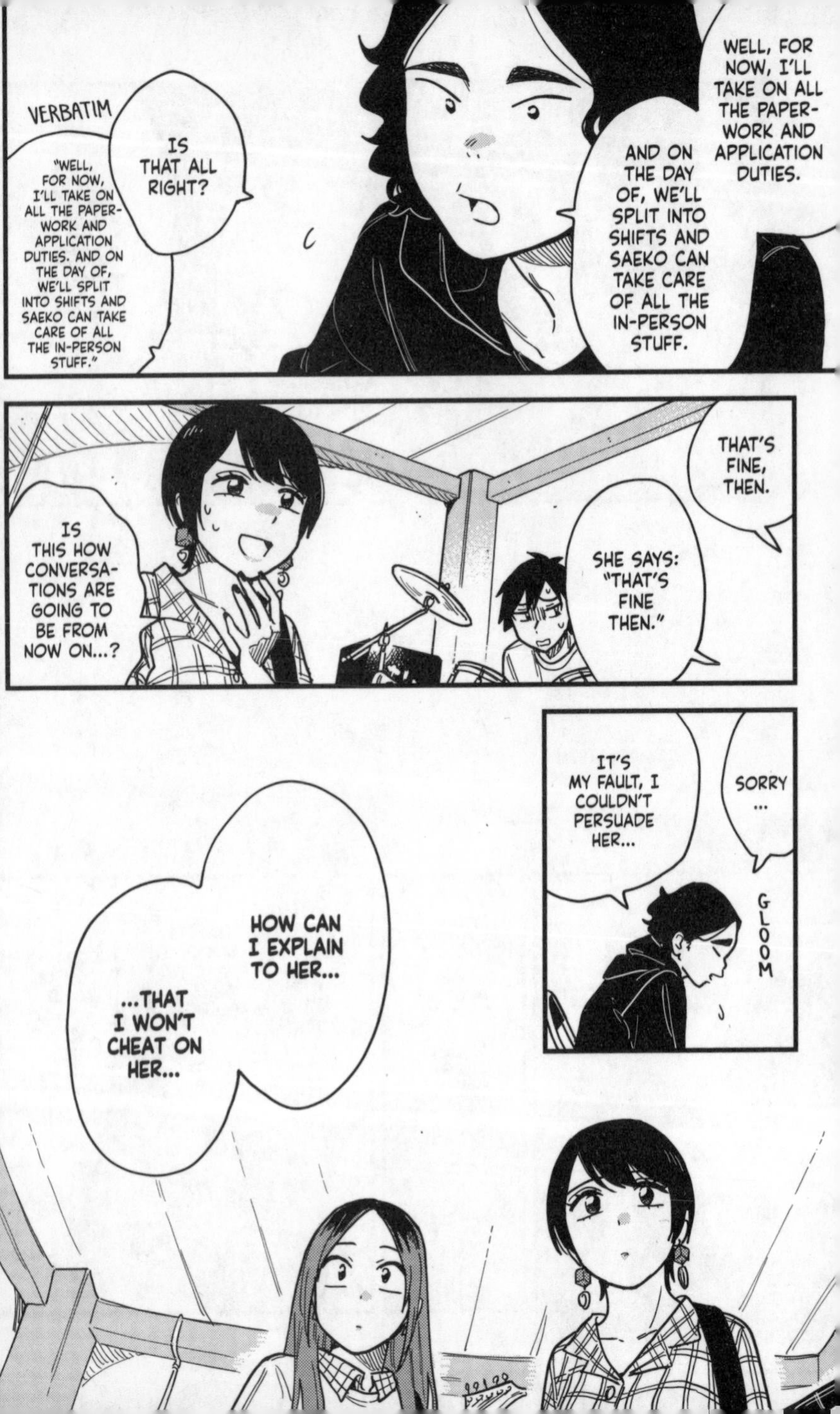
WELL, FOR NOW, I'LL TAKE ON ALL THE PAPER-WORK AND APPLICATION DUTIES.
AND ON THE DAY OF, WE'LL SPLIT INTO SHIFTS AND SAEKO CAN TAKE CARE OF ALL THE IN-PERSON STUFF.
IS THAT ALL RIGHT?
VERBATIM
"WELL, FOR NOW, I'LL TAKE ON ALL THE PAPER-WORK AND APPLICATION DUTIES. AND ON THE DAY OF, WE'LL SPLIT INTO SHIFTS AND SAEKO CAN TAKE CARE OF ALL THE IN-PERSON STUFF."
THAT'S FINE, THEN.
SHE SAYS: "THAT'S FINE THEN."
IS THIS HOW CONVERSA-TIONS ARE GOING TO BE FROM NOW ON...?
SORRY...
IT'S MY FAULT, I COULDN'T PERSUADE HER...
GLOOM
HOW CAN I EXPLAIN TO HER...
...THAT I WON'T CHEAT ON HER...

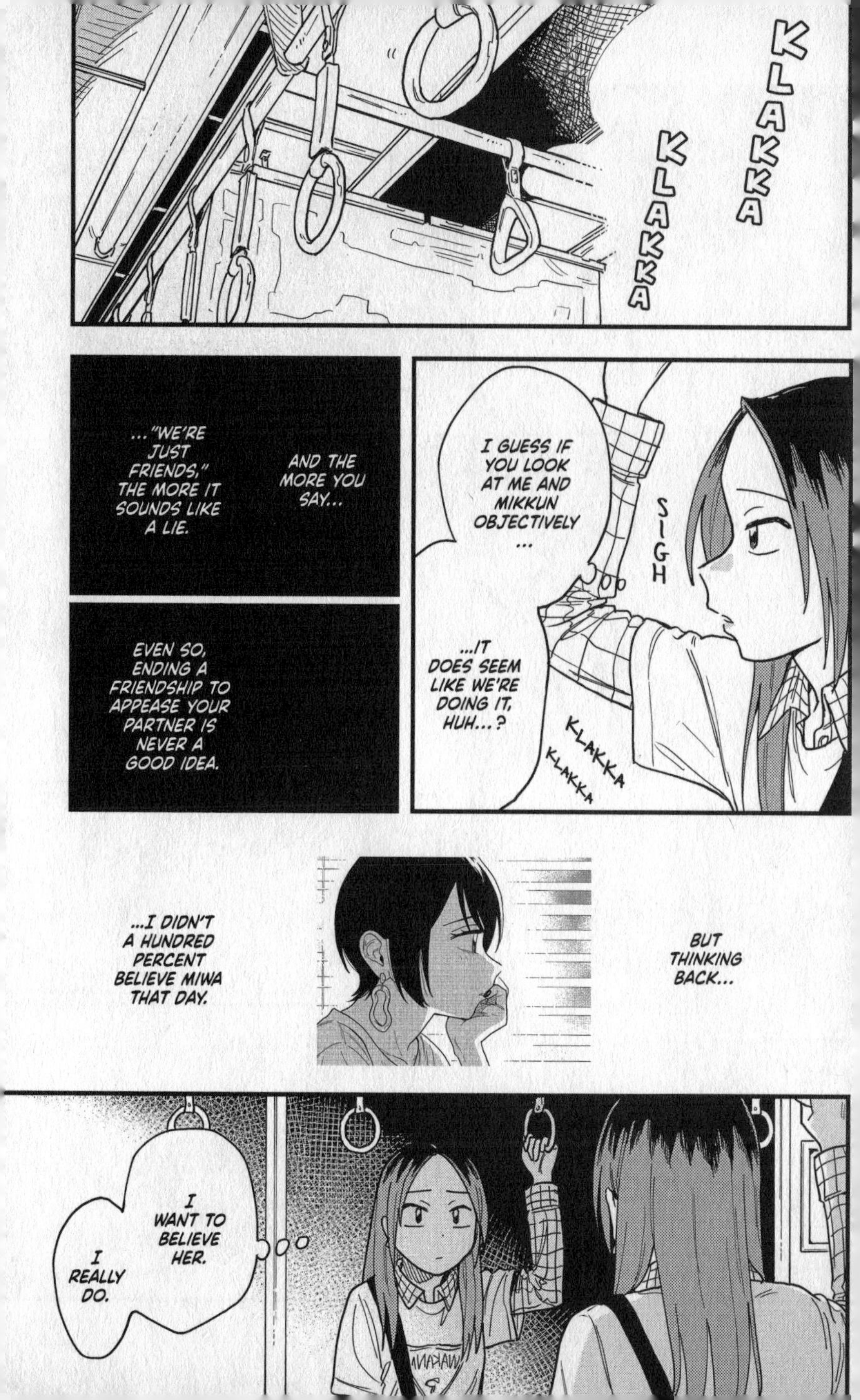
KLAKKA
KLAKKA
I GUESS IF YOU LOOK AT ME AND MIKKUN OBJECTIVELY...
SIGH
...IT DOES SEEM LIKE WE'RE DOING IT, HUH...?
KLAKKA
KLAKKA
AND THE MORE YOU SAY...
..."WE'RE JUST FRIENDS," THE MORE IT SOUNDS LIKE A LIE.
EVEN SO, ENDING A FRIENDSHIP TO APPEASE YOUR PARTNER IS NEVER A GOOD IDEA.
BUT THINKING BACK...
...I DIDN'T A HUNDRED PERCENT BELIEVE MIWA THAT DAY.
I WANT TO BELIEVE HER.
I REALLY DO.

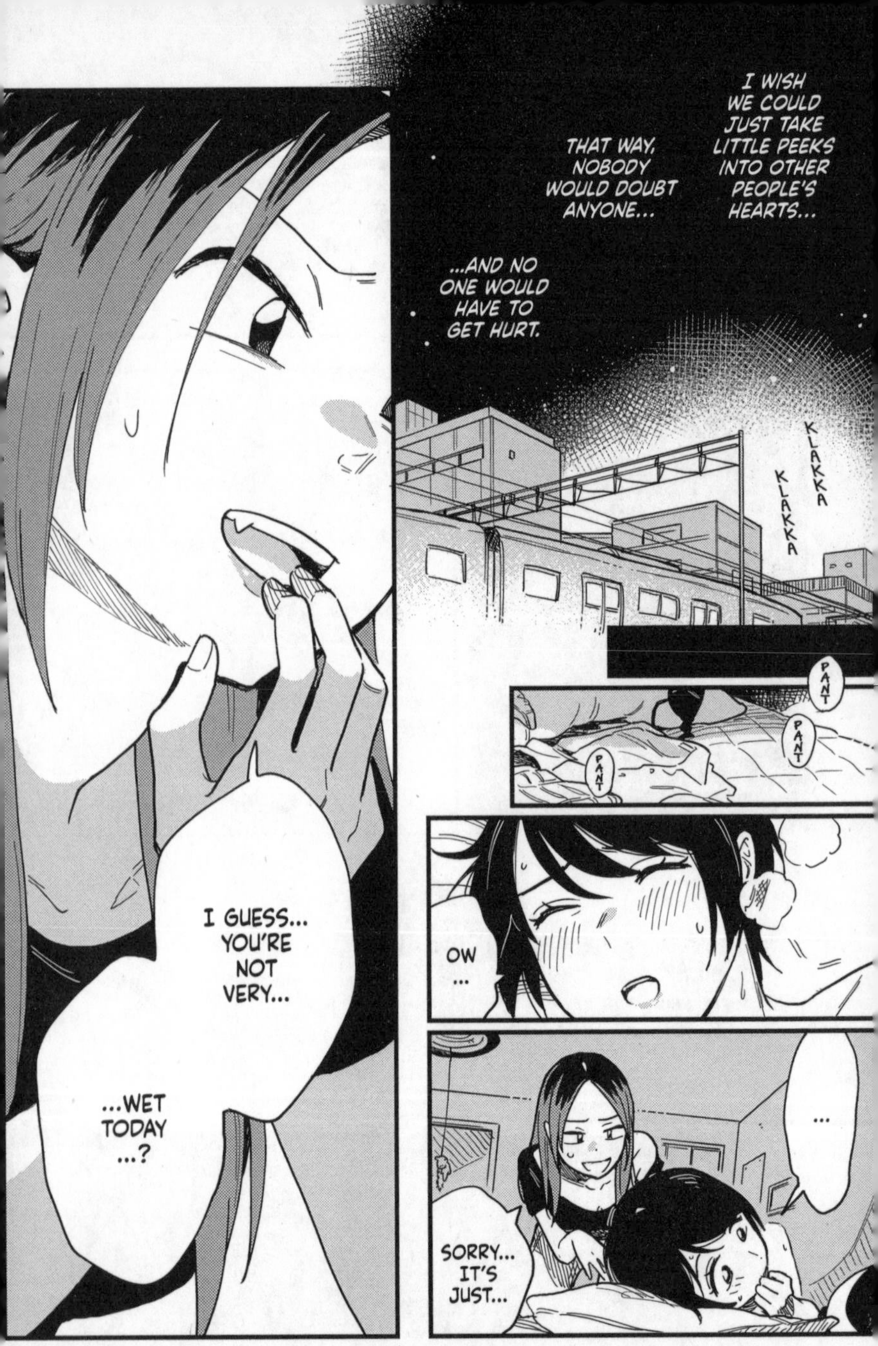
I WISH WE COULD JUST TAKE LITTLE PEEKS INTO OTHER PEOPLE'S HEARTS...
THAT WAY, NOBODY WOULD DOUBT ANYONE...
...AND NO ONE WOULD HAVE TO GET HURT.
KLAKKA
KLAKKA
PANT
PANT
PANT
OW ...
...
SORRY... IT'S JUST...
I GUESS... YOU'RE NOT VERY...
...WET TODAY ...?

HOW DO WE RELATIONSHIP?

HOW DO WE RELATIONSHIP?

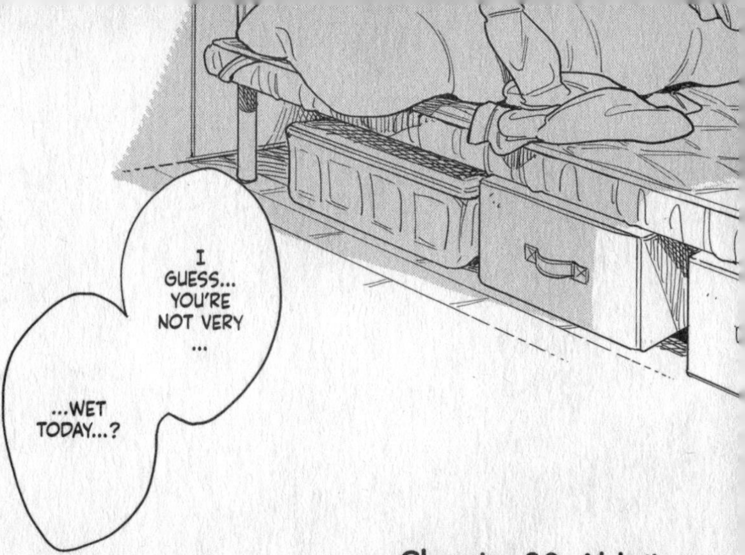
I GUESS... YOU'RE NOT VERY ...
...WET TODAY...?

Chapter 30: Ablutions

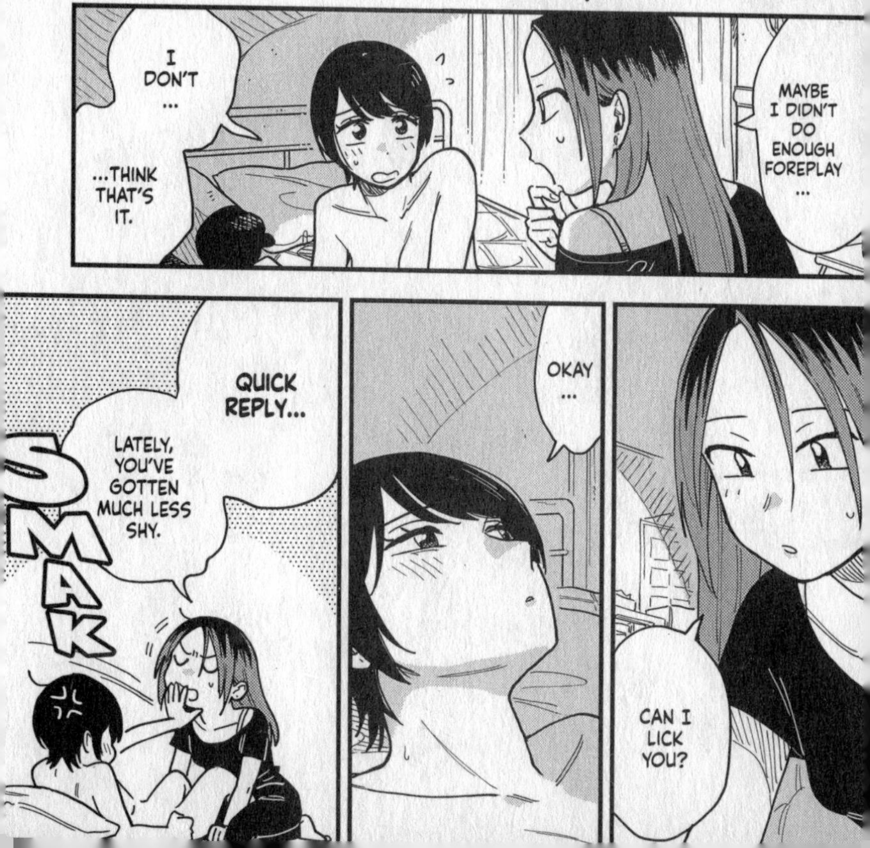
MAYBE I DIDN'T DO ENOUGH FOREPLAY ...
I DON'T ...
...THINK THAT'S IT.
CAN I LICK YOU?
OKAY ...
QUICK REPLY...
LATELY, YOU'VE GOTTEN MUCH LESS SHY.
SMAK

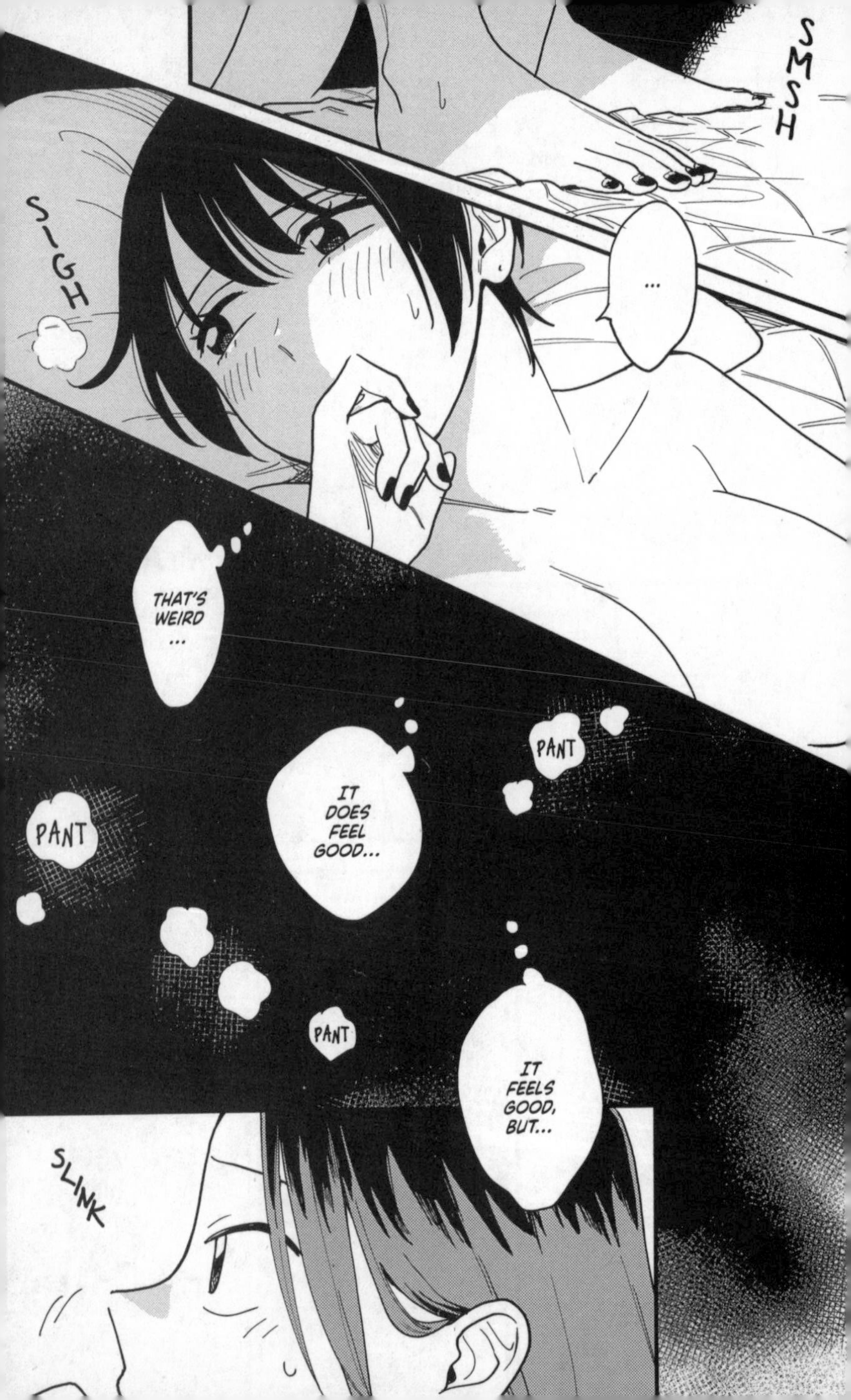
SMSH
...
SIGH
THAT'S WEIRD...
PANT
IT DOES FEEL GOOD...
PANT
PANT
IT FEELS GOOD, BUT...
SLINK

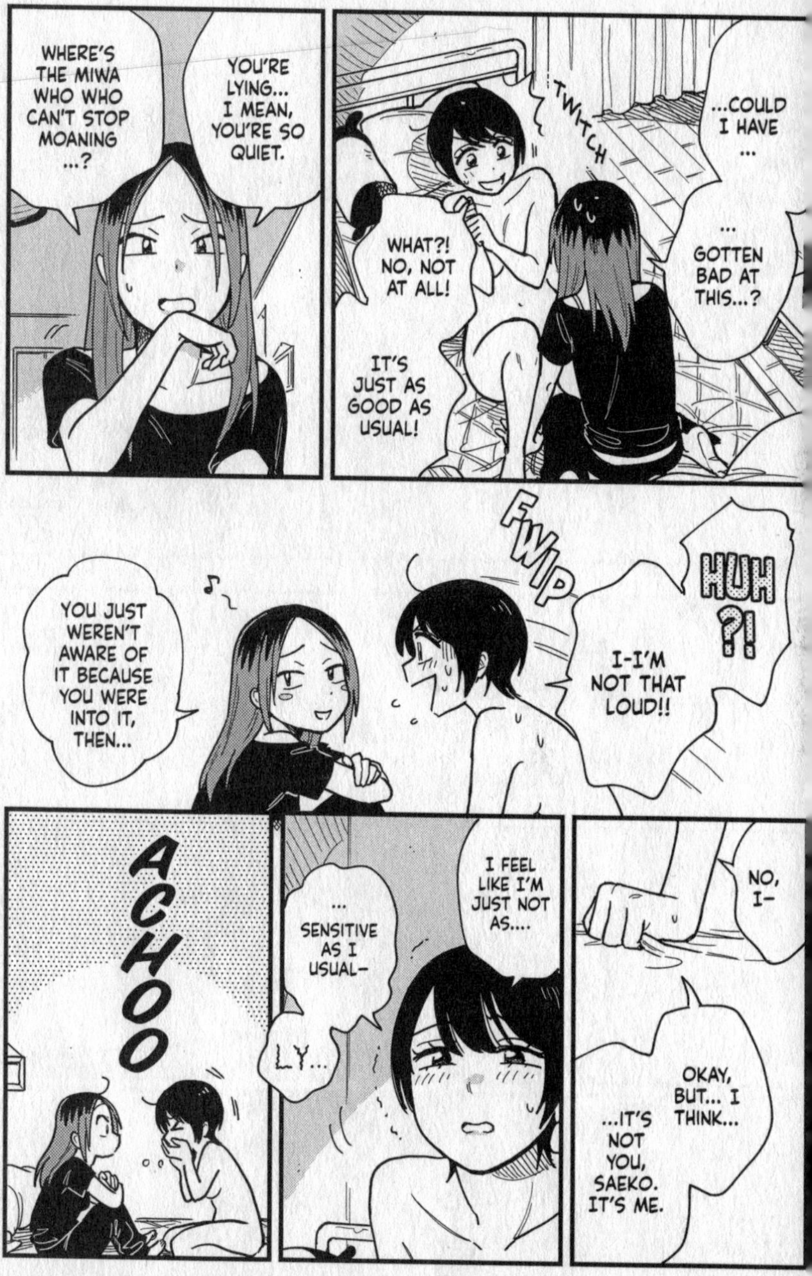
TWITCH
...COULD I HAVE ...
... GOTTEN BAD AT THIS...?
WHAT?! NO, NOT AT ALL!
IT'S JUST AS GOOD AS USUAL!
YOU'RE LYING... I MEAN, YOU'RE SO QUIET.
WHERE'S THE MIWA WHO WHO CAN'T STOP MOANING ...?
HUH ?!
FWIP
I-I'M NOT THAT LOUD!!
YOU JUST WEREN'T AWARE OF IT BECAUSE YOU WERE INTO IT, THEN...
NO, I-
OKAY, BUT... I THINK...
...IT'S NOT YOU, SAEKO. IT'S ME.
I FEEL LIKE I'M JUST NOT AS....
... SENSITIVE AS I USUAL-
LY...
ACHOO

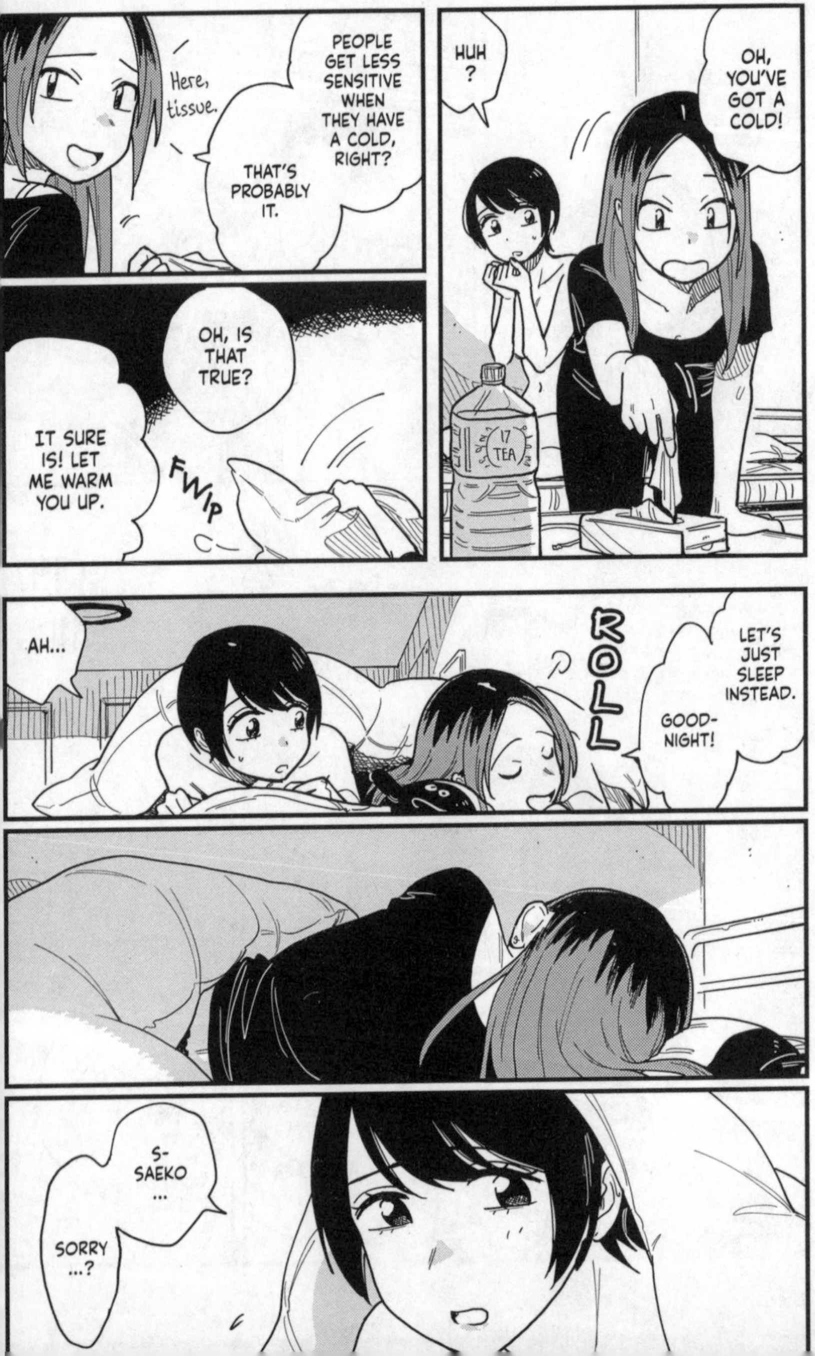
OH, YOU'VE GOT A COLD!
HUH?
17 TEA
PEOPLE GET LESS SENSITIVE WHEN THEY HAVE A COLD, RIGHT?
THAT'S PROBABLY IT.
Here, tissue.
OH, IS THAT TRUE?
IT SURE IS! LET ME WARM YOU UP.
FWIP
LET'S JUST SLEEP INSTEAD.
GOOD-NIGHT!
ROLL
AH...
S-SAEKO ...
SORRY ...?

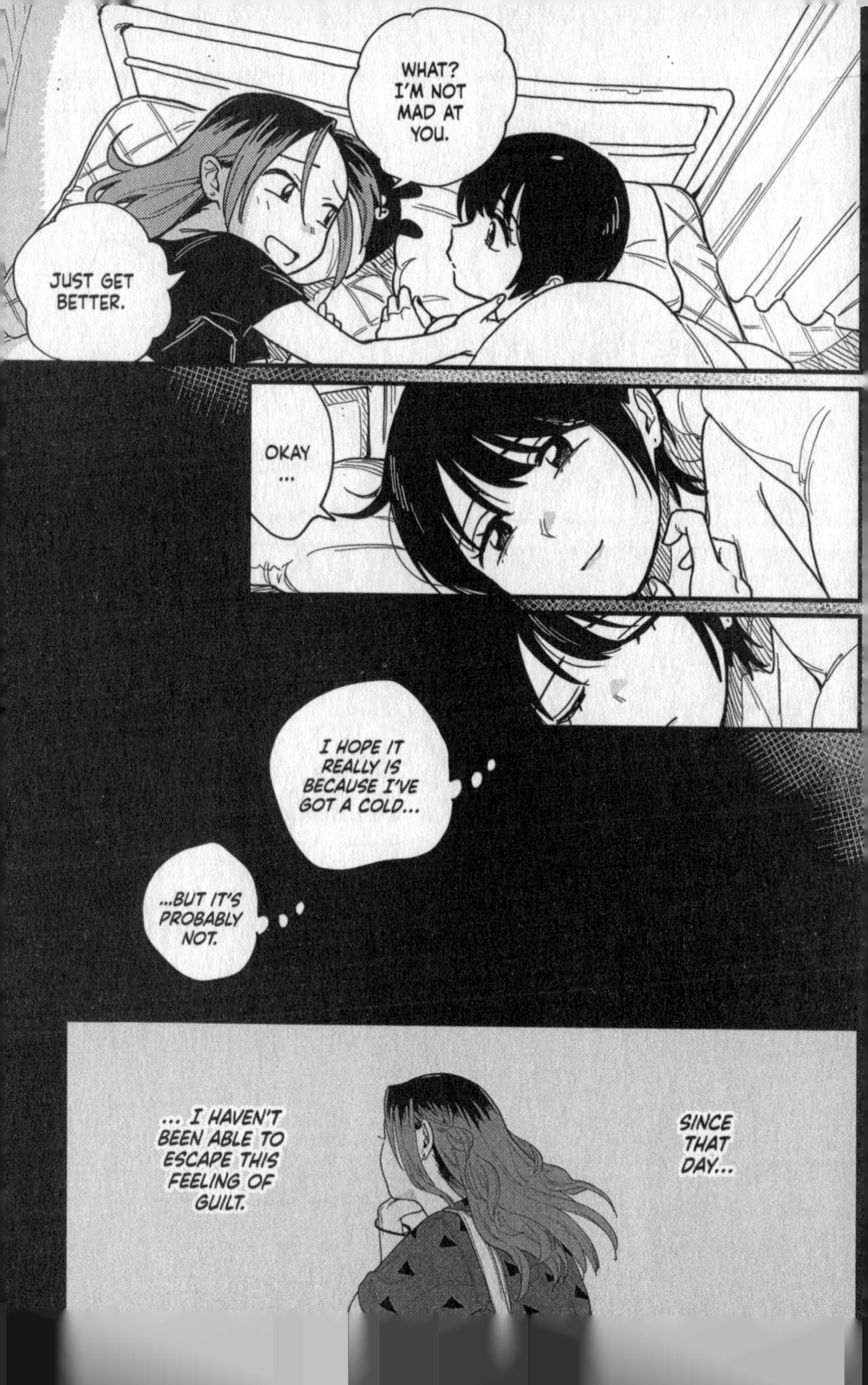
WHAT? I'M NOT MAD AT YOU.
JUST GET BETTER.
OKAY ...
I HOPE IT REALLY IS BECAUSE I'VE GOT A COLD...
...BUT IT'S PROBABLY NOT.
SINCE THAT DAY...
... I HAVEN'T BEEN ABLE TO ESCAPE THIS FEELING OF GUILT.

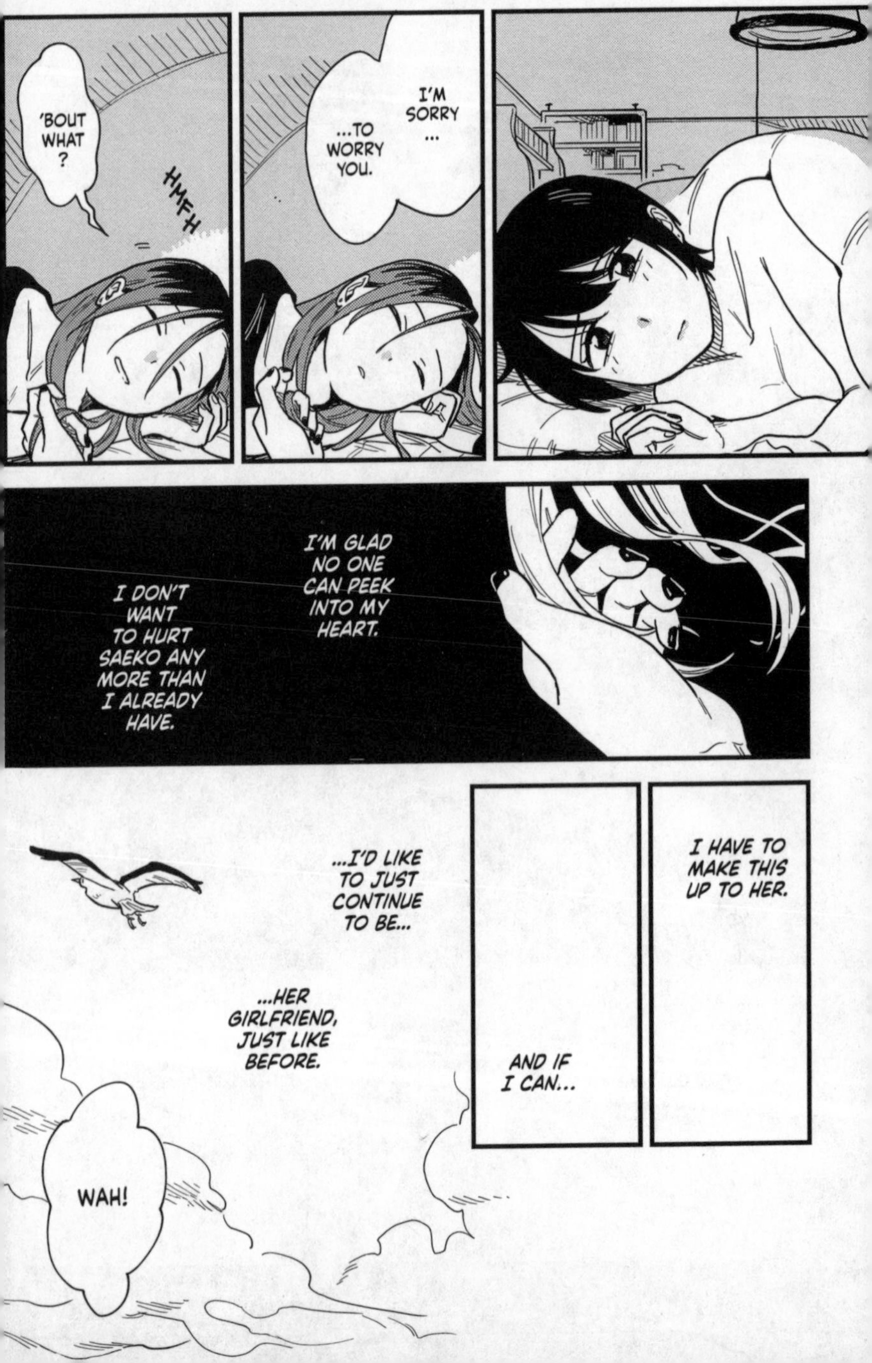
I'M SORRY ...
...TO WORRY YOU.
HMFH
'BOUT WHAT?
I'M GLAD NO ONE CAN PEEK INTO MY HEART.
I DON'T WANT TO HURT SAEKO ANY MORE THAN I ALREADY HAVE.
I HAVE TO MAKE THIS UP TO HER.
AND IF I CAN...
...I'D LIKE TO JUST CONTINUE TO BE...
...HER GIRLFRIEND, JUST LIKE BEFORE.
WAH!

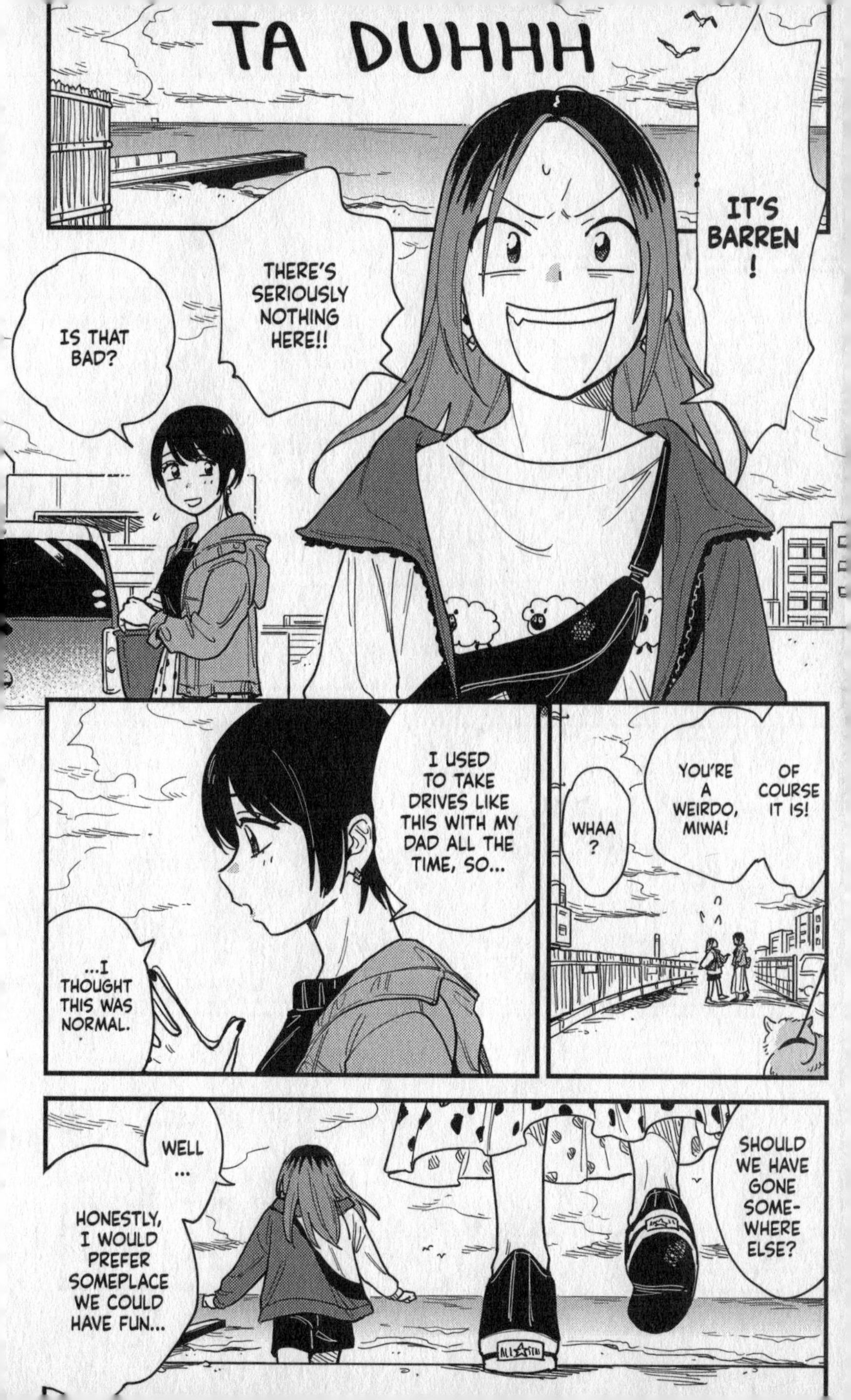
TA DUHHH
IT'S BARREN!
THERE'S SERIOUSLY NOTHING HERE!!
IS THAT BAD?
OF COURSE IT IS!
YOU'RE A WEIRDO, MIWA!
WHAA?
I USED TO TAKE DRIVES LIKE THIS WITH MY DAD ALL THE TIME, SO...
...I THOUGHT THIS WAS NORMAL.
SHOULD WE HAVE GONE SOME-WHERE ELSE?
WELL...
HONESTLY, I WOULD PREFER SOMEPLACE WE COULD HAVE FUN...

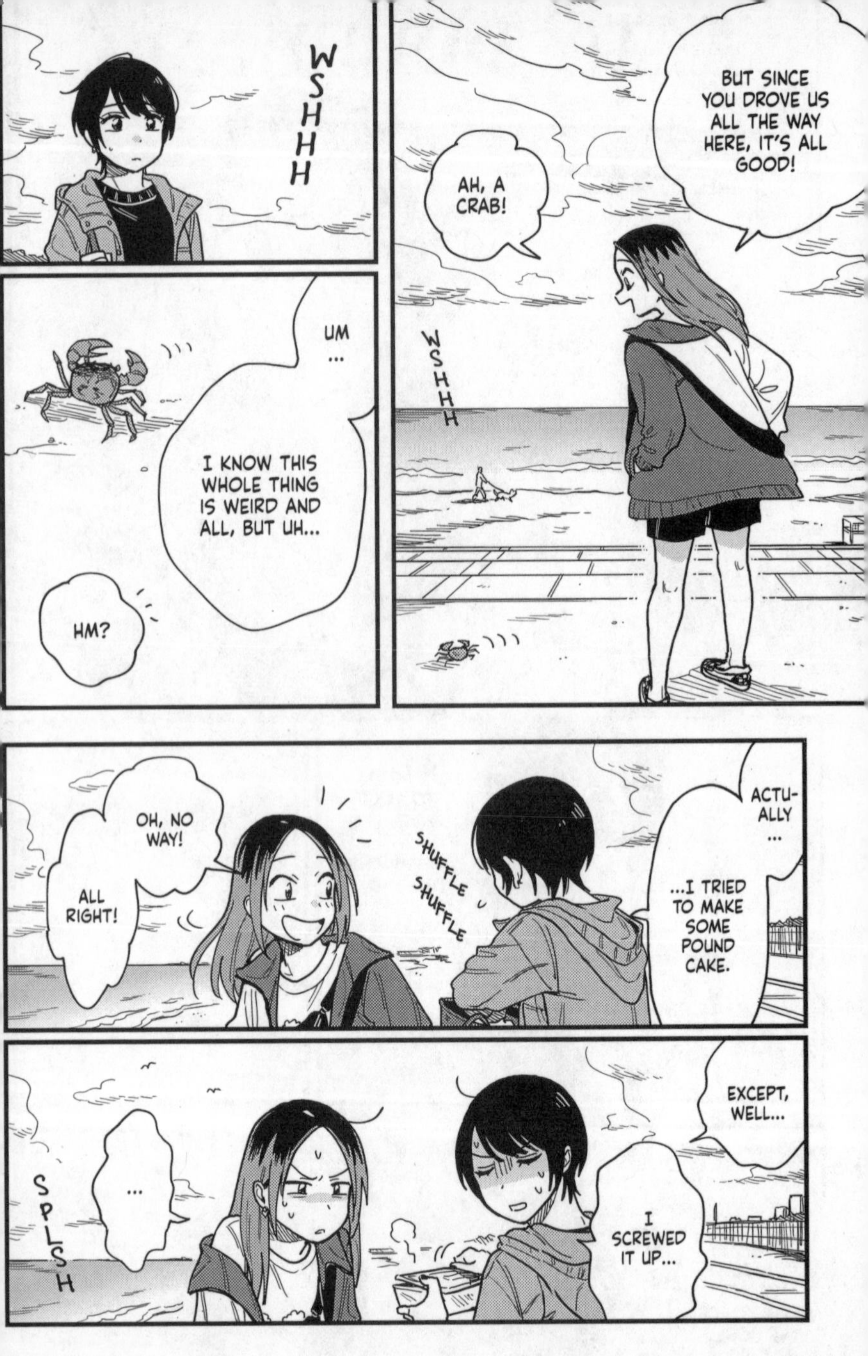
BUT SINCE YOU DROVE US ALL THE WAY HERE, IT'S ALL GOOD!
AH, A CRAB!
WSHHH
WSHHH
UM ...
I KNOW THIS WHOLE THING IS WEIRD AND ALL, BUT UH...
HM?
ACTU-ALLY ...
...I TRIED TO MAKE SOME POUND CAKE.
SHUFFLE SHUFFLE
OH, NO WAY!
ALL RIGHT!
EXCEPT, WELL...
I SCREWED IT UP...
...
SPLSH

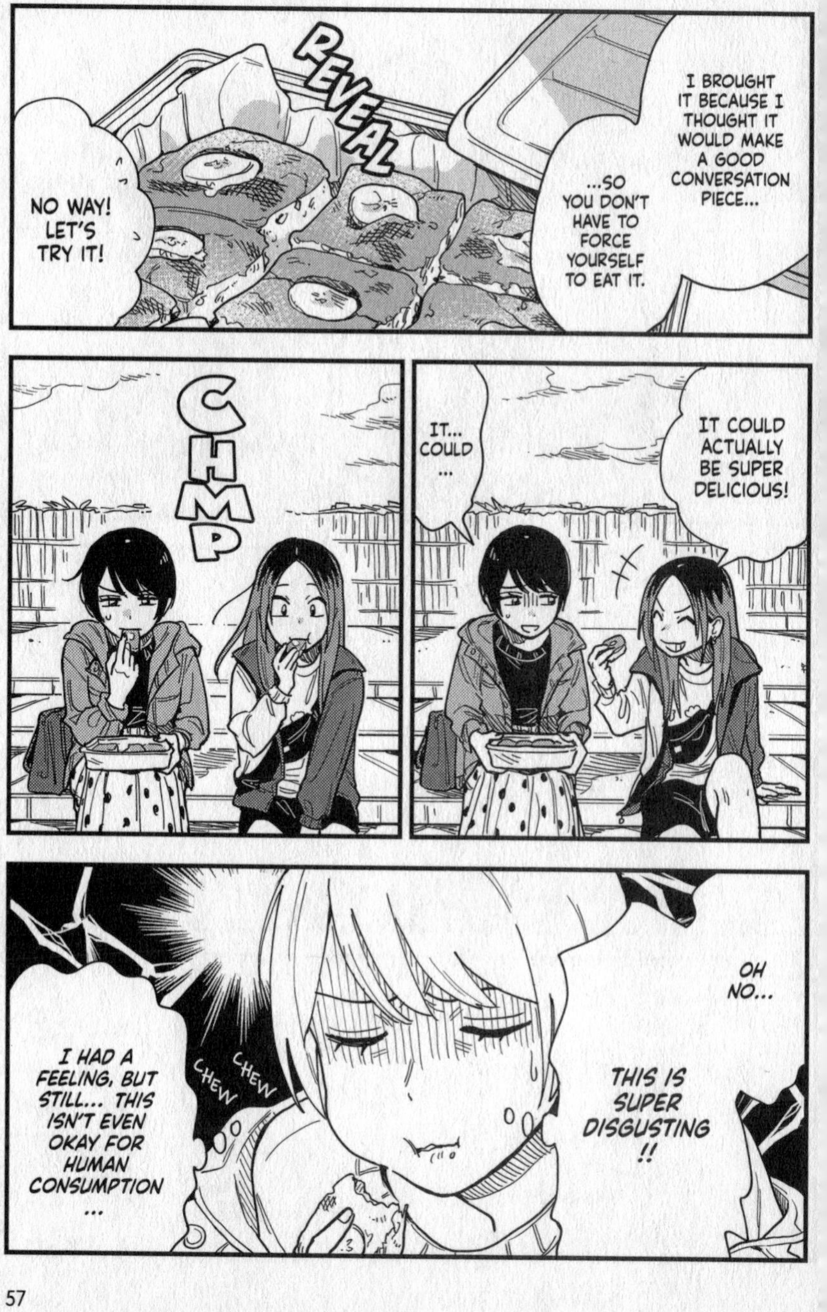
I BROUGHT IT BECAUSE I THOUGHT IT WOULD MAKE A GOOD CONVERSATION PIECE...
REVEAL
...SO YOU DON'T HAVE TO FORCE YOURSELF TO EAT IT.
NO WAY! LET'S TRY IT!
IT COULD ACTUALLY BE SUPER DELICIOUS!
IT... COULD ...
CHMP
OH NO...
THIS IS SUPER DISGUSTING !!
CHEW CHEW
I HAD A FEELING, BUT STILL... THIS ISN'T EVEN OKAY FOR HUMAN CONSUMPTION ...

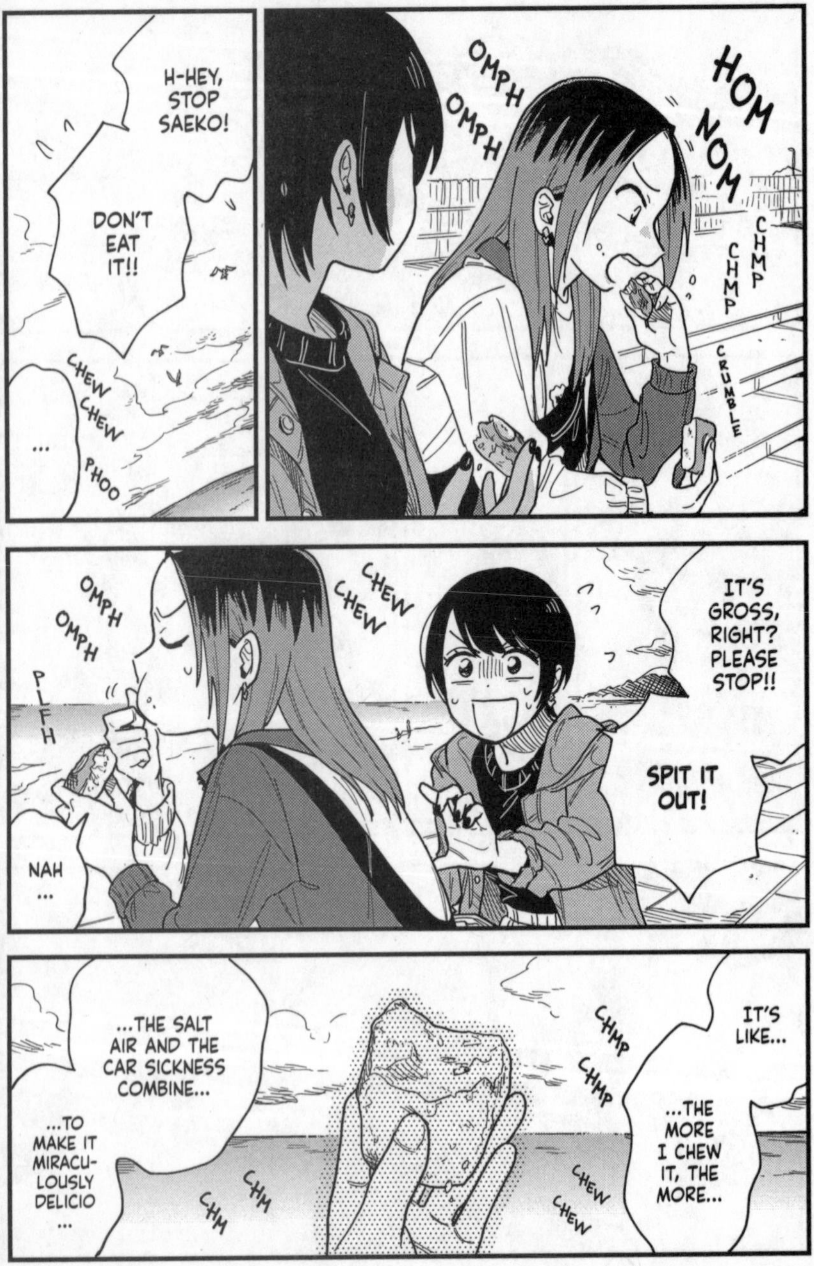
HOM NOM
OMPH OMPH
CHMP CHMP
CRUMBLE
H-HEY, STOP SAEKO!
DON'T EAT IT!!
CHEW CHEW
...
PHOO
IT'S GROSS, RIGHT? PLEASE STOP!!
SPIT IT OUT!
CHEW CHEW
OMPH OMPH
PLFH
NAH ...
IT'S LIKE...
...THE MORE I CHEW IT, THE MORE...
CHMP CHMP
CHEW CHEW
...THE SALT AIR AND THE CAR SICKNESS COMBINE...
CHM CHM
...TO MAKE IT MIRACU-LOUSLY DELICIO ...

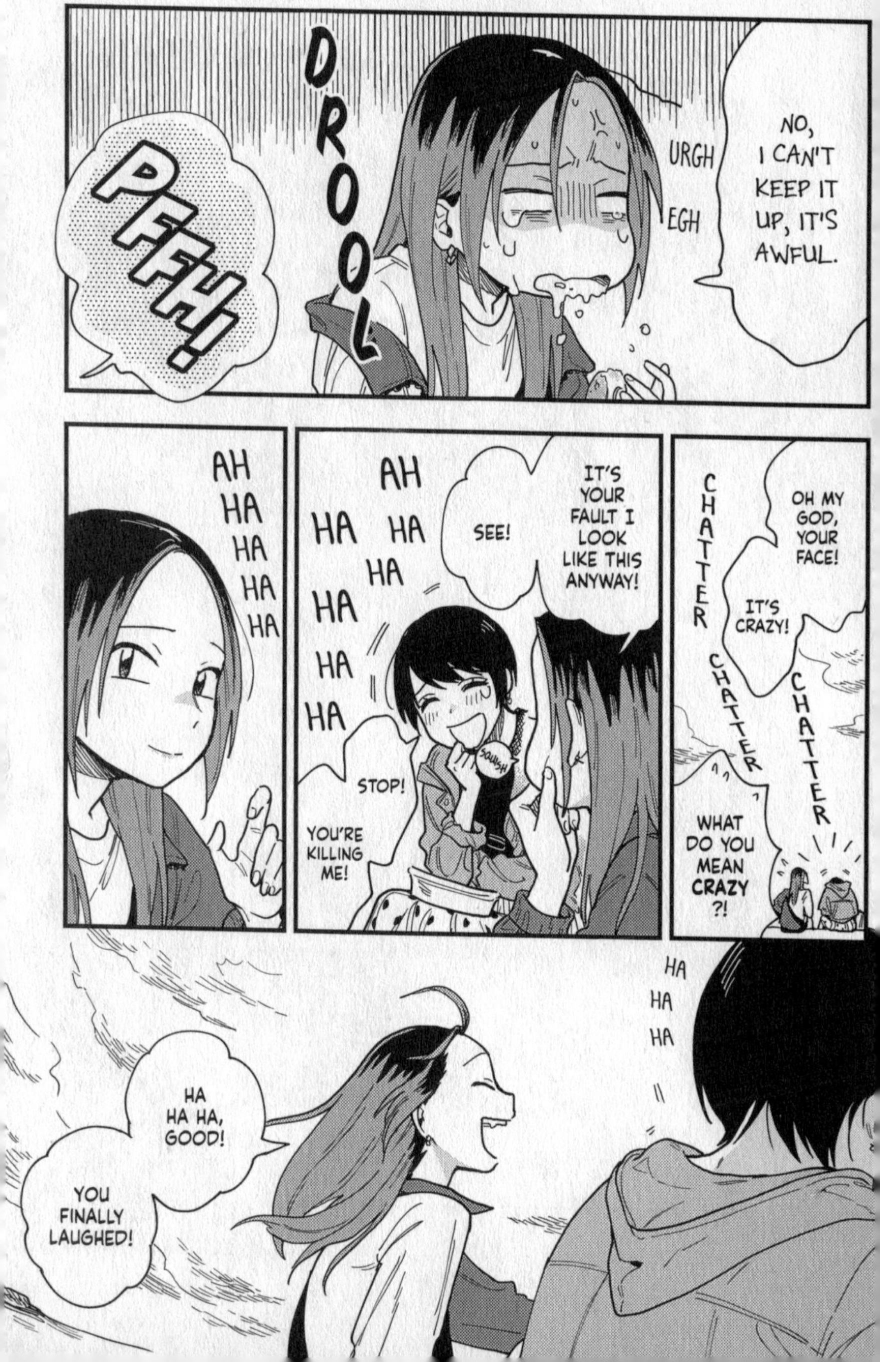
NO, I CAN'T KEEP IT UP, IT'S AWFUL.
URGH EGH
DROOL
PFFH!
OH MY GOD, YOUR FACE!
IT'S CRAZY!
CHATTER
CHATTER
CHATTER
WHAT DO YOU MEAN CRAZY?!
IT'S YOUR FAULT I LOOK LIKE THIS ANYWAY!
SEE!
AH HA HA HA HA HA HA
SQUISH
STOP!
YOU'RE KILLING ME!
AH HA HA HA HA
HA HA HA
HA HA HA, GOOD!
YOU FINALLY LAUGHED!

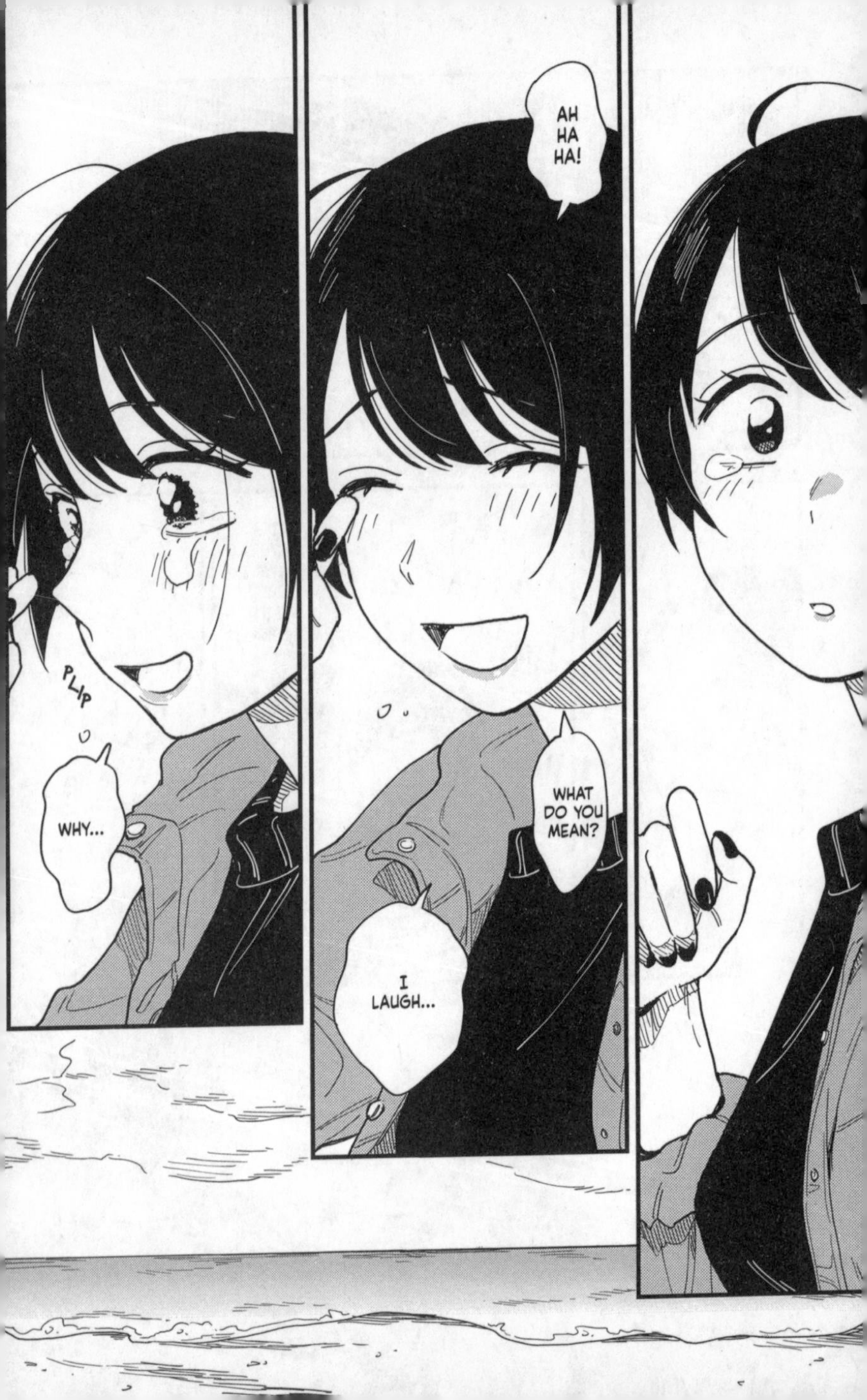
AH HA HA!
WHAT DO YOU MEAN?
I LAUGH...
PLIP
WHY...

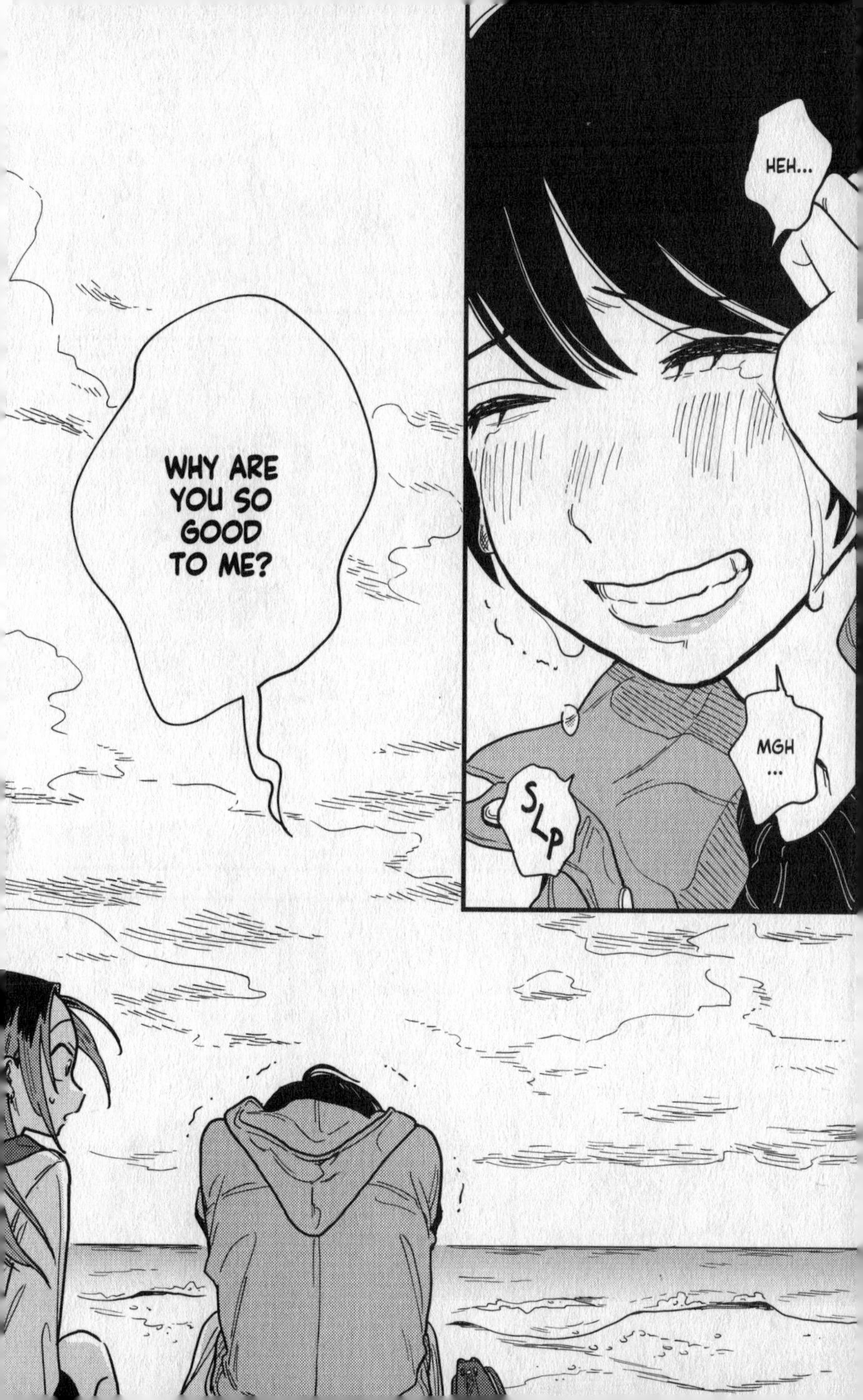
HEH...
MGH ...
SLP
WHY ARE YOU SO GOOD TO ME?

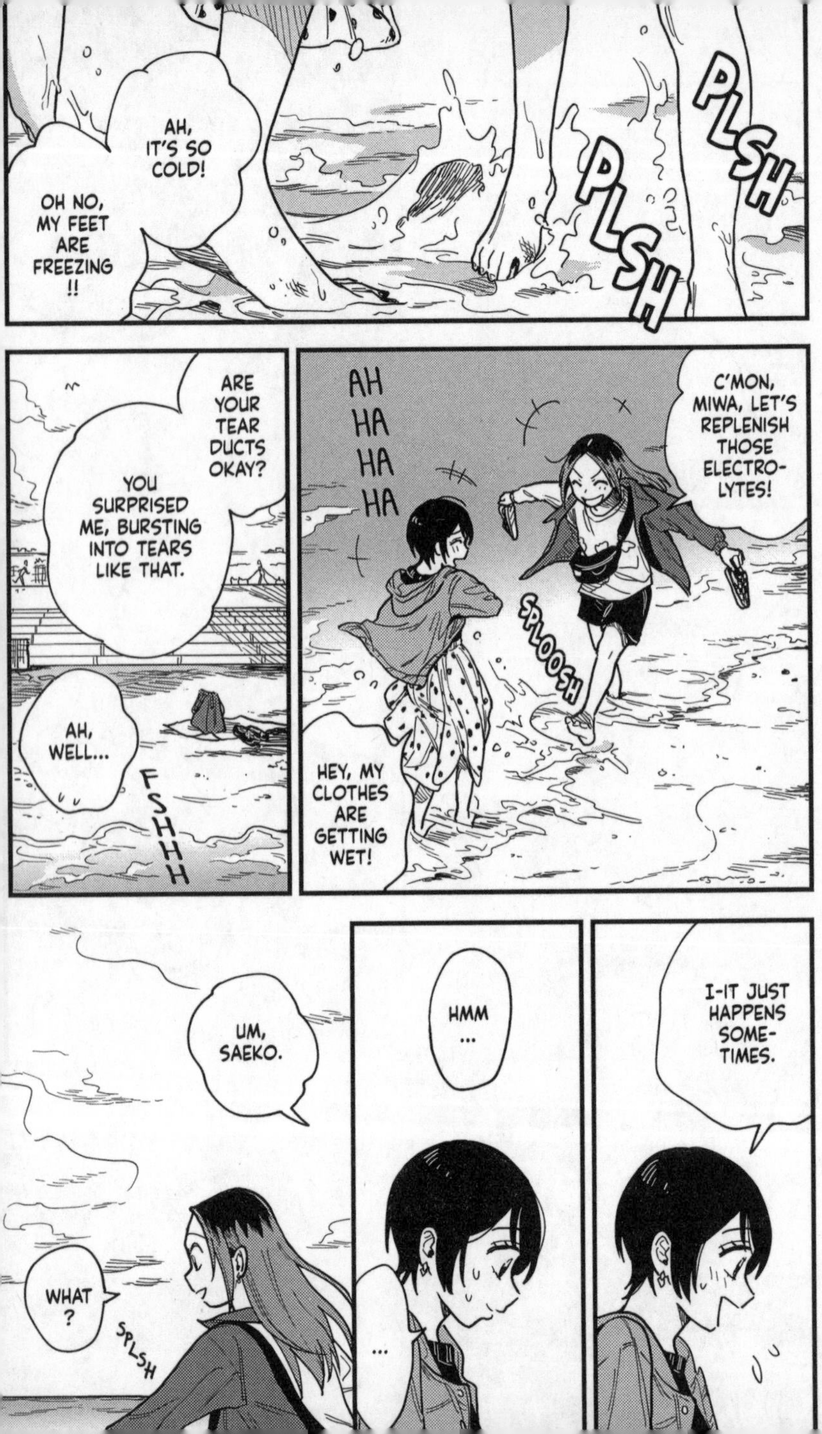
PLSH
PLSH
AH, IT'S SO COLD!
OH NO, MY FEET ARE FREEZING !!
C'MON, MIWA, LET'S REPLENISH THOSE ELECTRO-LYTES!
AH HA HA HA
SPLOOSH
HEY, MY CLOTHES ARE GETTING WET!
ARE YOUR TEAR DUCTS OKAY?
YOU SURPRISED ME, BURSTING INTO TEARS LIKE THAT.
AH, WELL...
FSHHH
I-IT JUST HAPPENS SOME-TIMES.
HMM ...
...
UM, SAEKO.
WHAT ?
SPLSH

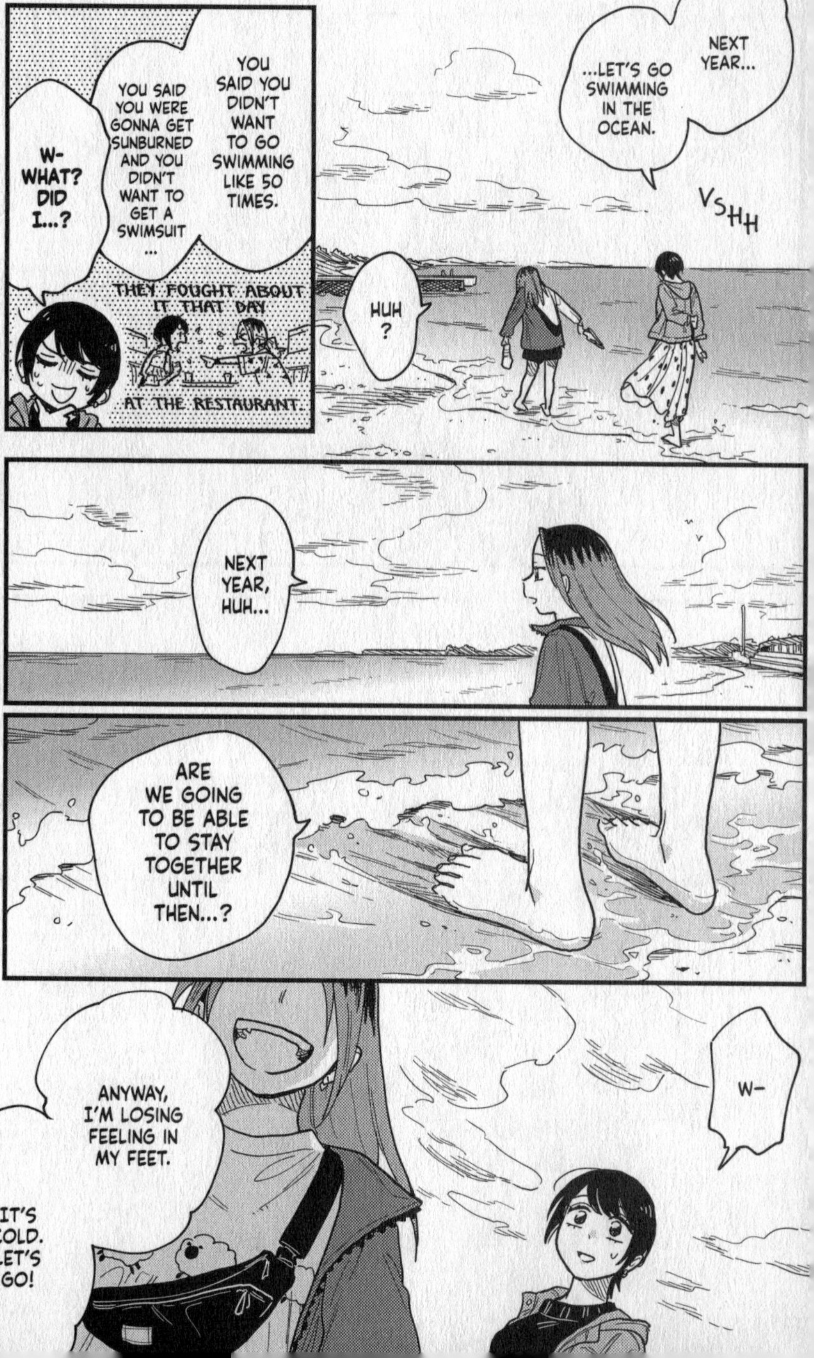
NEXT YEAR...
...LET'S GO SWIMMING IN THE OCEAN.
VSHH
HUH?
YOU SAID YOU DIDN'T WANT TO GO SWIMMING LIKE 50 TIMES.
YOU SAID YOU WERE GONNA GET SUNBURNED AND YOU DIDN'T WANT TO GET A SWIMSUIT...
W-WHAT? DID I...?
THEY FOUGHT ABOUT IT THAT DAY
AT THE RESTAURANT.
NEXT YEAR, HUH...
ARE WE GOING TO BE ABLE TO STAY TOGETHER UNTIL THEN...?
W-
ANYWAY, I'M LOSING FEELING IN MY FEET.
IT'S COLD. LET'S GO!

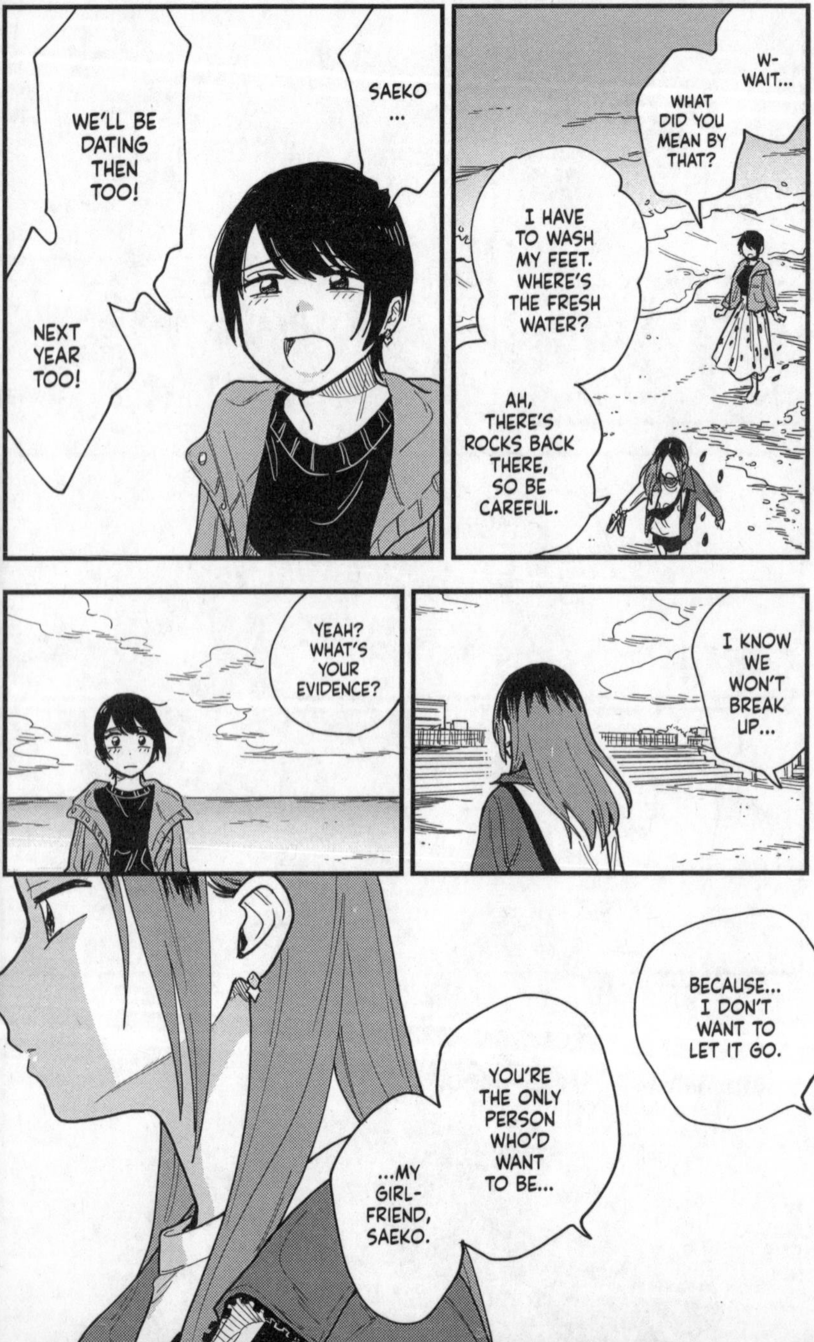
W- WAIT...
WHAT DID YOU MEAN BY THAT?
I HAVE TO WASH MY FEET. WHERE'S THE FRESH WATER?
AH, THERE'S ROCKS BACK THERE, SO BE CAREFUL.
SAEKO ...
WE'LL BE DATING THEN TOO!
NEXT YEAR TOO!
I KNOW WE WON'T BREAK UP...
YEAH? WHAT'S YOUR EVIDENCE?
BECAUSE... I DON'T WANT TO LET IT GO.
YOU'RE THE ONLY PERSON WHO'D WANT TO BE...
...MY GIRL-FRIEND, SAEKO.

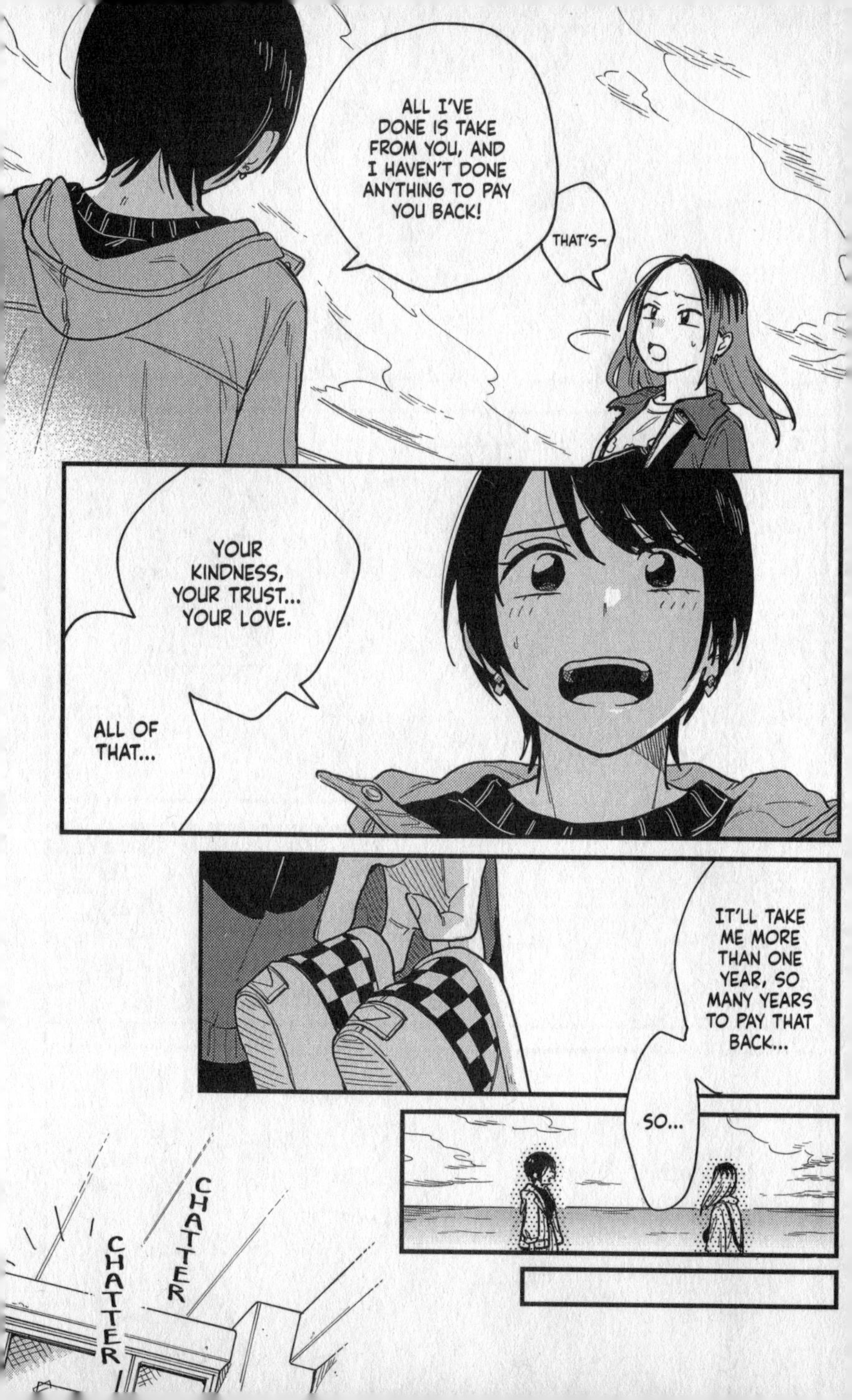
ALL I'VE DONE IS TAKE FROM YOU, AND I HAVEN'T DONE ANYTHING TO PAY YOU BACK!
THAT'S—
YOUR KINDNESS, YOUR TRUST... YOUR LOVE.
ALL OF THAT...
IT'LL TAKE ME MORE THAN ONE YEAR, SO MANY YEARS TO PAY THAT BACK...
SO...
CHATTER
CHATTER

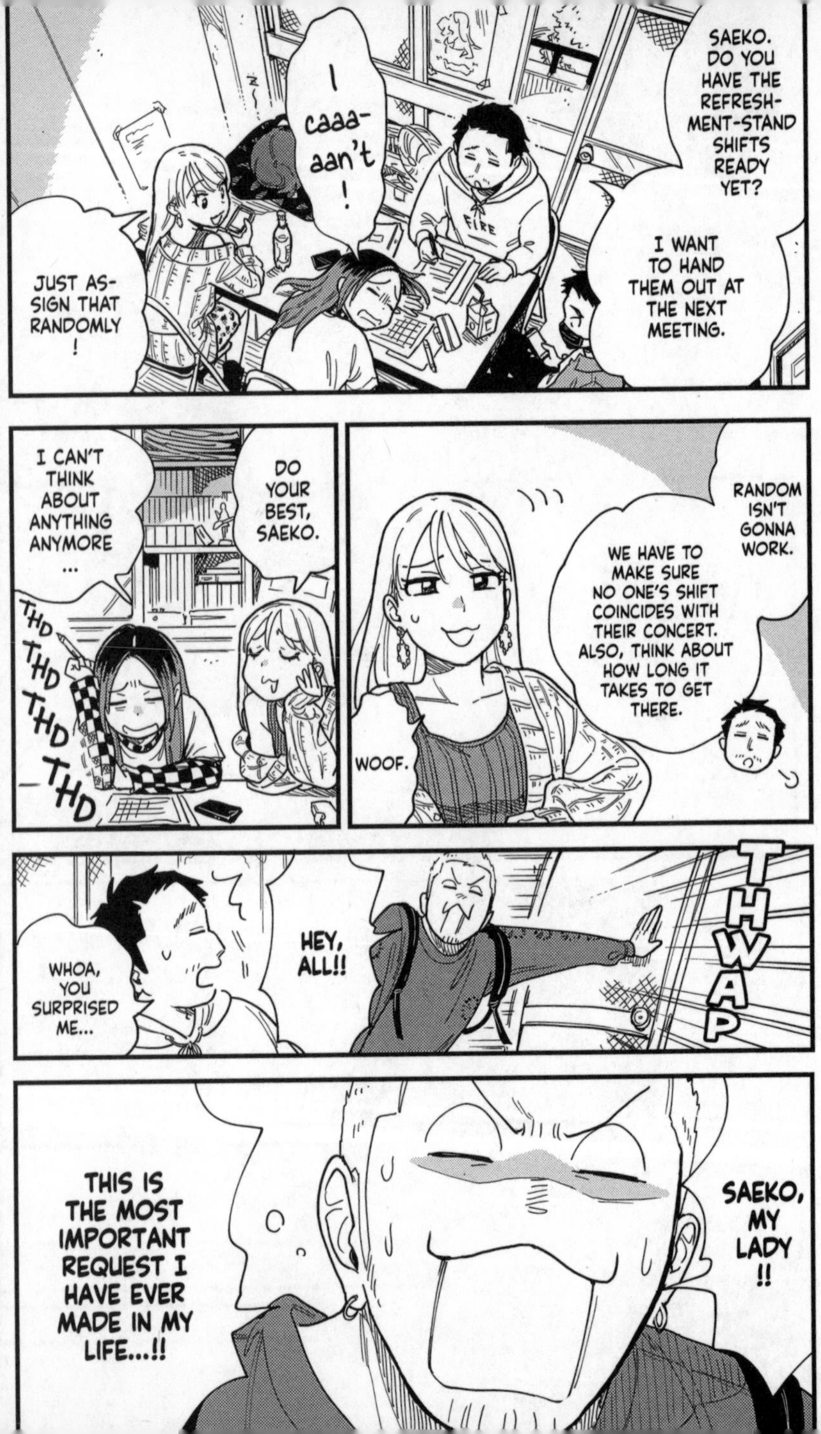
SAEKO. DO YOU HAVE THE REFRESHMENT-STAND SHIFTS READY YET?
I WANT TO HAND THEM OUT AT THE NEXT MEETING.
I caaa-aan't!
JUST ASSIGN THAT RANDOMLY!
RANDOM ISN'T GONNA WORK.
WE HAVE TO MAKE SURE NO ONE'S SHIFT COINCIDES WITH THEIR CONCERT. ALSO, THINK ABOUT HOW LONG IT TAKES TO GET THERE.
WOOF.
DO YOUR BEST, SAEKO.
I CAN'T THINK ABOUT ANYTHING ANYMORE...
THD THD THD THD THD
THWAP
HEY, ALL!!
WHOA, YOU SURPRISED ME...
SAEKO, MY LADY!!
THIS IS THE MOST IMPORTANT REQUEST I HAVE EVER MADE IN MY LIFE...!!

How Do We
Relationship?

HOW DO WE RELATIONSHIP?

Chapter 31: Whether To Escape or Avoid

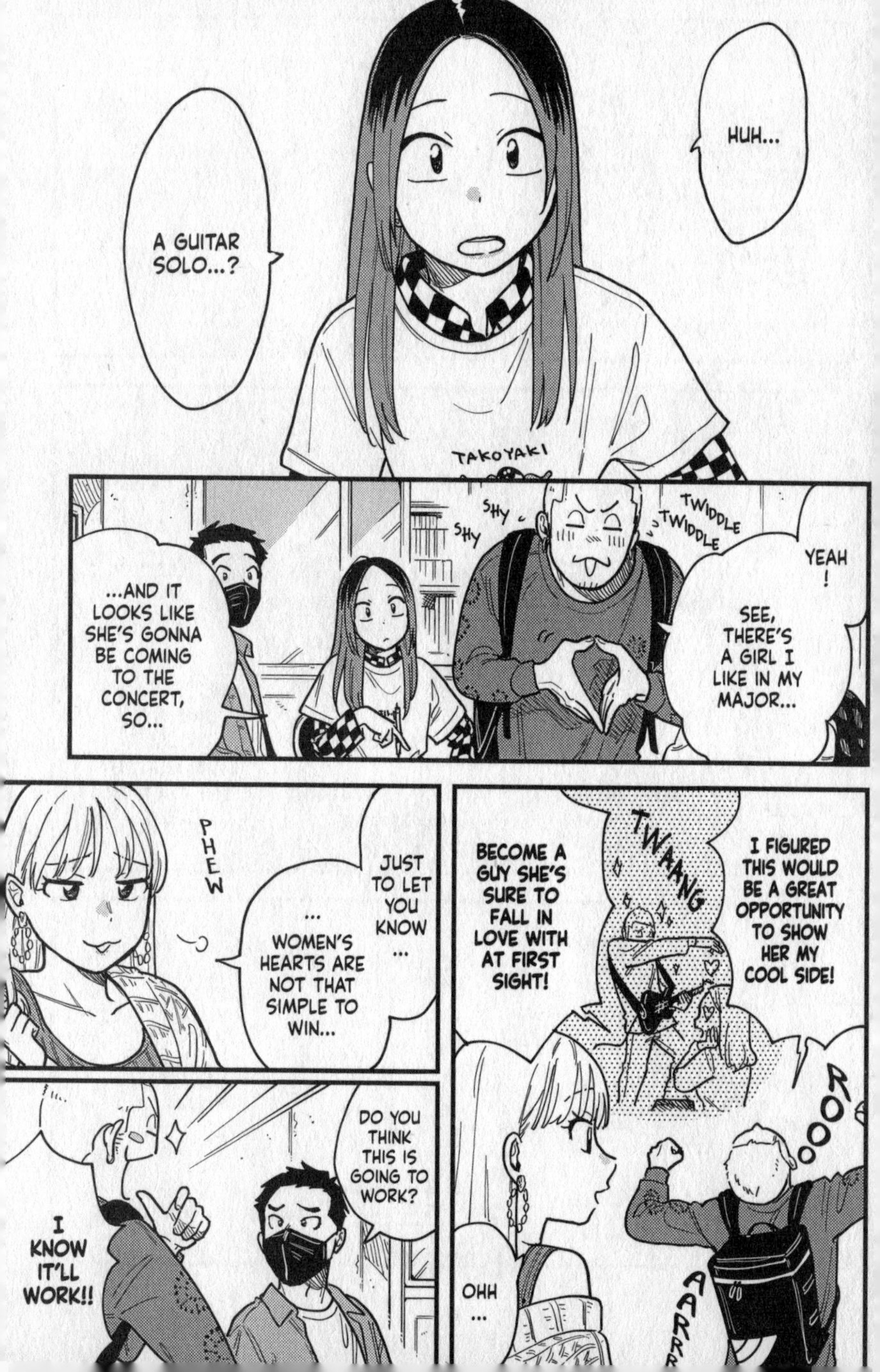
HUH...
A GUITAR SOLO...?
YEAH! SEE, THERE'S A GIRL I LIKE IN MY MAJOR...
TWIDDLE TWIDDLE
SHY SHY
TAKOYAKI
...AND IT LOOKS LIKE SHE'S GONNA BE COMING TO THE CONCERT, SO...
I FIGURED THIS WOULD BE A GREAT OPPORTUNITY TO SHOW HER MY COOL SIDE!
TWAAANG
BECOME A GUY SHE'S SURE TO FALL IN LOVE WITH AT FIRST SIGHT!
ROOOO
OHH...
AARRR
JUST TO LET YOU KNOW...
...WOMEN'S HEARTS ARE NOT THAT SIMPLE TO WIN...
PHEW
DO YOU THINK THIS IS GOING TO WORK?
I KNOW IT'LL WORK!!

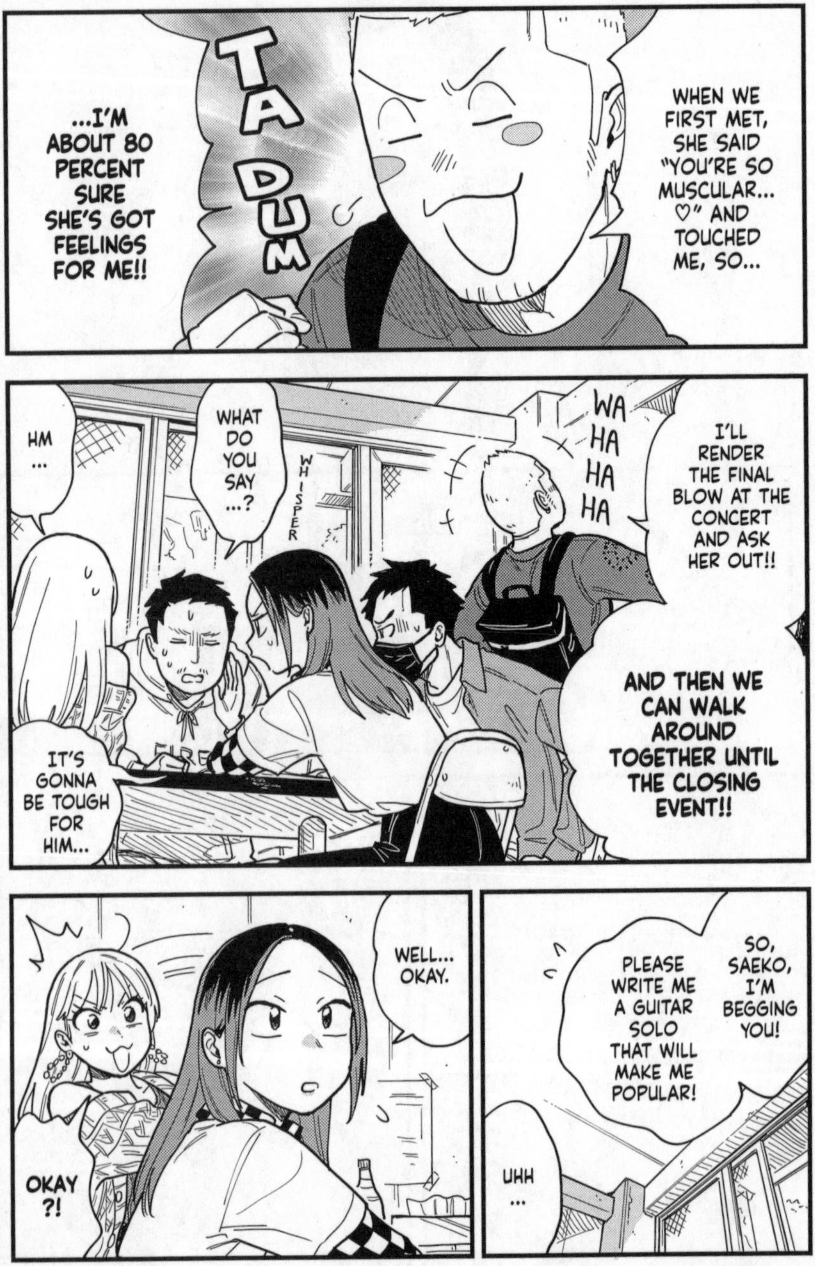
WHEN WE FIRST MET, SHE SAID "YOU'RE SO MUSCULAR... ♡" AND TOUCHED ME, SO...
TA DUM
...I'M ABOUT 80 PERCENT SURE SHE'S GOT FEELINGS FOR ME!!
I'LL RENDER THE FINAL BLOW AT THE CONCERT AND ASK HER OUT!!
WA HA HA HA
AND THEN WE CAN WALK AROUND TOGETHER UNTIL THE CLOSING EVENT!!
WHISPER
WHAT DO YOU SAY ...?
HM ...
IT'S GONNA BE TOUGH FOR HIM...
SO, SAEKO, I'M BEGGING YOU!
PLEASE WRITE ME A GUITAR SOLO THAT WILL MAKE ME POPULAR!
UHH ...
WELL... OKAY.
OKAY ?!

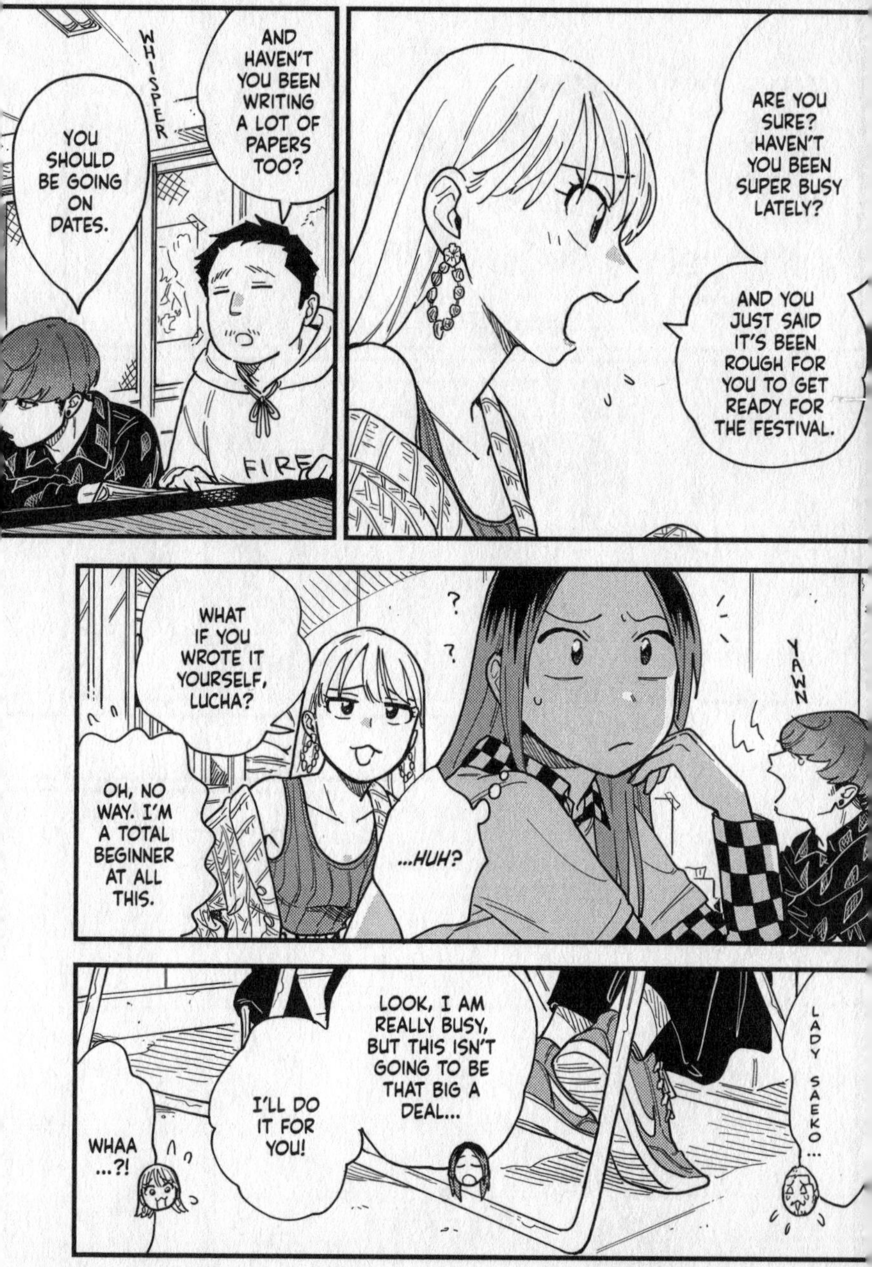
ARE YOU SURE? HAVEN'T YOU BEEN SUPER BUSY LATELY?
AND YOU JUST SAID IT'S BEEN ROUGH FOR YOU TO GET READY FOR THE FESTIVAL.
AND HAVEN'T YOU BEEN WRITING A LOT OF PAPERS TOO?
WHISPER
YOU SHOULD BE GOING ON DATES.
FIRE
YAWN
...HUH?
WHAT IF YOU WROTE IT YOURSELF, LUCHA?
OH, NO WAY. I'M A TOTAL BEGINNER AT ALL THIS.
LADY SAEKO...
LOOK, I AM REALLY BUSY, BUT THIS ISN'T GOING TO BE THAT BIG A DEAL...
I'LL DO IT FOR YOU!
WHAA ...?!

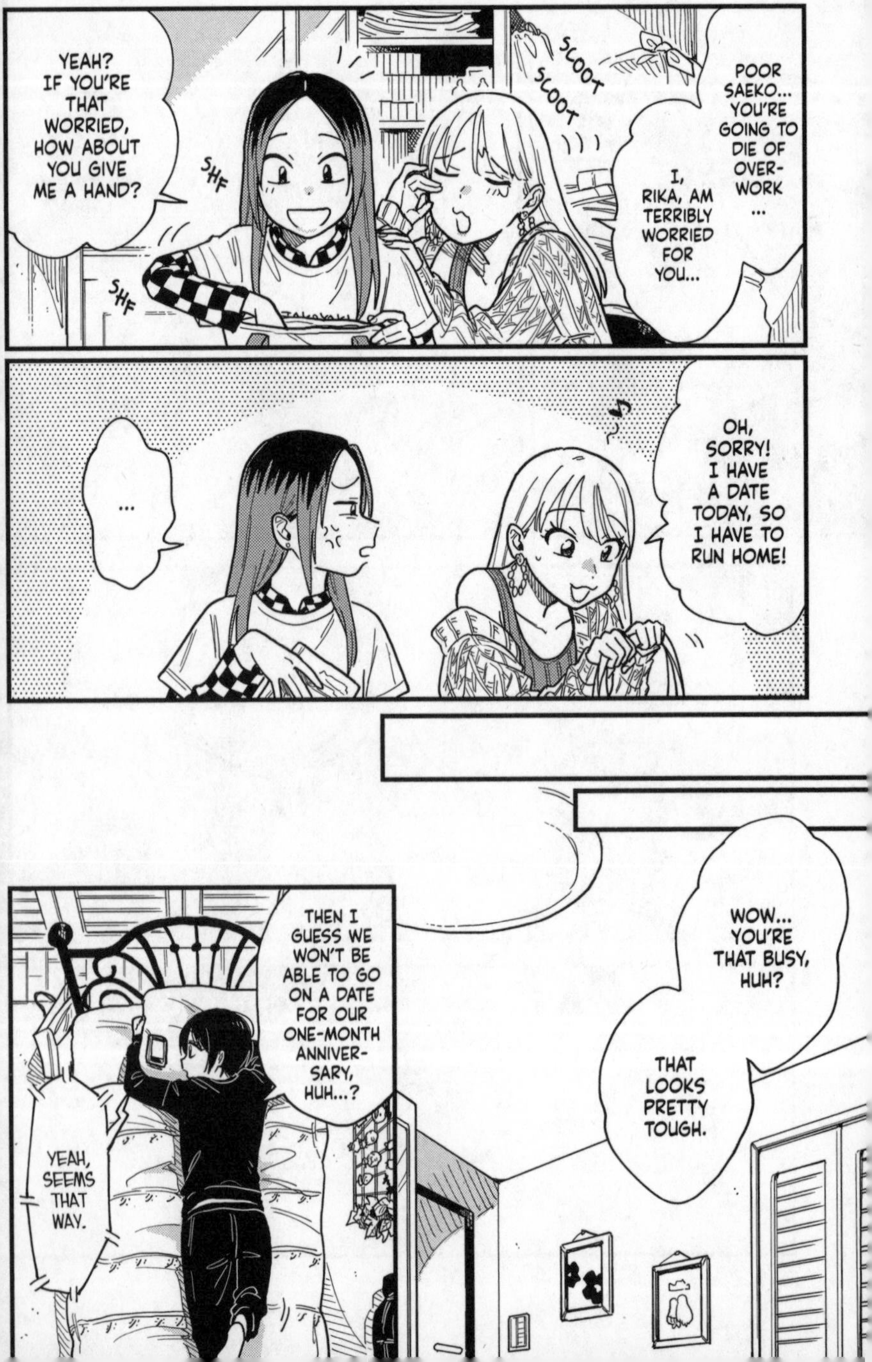
POOR SAEKO... YOU'RE GOING TO DIE OF OVER-WORK...
I, RIKA, AM TERRIBLY WORRIED FOR YOU...
SCOOT SCOOT
YEAH? IF YOU'RE THAT WORRIED, HOW ABOUT YOU GIVE ME A HAND?
SHF
SHF
OH, SORRY! I HAVE A DATE TODAY, SO I HAVE TO RUN HOME!
...
WOW... YOU'RE THAT BUSY, HUH?
THAT LOOKS PRETTY TOUGH.
THEN I GUESS WE WON'T BE ABLE TO GO ON A DATE FOR OUR ONE-MONTH ANNIVER-SARY, HUH...?
YEAH, SEEMS THAT WAY.

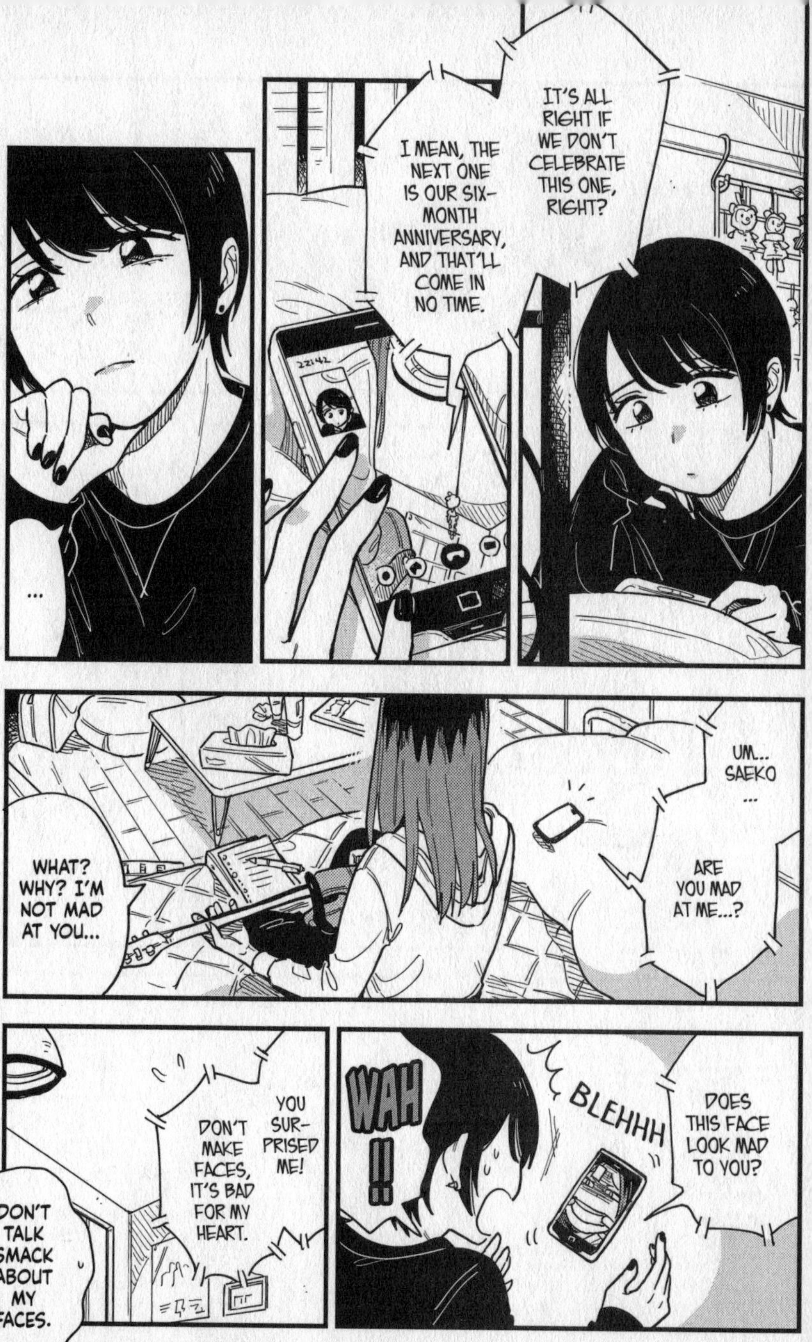
IT'S ALL RIGHT IF WE DON'T CELEBRATE THIS ONE, RIGHT?
I MEAN, THE NEXT ONE IS OUR SIX-MONTH ANNIVERSARY, AND THAT'LL COME IN NO TIME.
...
UM... SAEKO...
ARE YOU MAD AT ME...?
WHAT? WHY? I'M NOT MAD AT YOU...
DOES THIS FACE LOOK MAD TO YOU?
BLEHHH
WAH!!
YOU SURPRISED ME!
DON'T MAKE FACES, IT'S BAD FOR MY HEART.
DON'T TALK SMACK ABOUT MY FACES.

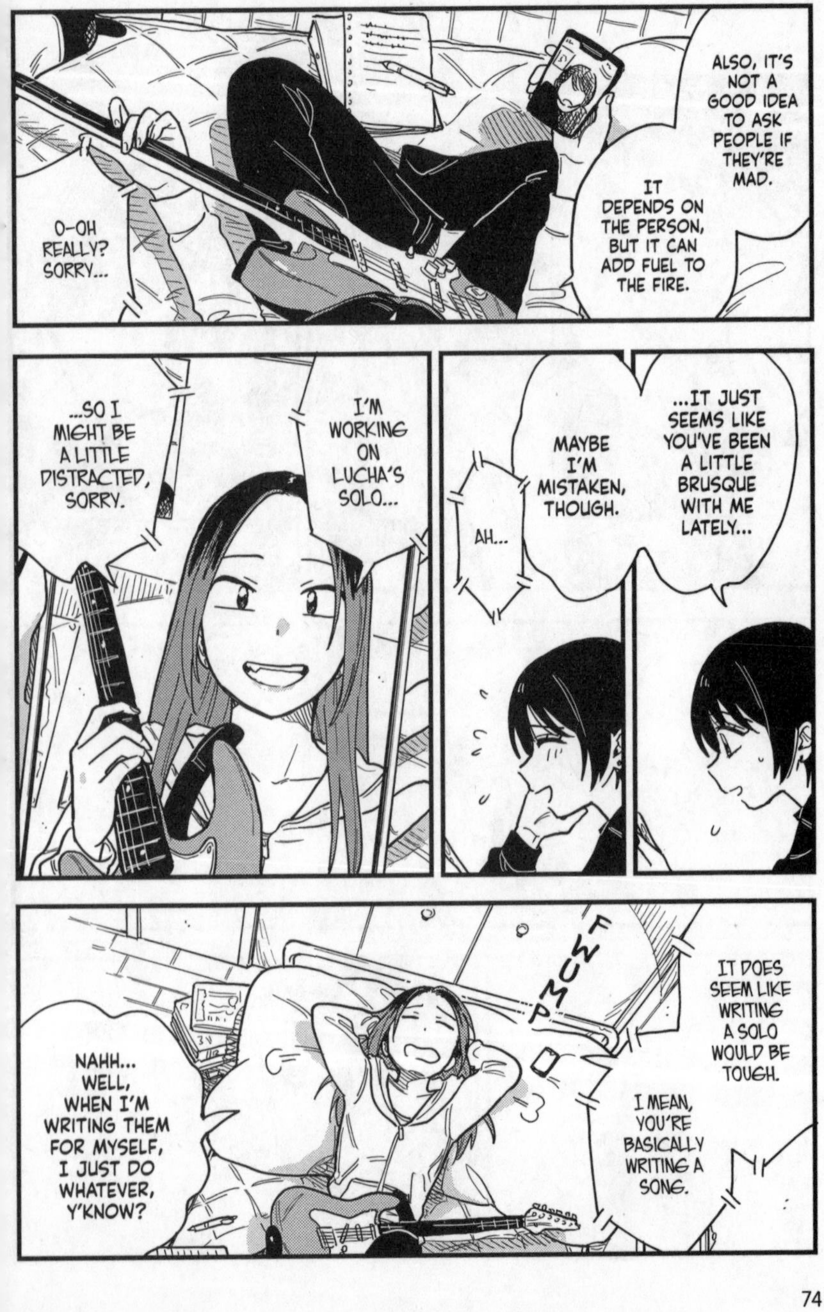
ALSO, IT'S NOT A GOOD IDEA TO ASK PEOPLE IF THEY'RE MAD.
IT DEPENDS ON THE PERSON, BUT IT CAN ADD FUEL TO THE FIRE.
O-OH REALLY? SORRY...
...IT JUST SEEMS LIKE YOU'VE BEEN A LITTLE BRUSQUE WITH ME LATELY...
MAYBE I'M MISTAKEN, THOUGH.
AH...
I'M WORKING ON LUCHA'S SOLO...
...SO I MIGHT BE A LITTLE DISTRACTED, SORRY.
IT DOES SEEM LIKE WRITING A SOLO WOULD BE TOUGH.
I MEAN, YOU'RE BASICALLY WRITING A SONG.
FWUMP
NAHH... WELL, WHEN I'M WRITING THEM FOR MYSELF, I JUST DO WHATEVER, Y'KNOW?

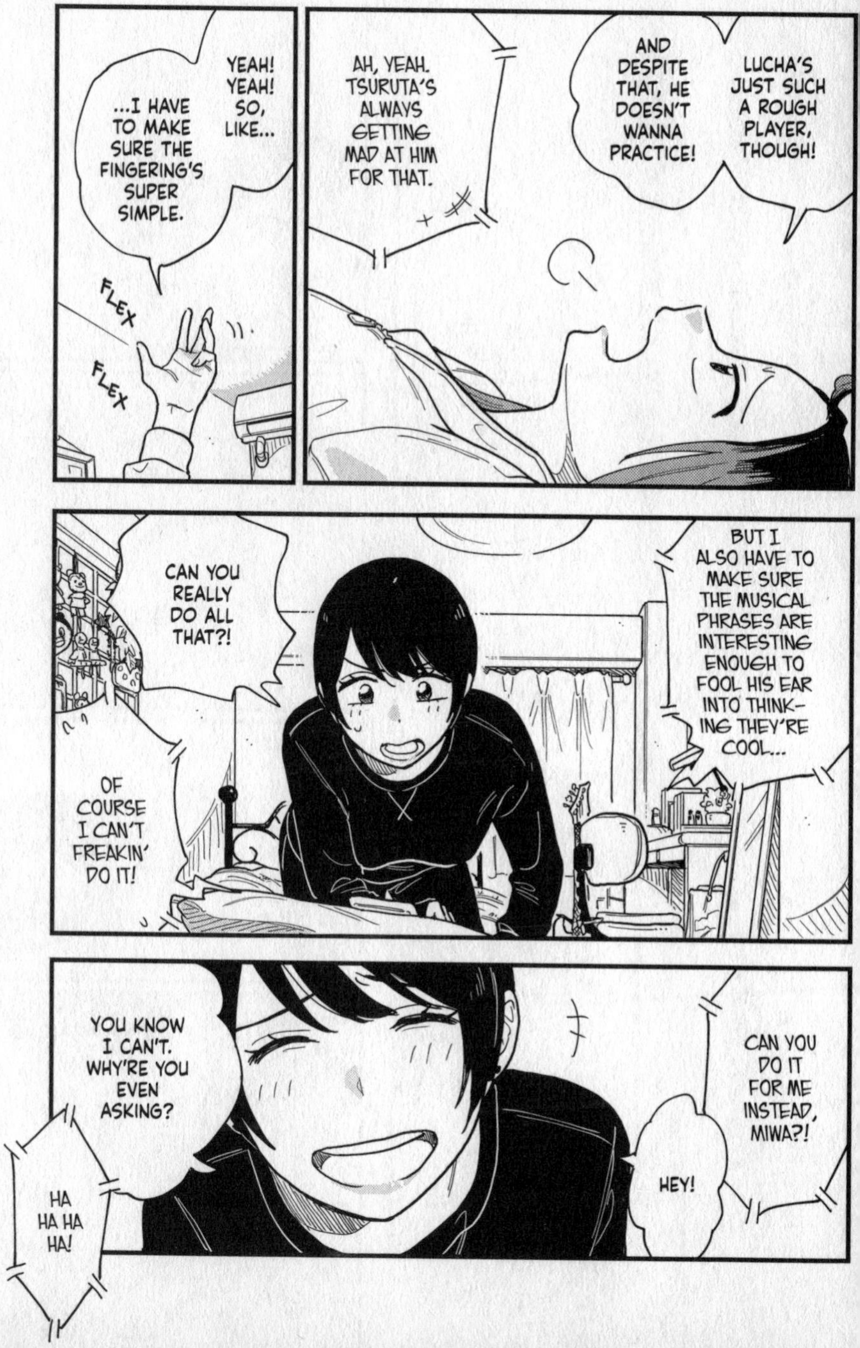
LUCHA'S JUST SUCH A ROUGH PLAYER, THOUGH!
AND DESPITE THAT, HE DOESN'T WANNA PRACTICE!
AH, YEAH. TSURUTA'S ALWAYS GETTING MAD AT HIM FOR THAT.
YEAH! YEAH! SO, LIKE...
...I HAVE TO MAKE SURE THE FINGERING'S SUPER SIMPLE.
FLEX
FLEX
BUT I ALSO HAVE TO MAKE SURE THE MUSICAL PHRASES ARE INTERESTING ENOUGH TO FOOL HIS EAR INTO THINKING THEY'RE COOL...
CAN YOU REALLY DO ALL THAT?!
OF COURSE I CAN'T FREAKIN' DO IT!
CAN YOU DO IT FOR ME INSTEAD, MIWA?!
HEY!
YOU KNOW I CAN'T. WHY'RE YOU EVEN ASKING?
HA HA HA HA!

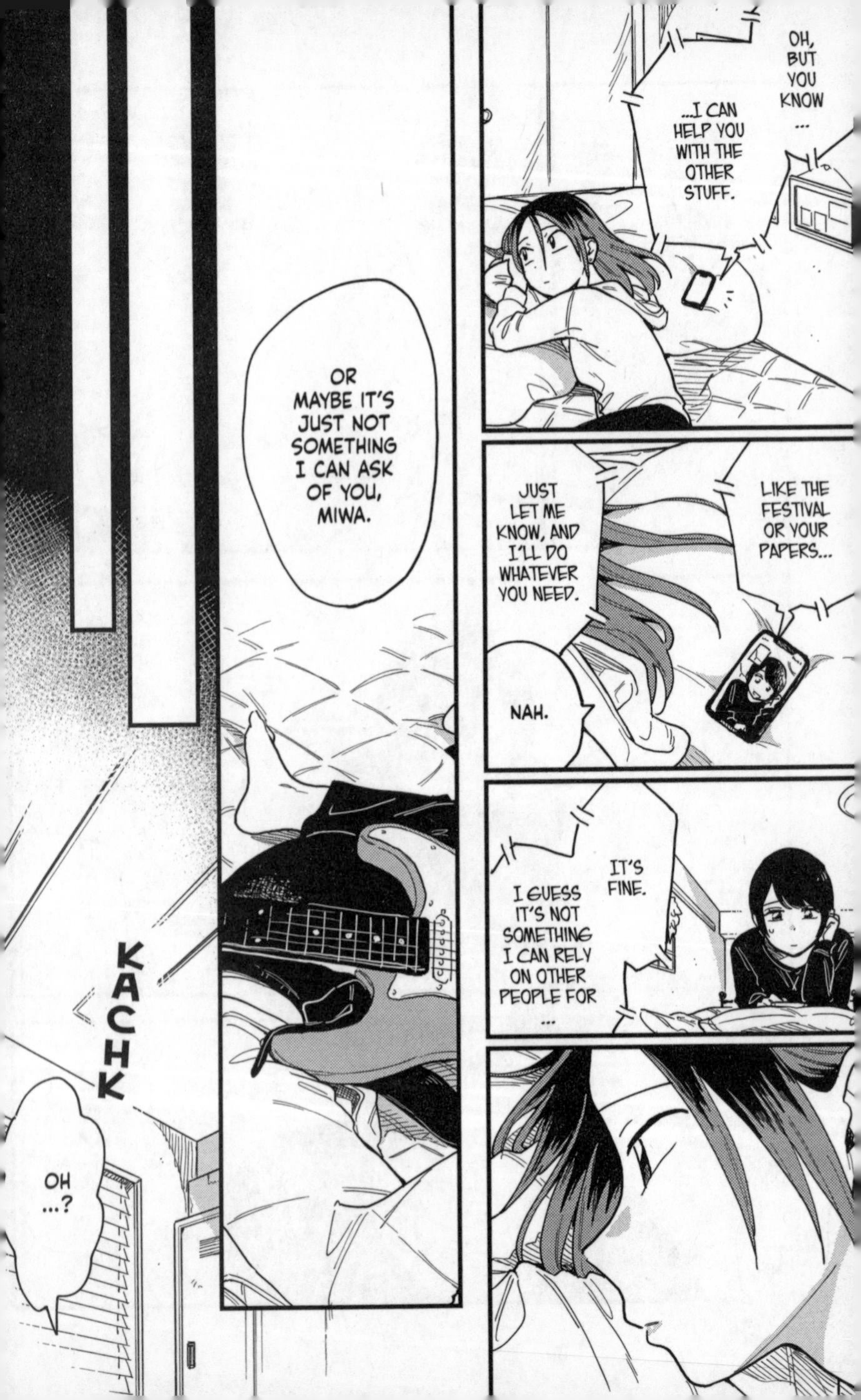
OH, BUT YOU KNOW...
...I CAN HELP YOU WITH THE OTHER STUFF.
LIKE THE FESTIVAL OR YOUR PAPERS...
JUST LET ME KNOW, AND I'LL DO WHATEVER YOU NEED.
NAH.
IT'S FINE.
I GUESS IT'S NOT SOMETHING I CAN RELY ON OTHER PEOPLE FOR...
OR MAYBE IT'S JUST NOT SOMETHING I CAN ASK OF YOU, MIWA.
KACHK
OH...?

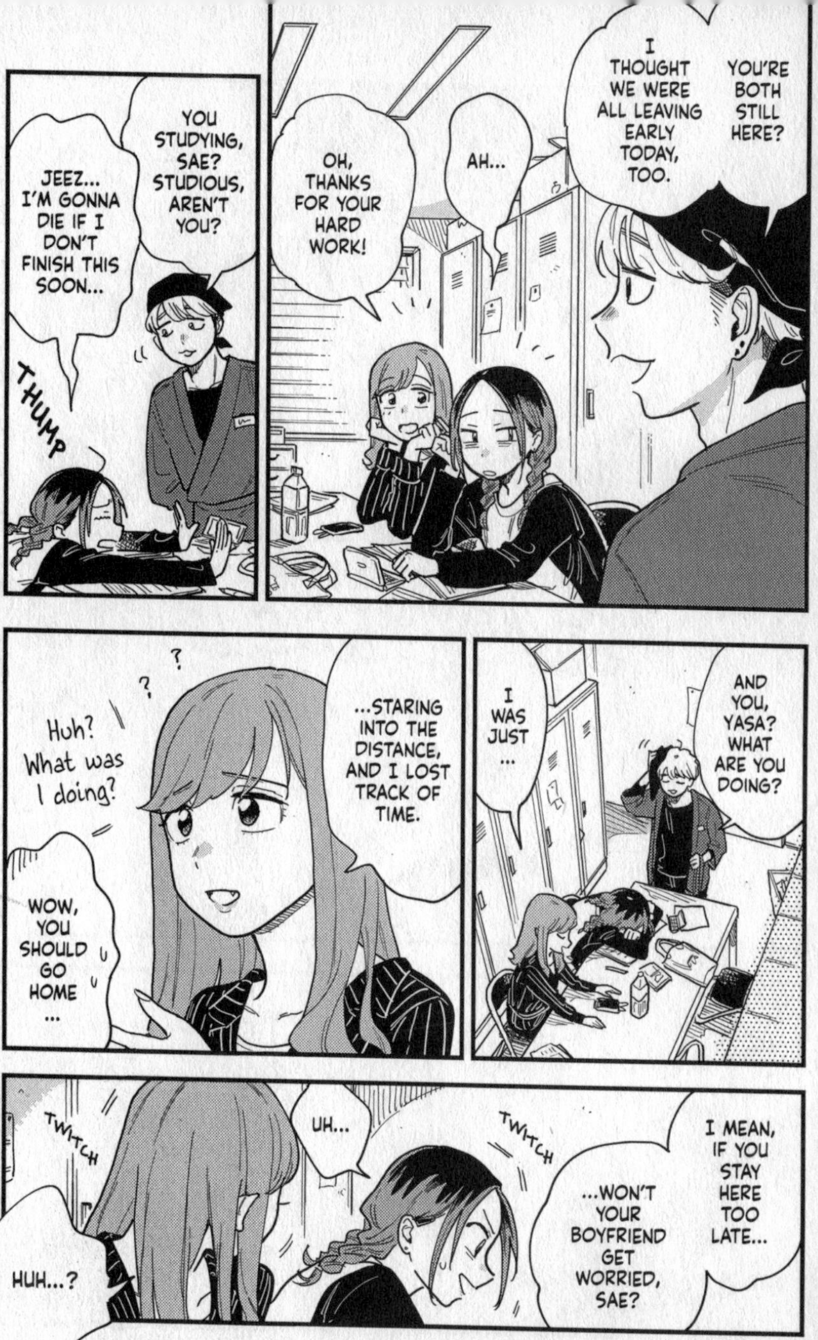
YOU'RE BOTH STILL HERE?
I THOUGHT WE WERE ALL LEAVING EARLY TODAY, TOO.
AH...
OH, THANKS FOR YOUR HARD WORK!
YOU STUDYING, SAE? STUDIOUS, AREN'T YOU?
JEEZ... I'M GONNA DIE IF I DON'T FINISH THIS SOON...
THUMP
AND YOU, YASA? WHAT ARE YOU DOING?
I WAS JUST ...
...STARING INTO THE DISTANCE, AND I LOST TRACK OF TIME.
Huh? What was I doing?
WOW, YOU SHOULD GO HOME ...
I MEAN, IF YOU STAY HERE TOO LATE...
...WON'T YOUR BOYFRIEND GET WORRIED, SAE?
TWITCH
UH...
TWITCH
HUH...?

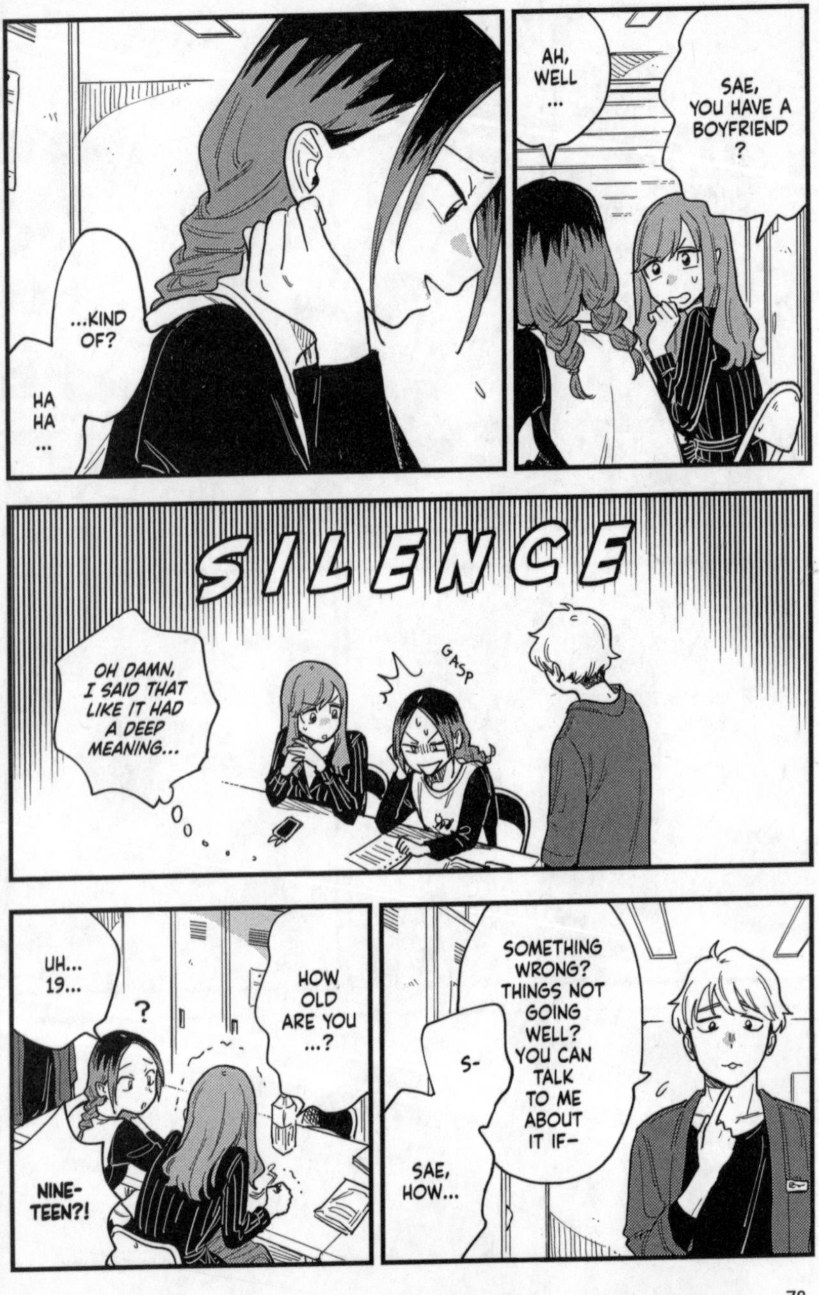
SAE, YOU HAVE A BOYFRIEND?
AH, WELL ...
...KIND OF?
HA HA ...
SILENCE
GASP
OH DAMN, I SAID THAT LIKE IT HAD A DEEP MEANING...
SOMETHING WRONG? THINGS NOT GOING WELL? YOU CAN TALK TO ME ABOUT IT IF–
S-
SAE, HOW...
HOW OLD ARE YOU ...?
UH... 19...
?
NINE-TEEN?!

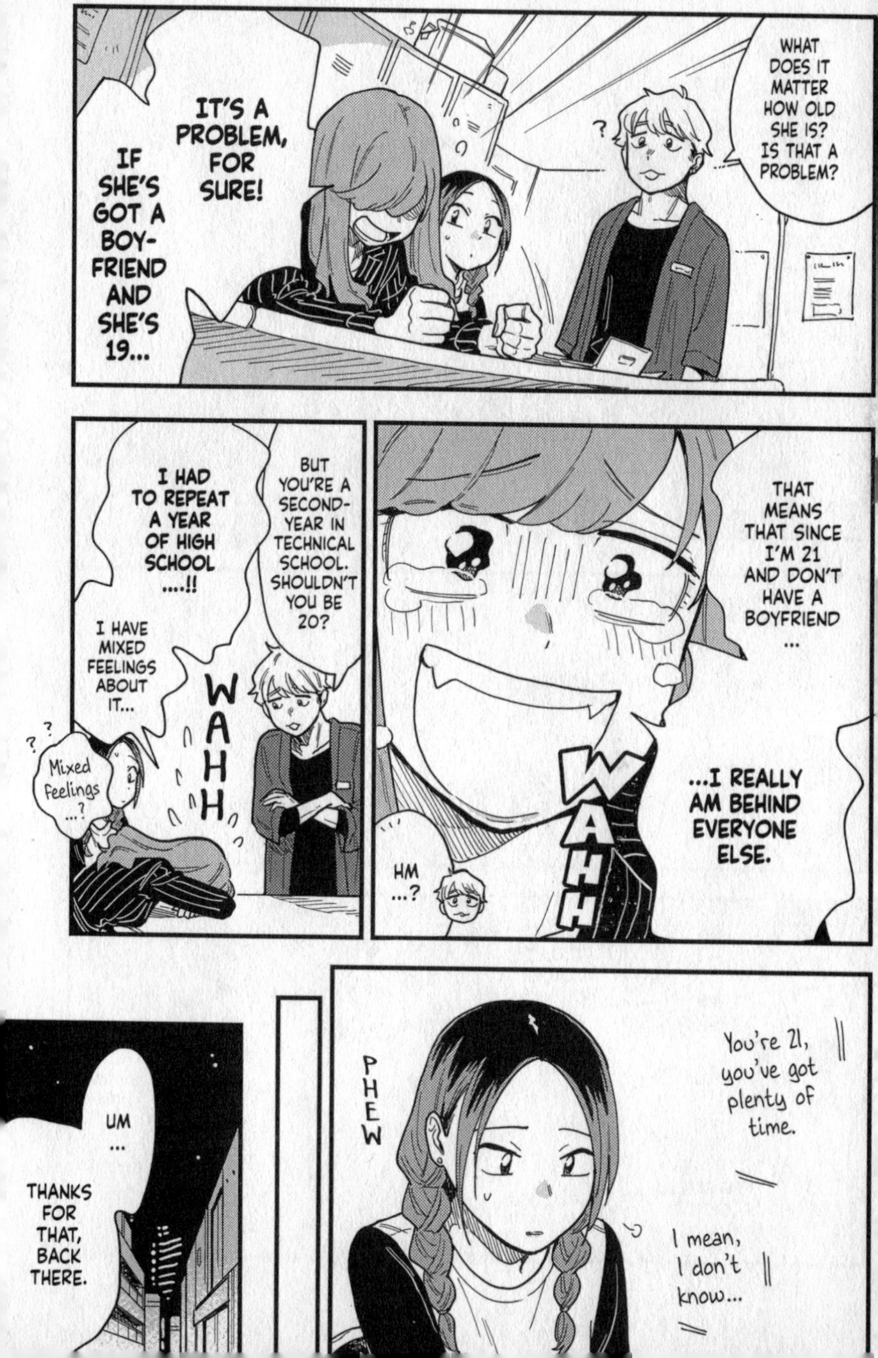
WHAT DOES IT MATTER HOW OLD SHE IS? IS THAT A PROBLEM?
IT'S A PROBLEM, FOR SURE!
IF SHE'S GOT A BOY-FRIEND AND SHE'S 19...
THAT MEANS THAT SINCE I'M 21 AND DON'T HAVE A BOYFRIEND ...
...I REALLY AM BEHIND EVERYONE ELSE.
WAHH
HM ...?
BUT YOU'RE A SECOND-YEAR IN TECHNICAL SCHOOL. SHOULDN'T YOU BE 20?
I HAD TO REPEAT A YEAR OF HIGH SCHOOL ....!!
I HAVE MIXED FEELINGS ABOUT IT...
WAHH
Mixed Feelings ...?
You're 21, you've got plenty of time.
PHEW
I mean, I don't know...
UM ...
THANKS FOR THAT, BACK THERE.

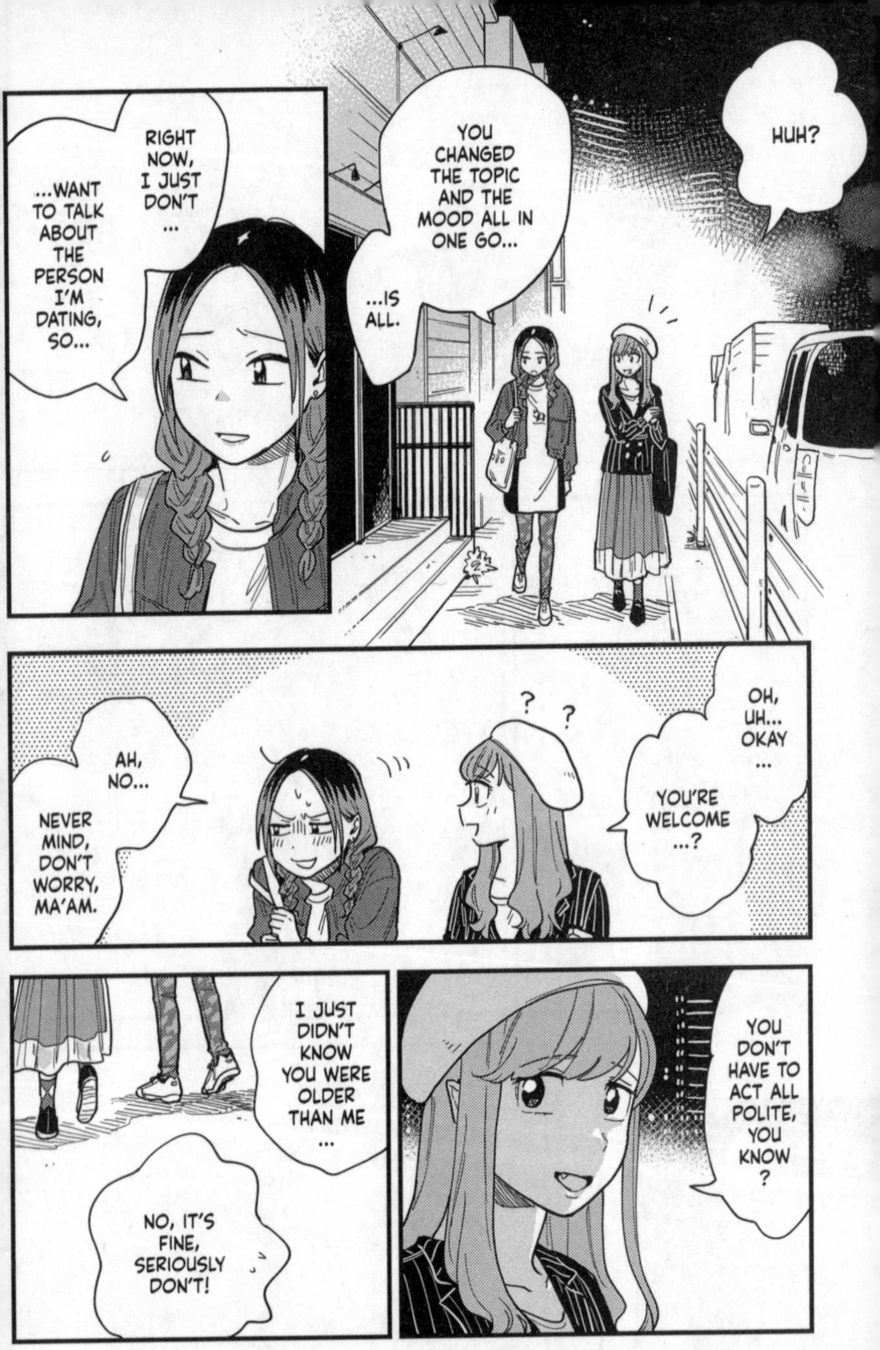
HUH?
YOU CHANGED THE TOPIC AND THE MOOD ALL IN ONE GO...
...IS ALL.
RIGHT NOW, I JUST DON'T ...
...WANT TO TALK ABOUT THE PERSON I'M DATING, SO...
OH, UH... OKAY ...
YOU'RE WELCOME ...?
AH, NO...
NEVER MIND, DON'T WORRY, MA'AM.
YOU DON'T HAVE TO ACT ALL POLITE, YOU KNOW ?
I JUST DIDN'T KNOW YOU WERE OLDER THAN ME ...
NO, IT'S FINE, SERIOUSLY DON'T!

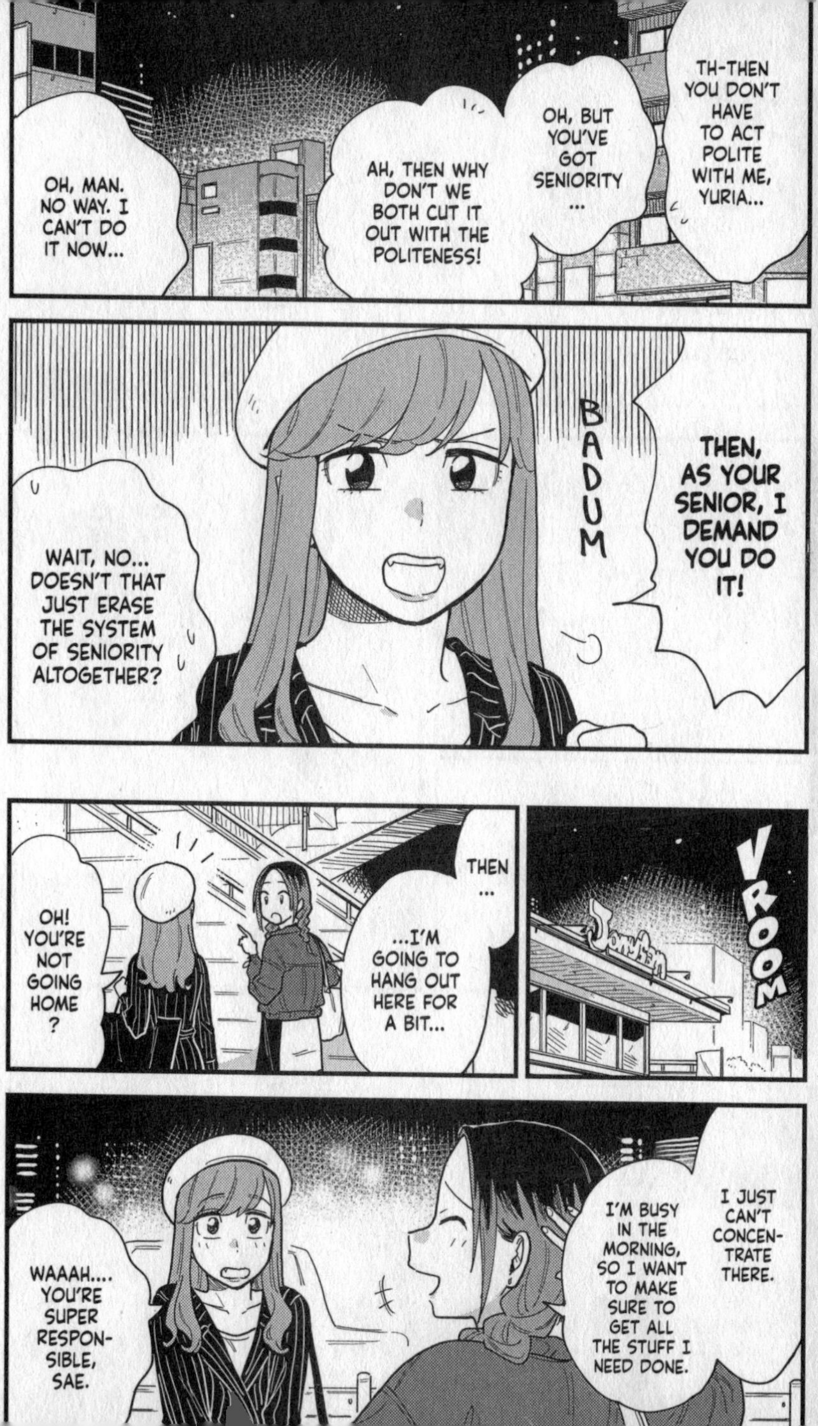
TH-THEN YOU DON'T HAVE TO ACT POLITE WITH ME, YURIA...
OH, BUT YOU'VE GOT SENIORITY ...
AH, THEN WHY DON'T WE BOTH CUT IT OUT WITH THE POLITENESS!
OH, MAN. NO WAY. I CAN'T DO IT NOW...
THEN, AS YOUR SENIOR, I DEMAND YOU DO IT!
BADUM
WAIT, NO... DOESN'T THAT JUST ERASE THE SYSTEM OF SENIORITY ALTOGETHER?
VROOM
THEN ...
...I'M GOING TO HANG OUT HERE FOR A BIT...
OH! YOU'RE NOT GOING HOME ?
I JUST CAN'T CONCEN-TRATE THERE.
I'M BUSY IN THE MORNING, SO I WANT TO MAKE SURE TO GET ALL THE STUFF I NEED DONE.
WAAAH.... YOU'RE SUPER RESPON-SIBLE, SAE.

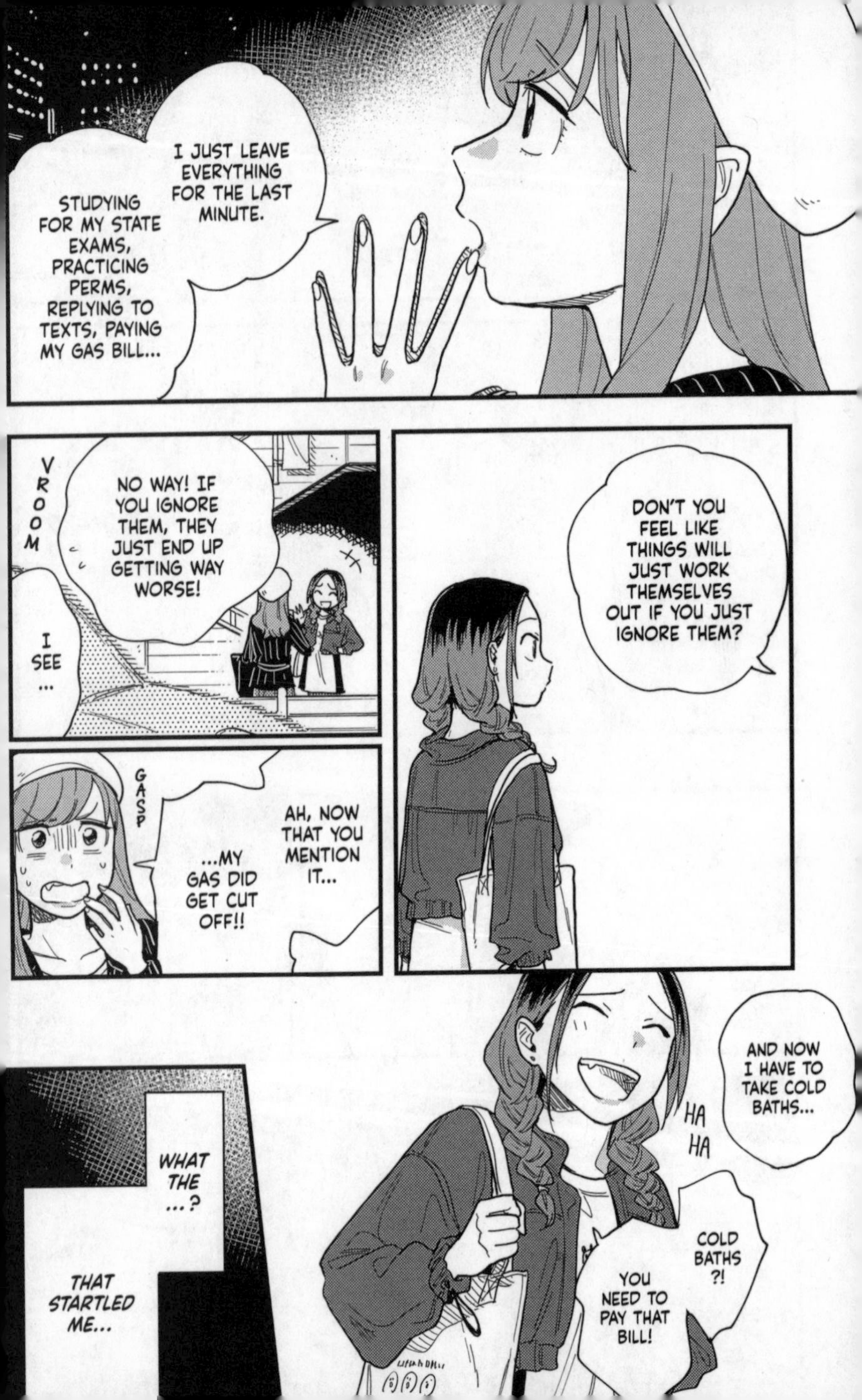
I JUST LEAVE EVERYTHING FOR THE LAST MINUTE.
STUDYING FOR MY STATE EXAMS, PRACTICING PERMS, REPLYING TO TEXTS, PAYING MY GAS BILL...
DON'T YOU FEEL LIKE THINGS WILL JUST WORK THEMSELVES OUT IF YOU JUST IGNORE THEM?
NO WAY! IF YOU IGNORE THEM, THEY JUST END UP GETTING WAY WORSE!
VROOM
I SEE...
AH, NOW THAT YOU MENTION IT...
...MY GAS DID GET CUT OFF!!
GASP
AND NOW I HAVE TO TAKE COLD BATHS...
HA HA
COLD BATHS?!
YOU NEED TO PAY THAT BILL!
WHAT THE ...?
THAT STARTLED ME...

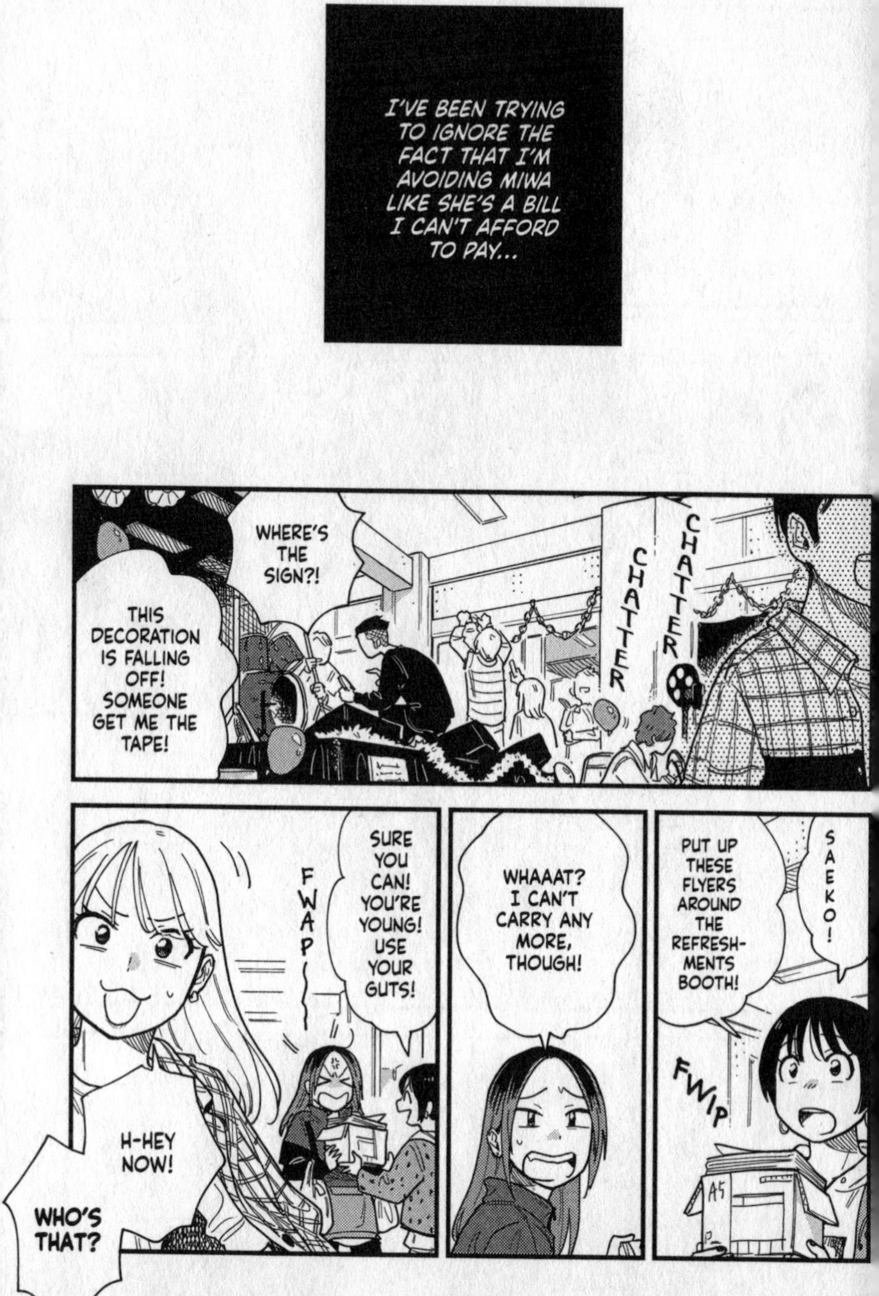
I'VE BEEN TRYING TO IGNORE THE FACT THAT I'M AVOIDING MIWA LIKE SHE'S A BILL I CAN'T AFFORD TO PAY...
CHATTER
CHATTER
WHERE'S THE SIGN?!
THIS DECORATION IS FALLING OFF! SOMEONE GET ME THE TAPE!
SAEKO!
PUT UP THESE FLYERS AROUND THE REFRESHMENTS BOOTH!
FWIP
WHAAAT? I CAN'T CARRY ANY MORE, THOUGH!
SURE YOU CAN! YOU'RE YOUNG! USE YOUR GUTS!
FWAP
H-HEY NOW!
WHO'S THAT?

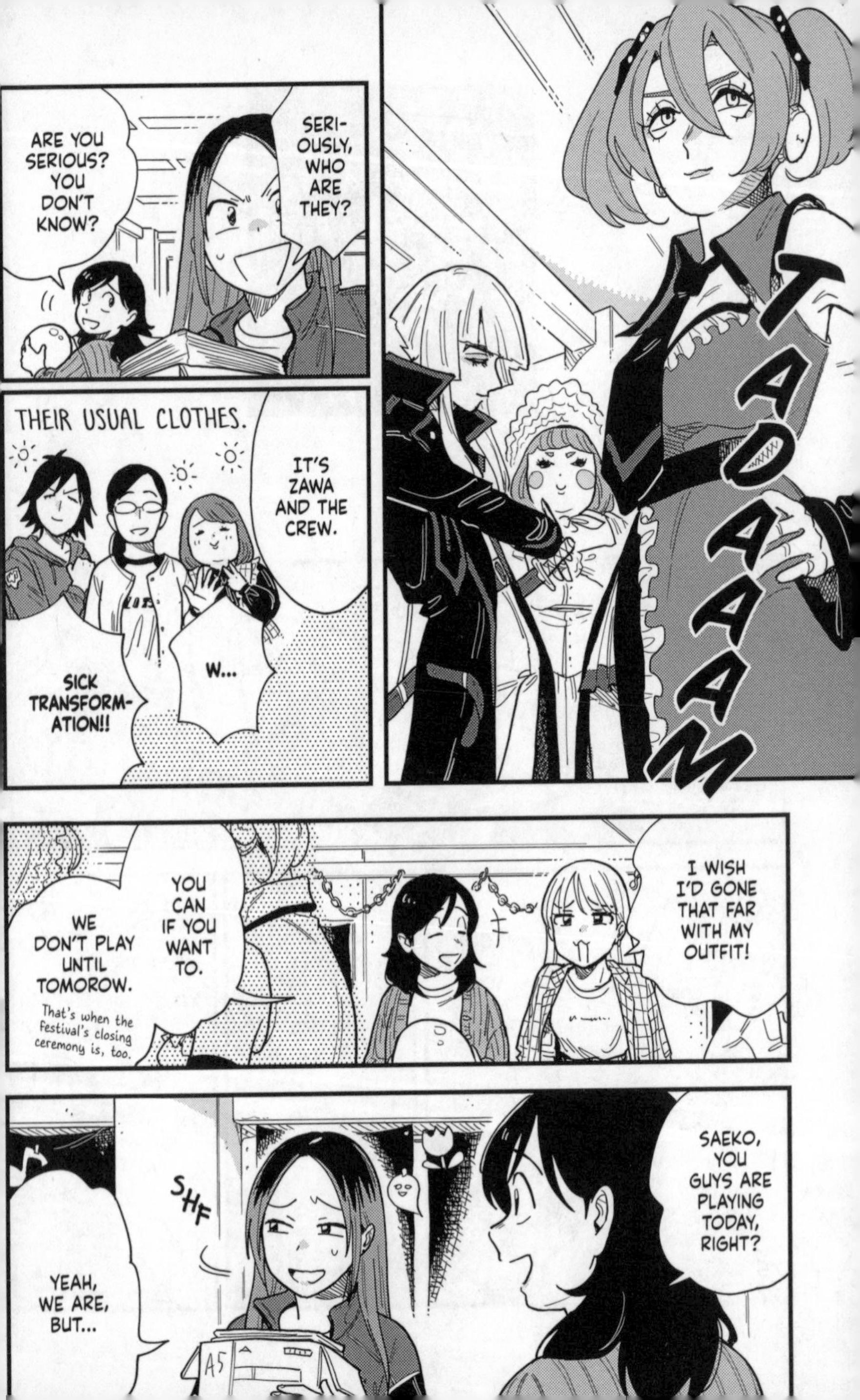
TADAAAAM
SERI-OUSLY, WHO ARE THEY?
ARE YOU SERIOUS? YOU DON'T KNOW?
IT'S ZAWA AND THE CREW.
THEIR USUAL CLOTHES.
W...
SICK TRANSFORM-ATION!!
I WISH I'D GONE THAT FAR WITH MY OUTFIT!
YOU CAN IF YOU WANT TO.
WE DON'T PLAY UNTIL TOMOROW.
That's when the Festival's closing ceremony is, too.
SAEKO, YOU GUYS ARE PLAYING TODAY, RIGHT?
SHF
YEAH, WE ARE, BUT...

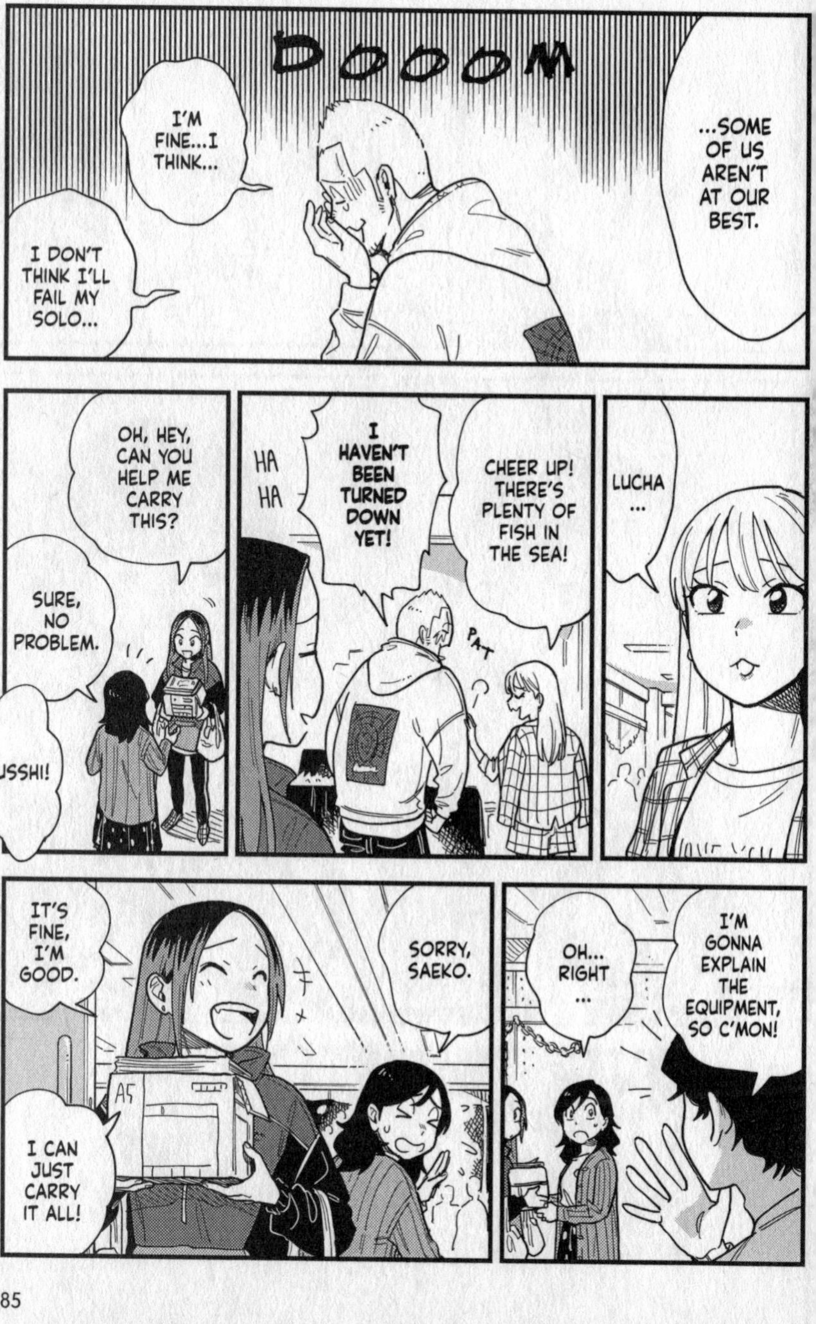
...SOME OF US AREN'T AT OUR BEST.
DOOOOM
I'M FINE...I THINK...
I DON'T THINK I'LL FAIL MY SOLO...
LUCHA ...
CHEER UP! THERE'S PLENTY OF FISH IN THE SEA!
PAT
I HAVEN'T BEEN TURNED DOWN YET!
HA HA
OH, HEY, CAN YOU HELP ME CARRY THIS?
SURE, NO PROBLEM.
USSHI!
I'M GONNA EXPLAIN THE EQUIPMENT, SO C'MON!
OH... RIGHT ...
SORRY, SAEKO.
IT'S FINE, I'M GOOD.
I CAN JUST CARRY IT ALL!

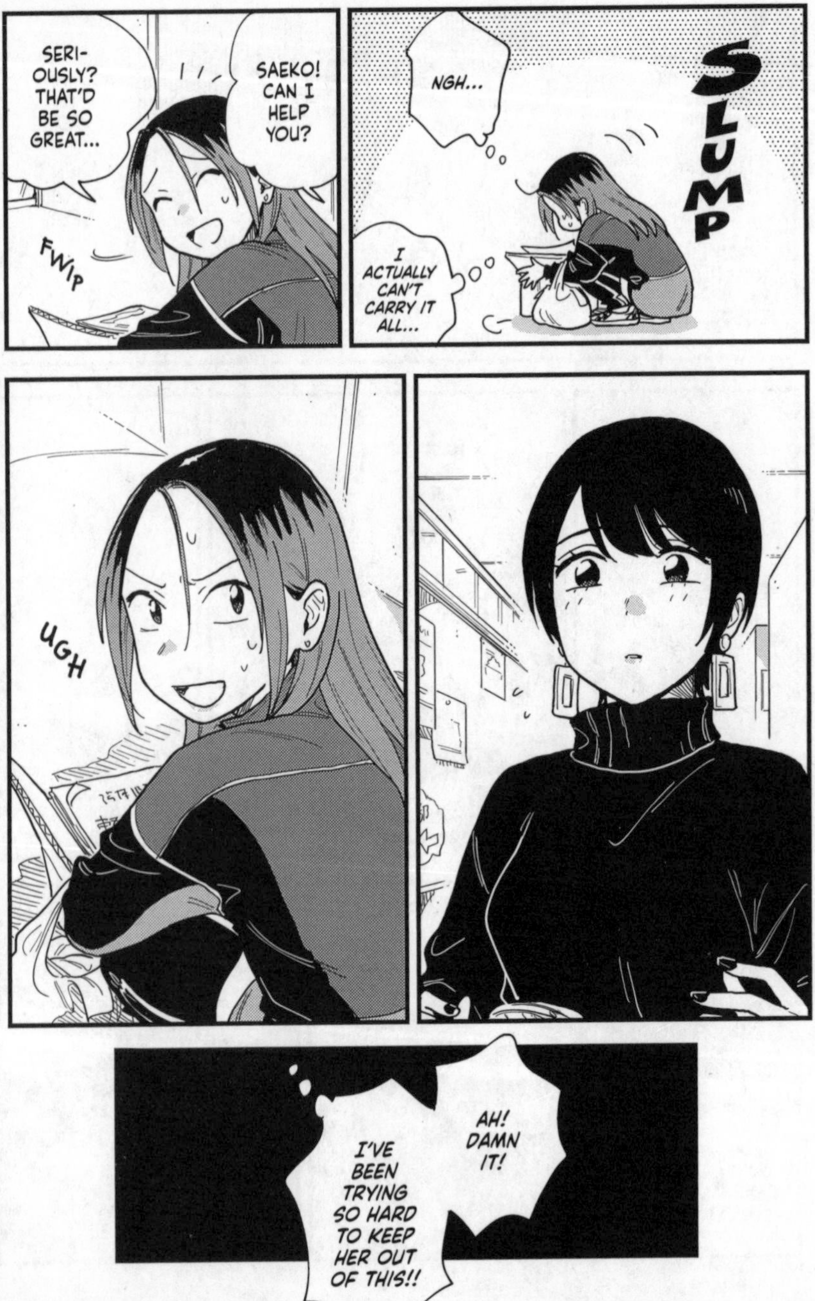
SLUMP
NGH...
I ACTUALLY CAN'T CARRY IT ALL...
SAEKO! CAN I HELP YOU?
SERI-OUSLY? THAT'D BE SO GREAT...
FWIP
UGH
AH! DAMN IT!
I'VE BEEN TRYING SO HARD TO KEEP HER OUT OF THIS!!

HOW DO WE RELATIONSHIP?

HOW DO WE RELATIONSHIP?

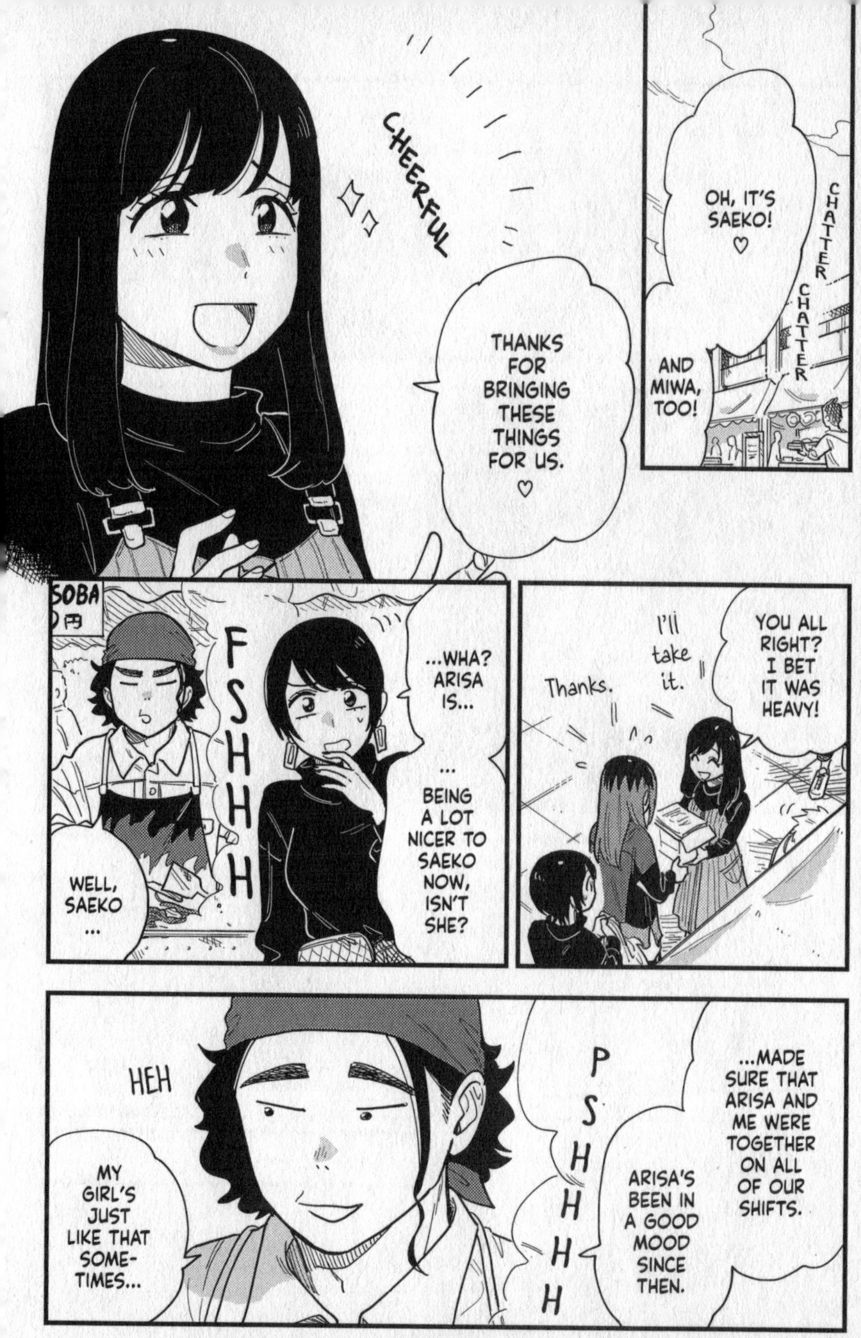
OH, IT'S SAEKO! ♡
CHATTER CHATTER
AND MIWA, TOO!
CHEERFUL
THANKS FOR BRINGING THESE THINGS FOR US. ♡
YOU ALL RIGHT? I BET IT WAS HEAVY!
I'll take it.
Thanks.
...WHA? ARISA IS...
...BEING A LOT NICER TO SAEKO NOW, ISN'T SHE?
FSHHHH
SOBA
WELL, SAEKO...
...MADE SURE THAT ARISA AND ME WERE TOGETHER ON ALL OF OUR SHIFTS.
ARISA'S BEEN IN A GOOD MOOD SINCE THEN.
PSHHHH
HEH
MY GIRL'S JUST LIKE THAT SOME-TIMES...

Chapter 32: A Closed Mouth...

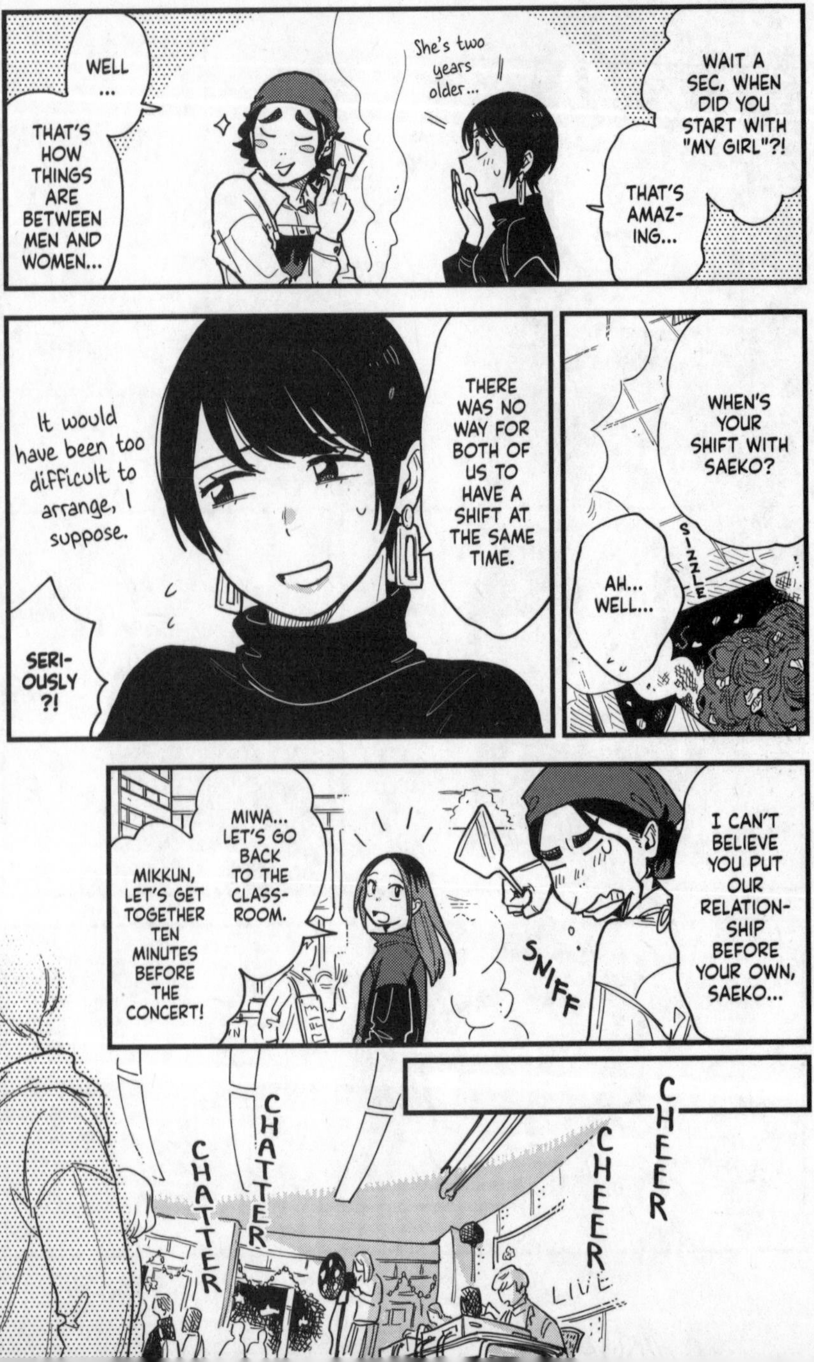
WAIT A SEC, WHEN DID YOU START WITH "MY GIRL"?!
THAT'S AMAZ-ING...
She's two years older...
WELL...
THAT'S HOW THINGS ARE BETWEEN MEN AND WOMEN...
WHEN'S YOUR SHIFT WITH SAEKO?
SIZZLE
AH... WELL...
THERE WAS NO WAY FOR BOTH OF US TO HAVE A SHIFT AT THE SAME TIME.
It would have been too difficult to arrange, I suppose.
SERI-OUSLY?!
I CAN'T BELIEVE YOU PUT OUR RELATION-SHIP BEFORE YOUR OWN, SAEKO...
SNIFF
MIWA... LET'S GO BACK TO THE CLASS-ROOM.
MIKKUN, LET'S GET TOGETHER TEN MINUTES BEFORE THE CONCERT!
CHEER
CHEER
CHATTER
CHATTER
LIVE

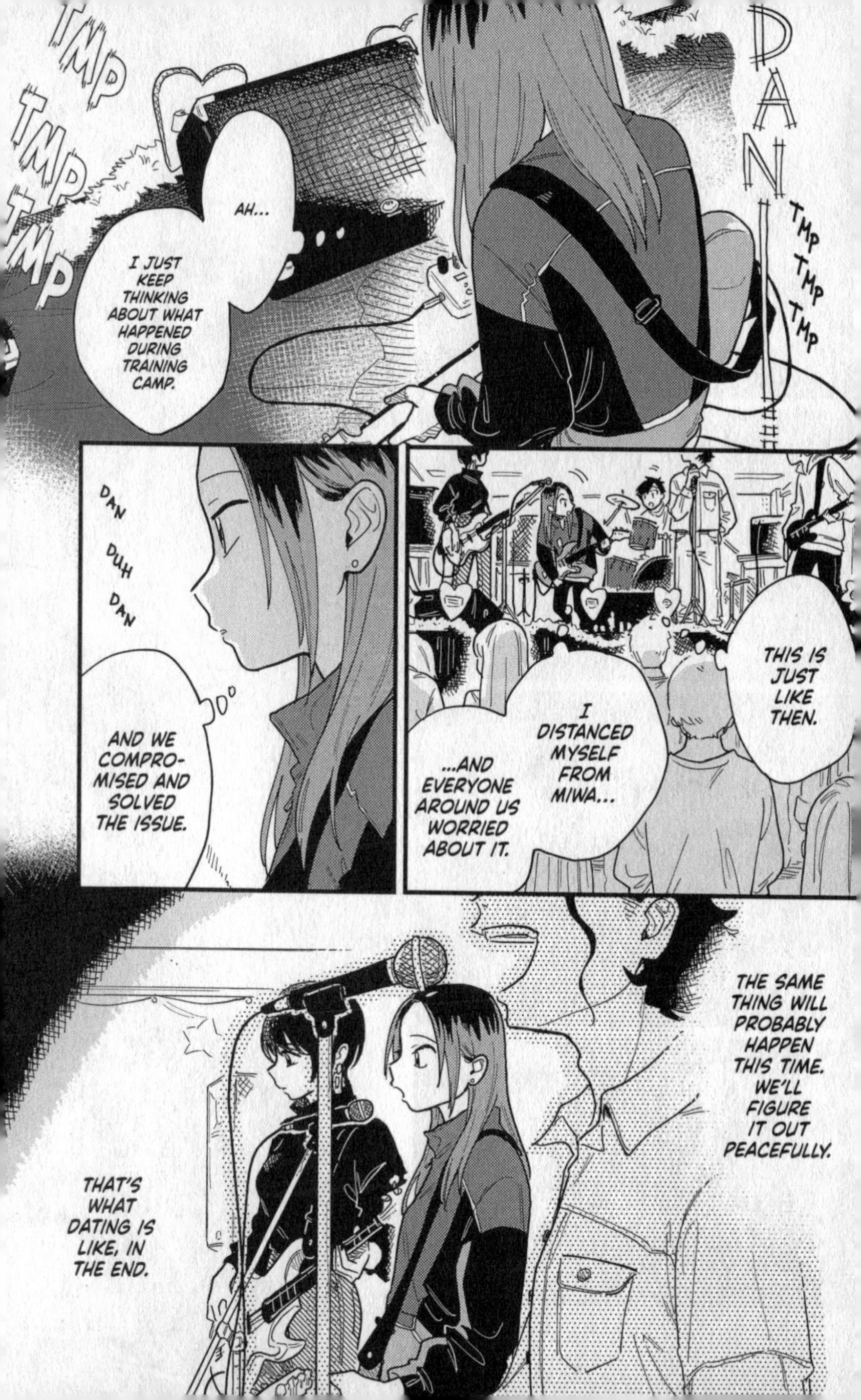
DAN
TMP TMP TMP
AH...
I JUST KEEP THINKING ABOUT WHAT HAPPENED DURING TRAINING CAMP.
TMP TMP TMP TMP
THIS IS JUST LIKE THEN.
I DISTANCED MYSELF FROM MIWA...
...AND EVERYONE AROUND US WORRIED ABOUT IT.
DAN DUH DAN
AND WE COMPRO-MISED AND SOLVED THE ISSUE.
THE SAME THING WILL PROBABLY HAPPEN THIS TIME. WE'LL FIGURE IT OUT PEACEFULLY.
THAT'S WHAT DATING IS LIKE, IN THE END.

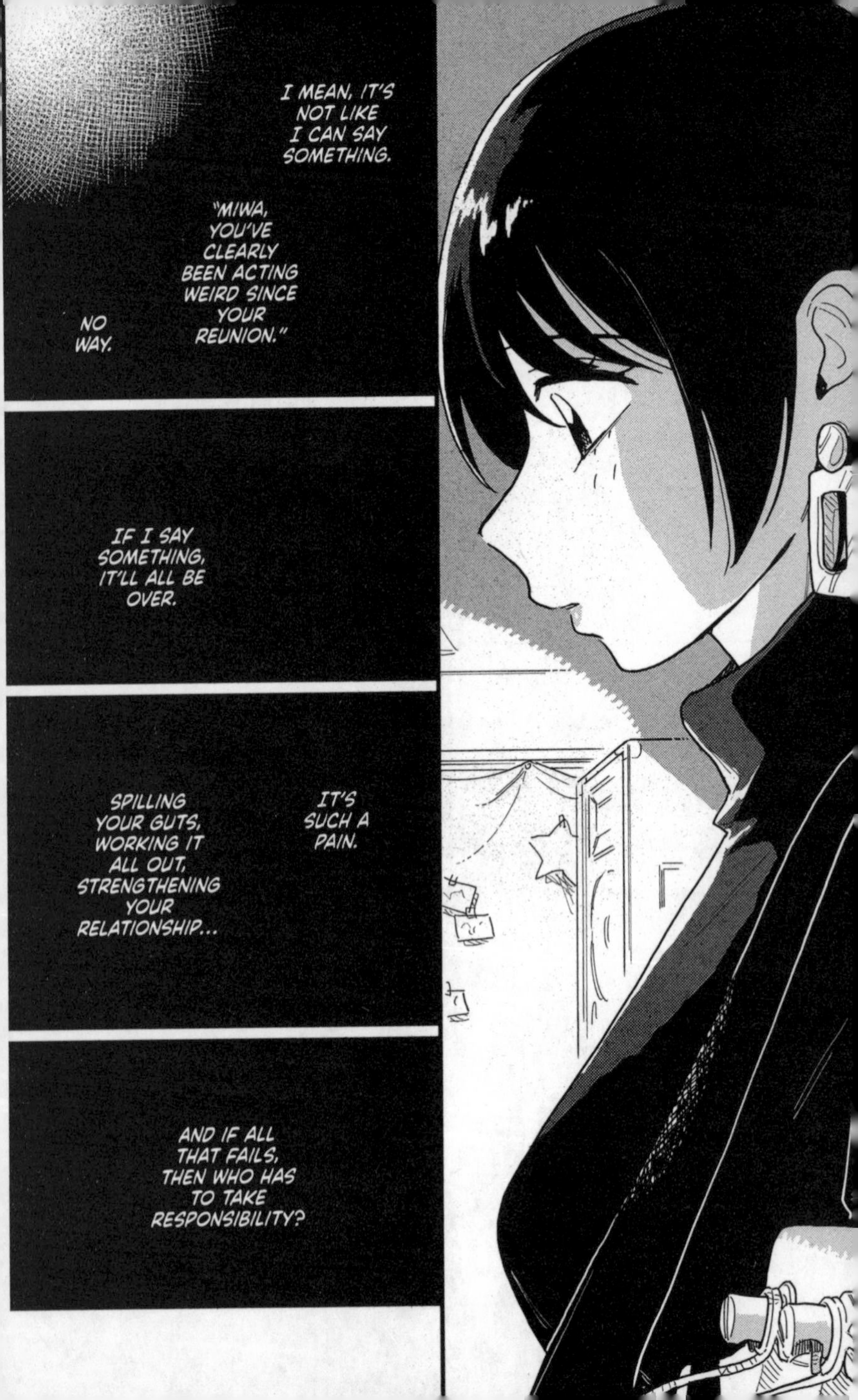

I MEAN, IT'S NOT LIKE I CAN SAY SOMETHING.
"MIWA, YOU'VE CLEARLY BEEN ACTING WEIRD SINCE YOUR REUNION."
NO WAY.
IF I SAY SOMETHING, IT'LL ALL BE OVER.
IT'S SUCH A PAIN.
SPILLING YOUR GUTS, WORKING IT ALL OUT, STRENGTHENING YOUR RELATIONSHIP...
AND IF ALL THAT FAILS, THEN WHO HAS TO TAKE RESPONSIBILITY?

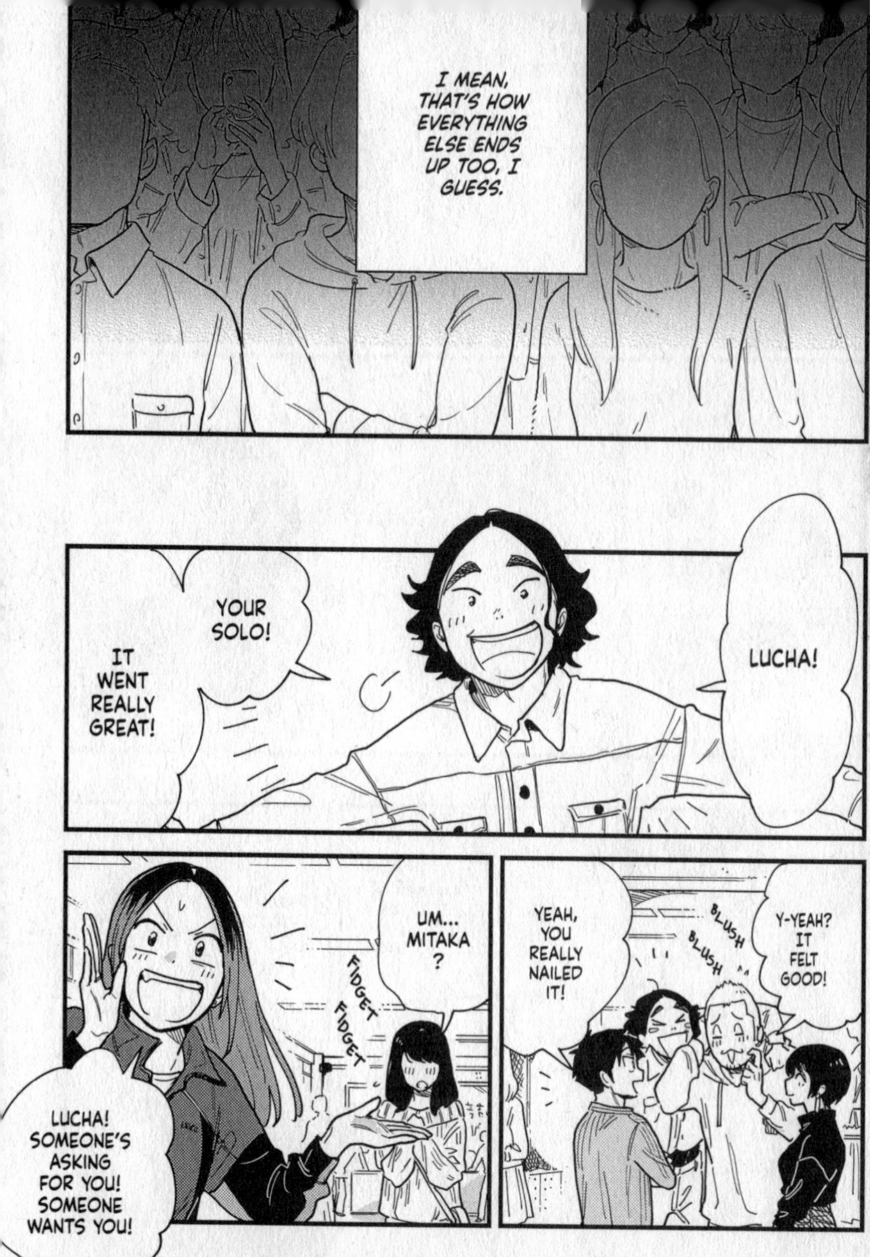
I MEAN, THAT'S HOW EVERYTHING ELSE ENDS UP TOO, I GUESS.
LUCHA!
YOUR SOLO!
IT WENT REALLY GREAT!
Y-YEAH? IT FELT GOOD!
BLUSH
BLUSH
YEAH, YOU REALLY NAILED IT!
UM... MITAKA?
FIDGET
FIDGET
LUCHA! SOMEONE'S ASKING FOR YOU! SOMEONE WANTS YOU!

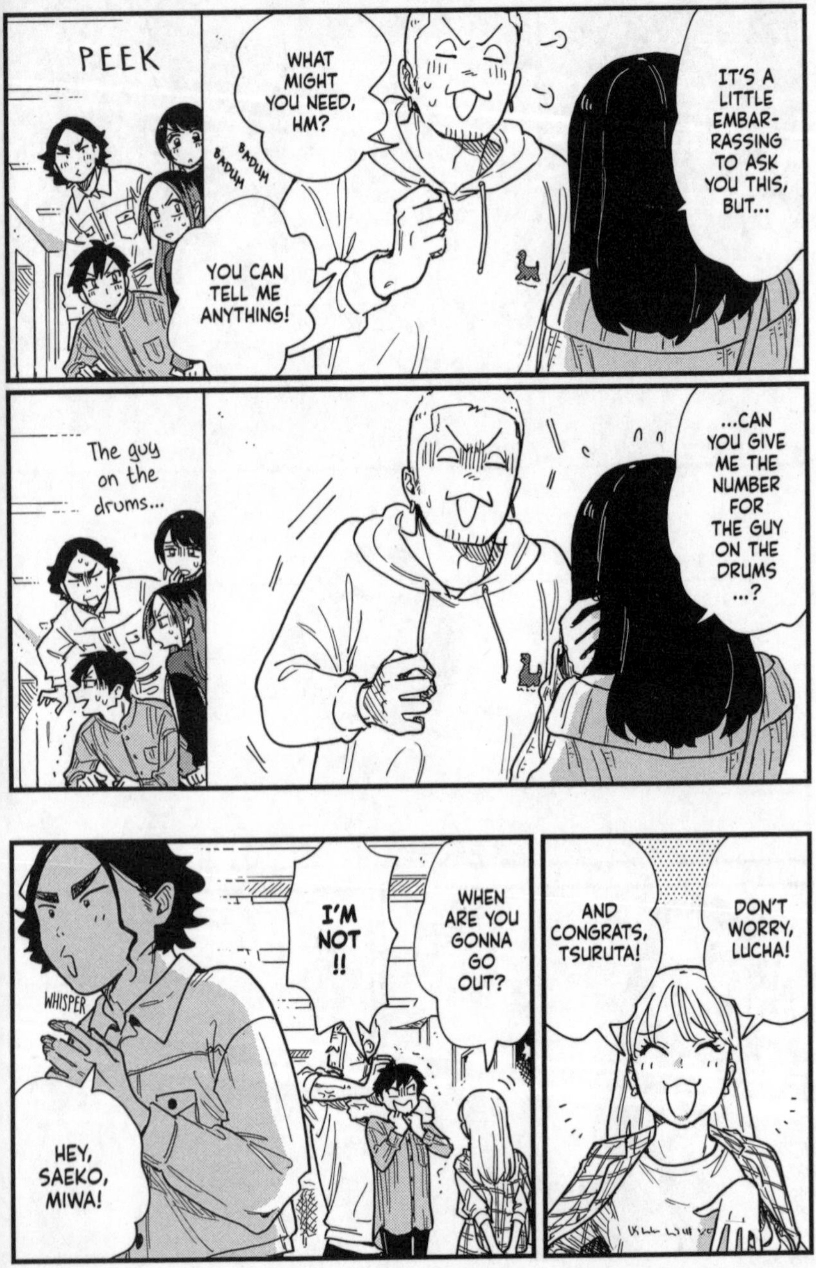
IT'S A LITTLE EMBARRASSING TO ASK YOU THIS, BUT...
WHAT MIGHT YOU NEED, HM?
BADUM BADUM
YOU CAN TELL ME ANYTHING!
PEEK
...CAN YOU GIVE ME THE NUMBER FOR THE GUY ON THE DRUMS ...?
The guy on the drums...
DON'T WORRY, LUCHA!
AND CONGRATS, TSURUTA!
WHEN ARE YOU GONNA GO OUT?
I'M NOT !!
WHISPER
HEY, SAEKO, MIWA!

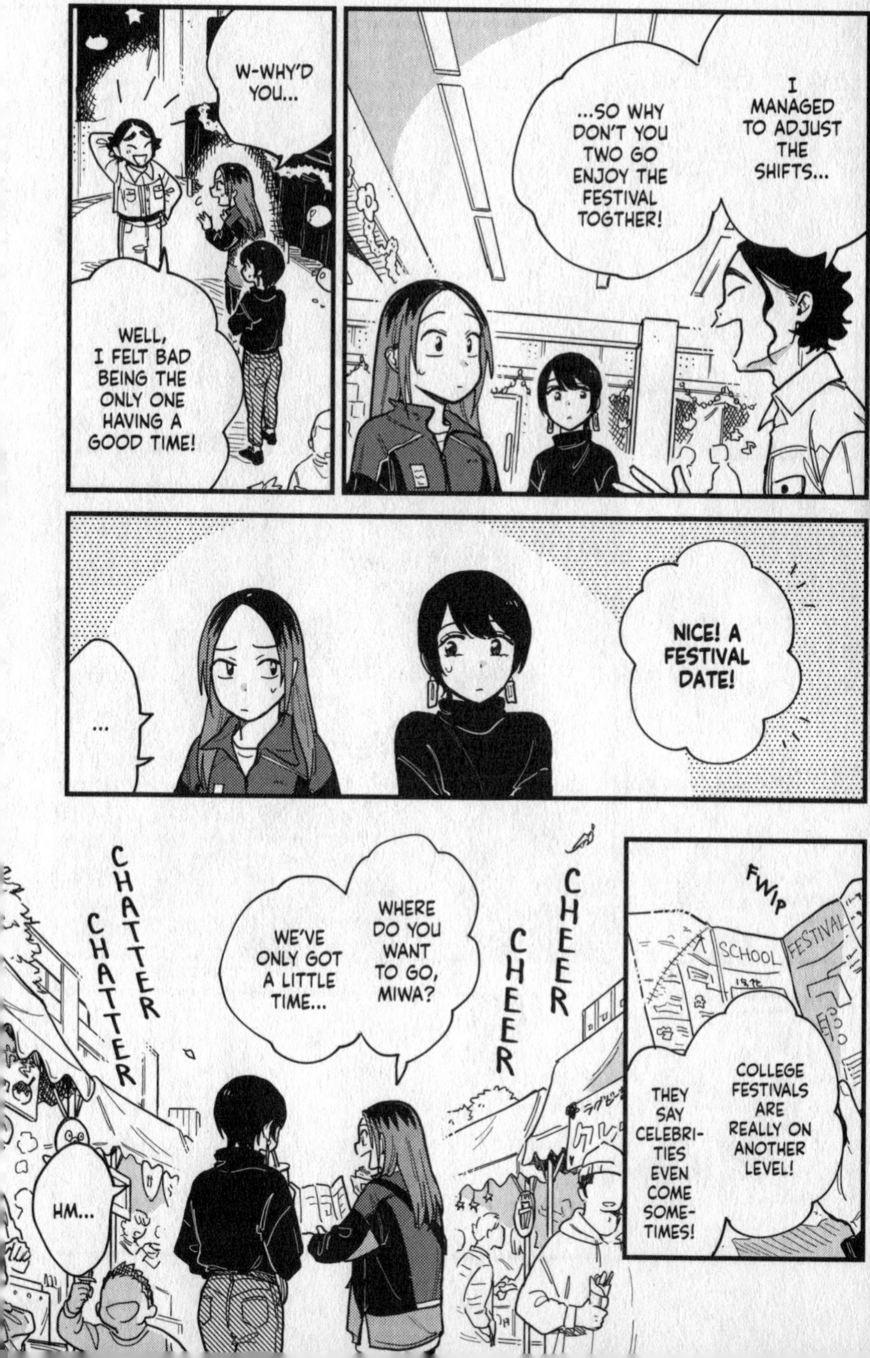
I MANAGED TO ADJUST THE SHIFTS...
...SO WHY DON'T YOU TWO GO ENJOY THE FESTIVAL TOGTHER!
W-WHY'D YOU...
WELL, I FELT BAD BEING THE ONLY ONE HAVING A GOOD TIME!
NICE! A FESTIVAL DATE!
...
FWIP
SCHOOL FESTIVAL
COLLEGE FESTIVALS ARE REALLY ON ANOTHER LEVEL!
THEY SAY CELEBRI-TIES EVEN COME SOME-TIMES!
CHEER CHEER
WHERE DO YOU WANT TO GO, MIWA?
WE'VE ONLY GOT A LITTLE TIME...
CHATTER CHATTER
HM...

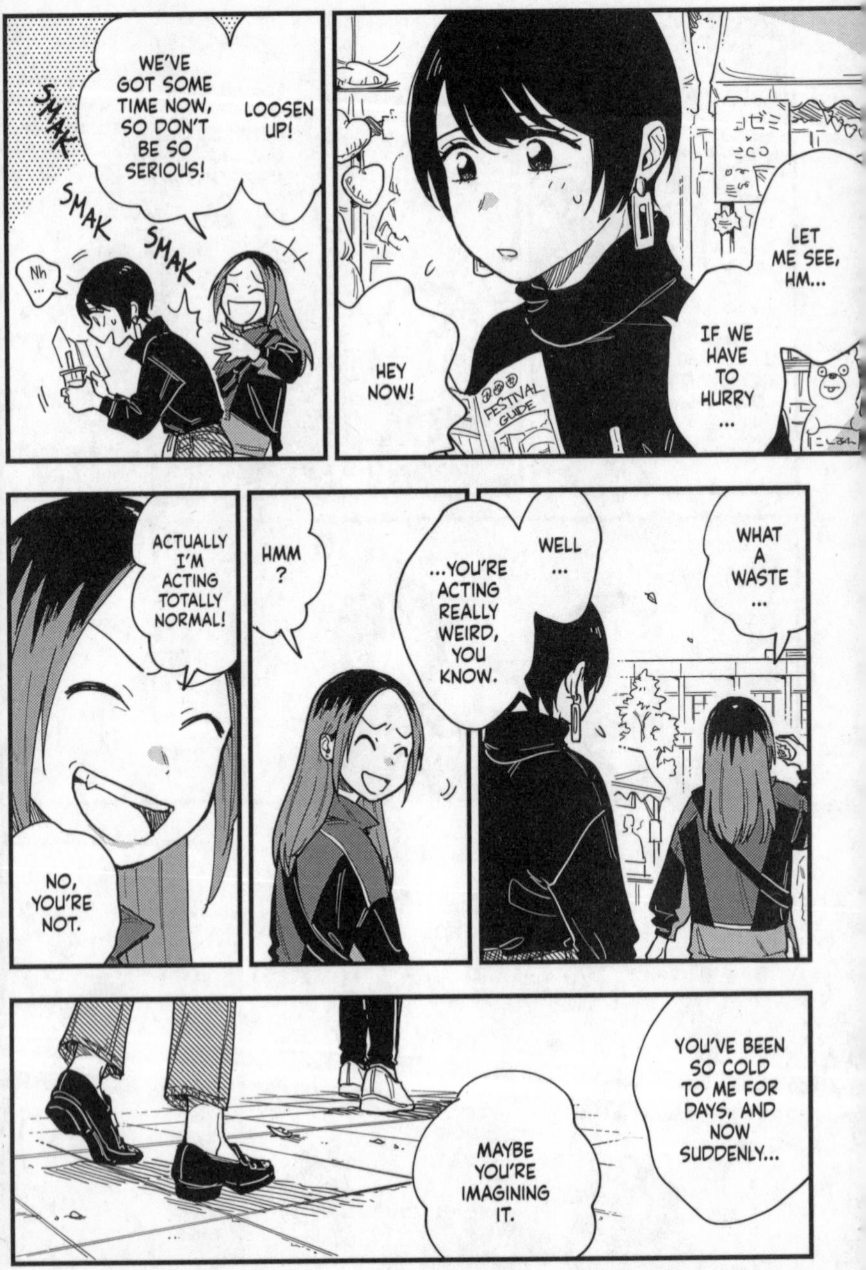
LET ME SEE, HM...
IF WE HAVE TO HURRY ...
FESTIVAL GUIDE
HEY NOW!
LOOSEN UP!
WE'VE GOT SOME TIME NOW, SO DON'T BE SO SERIOUS!
SMAK
SMAK
SMAK
Nh ...
WHAT A WASTE ...
WELL ...
...YOU'RE ACTING REALLY WEIRD, YOU KNOW.
HMM ?
ACTUALLY I'M ACTING TOTALLY NORMAL!
NO, YOU'RE NOT.
YOU'VE BEEN SO COLD TO ME FOR DAYS, AND NOW SUDDENLY...
MAYBE YOU'RE IMAGINING IT.
...

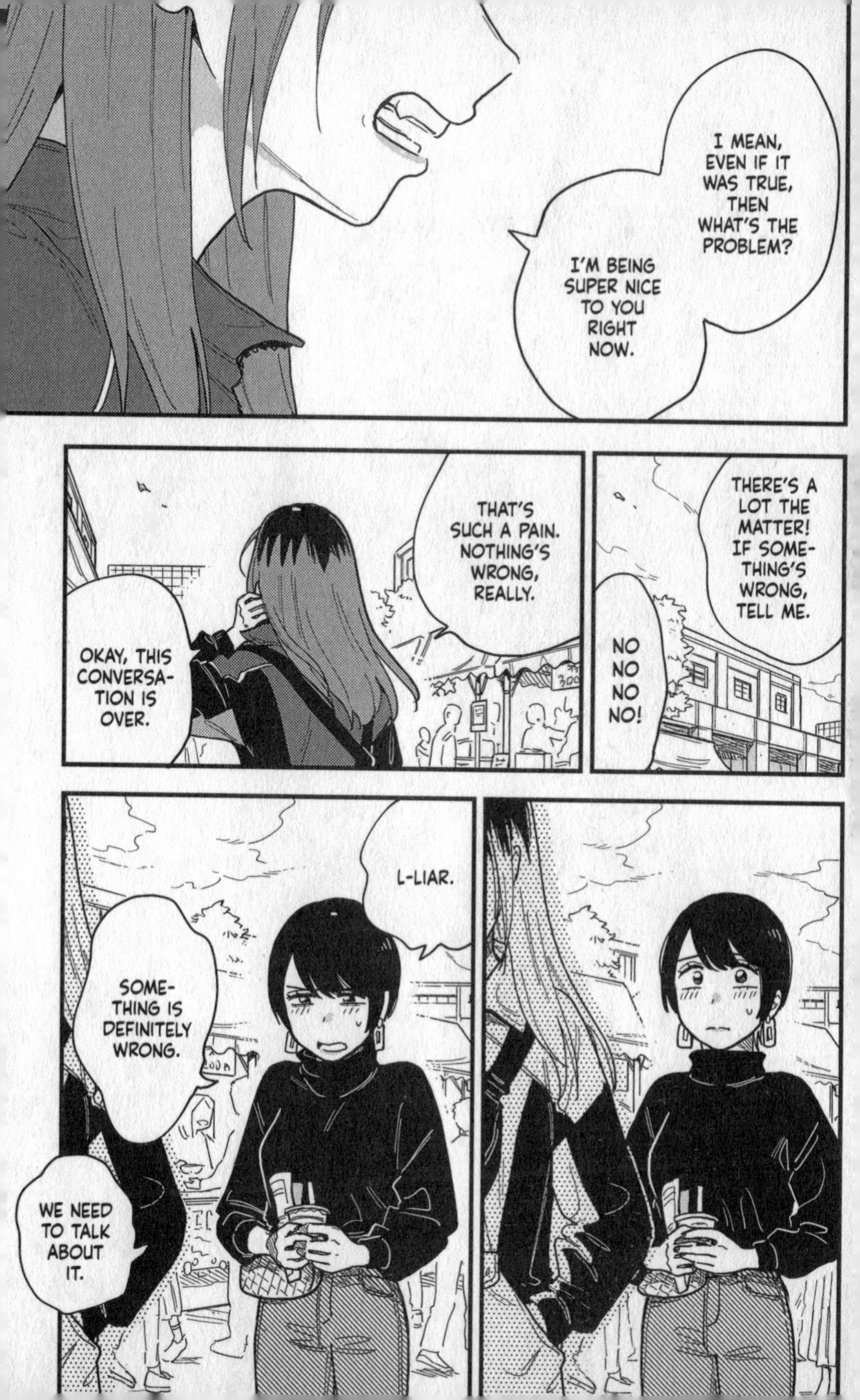
I MEAN, EVEN IF IT WAS TRUE, THEN WHAT'S THE PROBLEM?
I'M BEING SUPER NICE TO YOU RIGHT NOW.
THERE'S A LOT THE MATTER! IF SOMETHING'S WRONG, TELL ME.
NO NO NO NO!
THAT'S SUCH A PAIN. NOTHING'S WRONG, REALLY.
OKAY, THIS CONVERSATION IS OVER.
L-LIAR.
SOMETHING IS DEFINITELY WRONG.
WE NEED TO TALK ABOUT IT.

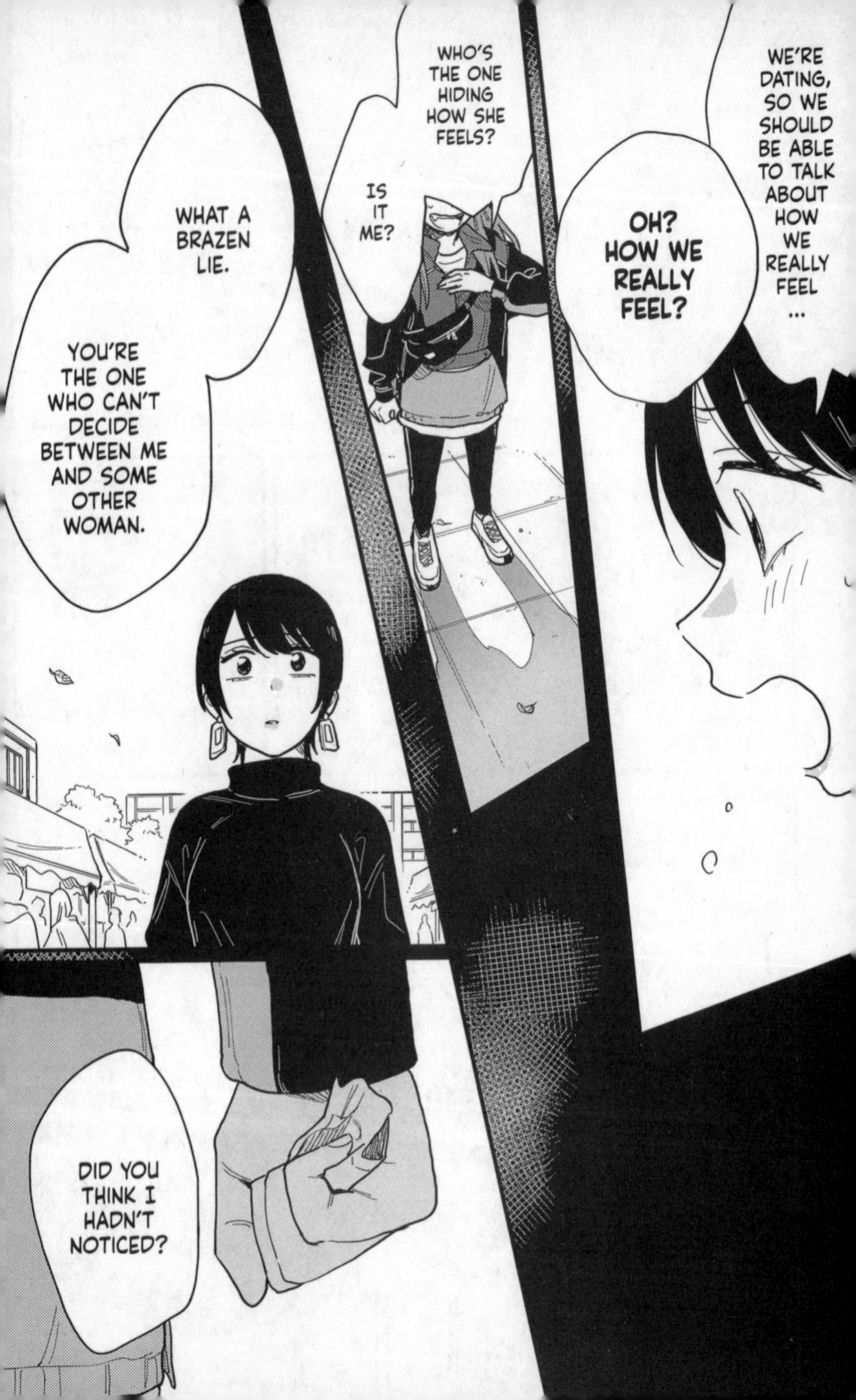
WE'RE DATING, SO WE SHOULD BE ABLE TO TALK ABOUT HOW WE REALLY FEEL ...
OH? HOW WE REALLY FEEL?
WHO'S THE ONE HIDING HOW SHE FEELS?
IS IT ME?
WHAT A BRAZEN LIE.
YOU'RE THE ONE WHO CAN'T DECIDE BETWEEN ME AND SOME OTHER WOMAN.
DID YOU THINK I HADN'T NOTICED?

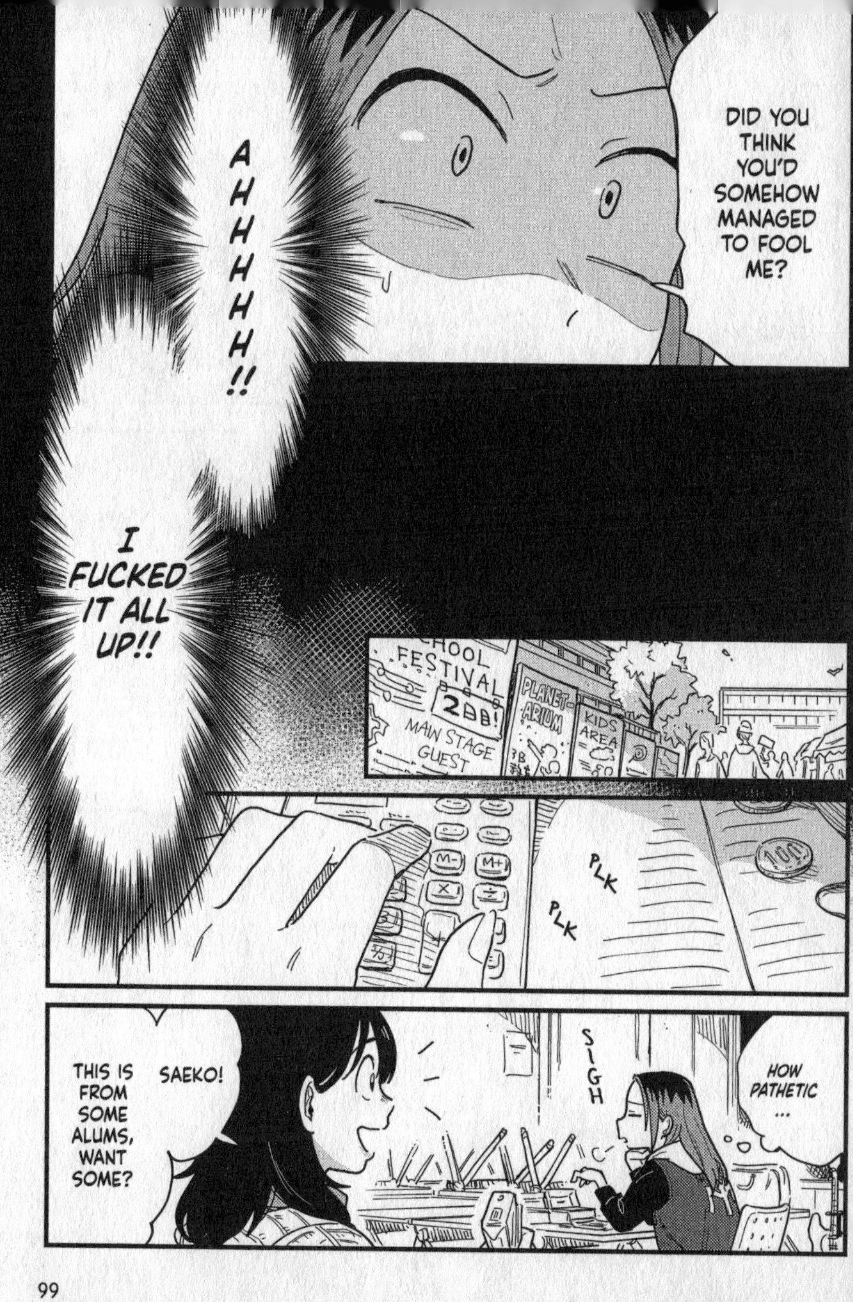
DID YOU THINK YOU'D SOMEHOW MANAGED TO FOOL ME?
AHHHHHH!!
I FUCKED IT ALL UP!!
CHOOL FESTIVAL
MAIN STAGE GUEST
PLANET-ARIUM
KIDS AREA
PLK
PLK
HOW PATHETIC ...
SIGH
SAEKO!
THIS IS FROM SOME ALUMS, WANT SOME?

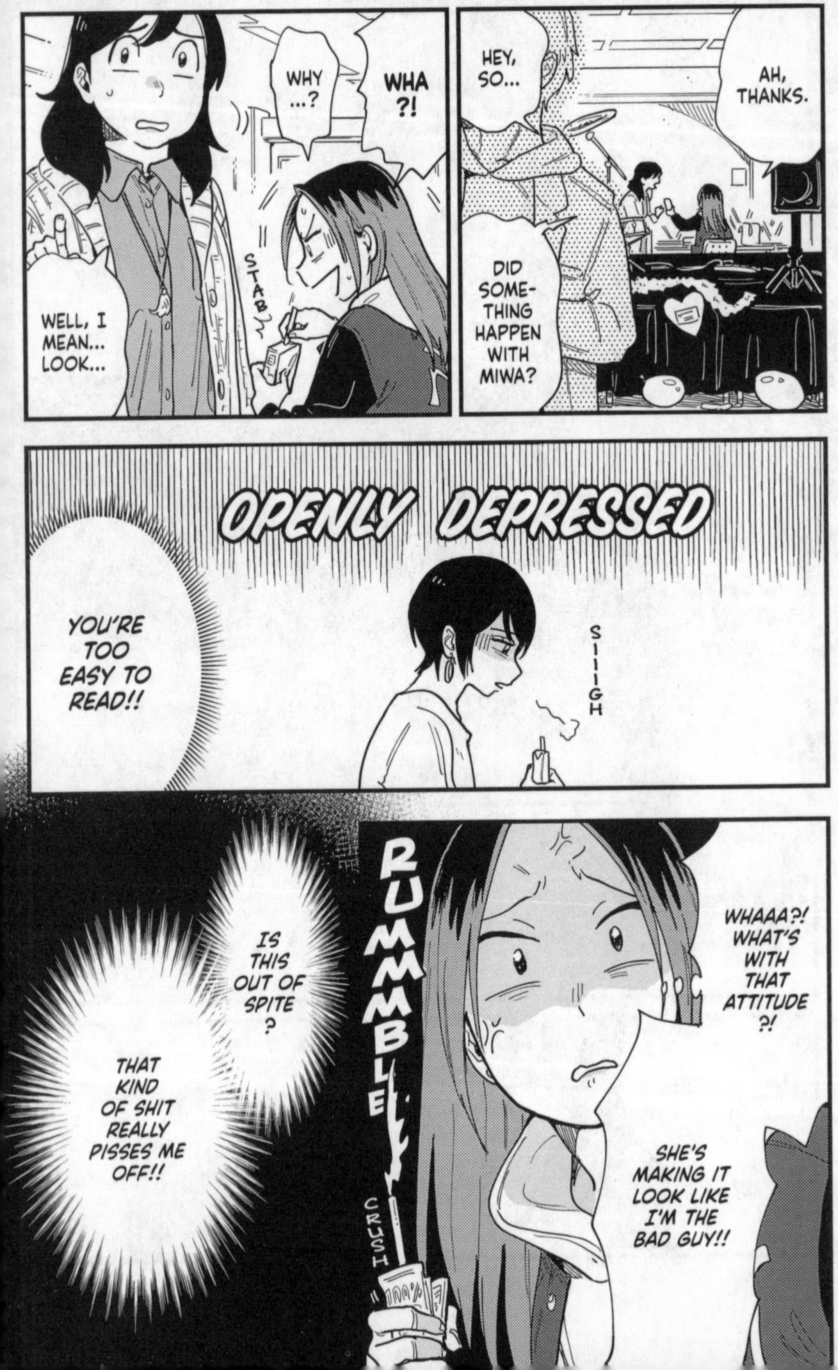
AH, THANKS.
HEY, SO...
DID SOMETHING HAPPEN WITH MIWA?
WHA ?!
WHY ...?
STAB
WELL, I MEAN... LOOK...
OPENLY DEPRESSED
SIIIGH
YOU'RE TOO EASY TO READ!!
WHAAA?! WHAT'S WITH THAT ATTITUDE ?!
RUMMBLE
IS THIS OUT OF SPITE ?
SHE'S MAKING IT LOOK LIKE I'M THE BAD GUY!!
CRUSH
THAT KIND OF SHIT REALLY PISSES ME OFF!!

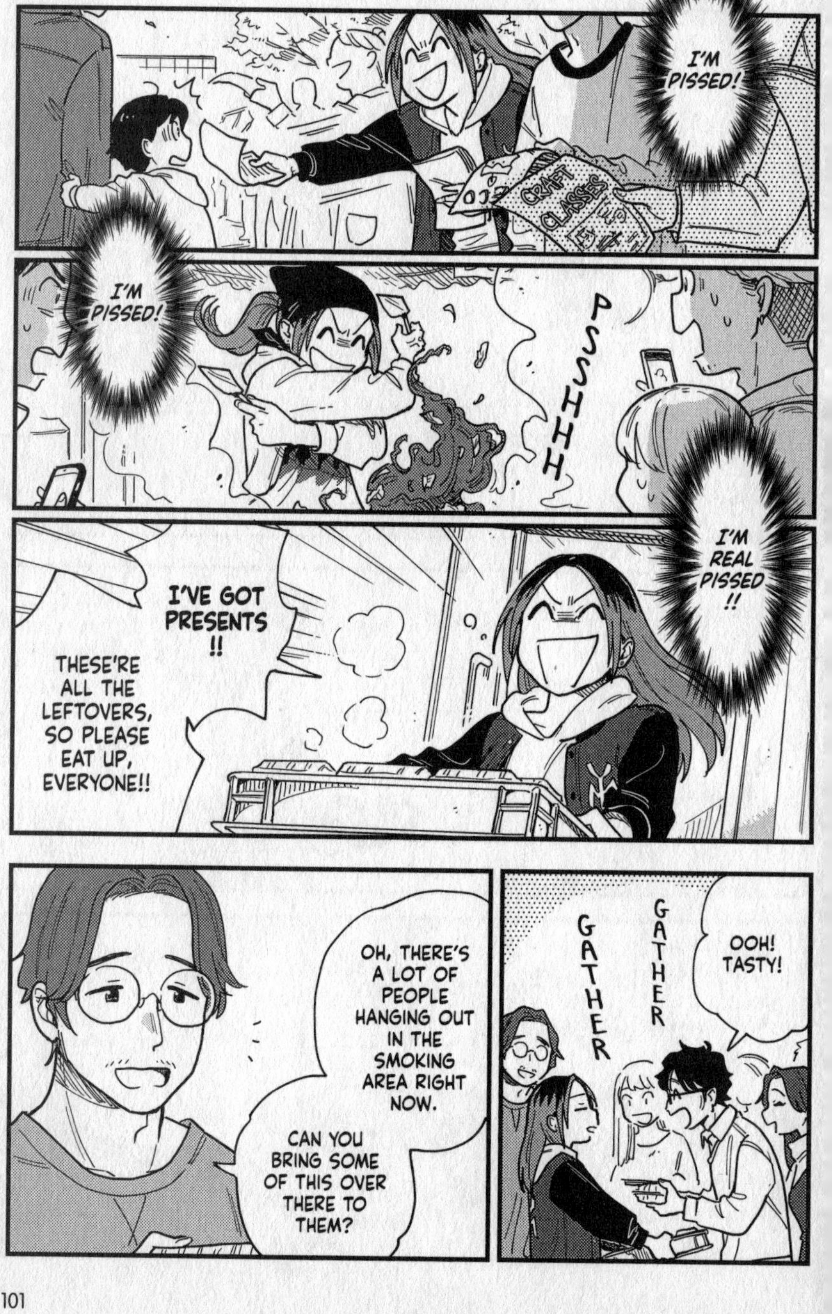
I'M PISSED!
PSSHHH
I'M PISSED!
I'M REAL PISSED!!
I'VE GOT PRESENTS!!
THESE'RE ALL THE LEFTOVERS, SO PLEASE EAT UP, EVERYONE!!
OOH! TASTY!
GATHER
GATHER
OH, THERE'S A LOT OF PEOPLE HANGING OUT IN THE SMOKING AREA RIGHT NOW.
CAN YOU BRING SOME OF THIS OVER THERE TO THEM?

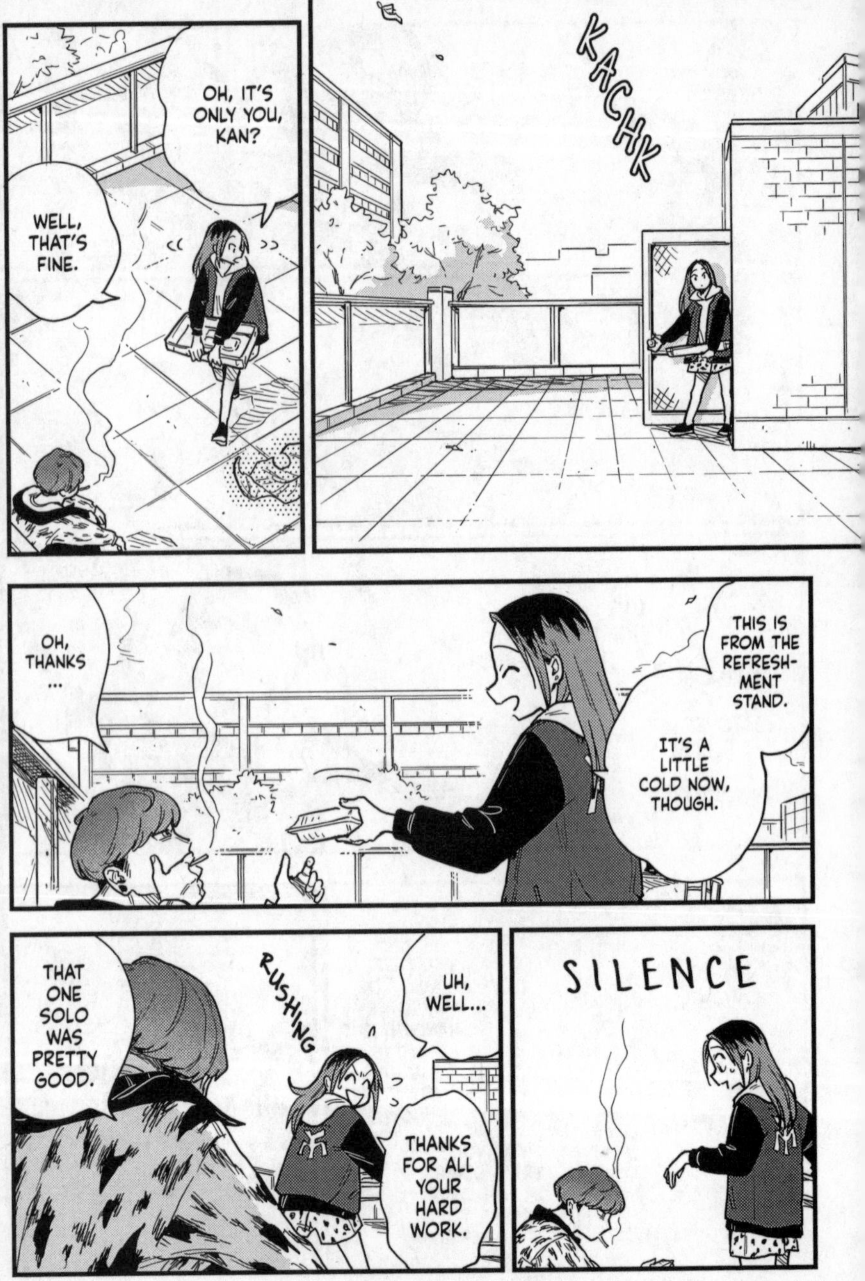
KACHK
OH, IT'S ONLY YOU, KAN?
WELL, THAT'S FINE.
THIS IS FROM THE REFRESHMENT STAND.
IT'S A LITTLE COLD NOW, THOUGH.
OH, THANKS...
SILENCE
UH, WELL...
THANKS FOR ALL YOUR HARD WORK.
RUSHING
THAT ONE SOLO WAS PRETTY GOOD.

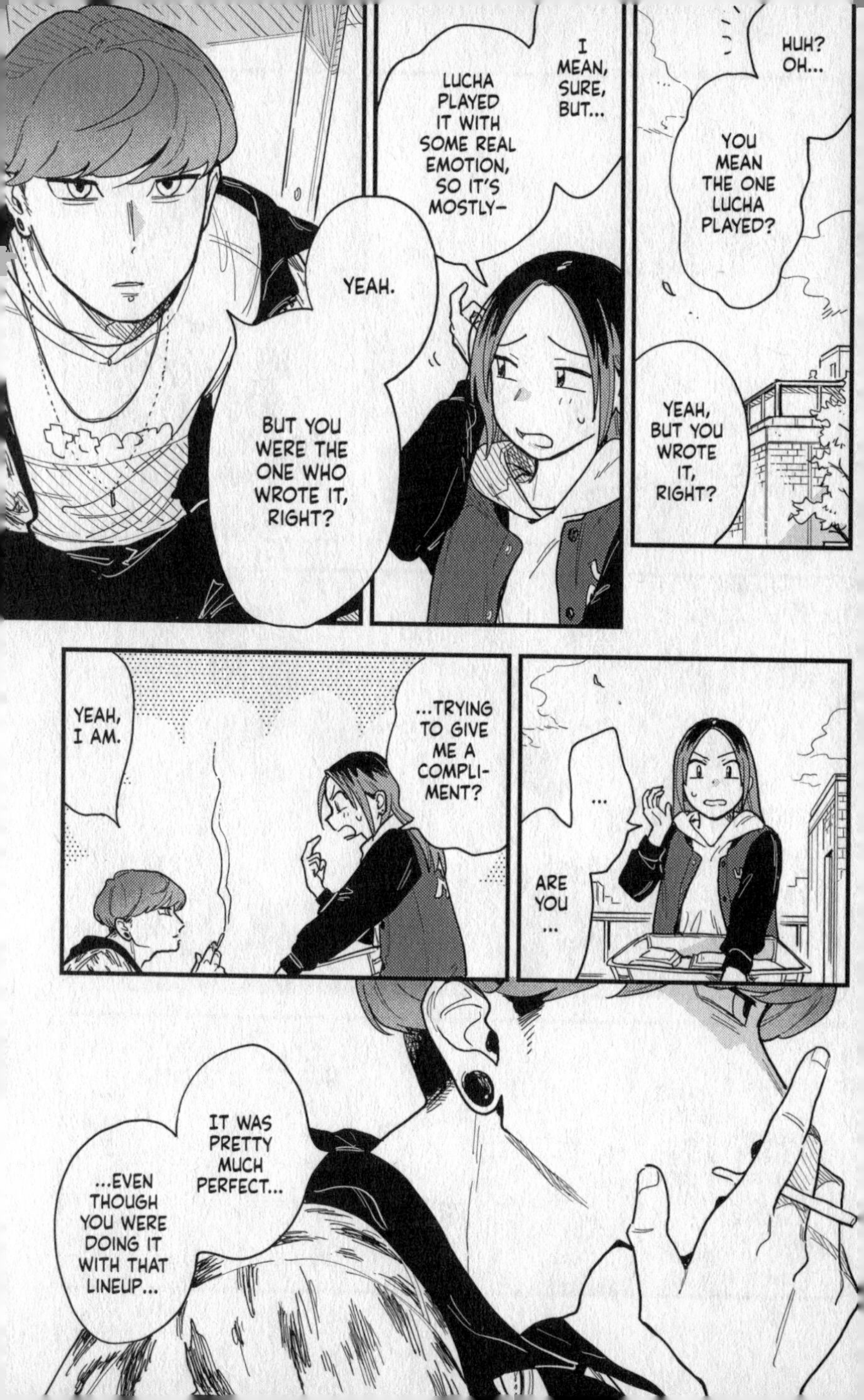
HUH? OH...
YOU MEAN THE ONE LUCHA PLAYED?
YEAH, BUT YOU WROTE IT, RIGHT?
I MEAN, SURE, BUT...
LUCHA PLAYED IT WITH SOME REAL EMOTION, SO IT'S MOSTLY—
YEAH.
BUT YOU WERE THE ONE WHO WROTE IT, RIGHT?
...
ARE YOU ...
...TRYING TO GIVE ME A COMPLIMENT?
YEAH, I AM.
IT WAS PRETTY MUCH PERFECT...
...EVEN THOUGH YOU WERE DOING IT WITH THAT LINEUP...

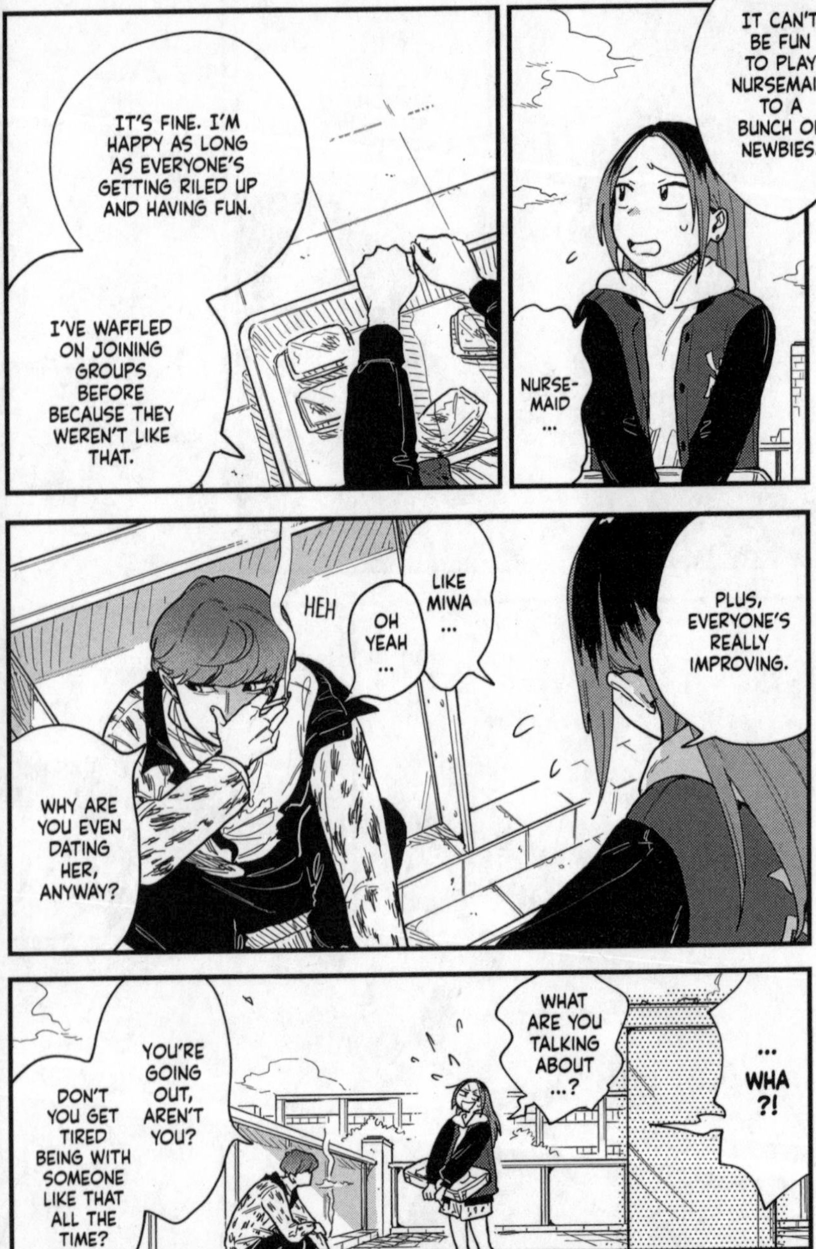
IT CAN'T BE FUN TO PLAY NURSEMAID TO A BUNCH OF NEWBIES.
NURSE-MAID...
IT'S FINE. I'M HAPPY AS LONG AS EVERYONE'S GETTING RILED UP AND HAVING FUN.
I'VE WAFFLED ON JOINING GROUPS BEFORE BECAUSE THEY WEREN'T LIKE THAT.
PLUS, EVERYONE'S REALLY IMPROVING.
LIKE MIWA...
OH YEAH...
HEH
WHY ARE YOU EVEN DATING HER, ANYWAY?
...WHA?!
WHAT ARE YOU TALKING ABOUT...?
YOU'RE GOING OUT, AREN'T YOU?
DON'T YOU GET TIRED BEING WITH SOMEONE LIKE THAT ALL THE TIME?

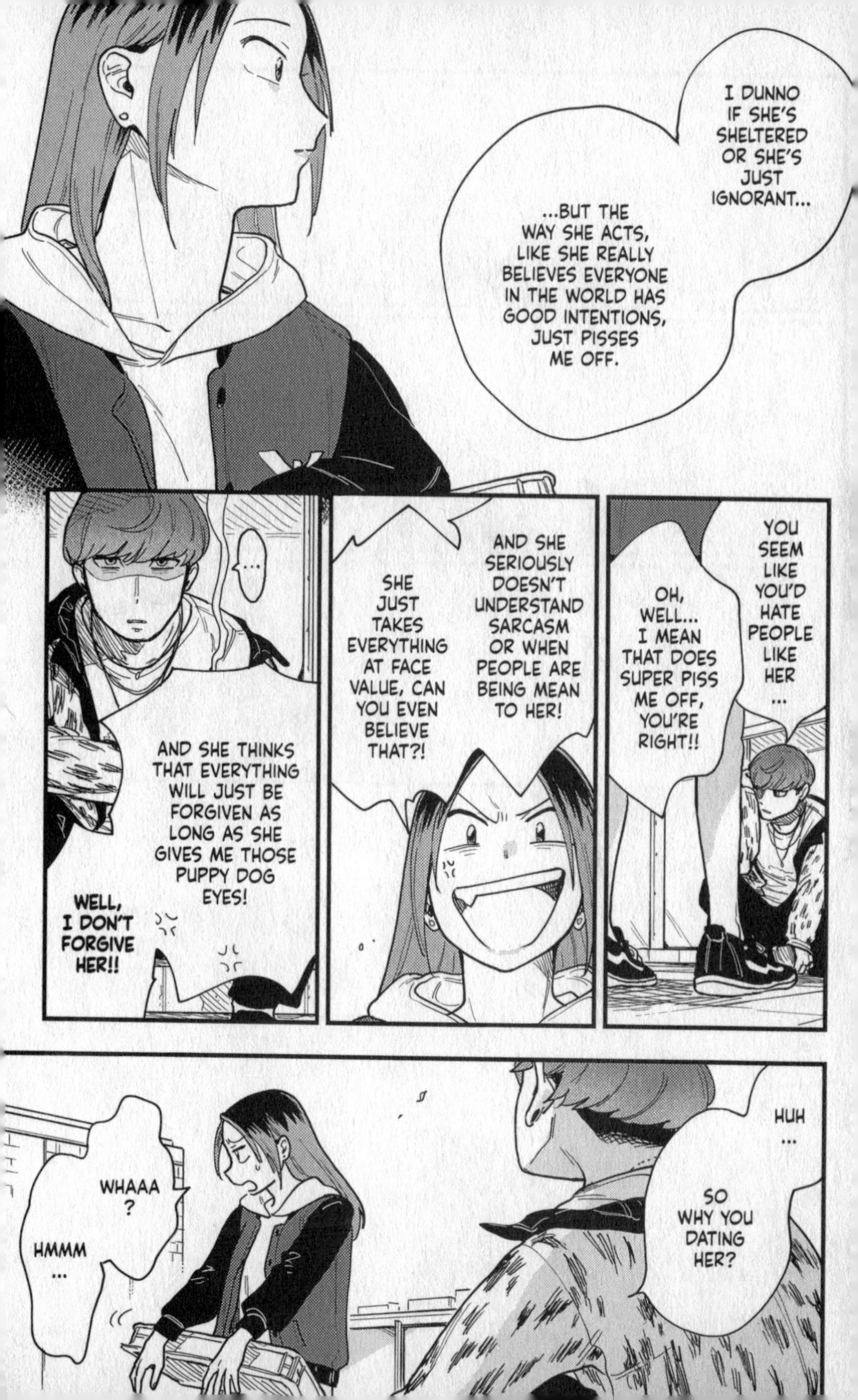
I DUNNO IF SHE'S SHELTERED OR SHE'S JUST IGNORANT...
...BUT THE WAY SHE ACTS, LIKE SHE REALLY BELIEVES EVERYONE IN THE WORLD HAS GOOD INTENTIONS, JUST PISSES ME OFF.
YOU SEEM LIKE YOU'D HATE PEOPLE LIKE HER ...
OH, WELL... I MEAN THAT DOES SUPER PISS ME OFF, YOU'RE RIGHT!!
AND SHE SERIOUSLY DOESN'T UNDERSTAND SARCASM OR WHEN PEOPLE ARE BEING MEAN TO HER!
SHE JUST TAKES EVERYTHING AT FACE VALUE, CAN YOU EVEN BELIEVE THAT?!
...
AND SHE THINKS THAT EVERYTHING WILL JUST BE FORGIVEN AS LONG AS SHE GIVES ME THOSE PUPPY DOG EYES!
WELL, I DON'T FORGIVE HER!!
HUH ...
SO WHY YOU DATING HER?
WHAAA ?
HMMM ...

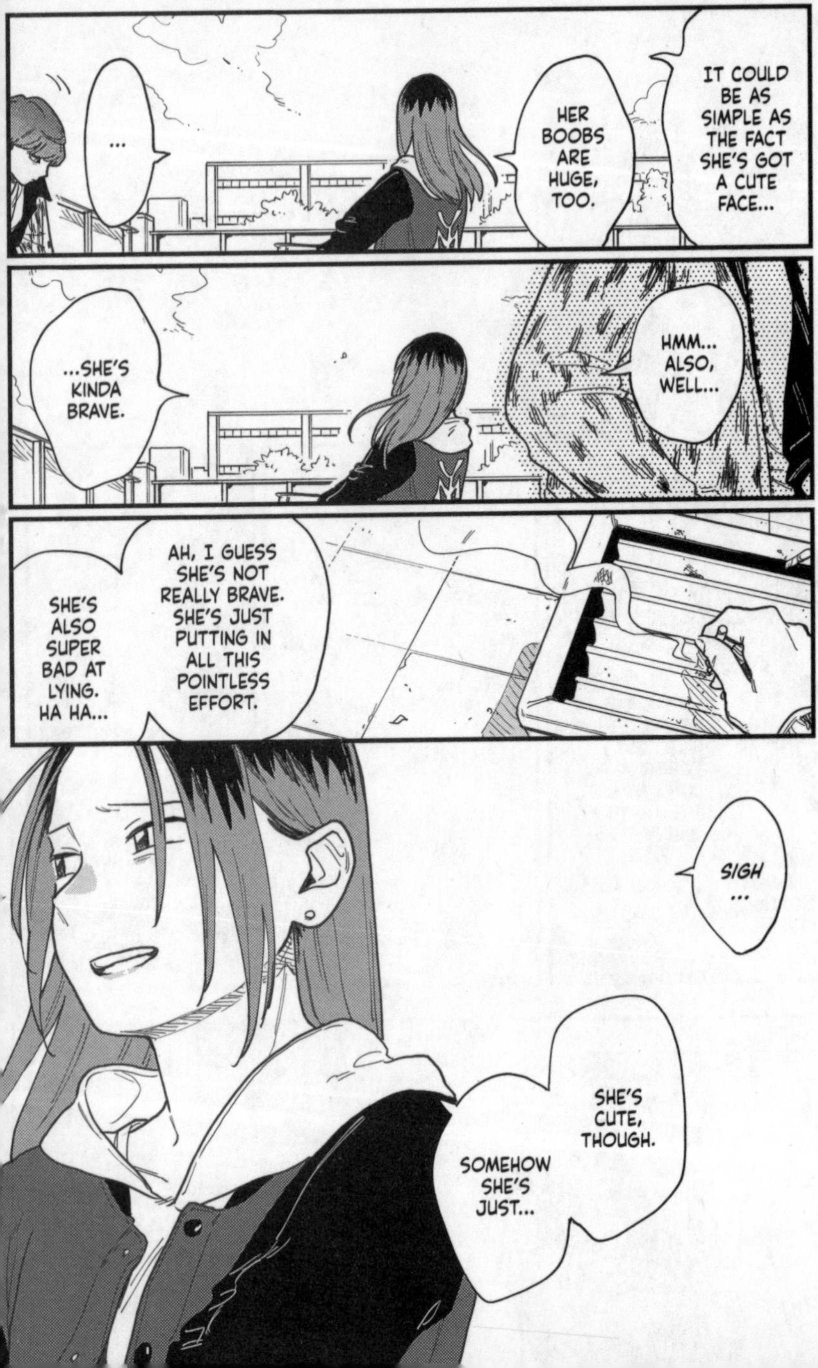
IT COULD BE AS SIMPLE AS THE FACT SHE'S GOT A CUTE FACE...
HER BOOBS ARE HUGE, TOO.
...
HMM... ALSO, WELL...
...SHE'S KINDA BRAVE.
AH, I GUESS SHE'S NOT REALLY BRAVE. SHE'S JUST PUTTING IN ALL THIS POINTLESS EFFORT.
SHE'S ALSO SUPER BAD AT LYING. HA HA...
SIGH...
SHE'S CUTE, THOUGH.
SOMEHOW SHE'S JUST...

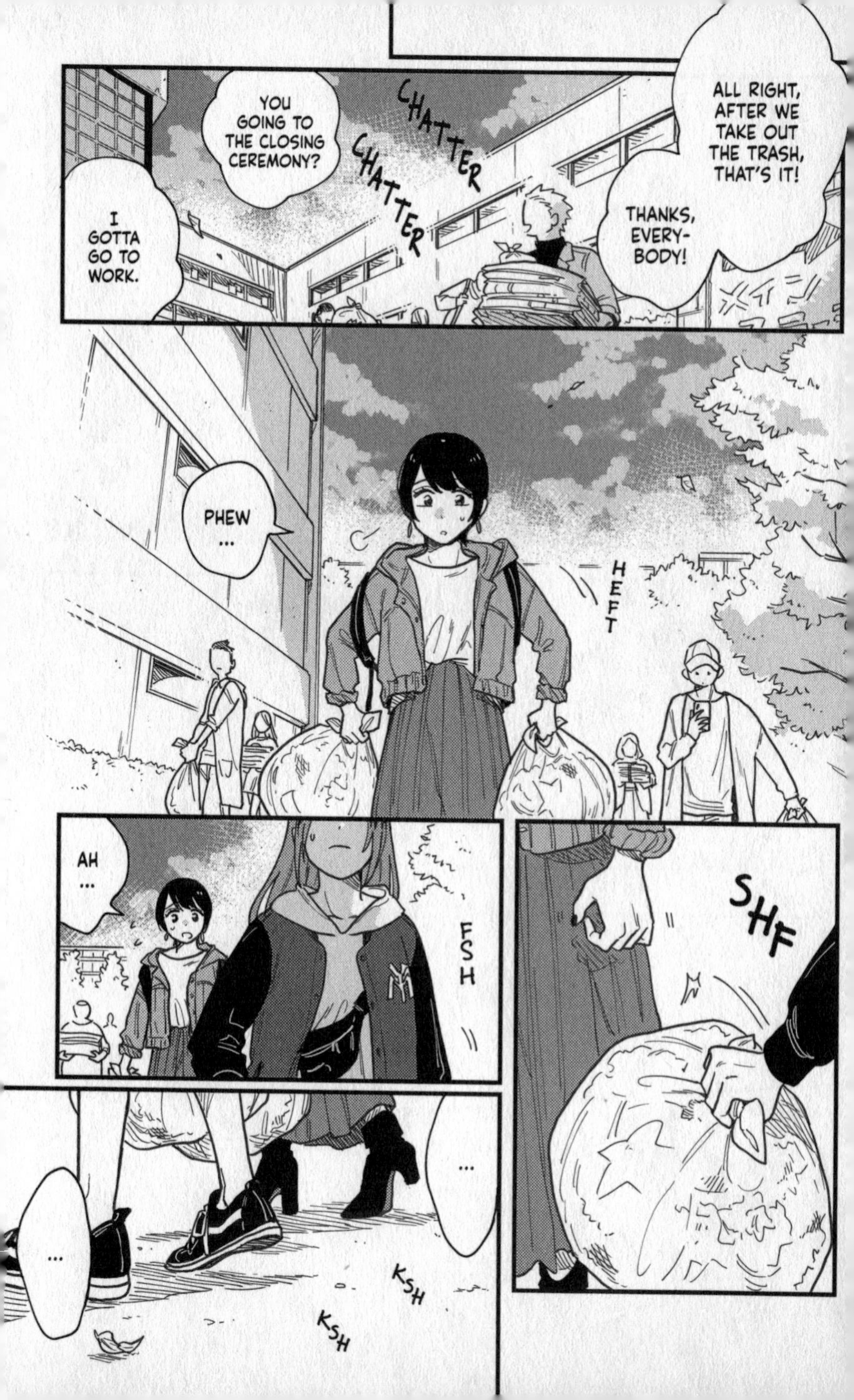
ALL RIGHT, AFTER WE TAKE OUT THE TRASH, THAT'S IT!
THANKS, EVERYBODY!
CHATTER
CHATTER
YOU GOING TO THE CLOSING CEREMONY?
I GOTTA GO TO WORK.
HEFT
PHEW ...
SHF
FSH
AH ...
...
KSH
KSH
...

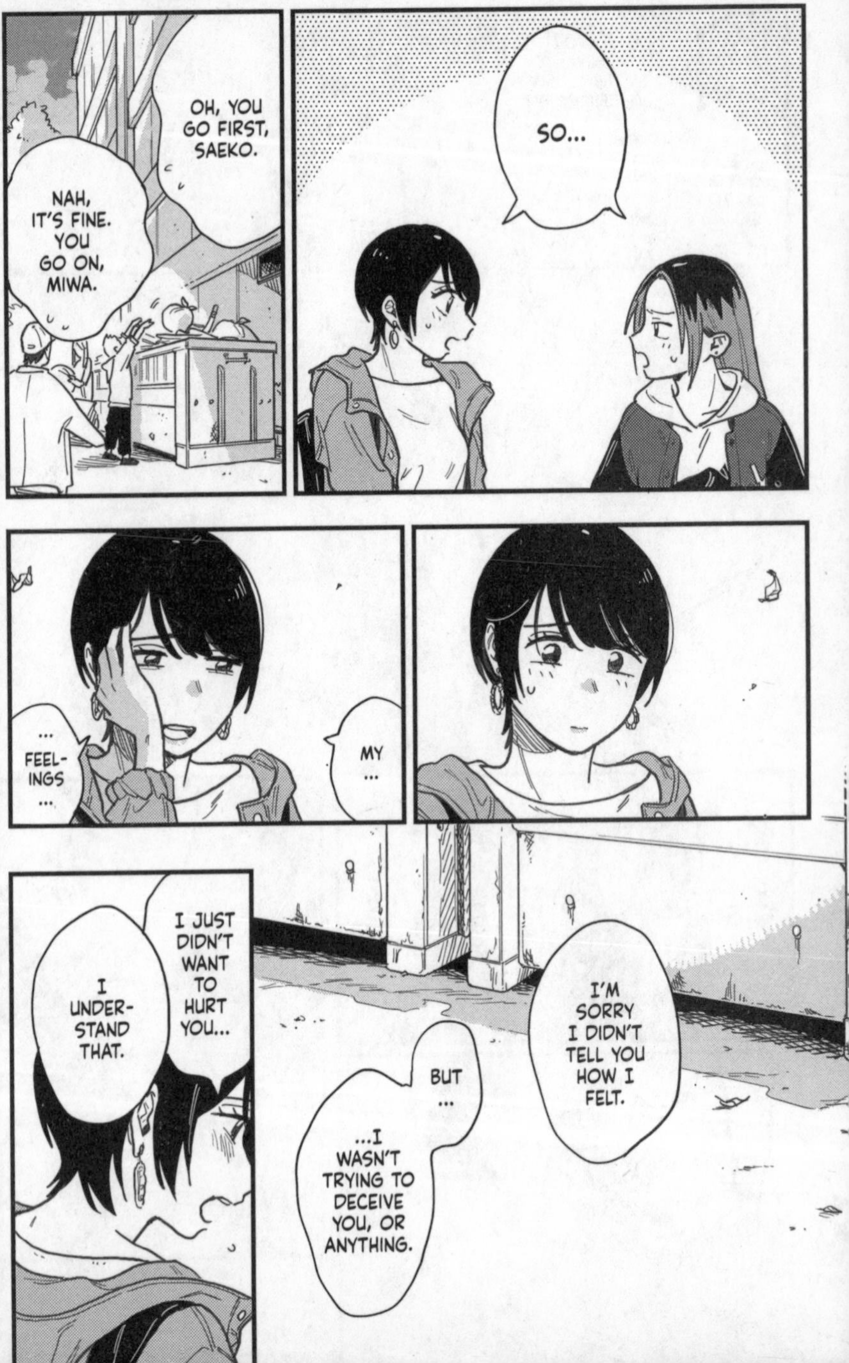
SO...
OH, YOU GO FIRST, SAEKO.
NAH, IT'S FINE. YOU GO ON, MIWA.
MY ...
... FEEL-INGS ...
I'M SORRY I DIDN'T TELL YOU HOW I FELT.
BUT ...
...I WASN'T TRYING TO DECEIVE YOU, OR ANYTHING.
I JUST DIDN'T WANT TO HURT YOU...
I UNDER-STAND THAT.

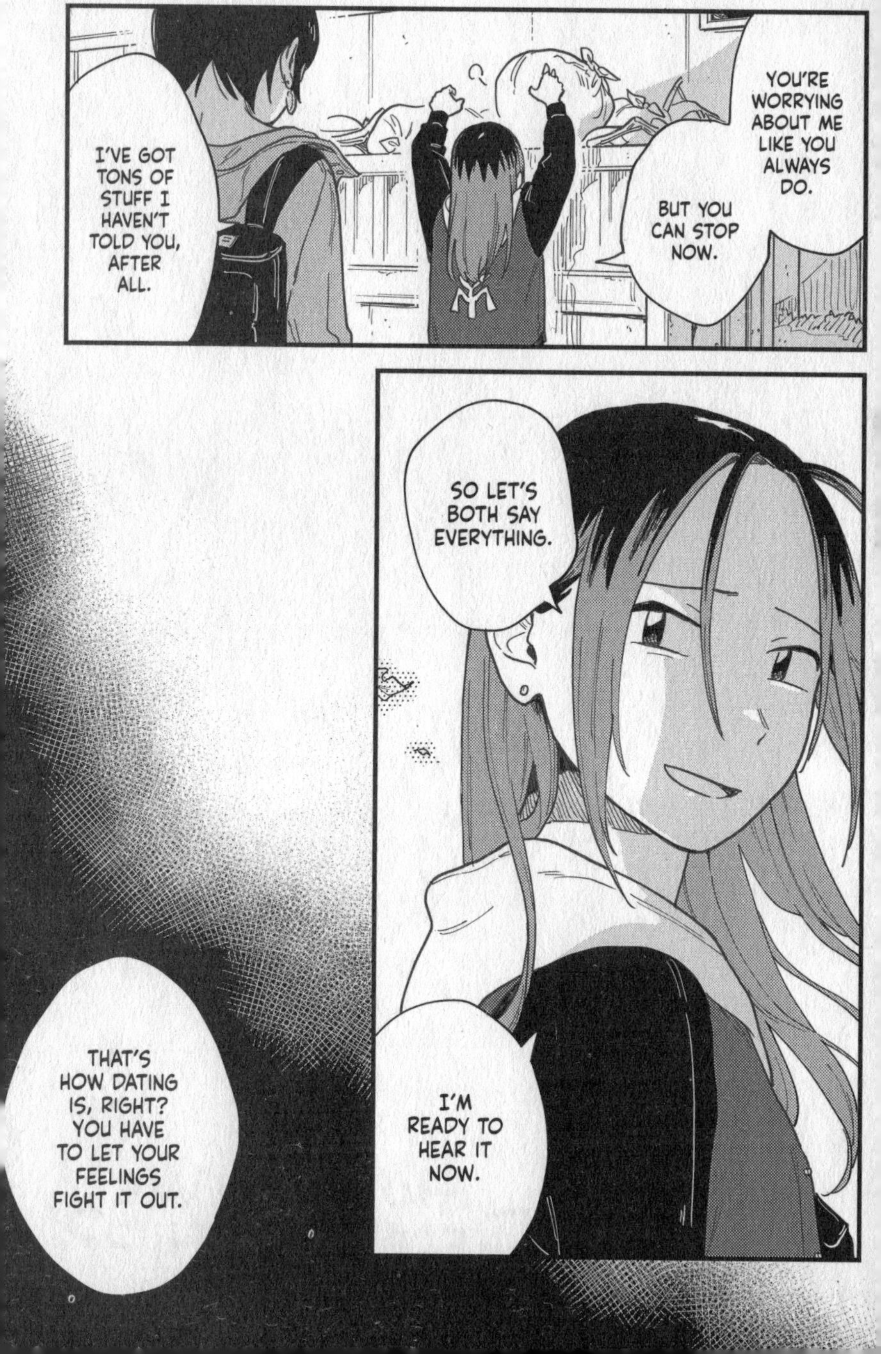
YOU'RE WORRYING ABOUT ME LIKE YOU ALWAYS DO.
BUT YOU CAN STOP NOW.
I'VE GOT TONS OF STUFF I HAVEN'T TOLD YOU, AFTER ALL.
SO LET'S BOTH SAY EVERYTHING.
I'M READY TO HEAR IT NOW.
THAT'S HOW DATING IS, RIGHT? YOU HAVE TO LET YOUR FEELINGS FIGHT IT OUT.

How Do We
Relationship?

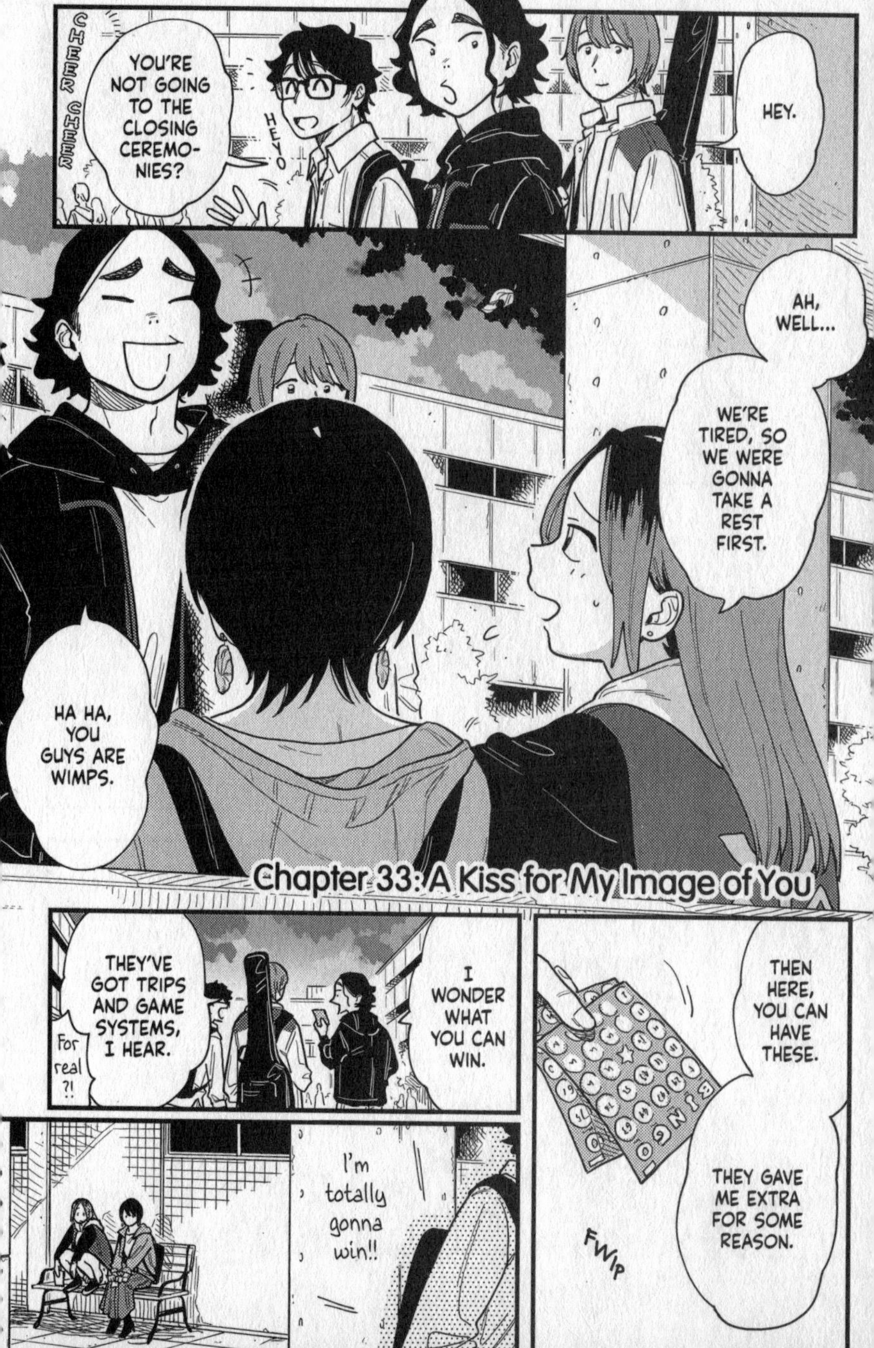
HEY.
YOU'RE NOT GOING TO THE CLOSING CEREMO-NIES?
HEYO
CHEER CHEER
AH, WELL...
WE'RE TIRED, SO WE WERE GONNA TAKE A REST FIRST.
HA HA, YOU GUYS ARE WIMPS.
Chapter 33: A Kiss for My Image of You
THEN HERE, YOU CAN HAVE THESE.
THEY GAVE ME EXTRA FOR SOME REASON.
FWIP
BINGO
I WONDER WHAT YOU CAN WIN.
THEY'VE GOT TRIPS AND GAME SYSTEMS, I HEAR.
For real?!
I'm totally gonna win!!

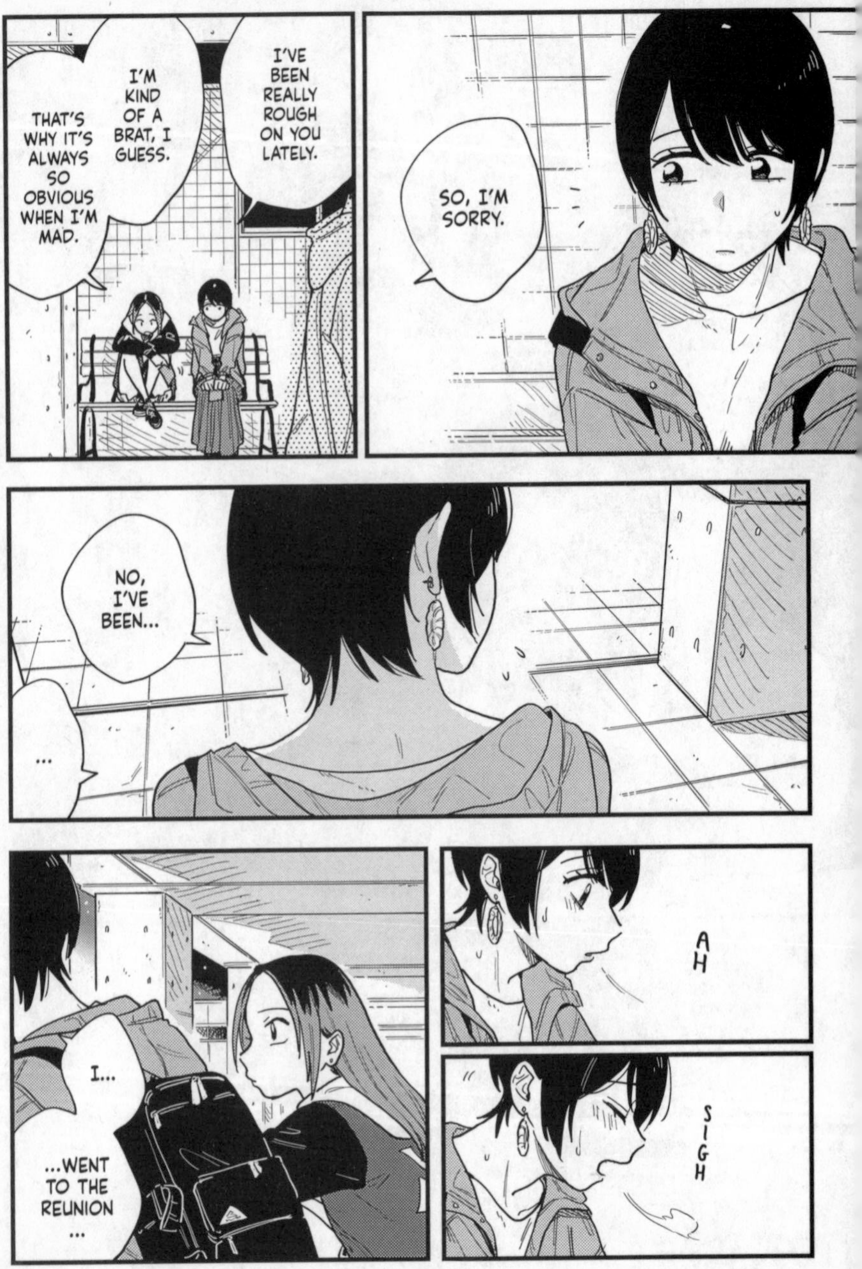
SO, I'M SORRY.
I'VE BEEN REALLY ROUGH ON YOU LATELY.
I'M KIND OF A BRAT, I GUESS.
THAT'S WHY IT'S ALWAYS SO OBVIOUS WHEN I'M MAD.
NO, I'VE BEEN...
...
AH
SIGH
I...
...WENT TO THE REUNION ...

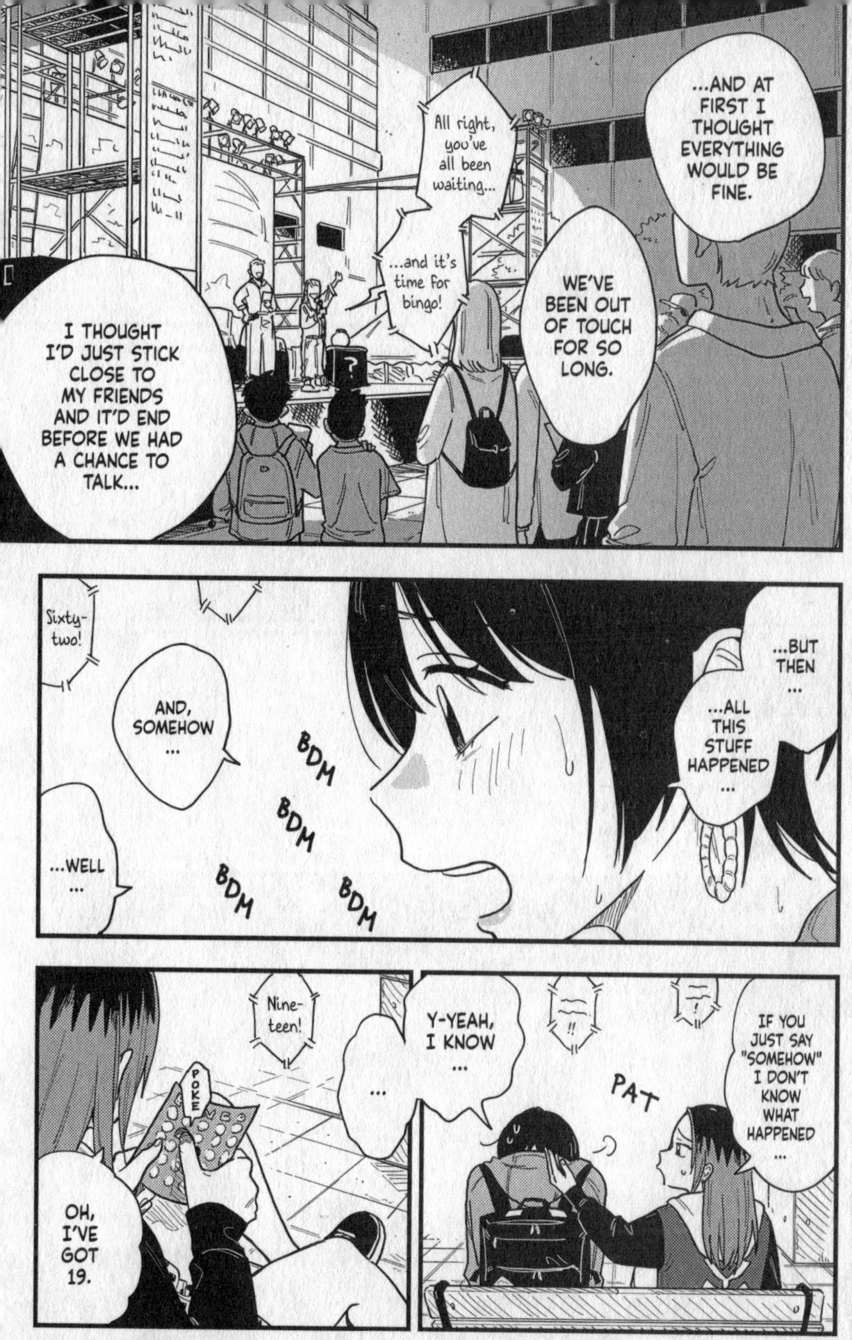
...AND AT FIRST I THOUGHT EVERYTHING WOULD BE FINE.
All right, you've all been waiting...
WE'VE BEEN OUT OF TOUCH FOR SO LONG.
...and it's time for bingo!
I THOUGHT I'D JUST STICK CLOSE TO MY FRIENDS AND IT'D END BEFORE WE HAD A CHANCE TO TALK...
...BUT THEN ...
...ALL THIS STUFF HAPPENED ...
Sixty-two!
AND, SOMEHOW ...
BDM
BDM
BDM
BDM
...WELL ...
!
!!
IF YOU JUST SAY "SOMEHOW" I DON'T KNOW WHAT HAPPENED ...
PAT
Y-YEAH, I KNOW ...
...
Nine-teen!
POKE
OH, I'VE GOT 19.

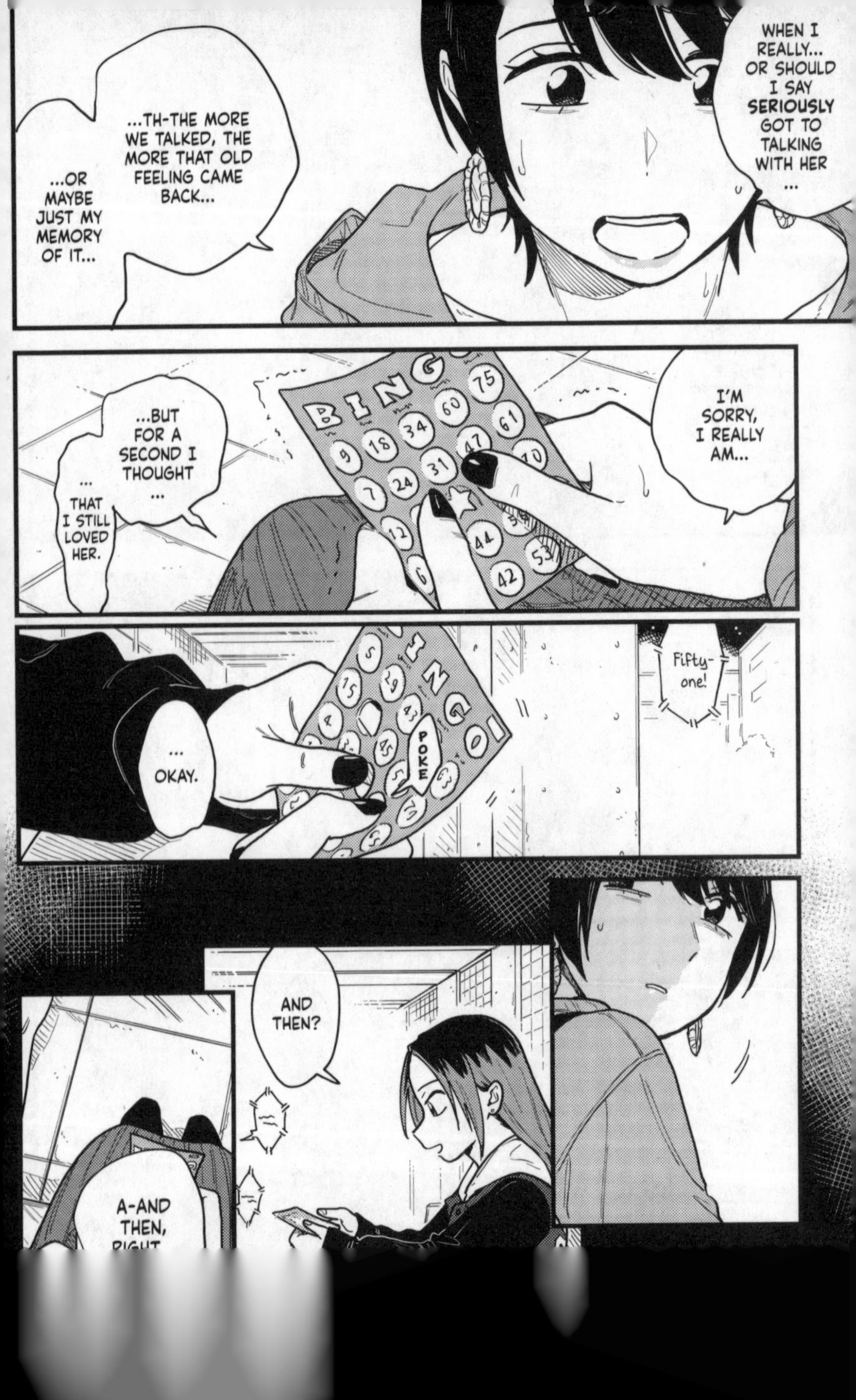
WHEN I REALLY... OR SHOULD I SAY SERIOUSLY GOT TO TALKING WITH HER ...
...TH-THE MORE WE TALKED, THE MORE THAT OLD FEELING CAME BACK...
...OR MAYBE JUST MY MEMORY OF IT...
I'M SORRY, I REALLY AM...
BINGO
...BUT FOR A SECOND I THOUGHT ...
... THAT I STILL LOVED HER.
Fifty-one!
POKE
... OKAY.
AND THEN?
A-AND THEN,

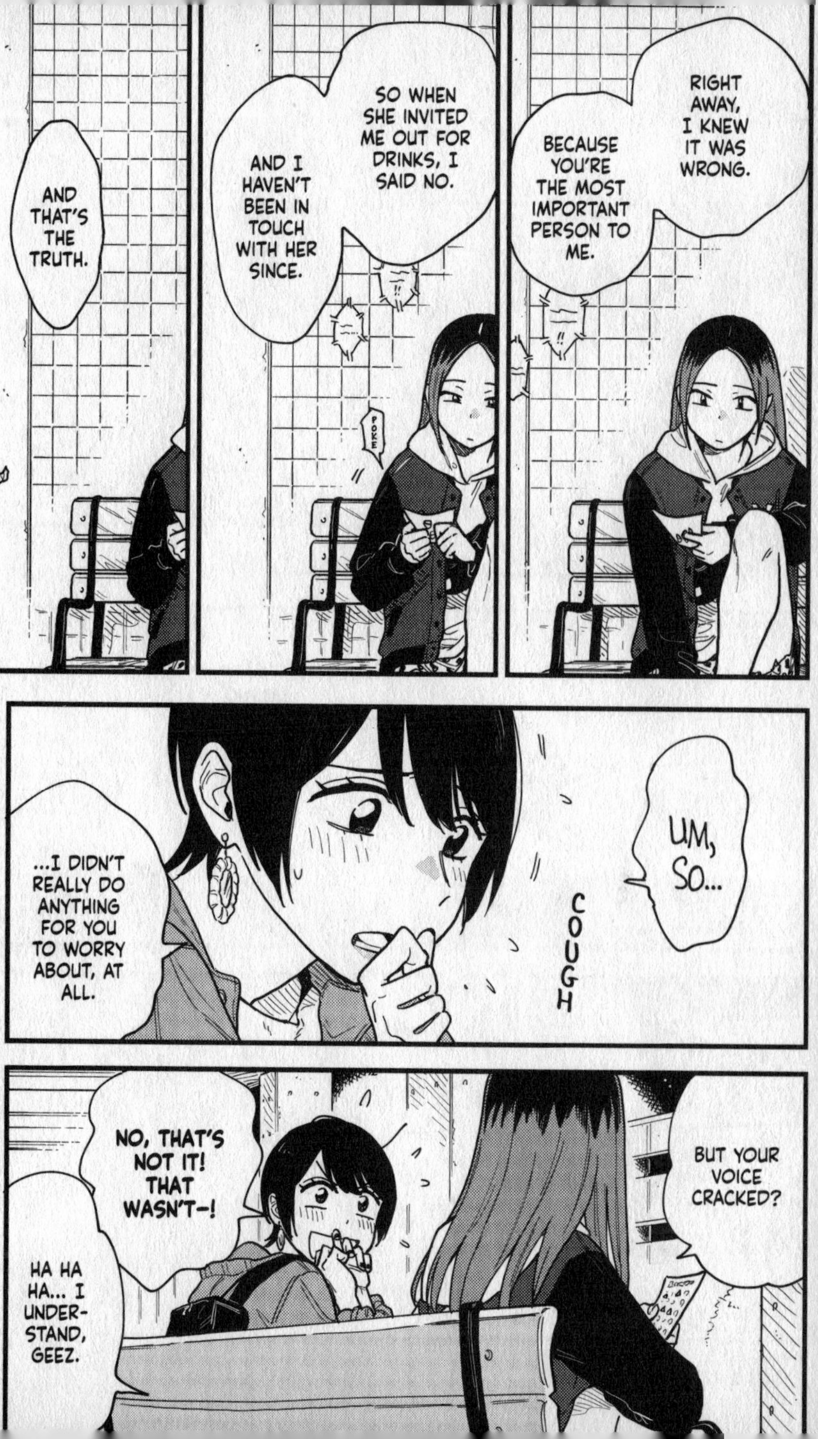
RIGHT AWAY, I KNEW IT WAS WRONG.
BECAUSE YOU'RE THE MOST IMPORTANT PERSON TO ME.
SO WHEN SHE INVITED ME OUT FOR DRINKS, I SAID NO.
AND I HAVEN'T BEEN IN TOUCH WITH HER SINCE.
POKE
AND THAT'S THE TRUTH.
UM, SO...
COUGH
...I DIDN'T REALLY DO ANYTHING FOR YOU TO WORRY ABOUT, AT ALL.
BUT YOUR VOICE CRACKED?
NO, THAT'S NOT IT! THAT WASN'T—!
HA HA HA... I UNDER-STAND, GEEZ.

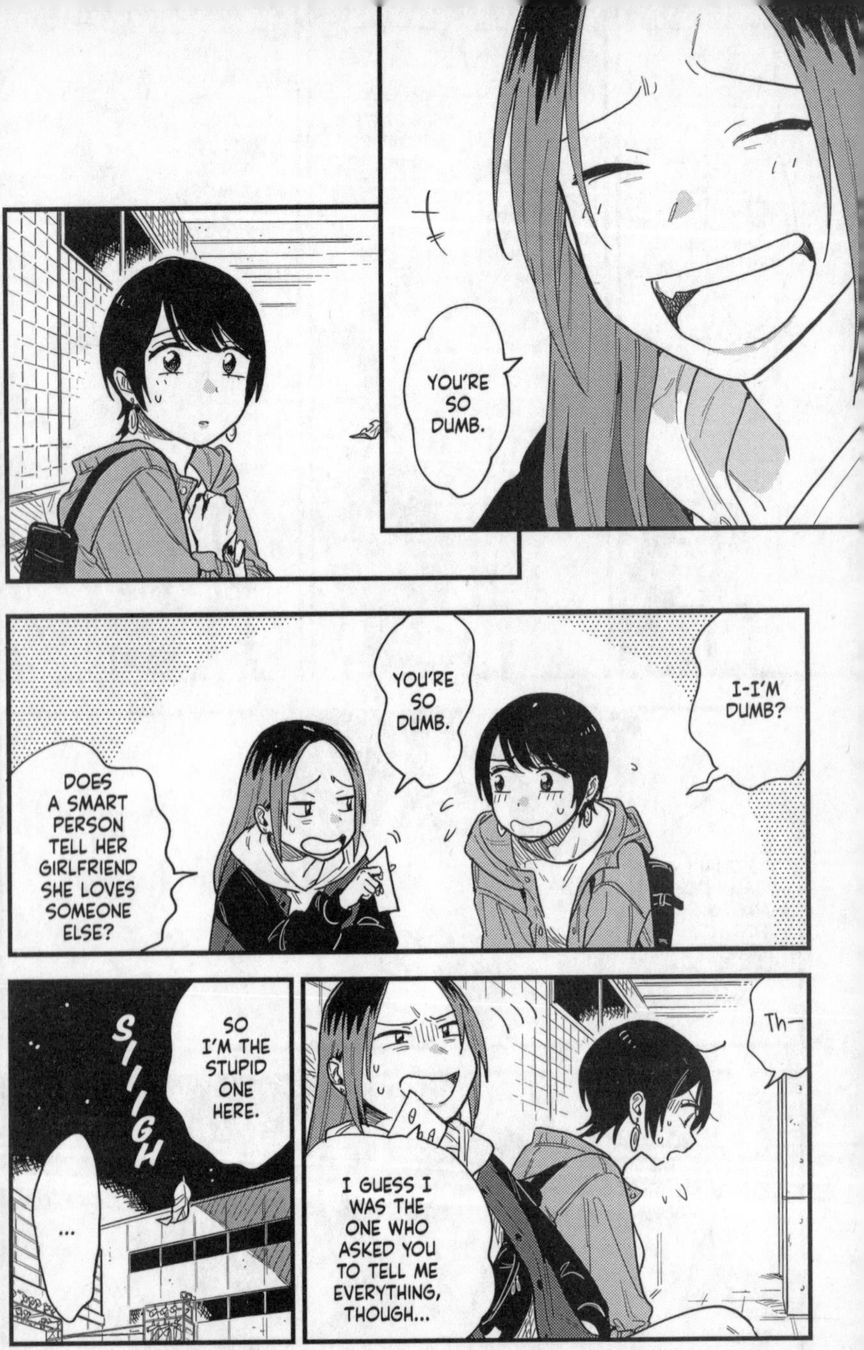
YOU'RE SO DUMB.
I-I'M DUMB?
YOU'RE SO DUMB.
DOES A SMART PERSON TELL HER GIRLFRIEND SHE LOVES SOMEONE ELSE?
Th—
I GUESS I WAS THE ONE WHO ASKED YOU TO TELL ME EVERYTHING, THOUGH...
SO I'M THE STUPID ONE HERE.
SIIIGH
...

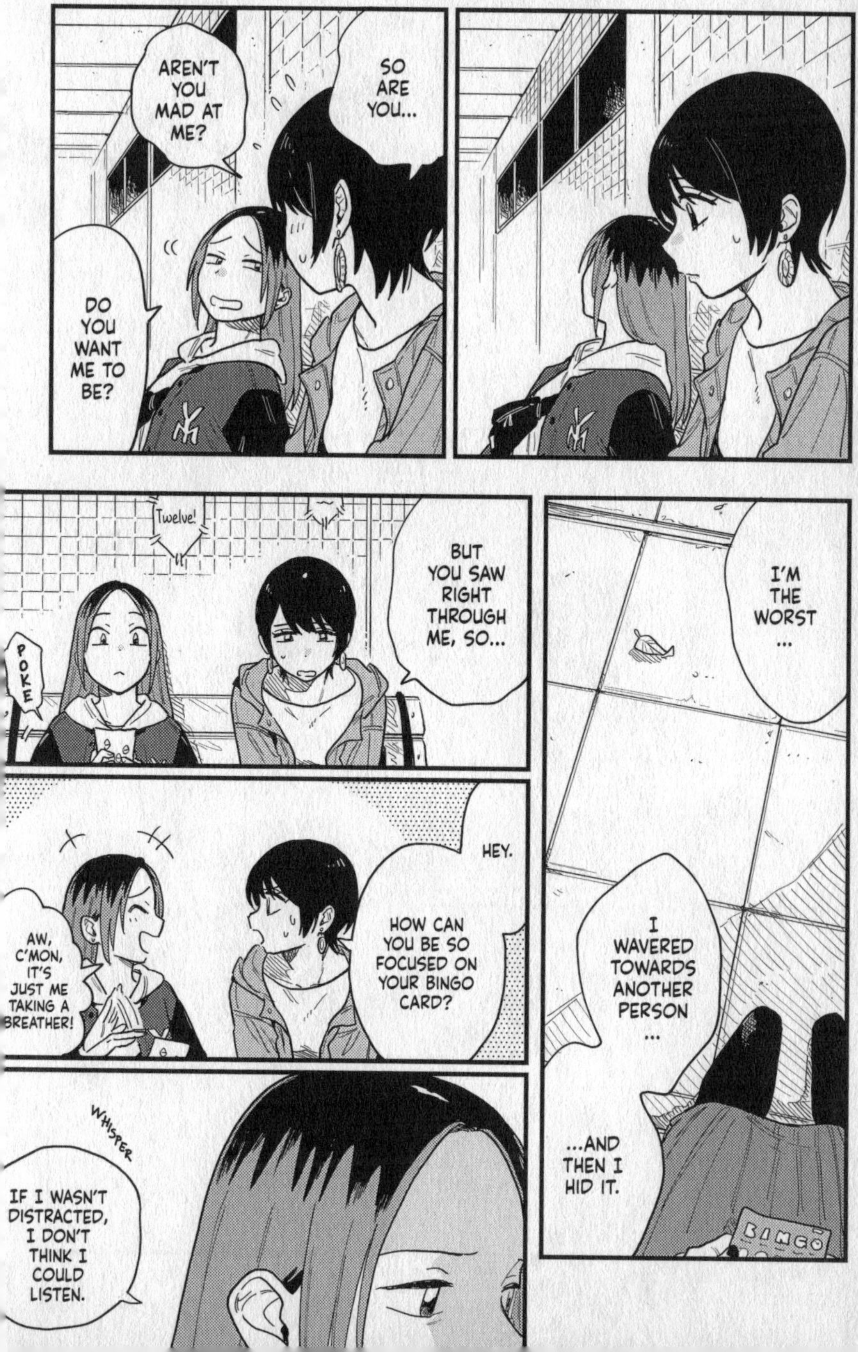
SO ARE YOU...
AREN'T YOU MAD AT ME?
DO YOU WANT ME TO BE?
I'M THE WORST...
I WAVERED TOWARDS ANOTHER PERSON...
...AND THEN I HID IT.
BINGO
Twelve!
BUT YOU SAW RIGHT THROUGH ME, SO...
POKE
HEY.
HOW CAN YOU BE SO FOCUSED ON YOUR BINGO CARD?
AW, C'MON, IT'S JUST ME TAKING A BREATHER!
WHISPER
IF I WASN'T DISTRACTED, I DON'T THINK I COULD LISTEN.

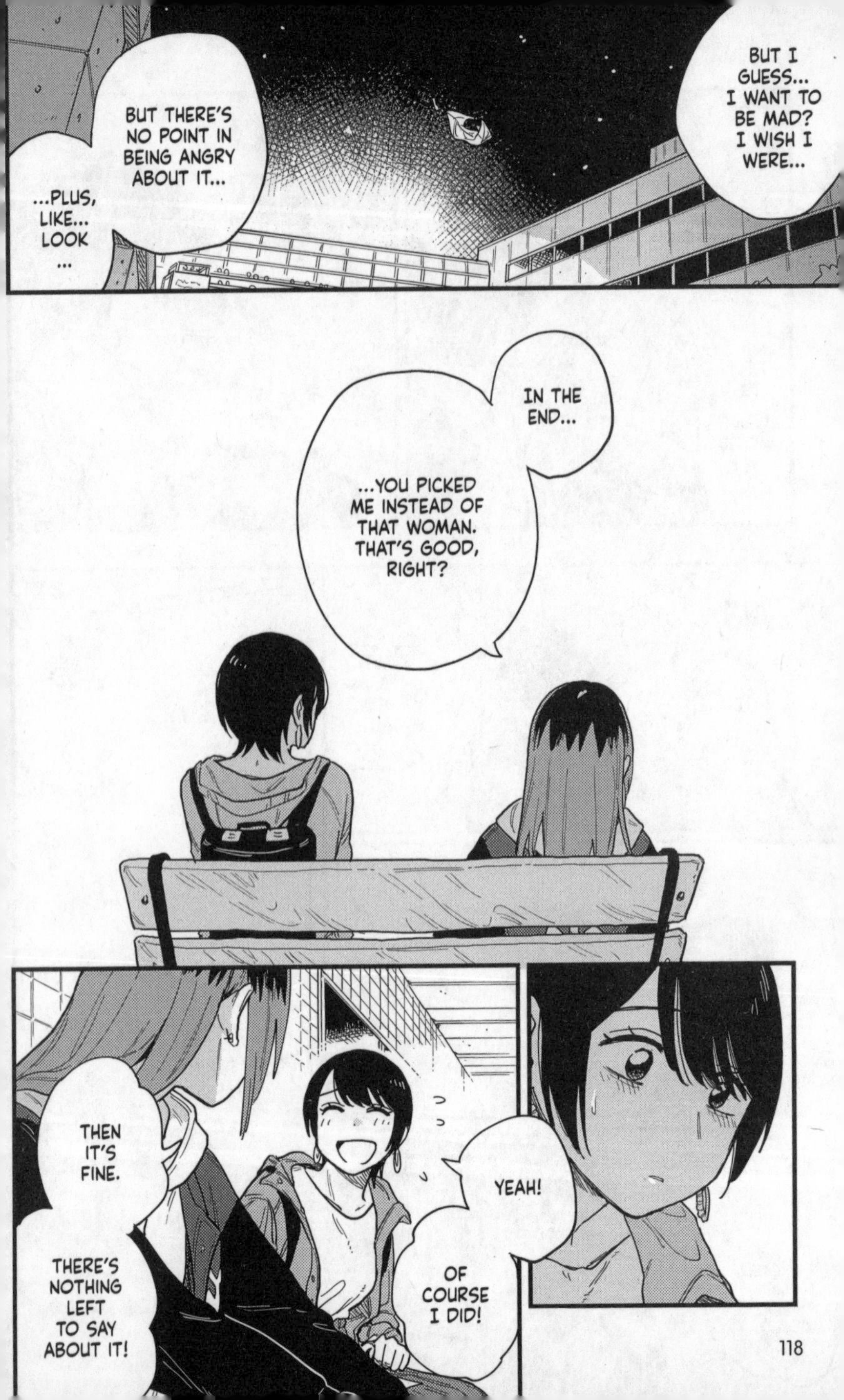
BUT I GUESS... I WANT TO BE MAD? I WISH I WERE...
BUT THERE'S NO POINT IN BEING ANGRY ABOUT IT...
...PLUS, LIKE... LOOK ...
IN THE END...
...YOU PICKED ME INSTEAD OF THAT WOMAN. THAT'S GOOD, RIGHT?
YEAH!
OF COURSE I DID!
THEN IT'S FINE.
THERE'S NOTHING LEFT TO SAY ABOUT IT!

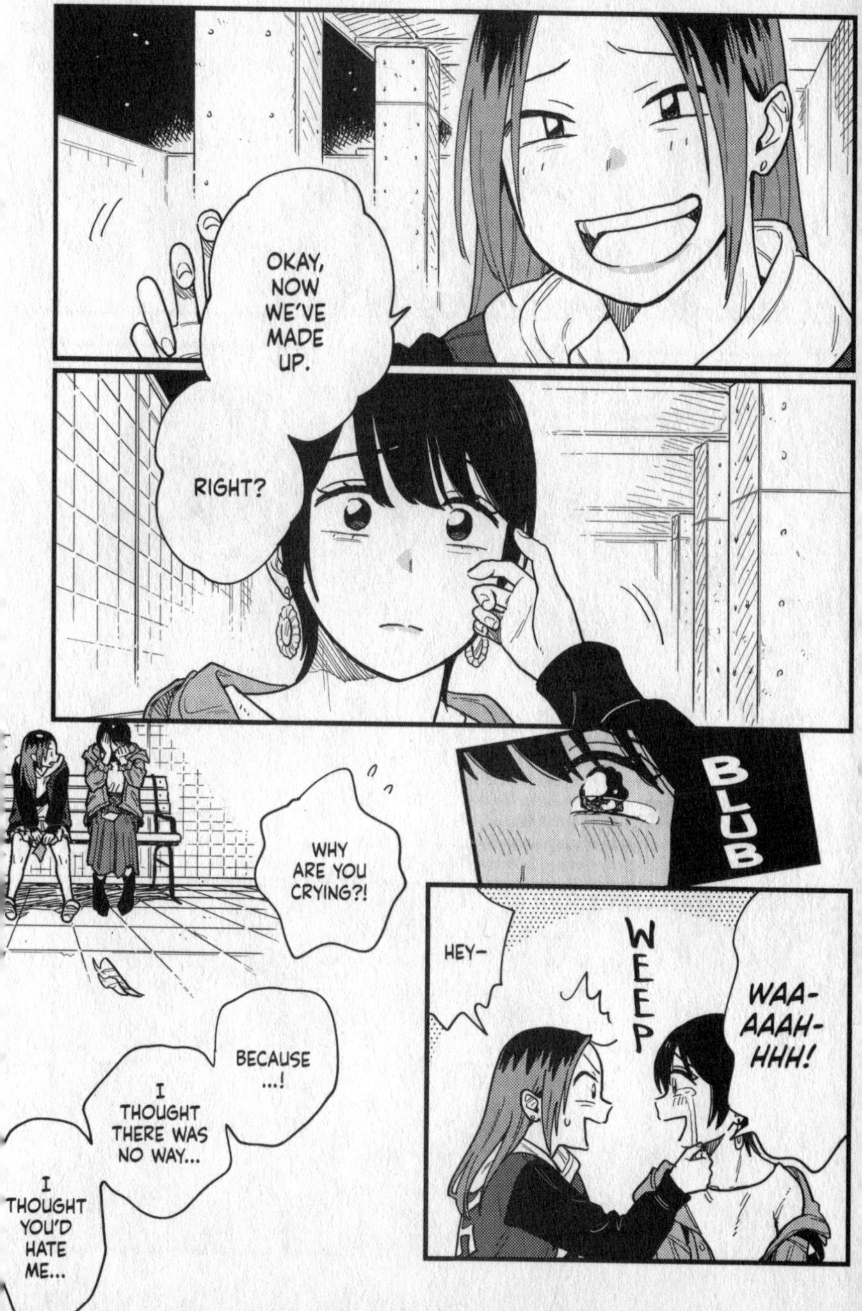
OKAY, NOW WE'VE MADE UP.
RIGHT?
BLUB
WAA-AAAH-HHH!
WEEP
HEY-
WHY ARE YOU CRYING?!
BECAUSE ...!
I THOUGHT THERE WAS NO WAY...
I THOUGHT YOU'D HATE ME...

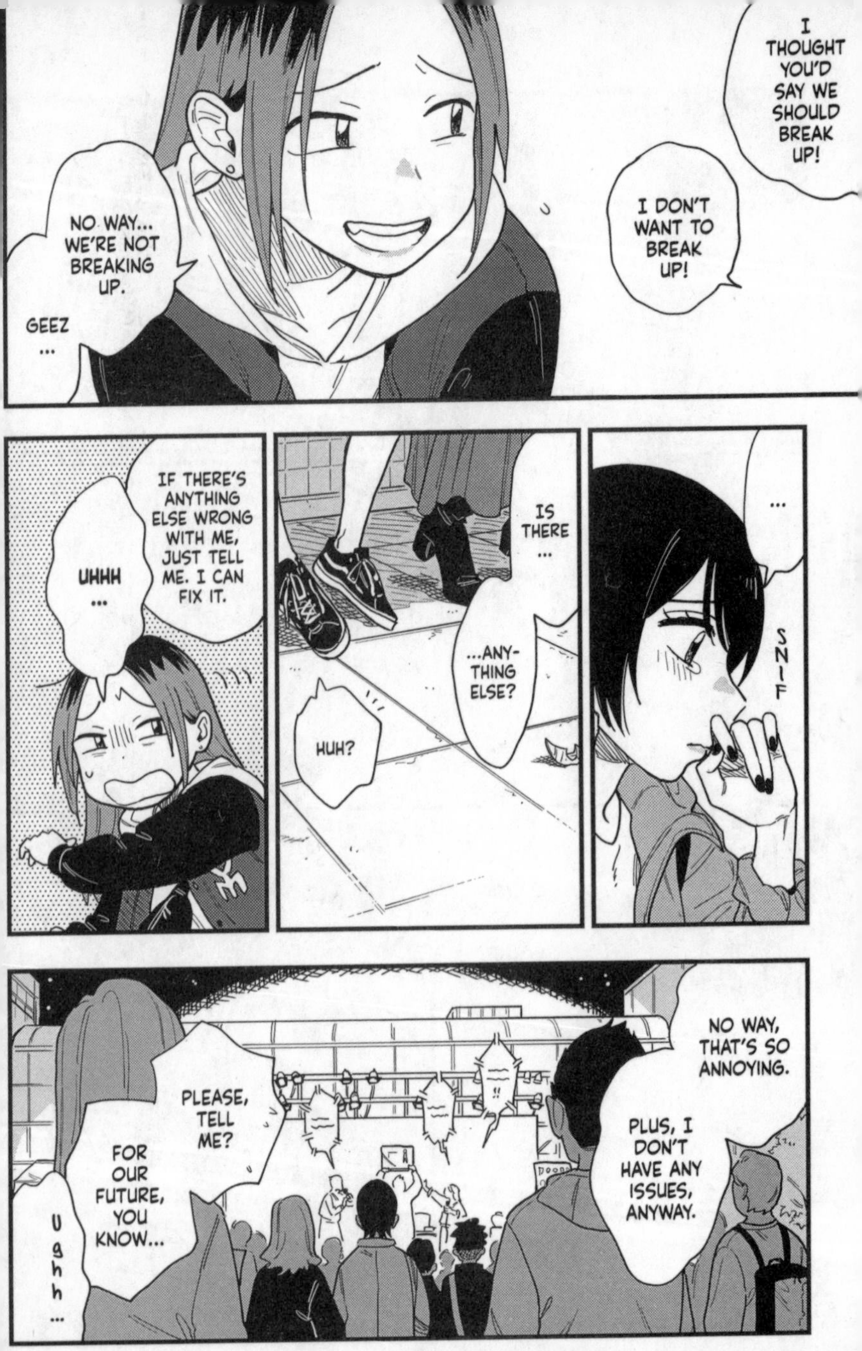
I THOUGHT YOU'D SAY WE SHOULD BREAK UP!
I DON'T WANT TO BREAK UP!
NO WAY... WE'RE NOT BREAKING UP.
GEEZ ...
...
SNIF
IS THERE ...
...ANYTHING ELSE?
HUH?
IF THERE'S ANYTHING ELSE WRONG WITH ME, JUST TELL ME. I CAN FIX IT.
UHHH ...
NO WAY, THAT'S SO ANNOYING.
PLUS, I DON'T HAVE ANY ISSUES, ANYWAY.
PLEASE, TELL ME?
FOR OUR FUTURE, YOU KNOW...
Ughh ...

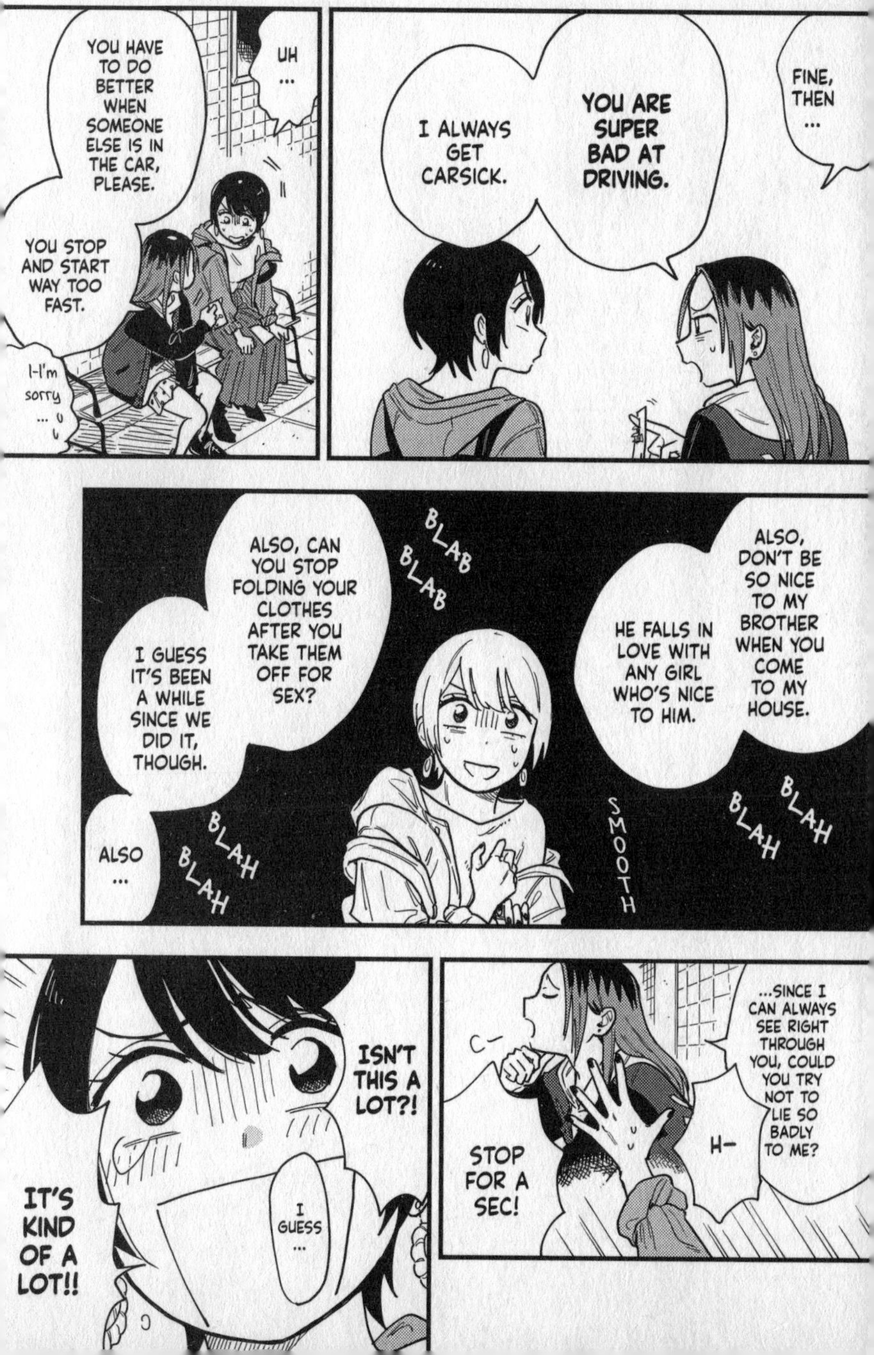
FINE, THEN ...
YOU ARE SUPER BAD AT DRIVING.
I ALWAYS GET CARSICK.
UH ...
YOU HAVE TO DO BETTER WHEN SOMEONE ELSE IS IN THE CAR, PLEASE.
YOU STOP AND START WAY TOO FAST.
I-I'm sorry ...
ALSO, DON'T BE SO NICE TO MY BROTHER WHEN YOU COME TO MY HOUSE.
HE FALLS IN LOVE WITH ANY GIRL WHO'S NICE TO HIM.
BLAH BLAH
SMOOTH
BLAB BLAB
ALSO, CAN YOU STOP FOLDING YOUR CLOTHES AFTER YOU TAKE THEM OFF FOR SEX?
I GUESS IT'S BEEN A WHILE SINCE WE DID IT, THOUGH.
ALSO ...
BLAH BLAH
...SINCE I CAN ALWAYS SEE RIGHT THROUGH YOU, COULD YOU TRY NOT TO LIE SO BADLY TO ME?
H-
C-
STOP FOR A SEC!
ISN'T THIS A LOT?!
I GUESS ...
IT'S KIND OF A LOT!!

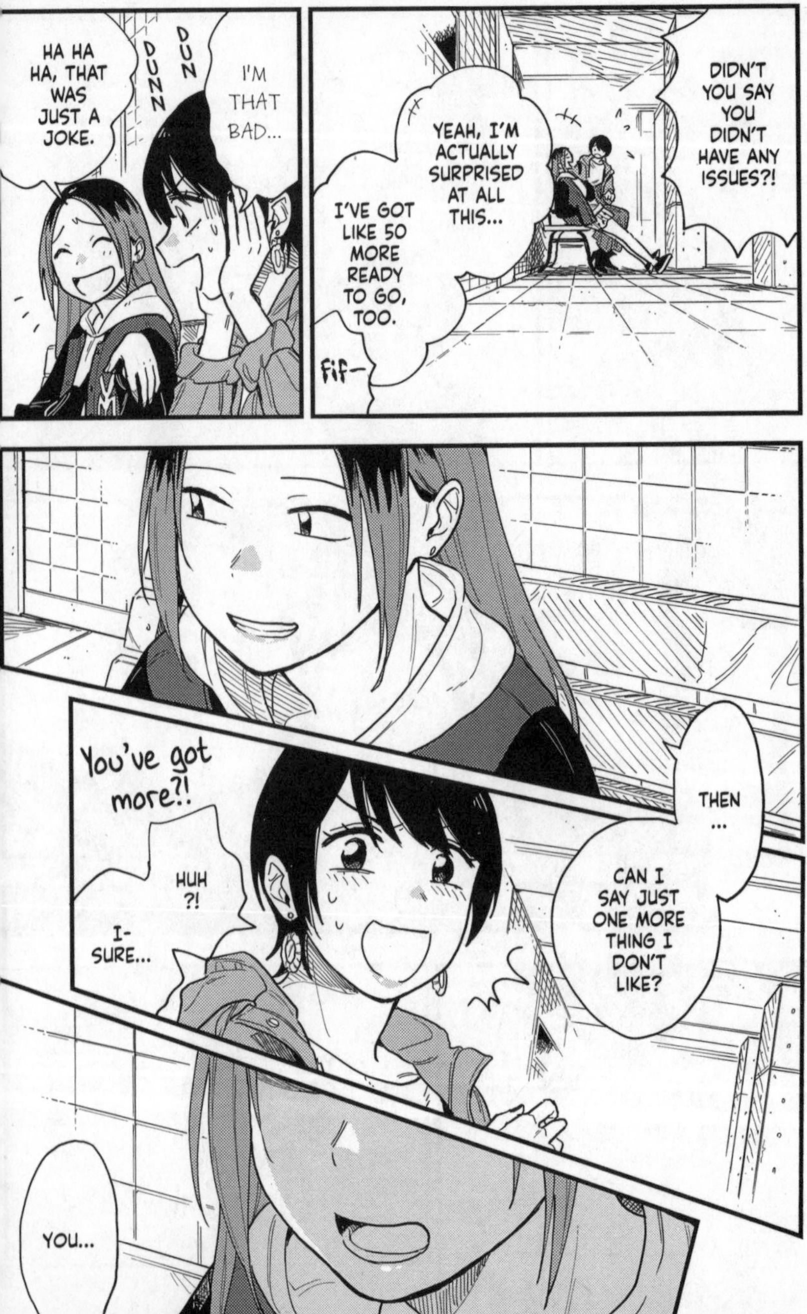
DIDN'T YOU SAY YOU DIDN'T HAVE ANY ISSUES?!
YEAH, I'M ACTUALLY SURPRISED AT ALL THIS...
I'VE GOT LIKE 50 MORE READY TO GO, TOO.
Fif—
I'M THAT BAD...
DUN
DUNN
HA HA HA, THAT WAS JUST A JOKE.
THEN ...
CAN I SAY JUST ONE MORE THING I DON'T LIKE?
You've got more?!
HUH ?!
I- SURE...
YOU...

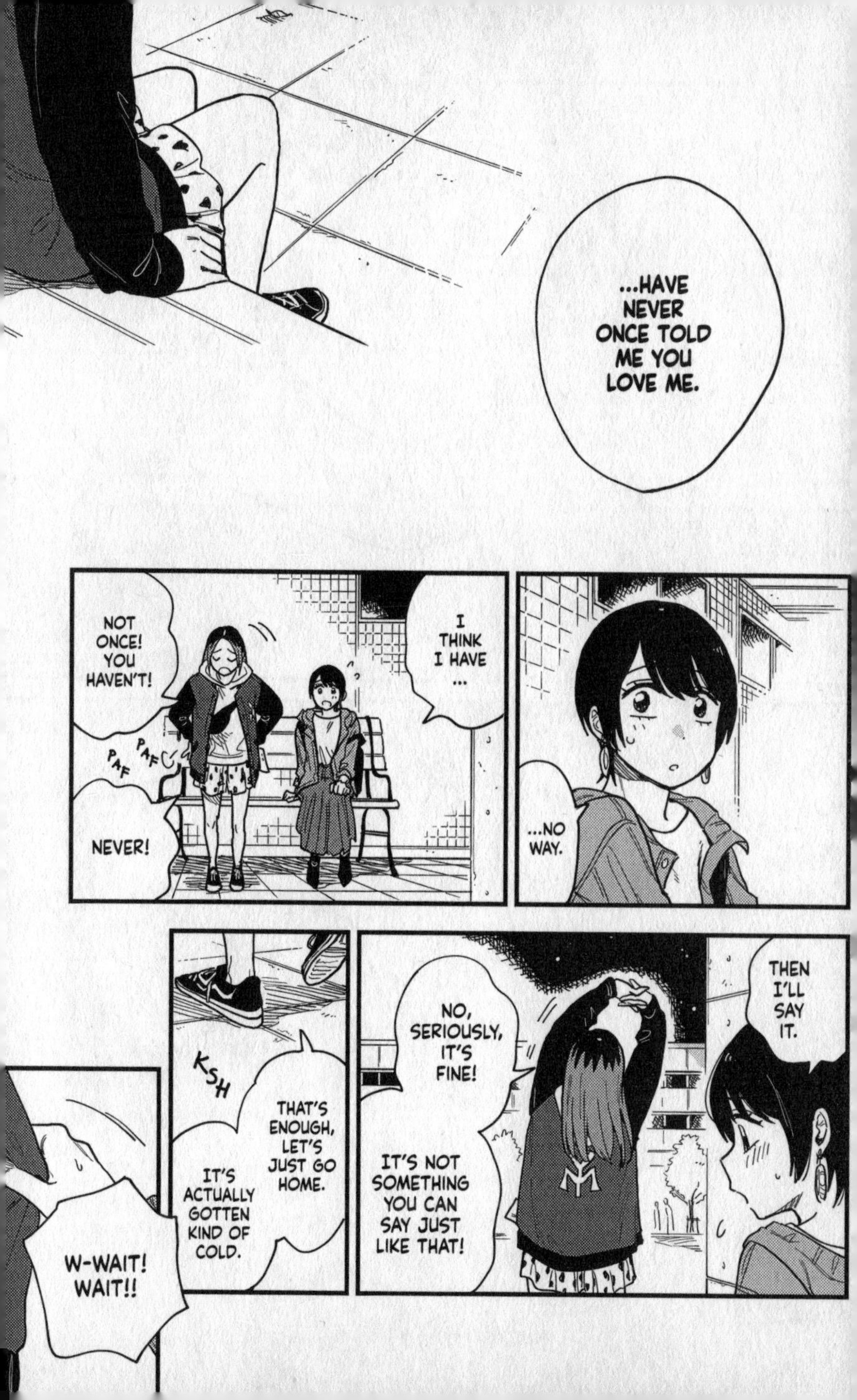
...HAVE NEVER ONCE TOLD ME YOU LOVE ME.
...NO WAY.
I THINK I HAVE ...
NOT ONCE! YOU HAVEN'T!
PAF PAF
NEVER!
THEN I'LL SAY IT.
NO, SERIOUSLY, IT'S FINE!
IT'S NOT SOMETHING YOU CAN SAY JUST LIKE THAT!
KSH
THAT'S ENOUGH, LET'S JUST GO HOME.
IT'S ACTUALLY GOTTEN KIND OF COLD.
W-WAIT! WAIT!!

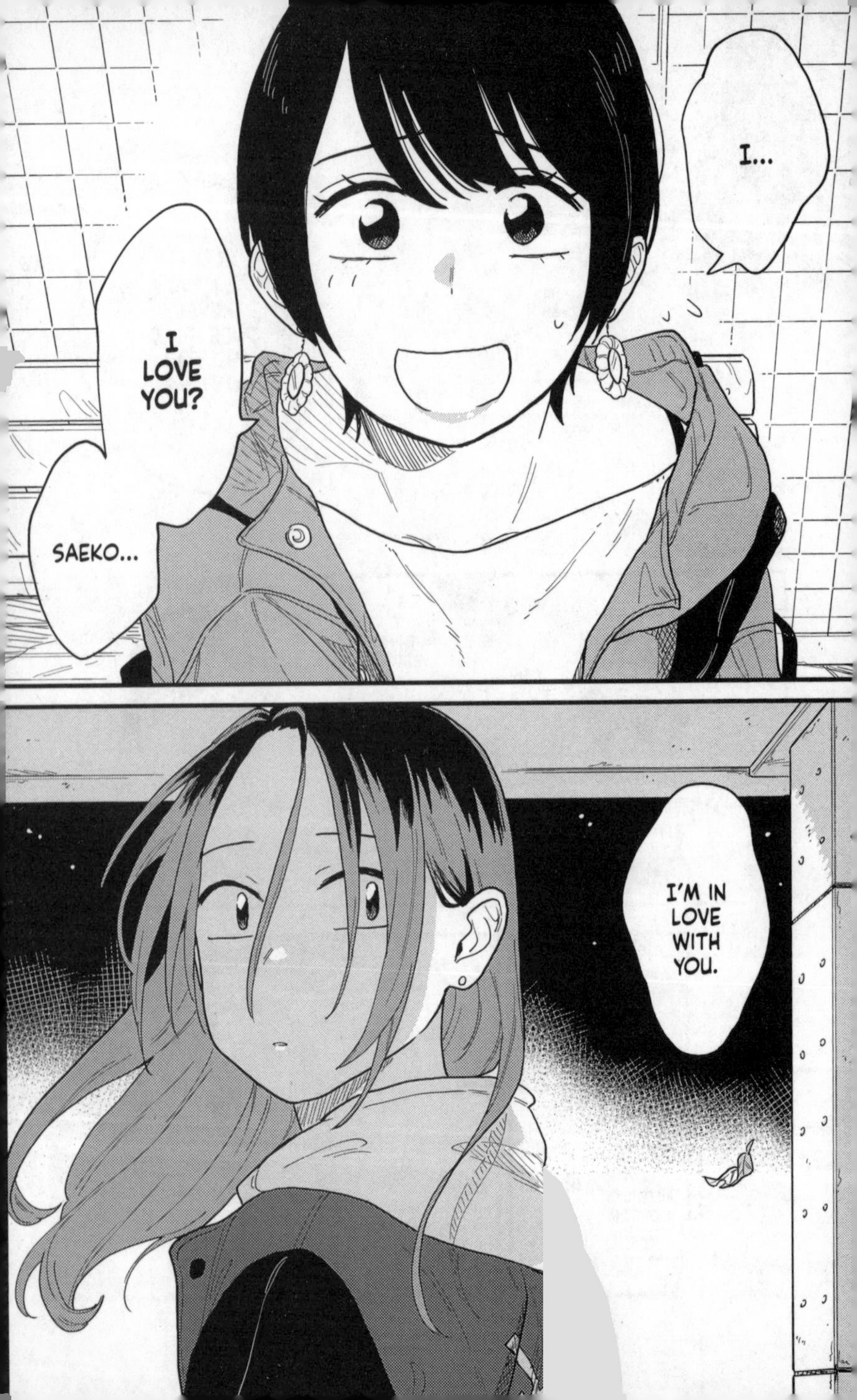
I...
I LOVE YOU?
SAEKO...
I'M IN LOVE WITH YOU.

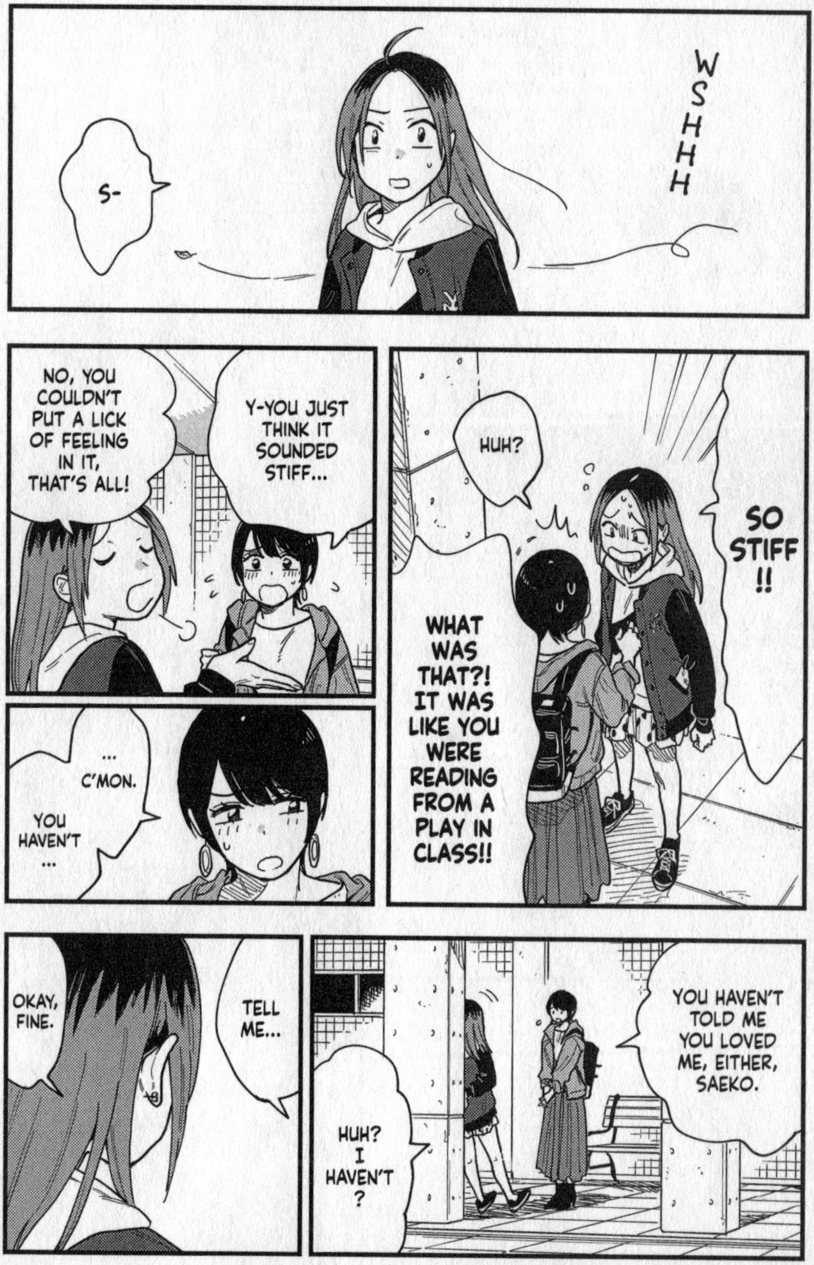
WSHHH
S-
SO STIFF!!
HUH?
WHAT WAS THAT?! IT WAS LIKE YOU WERE READING FROM A PLAY IN CLASS!!
Y-YOU JUST THINK IT SOUNDED STIFF...
NO, YOU COULDN'T PUT A LICK OF FEELING IN IT, THAT'S ALL!
... C'MON.
YOU HAVEN'T ...
YOU HAVEN'T TOLD ME YOU LOVED ME, EITHER, SAEKO.
HUH? I HAVEN'T ?
TELL ME...
OKAY, FINE.

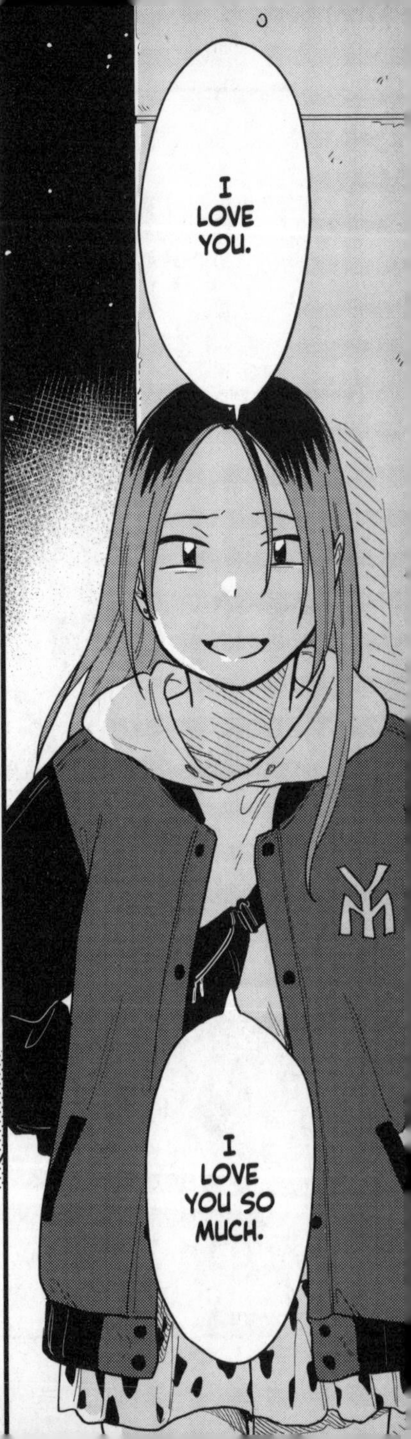
I LOVE YOU.
I LOVE YOU SO MUCH.

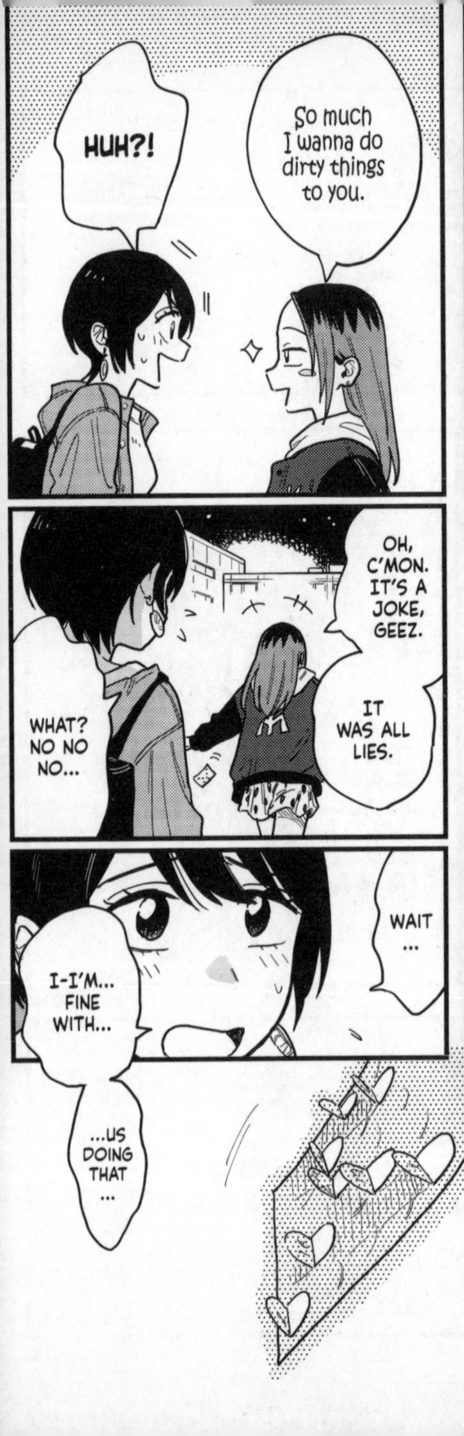
So much I wanna do dirty things to you.
HUH?!
OH, C'MON. IT'S A JOKE, GEEZ.
IT WAS ALL LIES.
WHAT? NO NO NO...
WAIT...
I-I'M... FINE WITH...
...US DOING THAT...

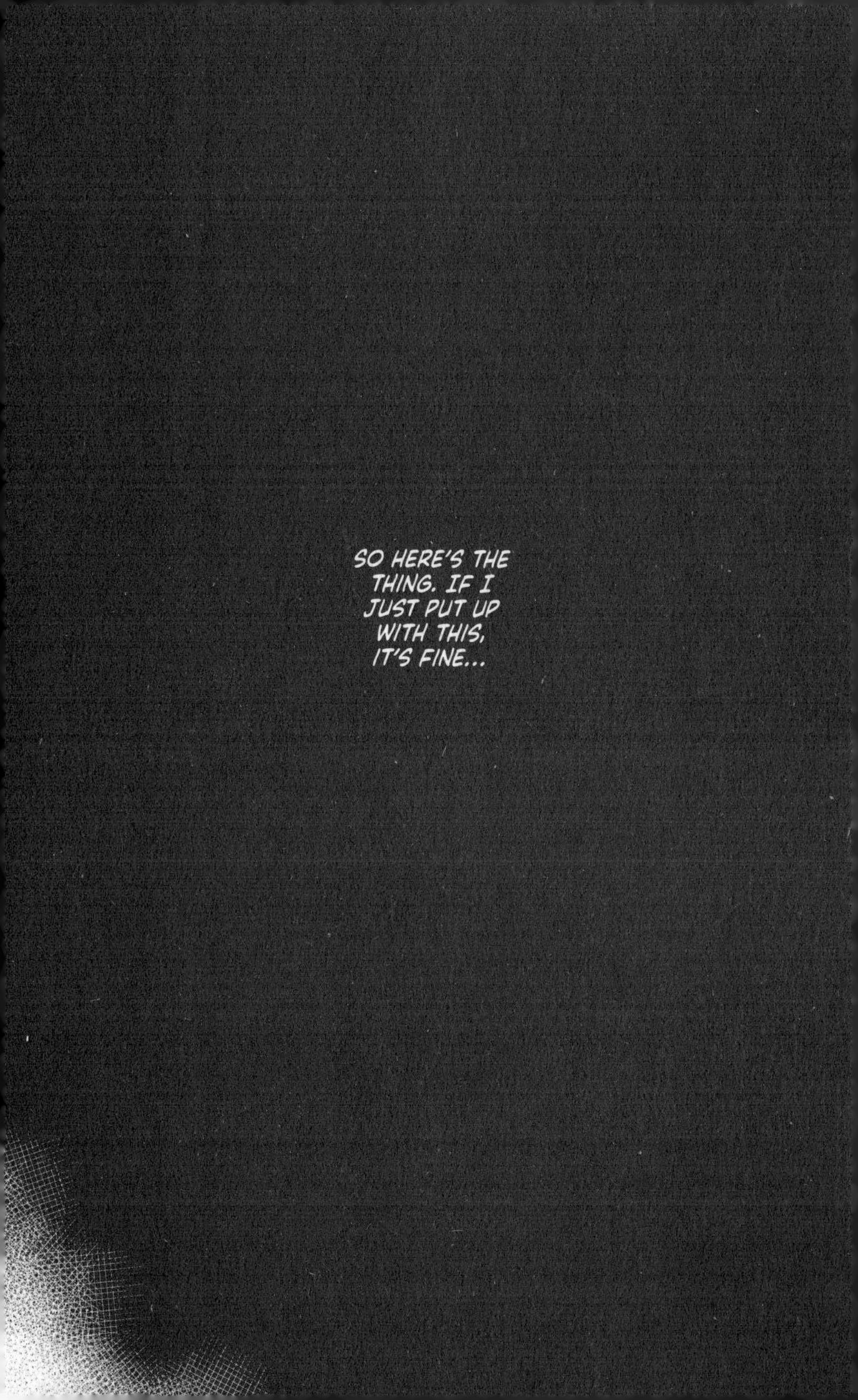
SO HERE'S THE THING. IF I JUST PUT UP WITH THIS, IT'S FINE...

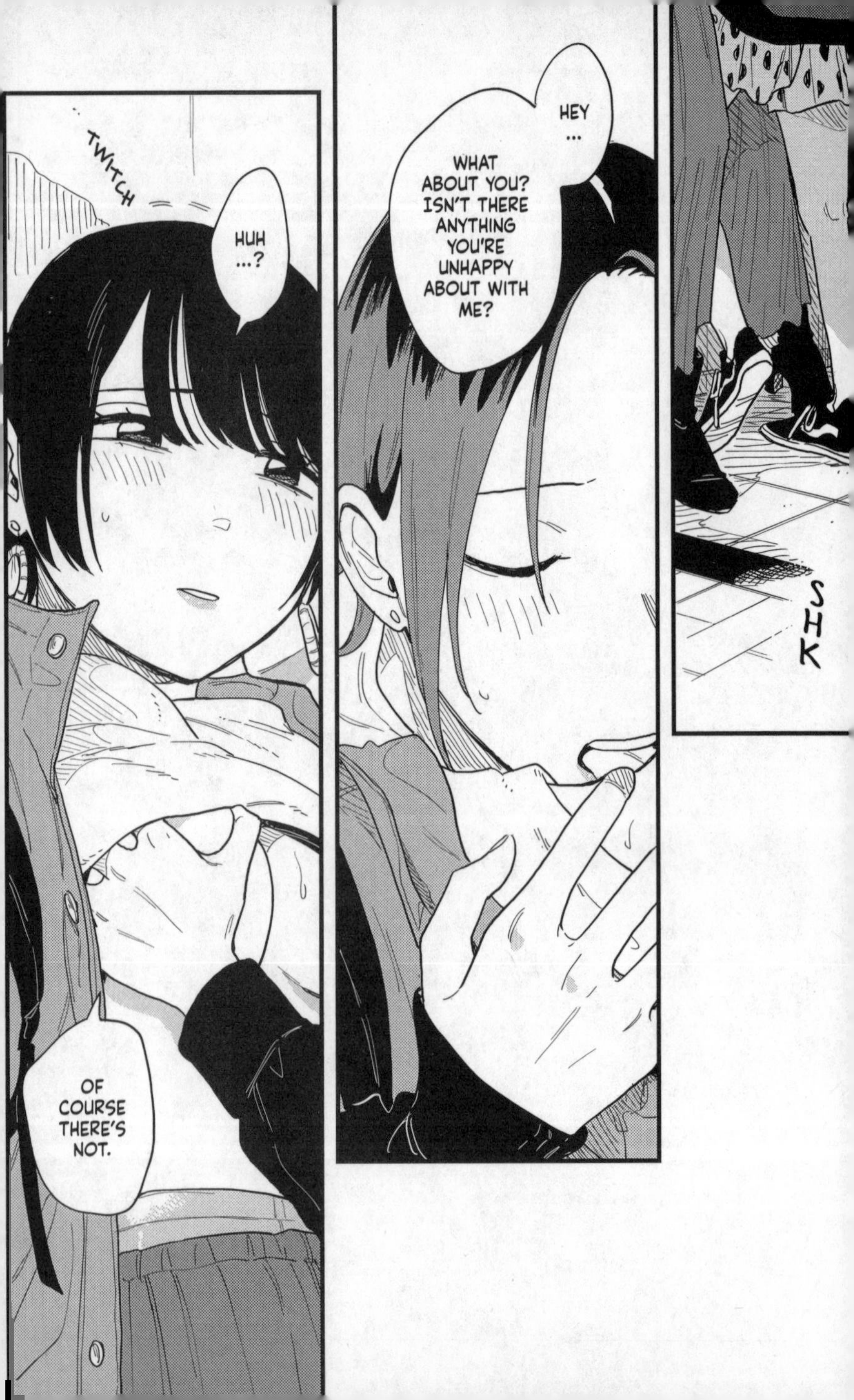
SHK
HEY ...
WHAT ABOUT YOU? ISN'T THERE ANYTHING YOU'RE UNHAPPY ABOUT WITH ME?
TWITCH
HUH ...?
OF COURSE THERE'S NOT.

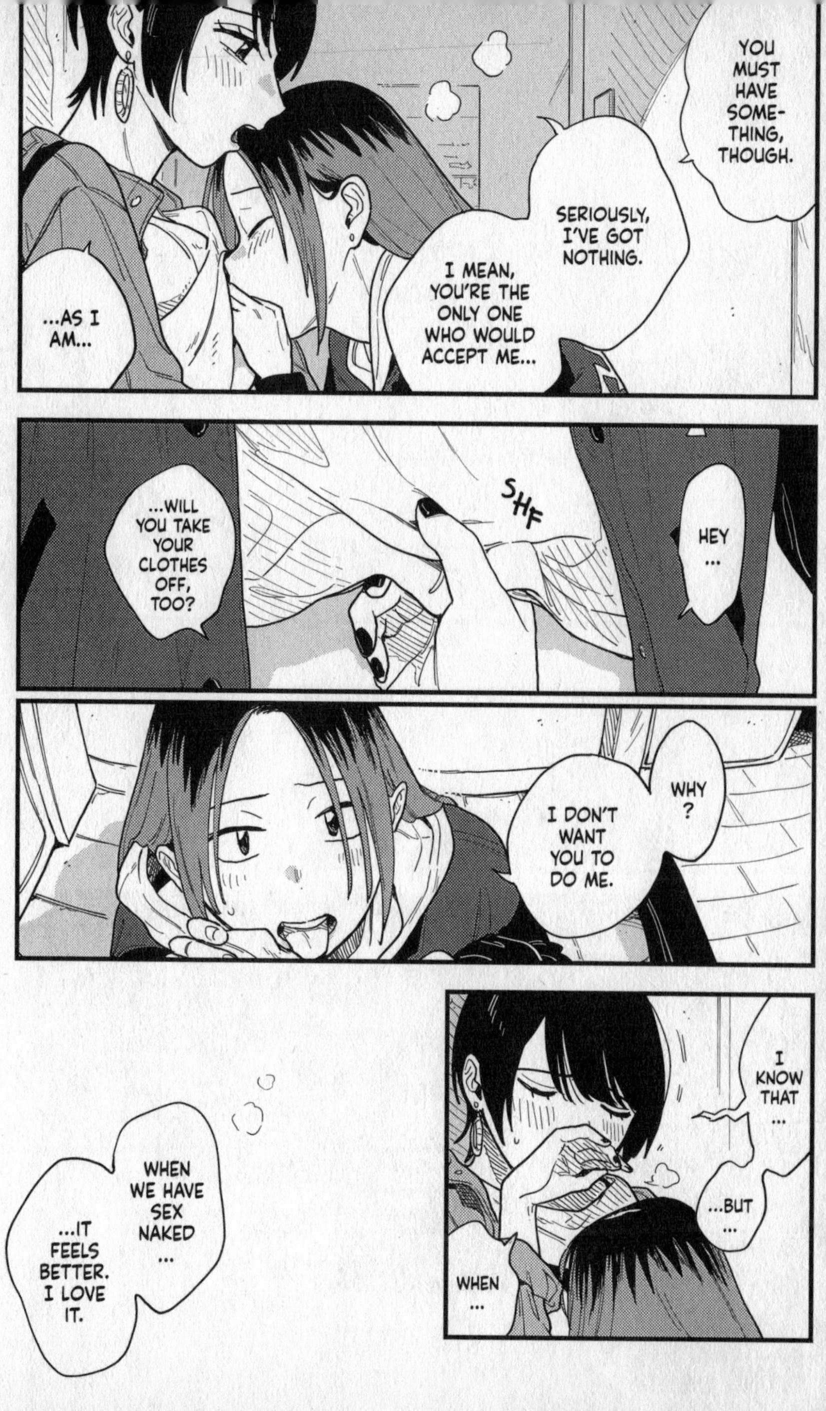
YOU MUST HAVE SOME-THING, THOUGH.
SERIOUSLY, I'VE GOT NOTHING.
I MEAN, YOU'RE THE ONLY ONE WHO WOULD ACCEPT ME...
...AS I AM...
HEY...
SHF
...WILL YOU TAKE YOUR CLOTHES OFF, TOO?
WHY?
I DON'T WANT YOU TO DO ME.
I KNOW THAT...
...BUT...
WHEN...
WHEN WE HAVE SEX NAKED...
...IT FEELS BETTER. I LOVE IT.

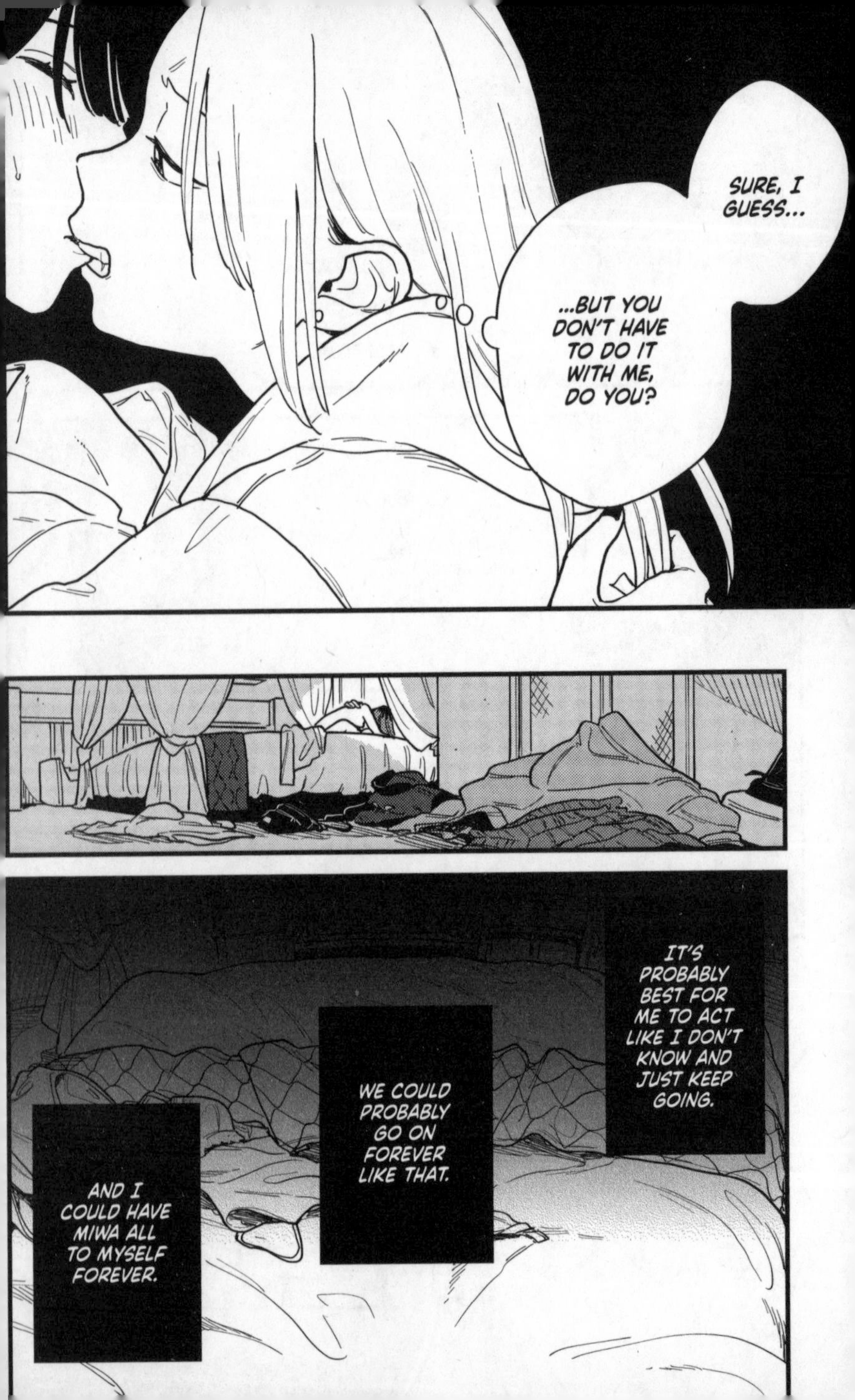
SURE, I GUESS...
...BUT YOU DON'T HAVE TO DO IT WITH ME, DO YOU?
IT'S PROBABLY BEST FOR ME TO ACT LIKE I DON'T KNOW AND JUST KEEP GOING.
WE COULD PROBABLY GO ON FOREVER LIKE THAT.
AND I COULD HAVE MIWA ALL TO MYSELF FOREVER.

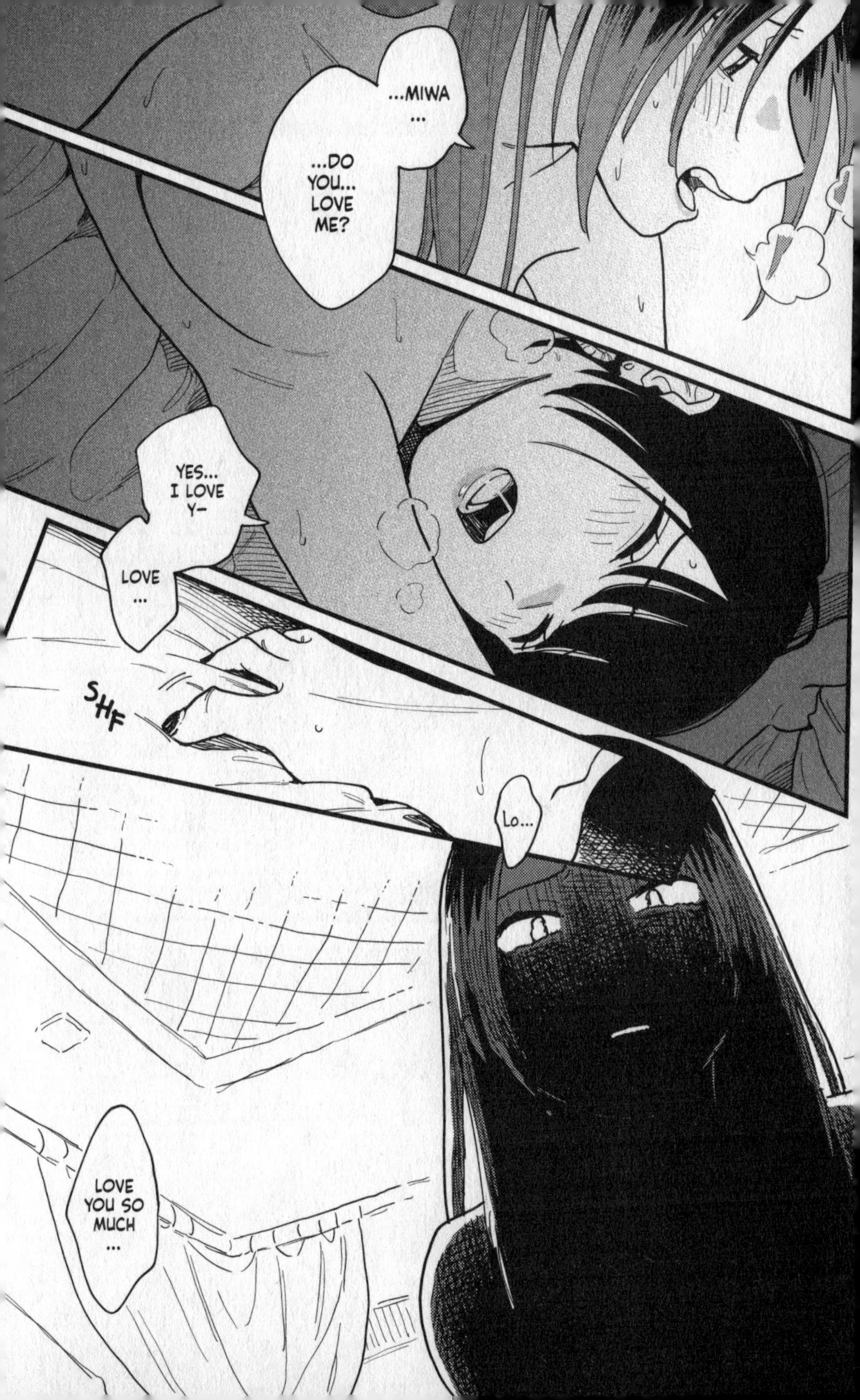
...MIWA ...
...DO YOU... LOVE ME?
YES... I LOVE Y-
LOVE ...
SHF
Lo...
LOVE YOU SO MUCH ...

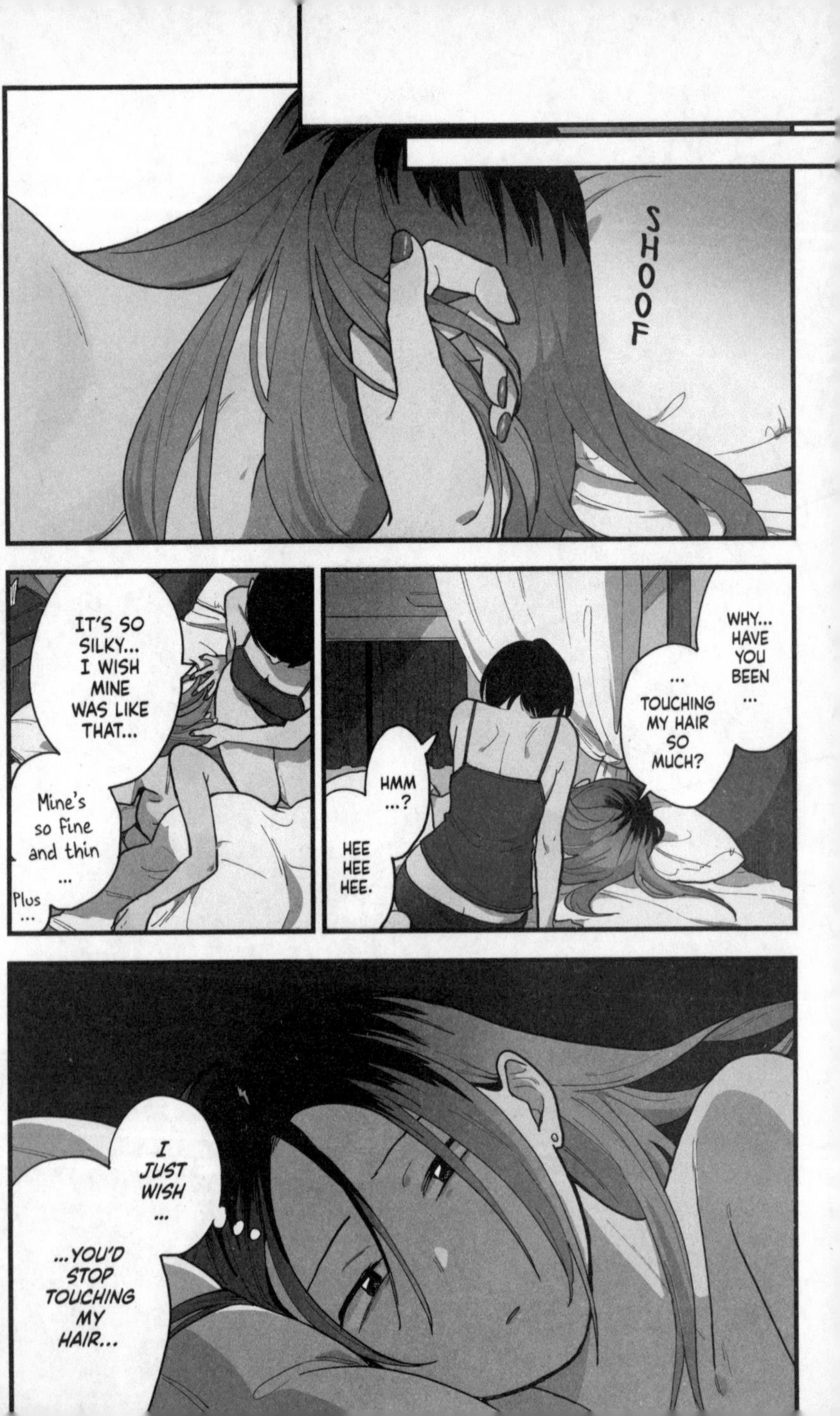
SHOOF
WHY... HAVE YOU BEEN ... ... TOUCHING MY HAIR SO MUCH?
HMM ...?
HEE HEE HEE.
IT'S SO SILKY... I WISH MINE WAS LIKE THAT...
Mine's so fine and thin ...
Plus ...
I JUST WISH ...
...YOU'D STOP TOUCHING MY HAIR...

How Do We
Relationship?

HOW DO WE
RELATIONSHIP?

Chapter 34: I Love You, I Loved You

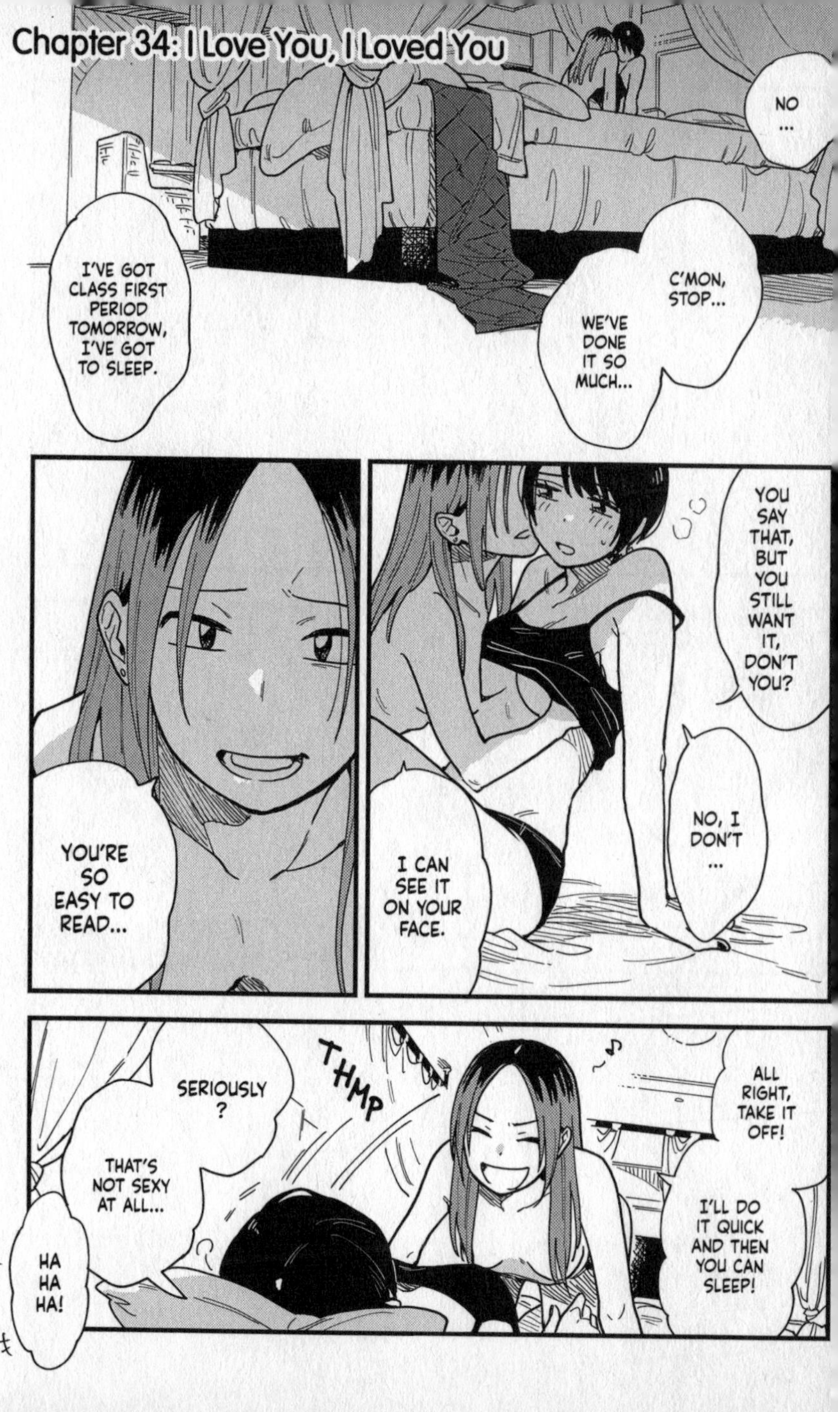

NO ...
C'MON, STOP...
WE'VE DONE IT SO MUCH...
I'VE GOT CLASS FIRST PERIOD TOMORROW, I'VE GOT TO SLEEP.
YOU SAY THAT, BUT YOU STILL WANT IT, DON'T YOU?
NO, I DON'T ...
I CAN SEE IT ON YOUR FACE.
YOU'RE SO EASY TO READ...
ALL RIGHT, TAKE IT OFF!
I'LL DO IT QUICK AND THEN YOU CAN SLEEP!
THMP
SERIOUSLY?
THAT'S NOT SEXY AT ALL...
HA HA HA!

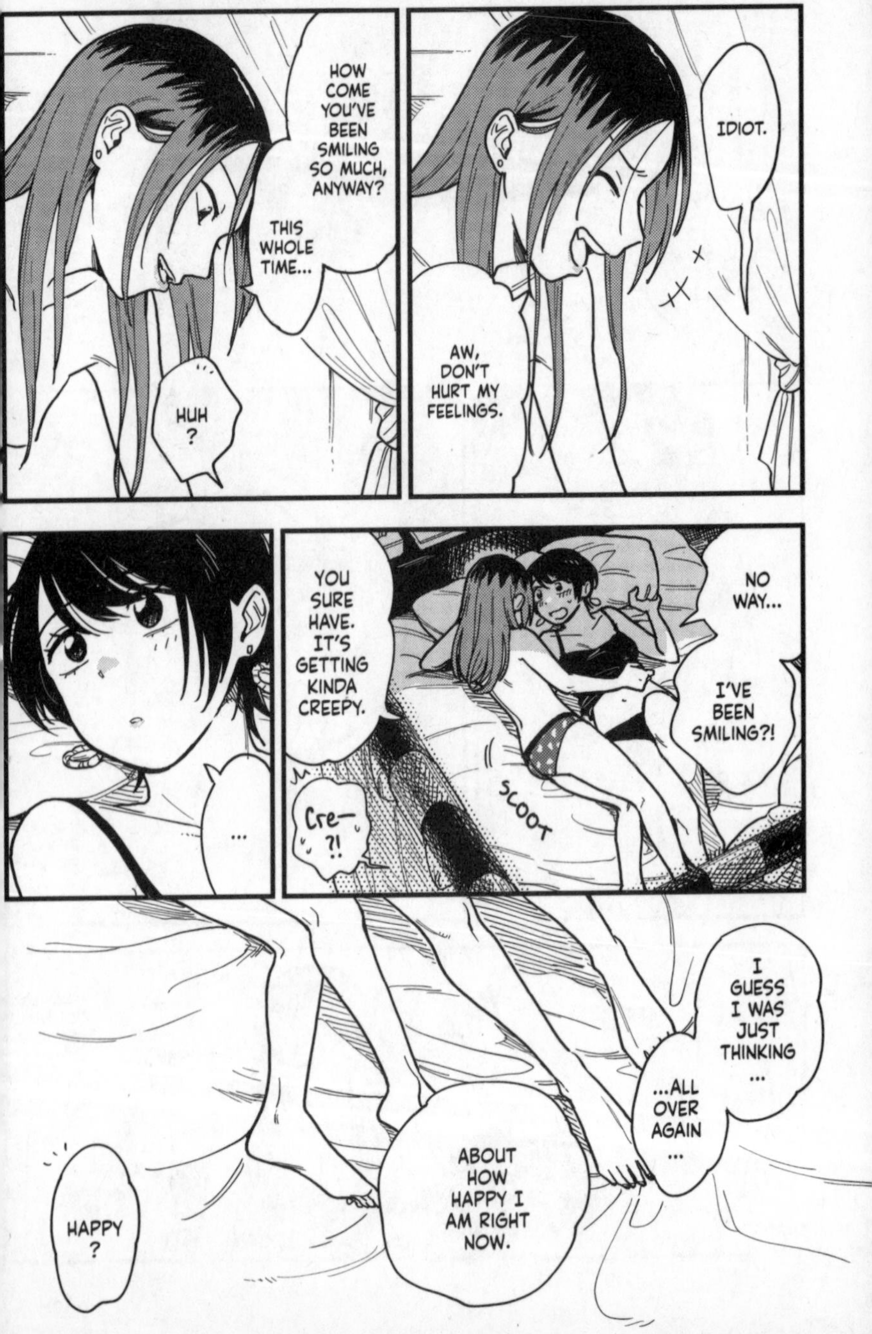
IDIOT.
AW, DON'T HURT MY FEELINGS.
HOW COME YOU'VE BEEN SMILING SO MUCH, ANYWAY?
THIS WHOLE TIME...
HUH?
NO WAY...
I'VE BEEN SMILING?!
YOU SURE HAVE. IT'S GETTING KINDA CREEPY.
SCOOT
Cre— ?!
...
I GUESS I WAS JUST THINKING...
...ALL OVER AGAIN...
ABOUT HOW HAPPY I AM RIGHT NOW.
HAPPY?

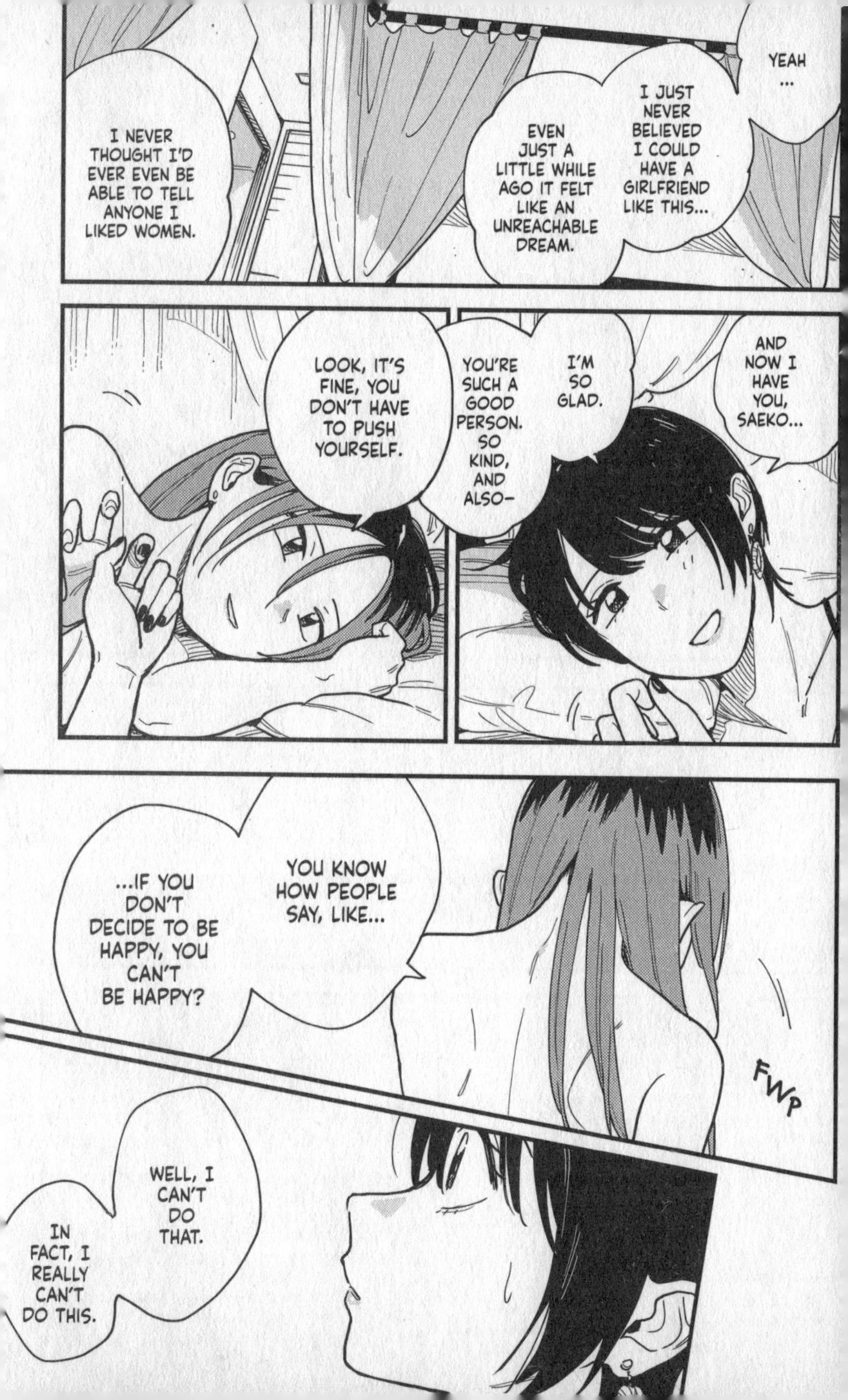
YEAH ...
I JUST NEVER BELIEVED I COULD HAVE A GIRLFRIEND LIKE THIS...
EVEN JUST A LITTLE WHILE AGO IT FELT LIKE AN UNREACHABLE DREAM.
I NEVER THOUGHT I'D EVER EVEN BE ABLE TO TELL ANYONE I LIKED WOMEN.
AND NOW I HAVE YOU, SAEKO...
I'M SO GLAD.
YOU'RE SUCH A GOOD PERSON. SO KIND, AND ALSO—
LOOK, IT'S FINE, YOU DON'T HAVE TO PUSH YOURSELF.
YOU KNOW HOW PEOPLE SAY, LIKE...
...IF YOU DON'T DECIDE TO BE HAPPY, YOU CAN'T BE HAPPY?
FWP
WELL, I CAN'T DO THAT.
IN FACT, I REALLY CAN'T DO THIS.

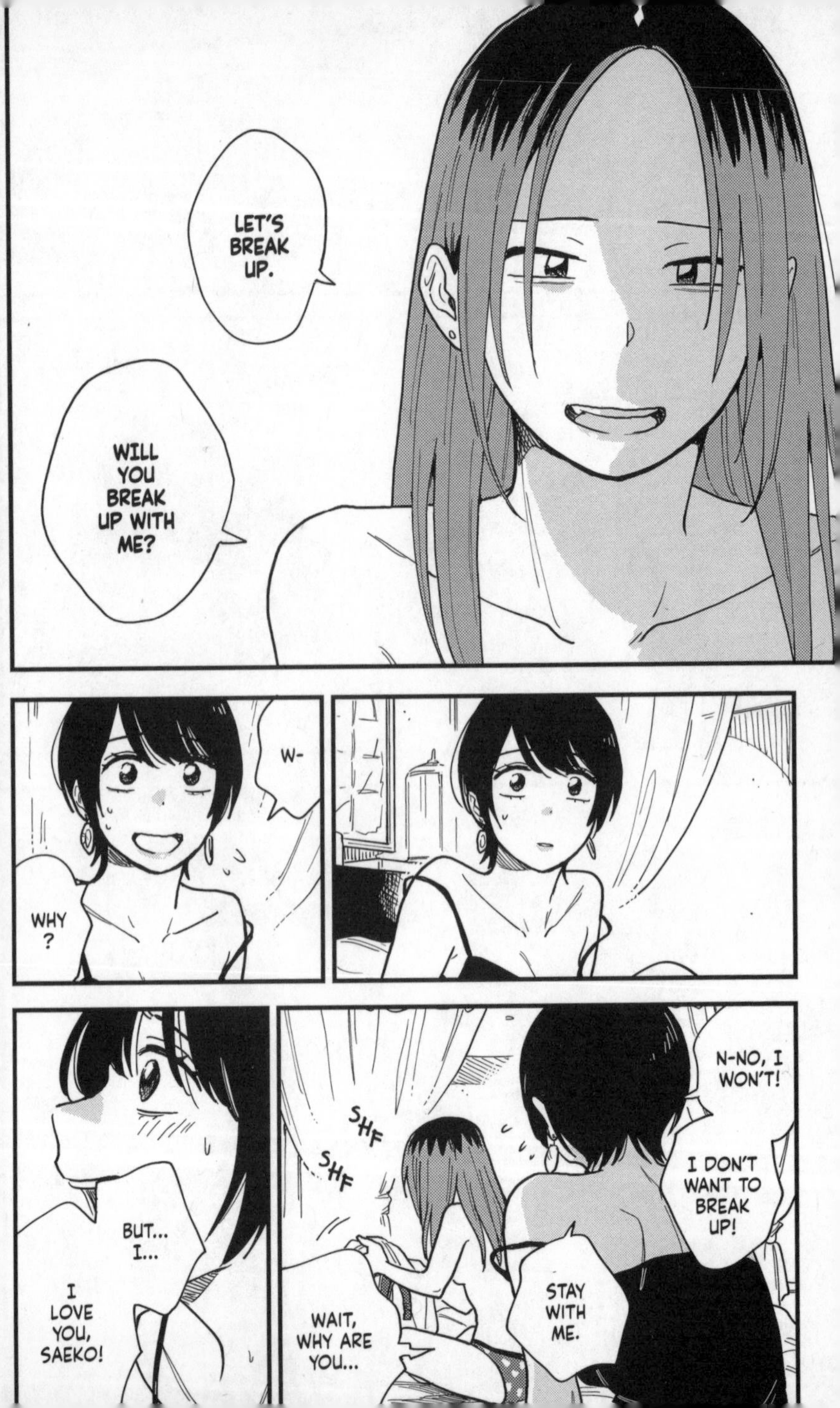
LET'S BREAK UP.
WILL YOU BREAK UP WITH ME?
W-
WHY?
N-NO, I WON'T!
I DON'T WANT TO BREAK UP!
SHF
SHF
STAY WITH ME.
WAIT, WHY ARE YOU...
BUT... I...
I LOVE YOU, SAEKO!

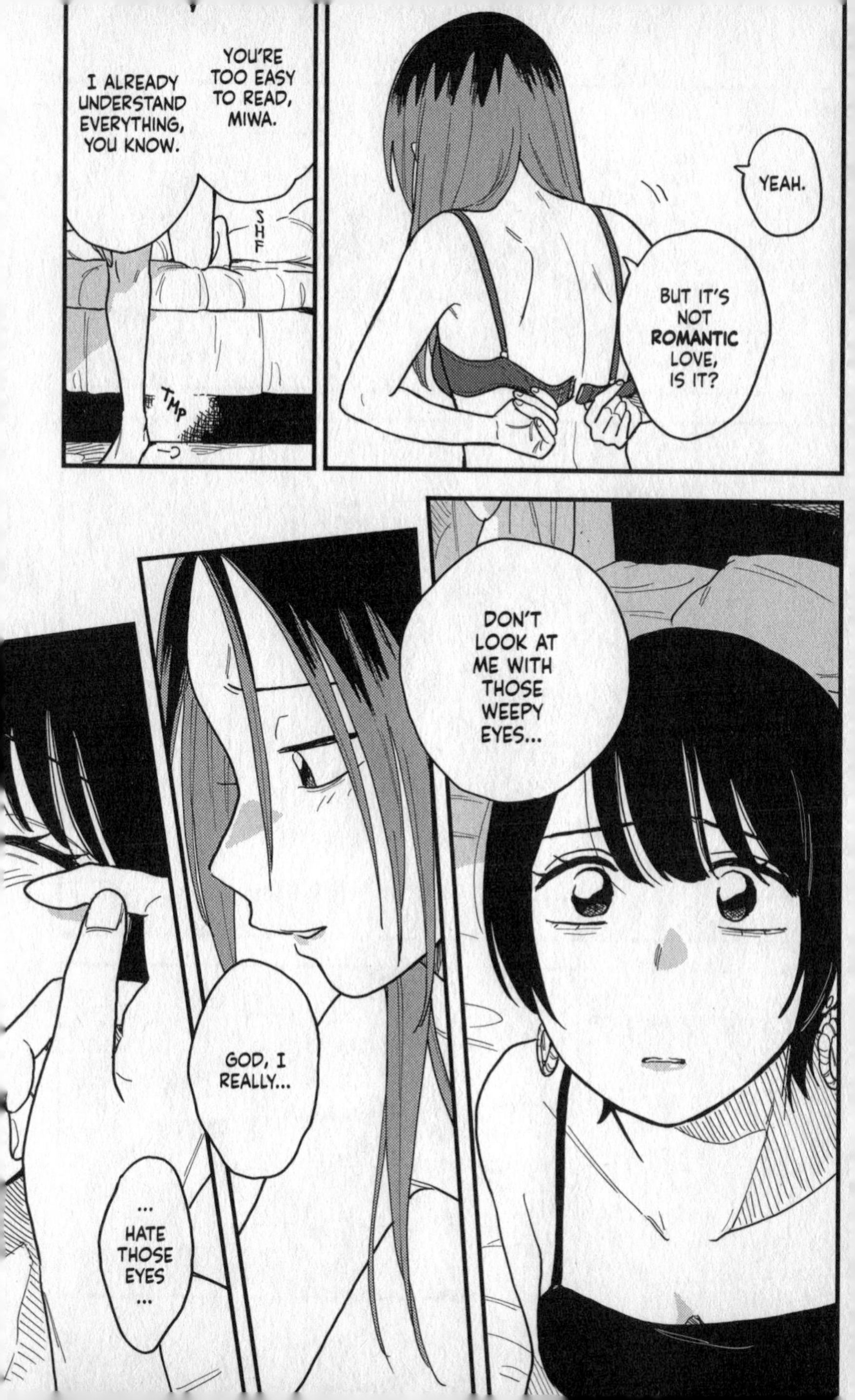
YEAH.
BUT IT'S NOT ROMANTIC LOVE, IS IT?
YOU'RE TOO EASY TO READ, MIWA.
I ALREADY UNDERSTAND EVERYTHING, YOU KNOW.
SHF
TMP
DON'T LOOK AT ME WITH THOSE WEEPY EYES...
GOD, I REALLY...
... HATE THOSE EYES ...

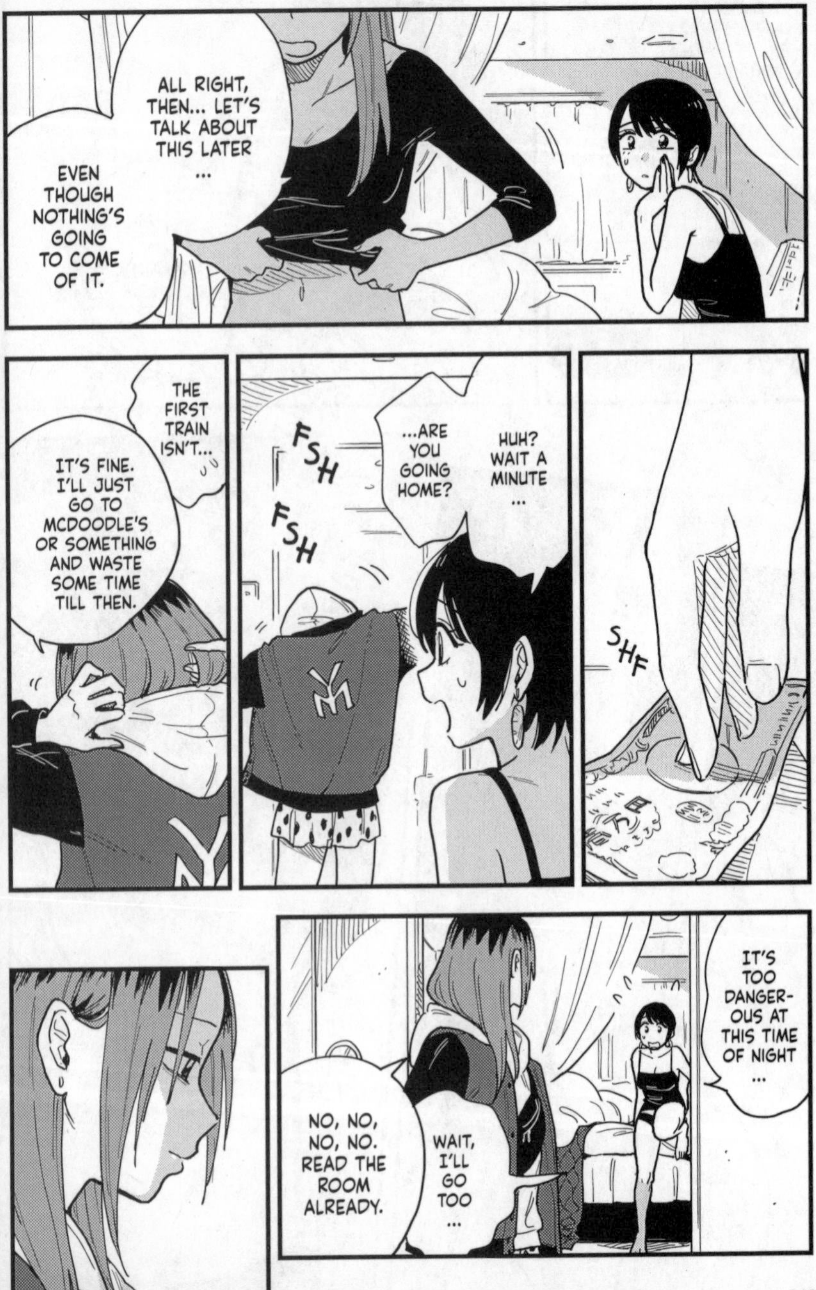
ALL RIGHT, THEN... LET'S TALK ABOUT THIS LATER ...
EVEN THOUGH NOTHING'S GOING TO COME OF IT.
SHF
HUH? WAIT A MINUTE ...
...ARE YOU GOING HOME?
FSH
FSH
THE FIRST TRAIN ISN'T...
IT'S FINE. I'LL JUST GO TO MCDOODLE'S OR SOMETHING AND WASTE SOME TIME TILL THEN.
IT'S TOO DANGER-OUS AT THIS TIME OF NIGHT ...
WAIT, I'LL GO TOO ...
NO, NO, NO, NO. READ THE ROOM ALREADY.

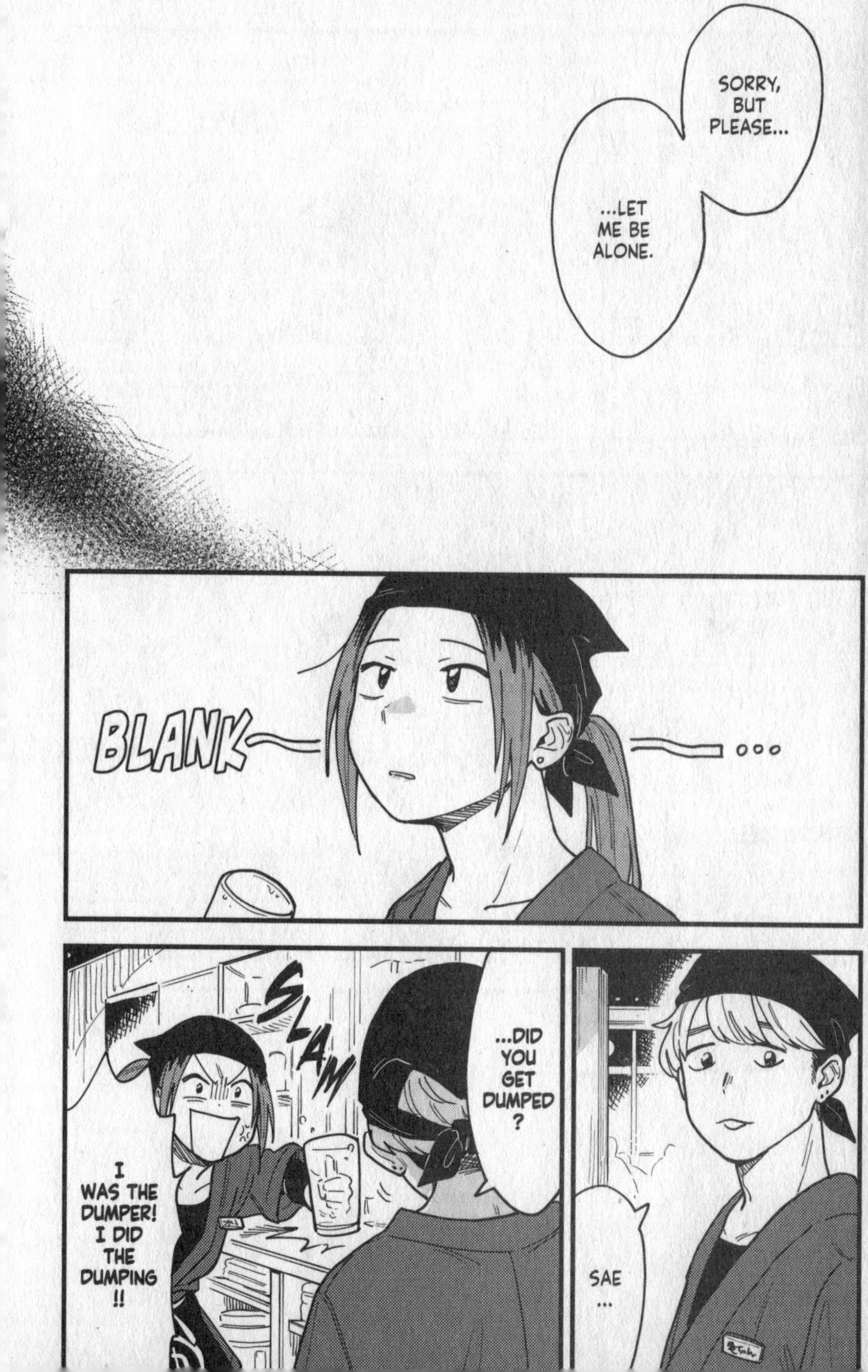
SORRY, BUT PLEASE...
...LET ME BE ALONE.
BLANK
...
SAE ...
...DID YOU GET DUMPED ?
SLAM
I WAS THE DUMPER! I DID THE DUMPING !!

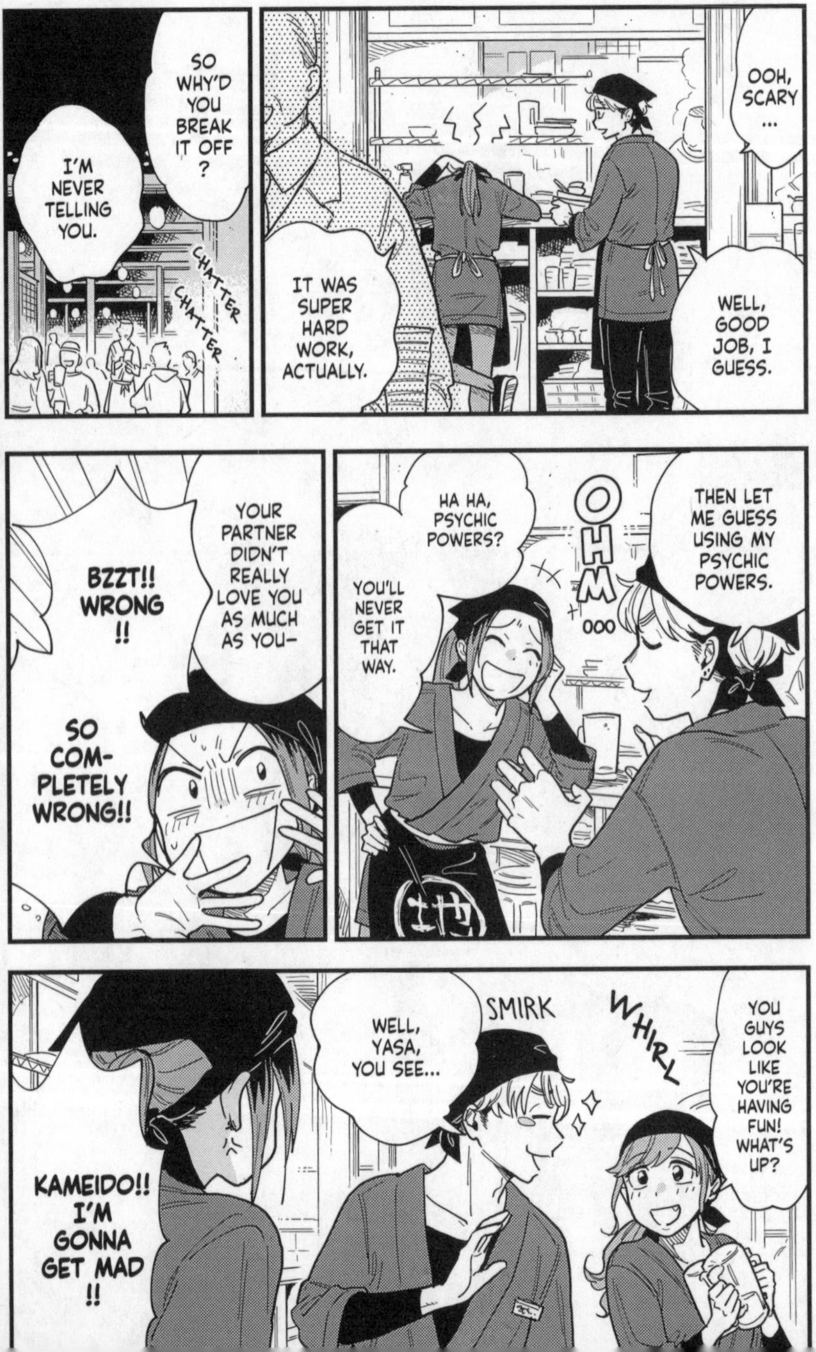
OOH, SCARY ...
WELL, GOOD JOB, I GUESS.
IT WAS SUPER HARD WORK, ACTUALLY.
SO WHY'D YOU BREAK IT OFF ?
I'M NEVER TELLING YOU.
CHATTER CHATTER
THEN LET ME GUESS USING MY PSYCHIC POWERS.
OHM
OOO
HA HA, PSYCHIC POWERS?
YOU'LL NEVER GET IT THAT WAY.
YOUR PARTNER DIDN'T REALLY LOVE YOU AS MUCH AS YOU—
BZZT!! WRONG !!
SO COM-PLETELY WRONG!!
YOU GUYS LOOK LIKE YOU'RE HAVING FUN! WHAT'S UP?
WHIRL
SMIRK
WELL, YASA, YOU SEE...
KAMEIDO!! I'M GONNA GET MAD !!

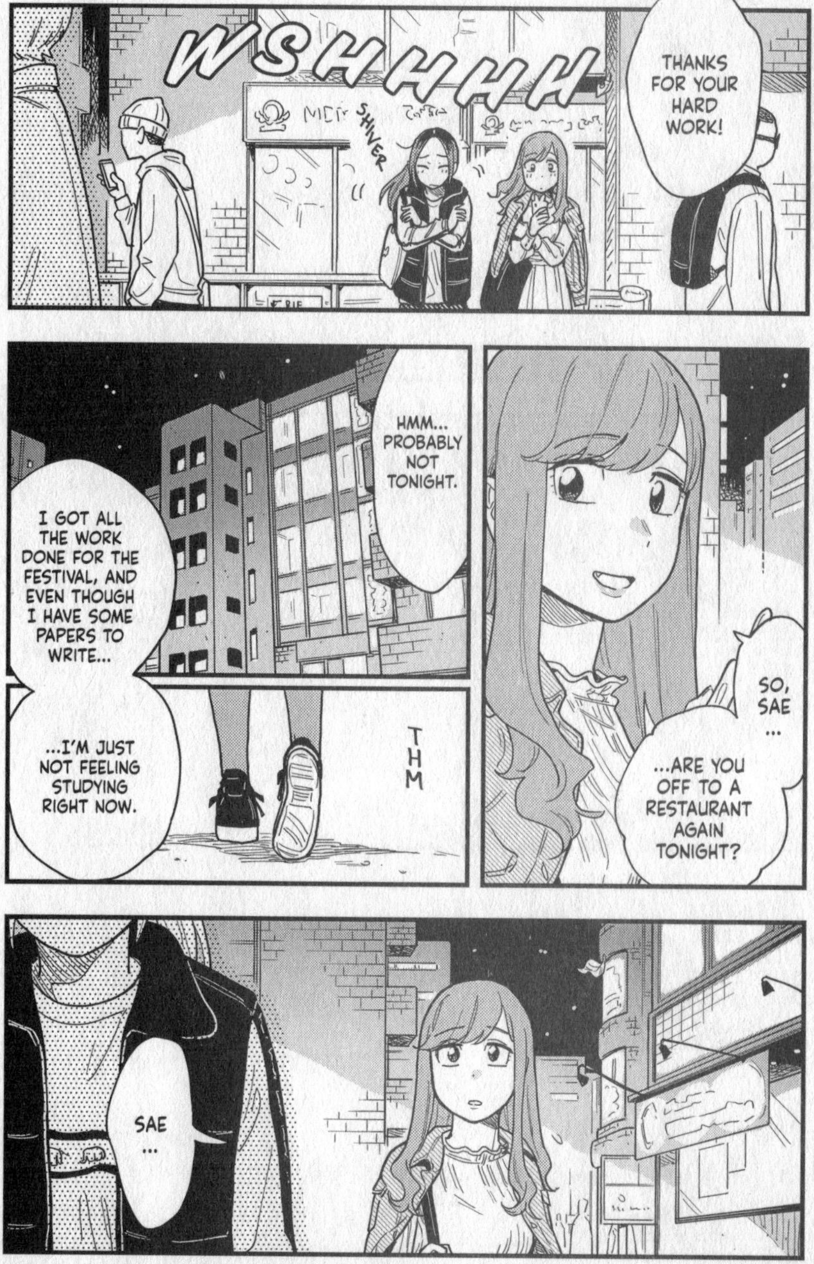
THANKS FOR YOUR HARD WORK!
WSHHHHH
SHIVER
SO, SAE...
...ARE YOU OFF TO A RESTAURANT AGAIN TONIGHT?
HMM... PROBABLY NOT TONIGHT.
I GOT ALL THE WORK DONE FOR THE FESTIVAL, AND EVEN THOUGH I HAVE SOME PAPERS TO WRITE...
THM
...I'M JUST NOT FEELING STUDYING RIGHT NOW.
SAE...

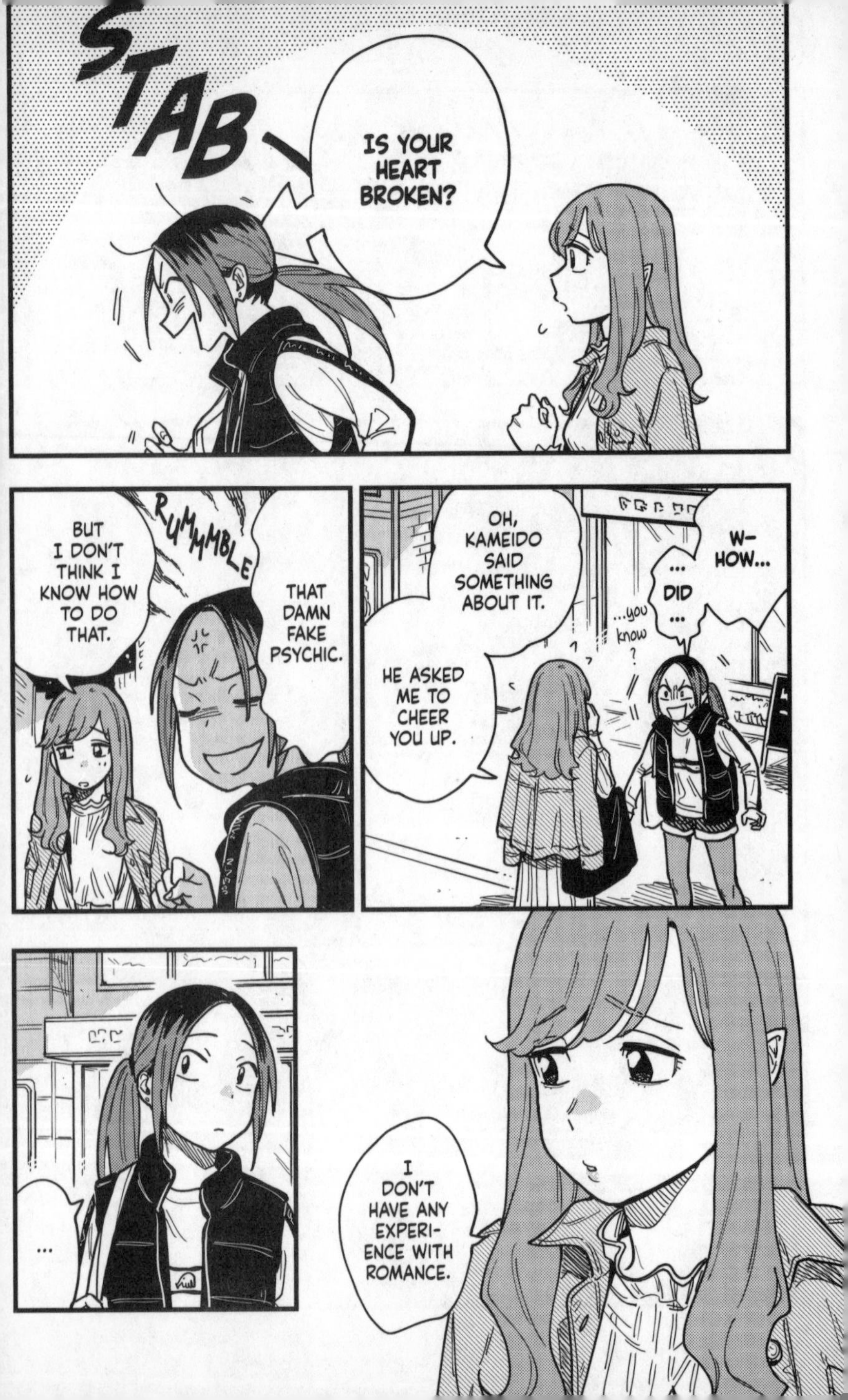
IS YOUR HEART BROKEN?
STAB
W- HOW...
... DID ...
...you know?
OH, KAMEIDO SAID SOMETHING ABOUT IT.
HE ASKED ME TO CHEER YOU UP.
THAT DAMN FAKE PSYCHIC.
RUMMMBLE
BUT I DON'T THINK I KNOW HOW TO DO THAT.
I DON'T HAVE ANY EXPERI- ENCE WITH ROMANCE.
...

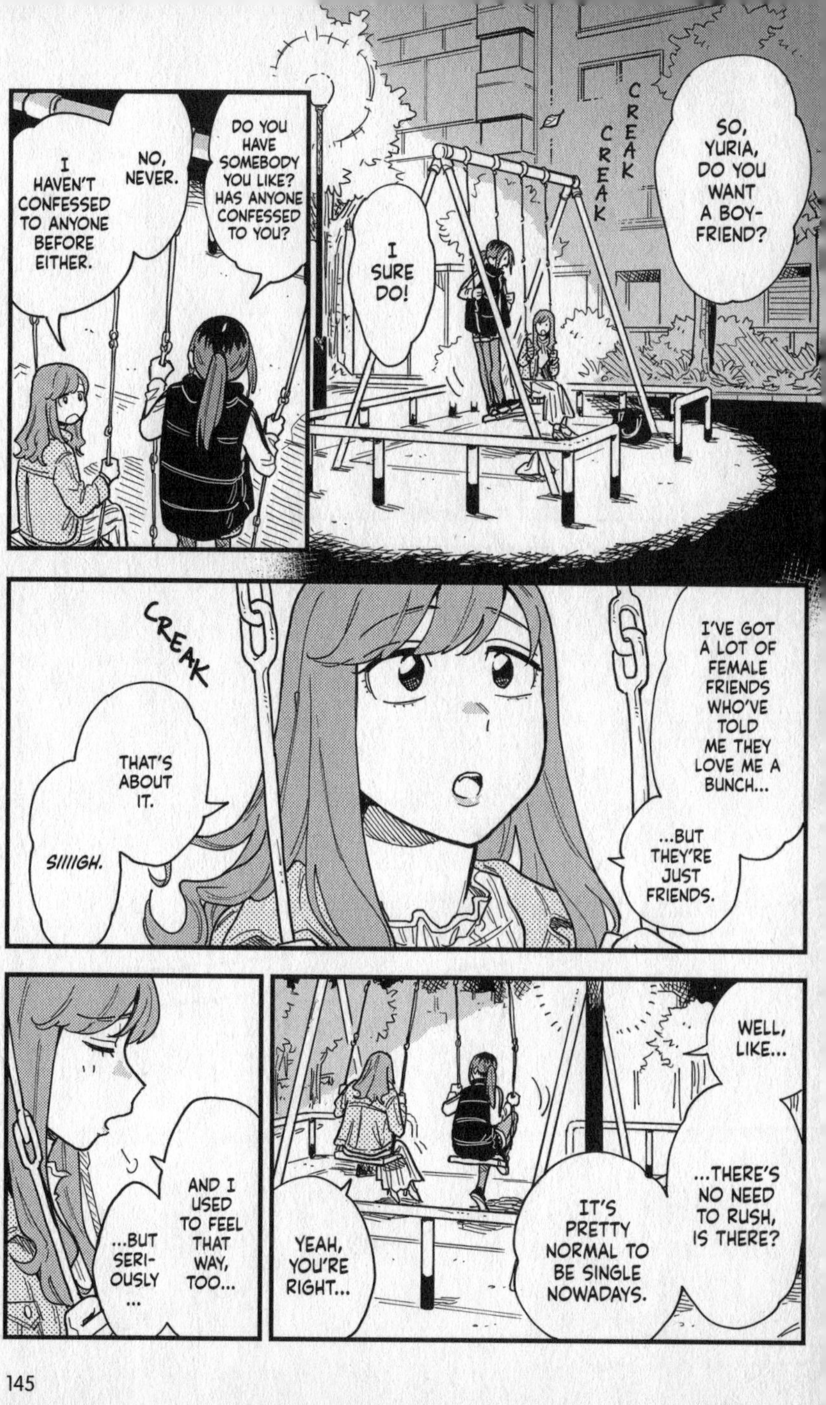
SO, YURIA, DO YOU WANT A BOY-FRIEND?
CREAK
CREAK
I SURE DO!
DO YOU HAVE SOMEBODY YOU LIKE? HAS ANYONE CONFESSED TO YOU?
NO, NEVER.
I HAVEN'T CONFESSED TO ANYONE BEFORE EITHER.
I'VE GOT A LOT OF FEMALE FRIENDS WHO'VE TOLD ME THEY LOVE ME A BUNCH...
...BUT THEY'RE JUST FRIENDS.
CREAK
THAT'S ABOUT IT.
SIIIGH.
WELL, LIKE...
...THERE'S NO NEED TO RUSH, IS THERE?
IT'S PRETTY NORMAL TO BE SINGLE NOWADAYS.
YEAH, YOU'RE RIGHT...
AND I USED TO FEEL THAT WAY, TOO...
...BUT SERI-OUSLY...

I'M STARTING TO FEEL LIKE I'M THE ONLY ONE OUT THERE WHO NOBODY REALLY LOVES.

AND I FEEL LIKE RUSHING ...

AH, WELL... YOU KNOW...

I WAS IN A RELATIONSHIP, AND I STILL FELT...

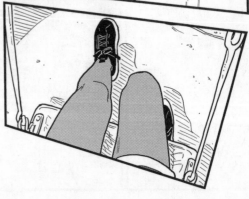

...LIKE NOBODY LOVED ME.

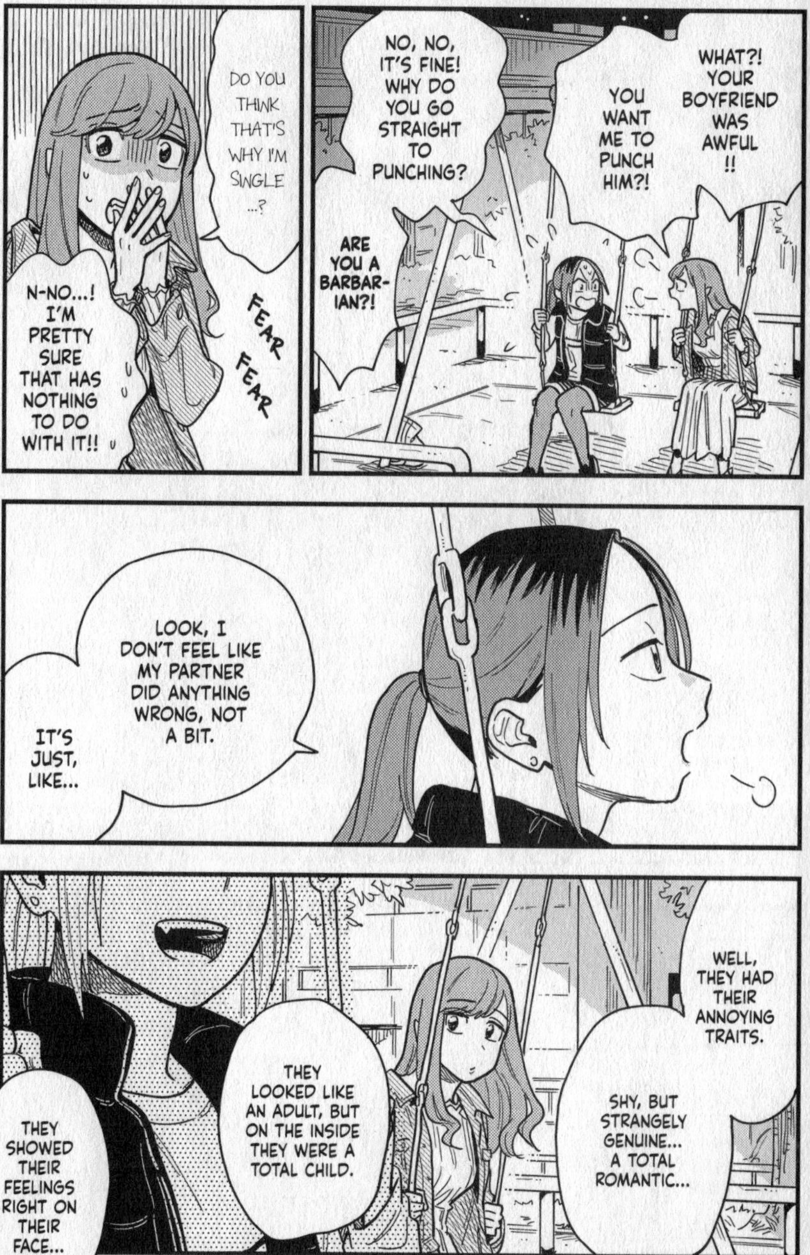
WHAT?! YOUR BOYFRIEND WAS AWFUL !!
YOU WANT ME TO PUNCH HIM?!
NO, NO, IT'S FINE! WHY DO YOU GO STRAIGHT TO PUNCHING?
ARE YOU A BARBARIAN?!
DO YOU THINK THAT'S WHY I'M SINGLE ...?
FEAR FEAR
N-NO...! I'M PRETTY SURE THAT HAS NOTHING TO DO WITH IT!!
LOOK, I DON'T FEEL LIKE MY PARTNER DID ANYTHING WRONG, NOT A BIT.
IT'S JUST, LIKE...
WELL, THEY HAD THEIR ANNOYING TRAITS.
SHY, BUT STRANGELY GENUINE... A TOTAL ROMANTIC...
THEY LOOKED LIKE AN ADULT, BUT ON THE INSIDE THEY WERE A TOTAL CHILD.
THEY SHOWED THEIR FEELINGS RIGHT ON THEIR FACE...

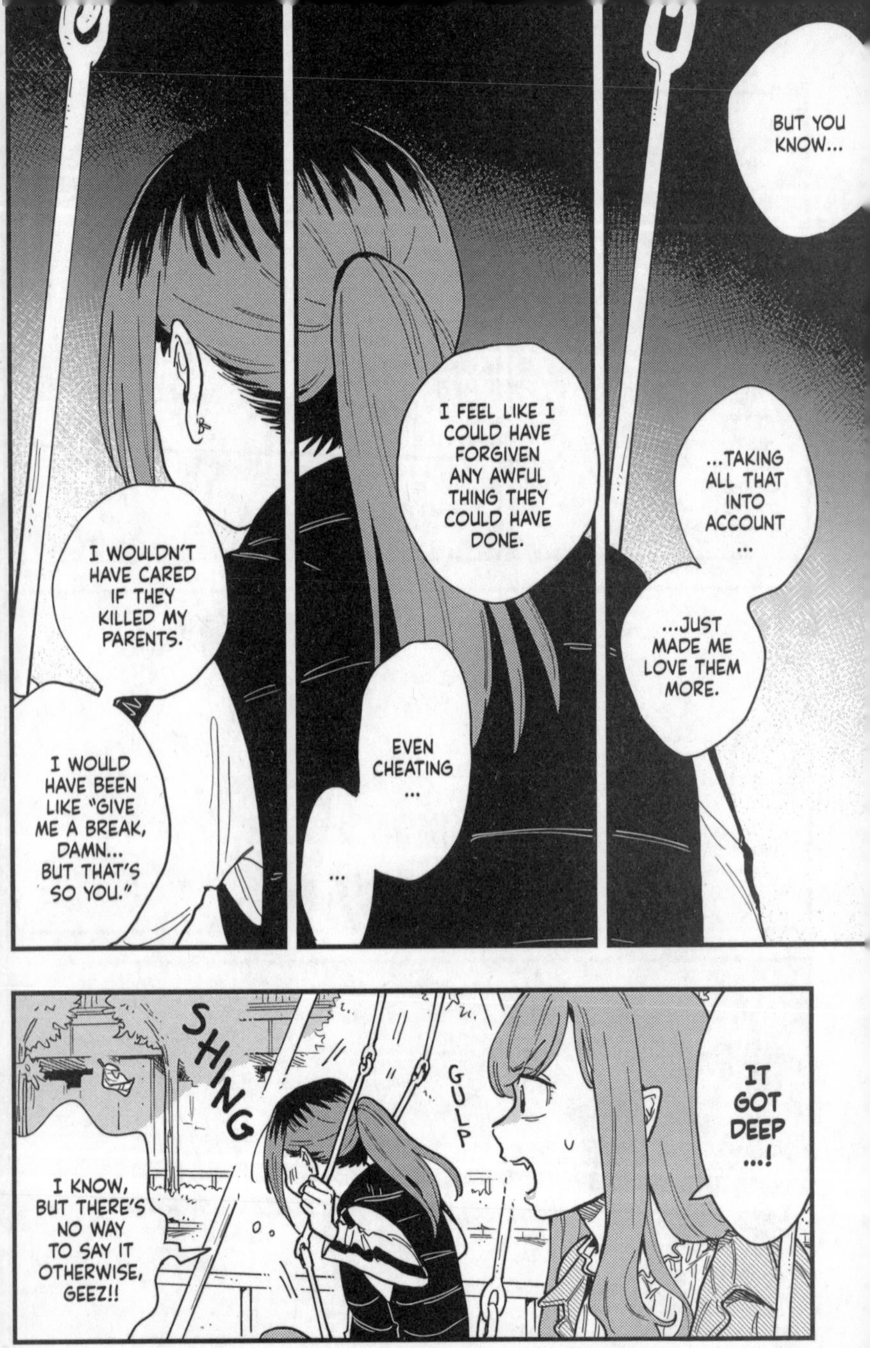
BUT YOU KNOW...
...TAKING ALL THAT INTO ACCOUNT...
...JUST MADE ME LOVE THEM MORE.
I FEEL LIKE I COULD HAVE FORGIVEN ANY AWFUL THING THEY COULD HAVE DONE.
EVEN CHEATING...
...
I WOULDN'T HAVE CARED IF THEY KILLED MY PARENTS.
I WOULD HAVE BEEN LIKE "GIVE ME A BREAK, DAMN... BUT THAT'S SO YOU."
IT GOT DEEP...!
GULP
SHING
I KNOW, BUT THERE'S NO WAY TO SAY IT OTHERWISE, GEEZ!!

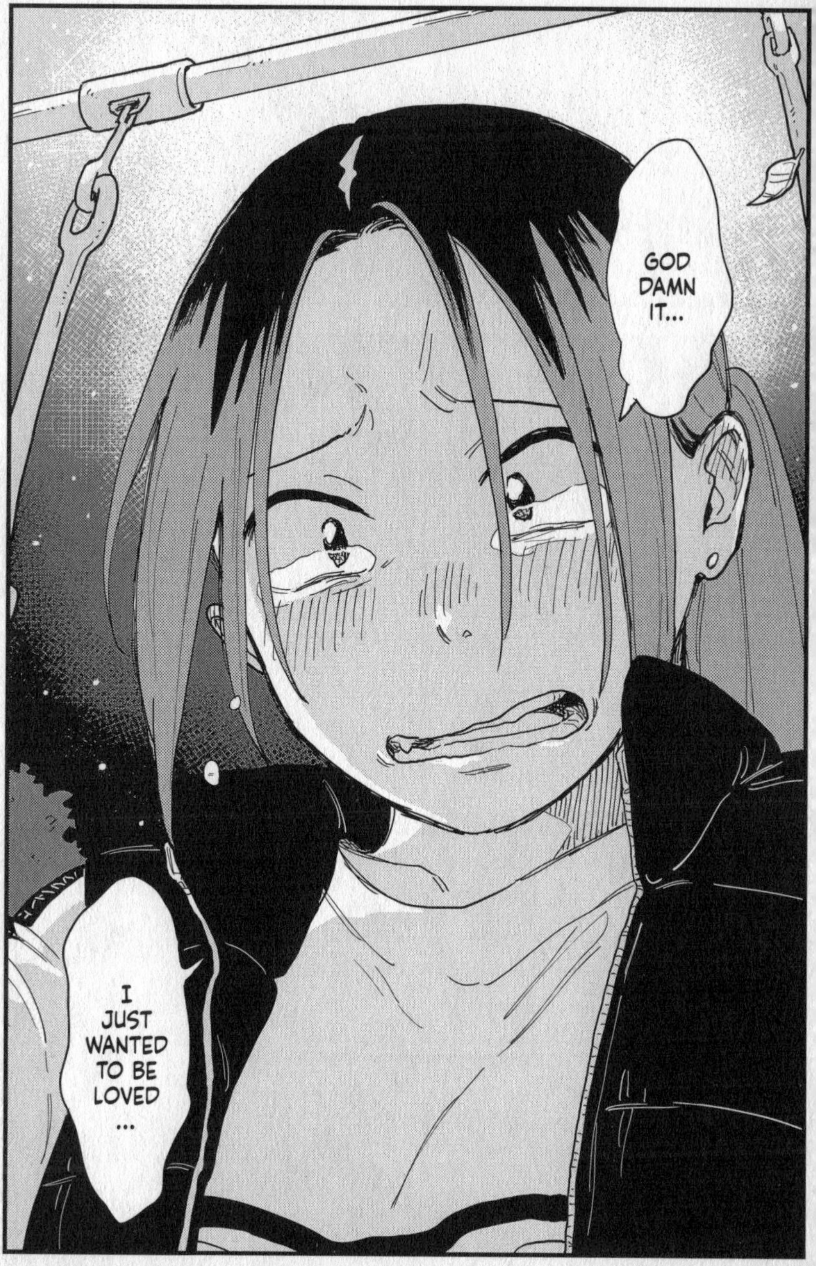
GOD DAMN IT...
I JUST WANTED TO BE LOVED ...

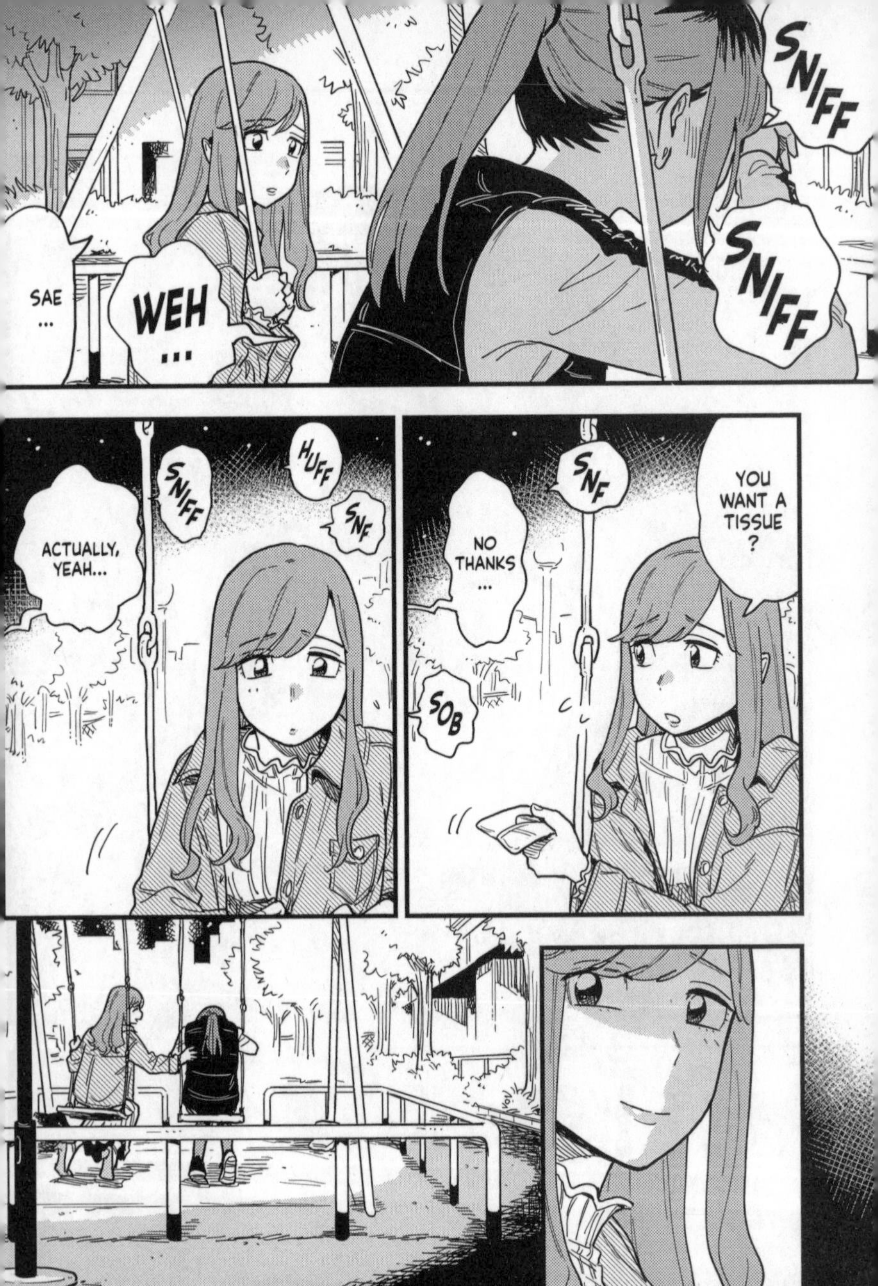
SNIFF
SNIFF
WEH ...
SAE ...
YOU WANT A TISSUE?
SNF
NO THANKS ...
SOB
HUFF
SNF
SNIFF
ACTUALLY, YEAH...

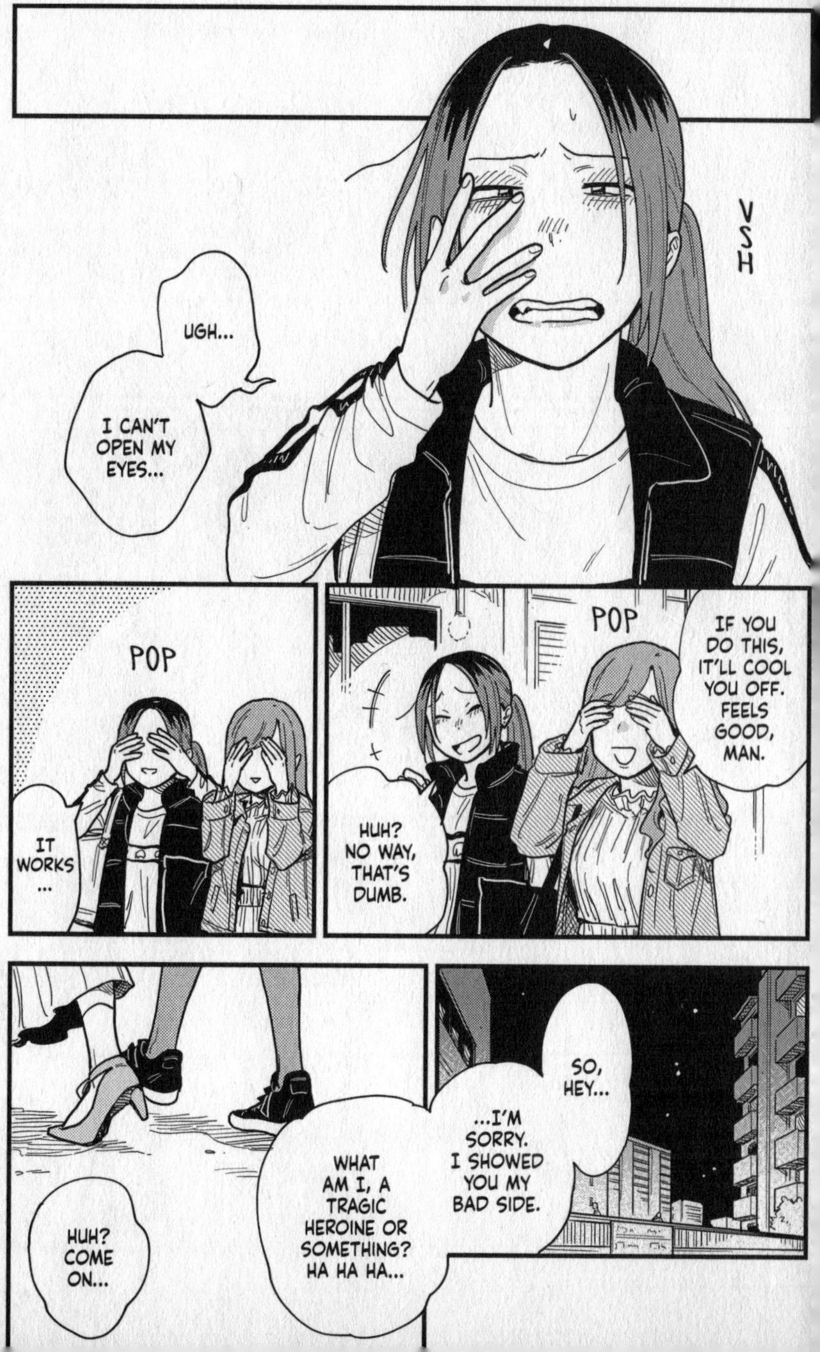
VSH
UGH...
I CAN'T OPEN MY EYES...
POP
IF YOU DO THIS, IT'LL COOL YOU OFF. FEELS GOOD, MAN.
HUH? NO WAY, THAT'S DUMB.
POP
IT WORKS ...
SO, HEY...
...I'M SORRY. I SHOWED YOU MY BAD SIDE.
WHAT AM I, A TRAGIC HEROINE OR SOMETHING? HA HA HA...
HUH? COME ON...

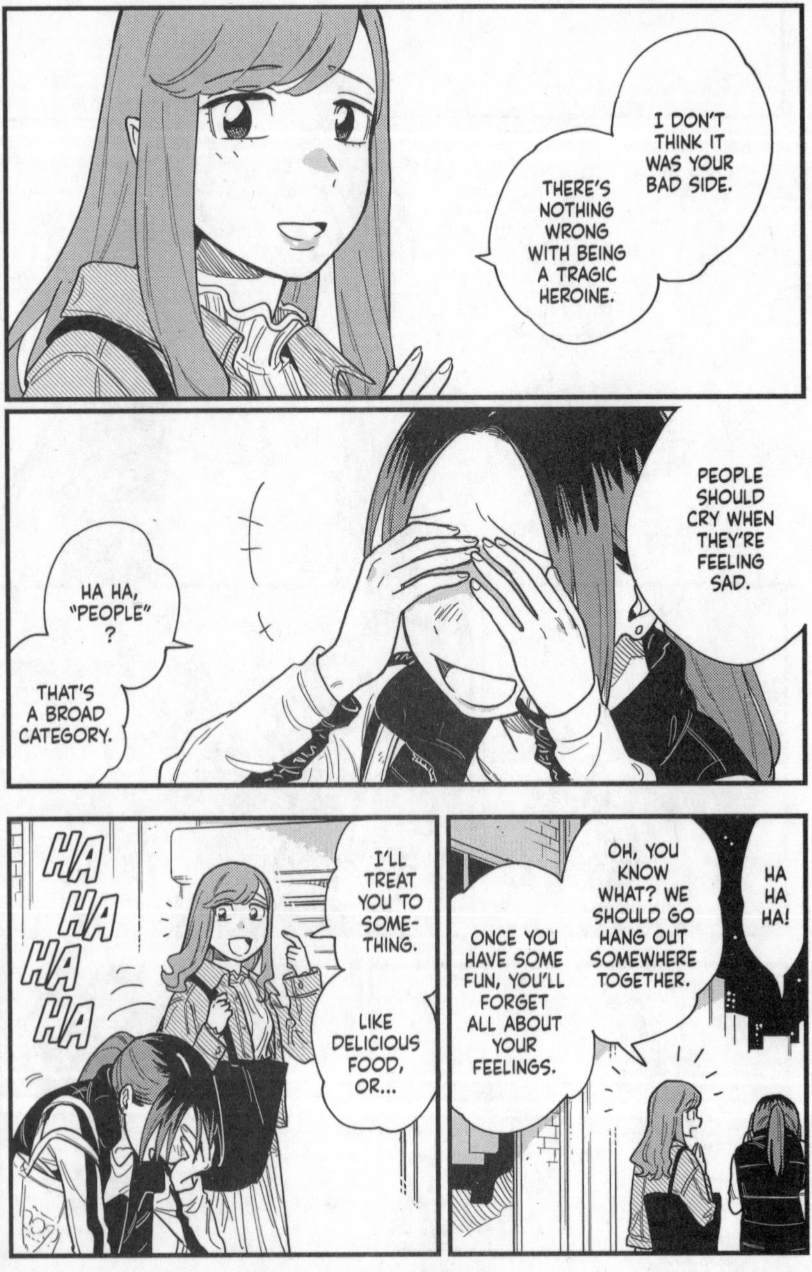
I DON'T THINK IT WAS YOUR BAD SIDE.
THERE'S NOTHING WRONG WITH BEING A TRAGIC HEROINE.
PEOPLE SHOULD CRY WHEN THEY'RE FEELING SAD.
HA HA, "PEOPLE"?
THAT'S A BROAD CATEGORY.
HA HA HA!
OH, YOU KNOW WHAT? WE SHOULD GO HANG OUT SOMEWHERE TOGETHER.
ONCE YOU HAVE SOME FUN, YOU'LL FORGET ALL ABOUT YOUR FEELINGS.
I'LL TREAT YOU TO SOME-THING.
LIKE DELICIOUS FOOD, OR...
HA HA HA HA

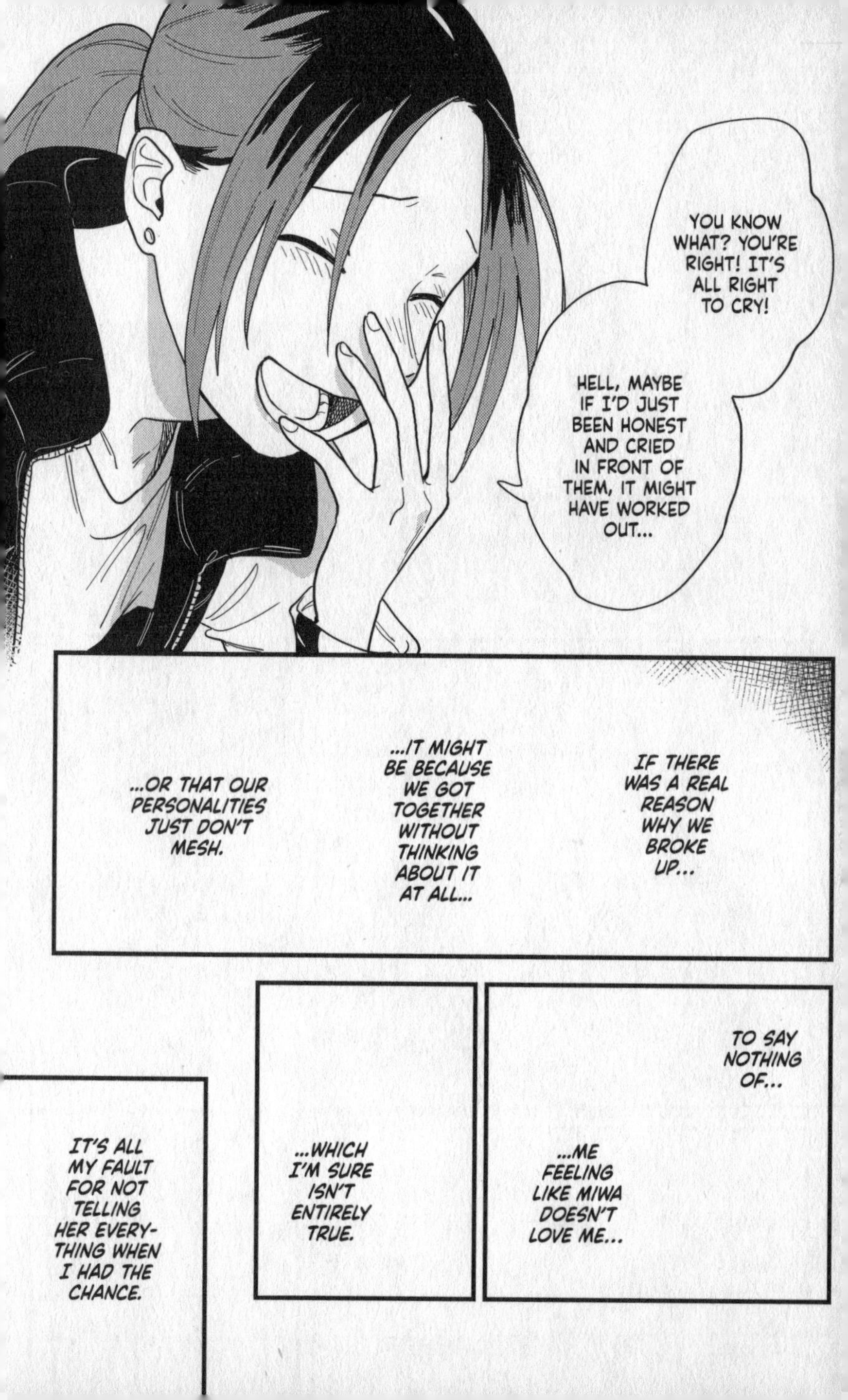
YOU KNOW WHAT? YOU'RE RIGHT! IT'S ALL RIGHT TO CRY!
HELL, MAYBE IF I'D JUST BEEN HONEST AND CRIED IN FRONT OF THEM, IT MIGHT HAVE WORKED OUT...
IF THERE WAS A REAL REASON WHY WE BROKE UP...
...IT MIGHT BE BECAUSE WE GOT TOGETHER WITHOUT THINKING ABOUT IT AT ALL...
...OR THAT OUR PERSONALITIES JUST DON'T MESH.
TO SAY NOTHING OF...
...ME FEELING LIKE MIWA DOESN'T LOVE ME...
...WHICH I'M SURE ISN'T ENTIRELY TRUE.
IT'S ALL MY FAULT FOR NOT TELLING HER EVERY-THING WHEN I HAD THE CHANCE.

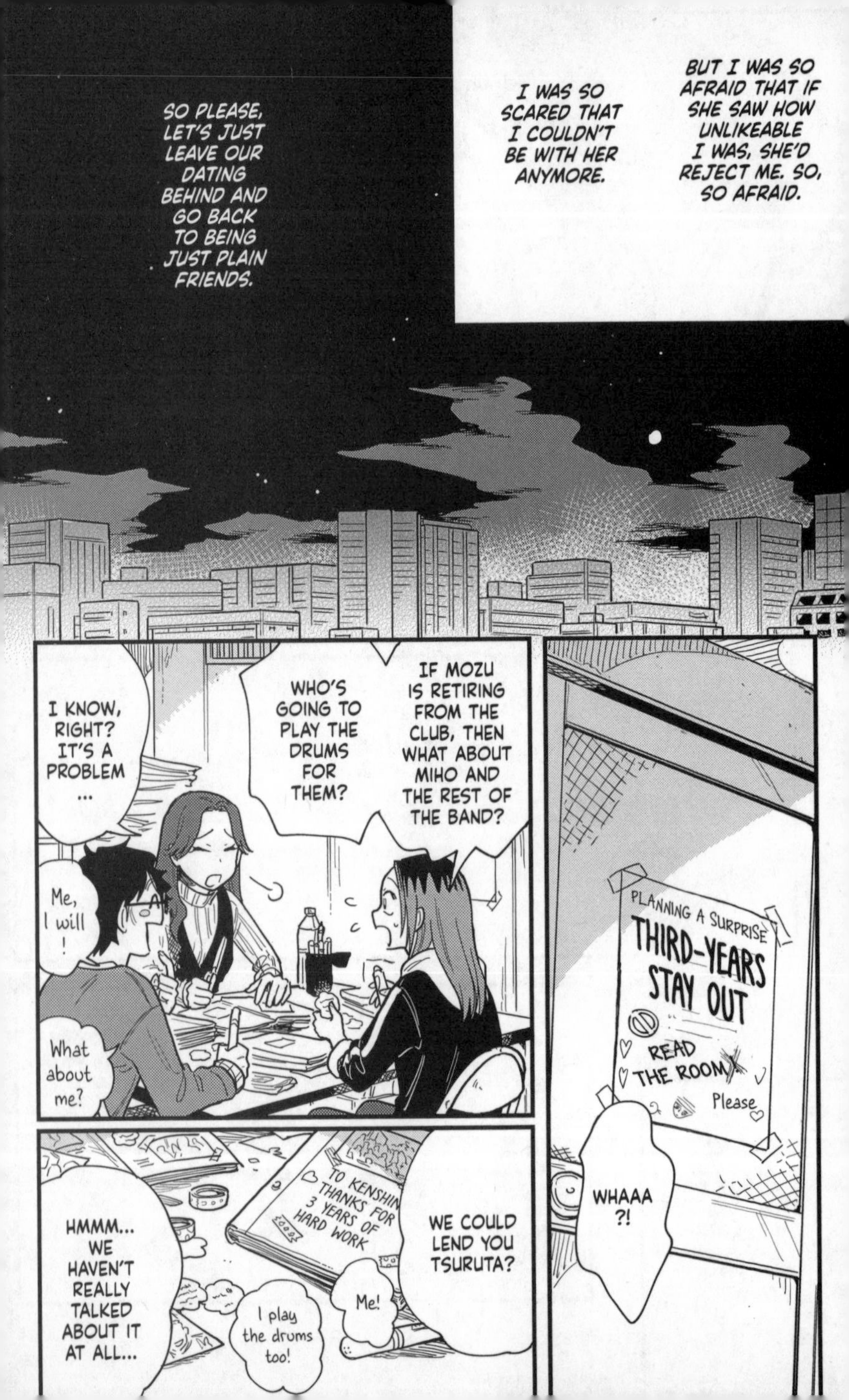
BUT I WAS SO AFRAID THAT IF SHE SAW HOW UNLIKEABLE I WAS, SHE'D REJECT ME. SO, SO AFRAID.
I WAS SO SCARED THAT I COULDN'T BE WITH HER ANYMORE.
SO PLEASE, LET'S JUST LEAVE OUR DATING BEHIND AND GO BACK TO BEING JUST PLAIN FRIENDS.
PLANNING A SURPRISE
THIRD-YEARS STAY OUT
READ THE ROOM
Please
WHAAA ?!
IF MOZU IS RETIRING FROM THE CLUB, THEN WHAT ABOUT MIHO AND THE REST OF THE BAND?
WHO'S GOING TO PLAY THE DRUMS FOR THEM?
I KNOW, RIGHT? IT'S A PROBLEM ...
Me, I will!
What about me?
WE COULD LEND YOU TSURUTA?
Me!
I play the drums too!
TO KENSHIN THANKS FOR 3 YEARS OF HARD WORK
HMMM... WE HAVEN'T REALLY TALKED ABOUT IT AT ALL...

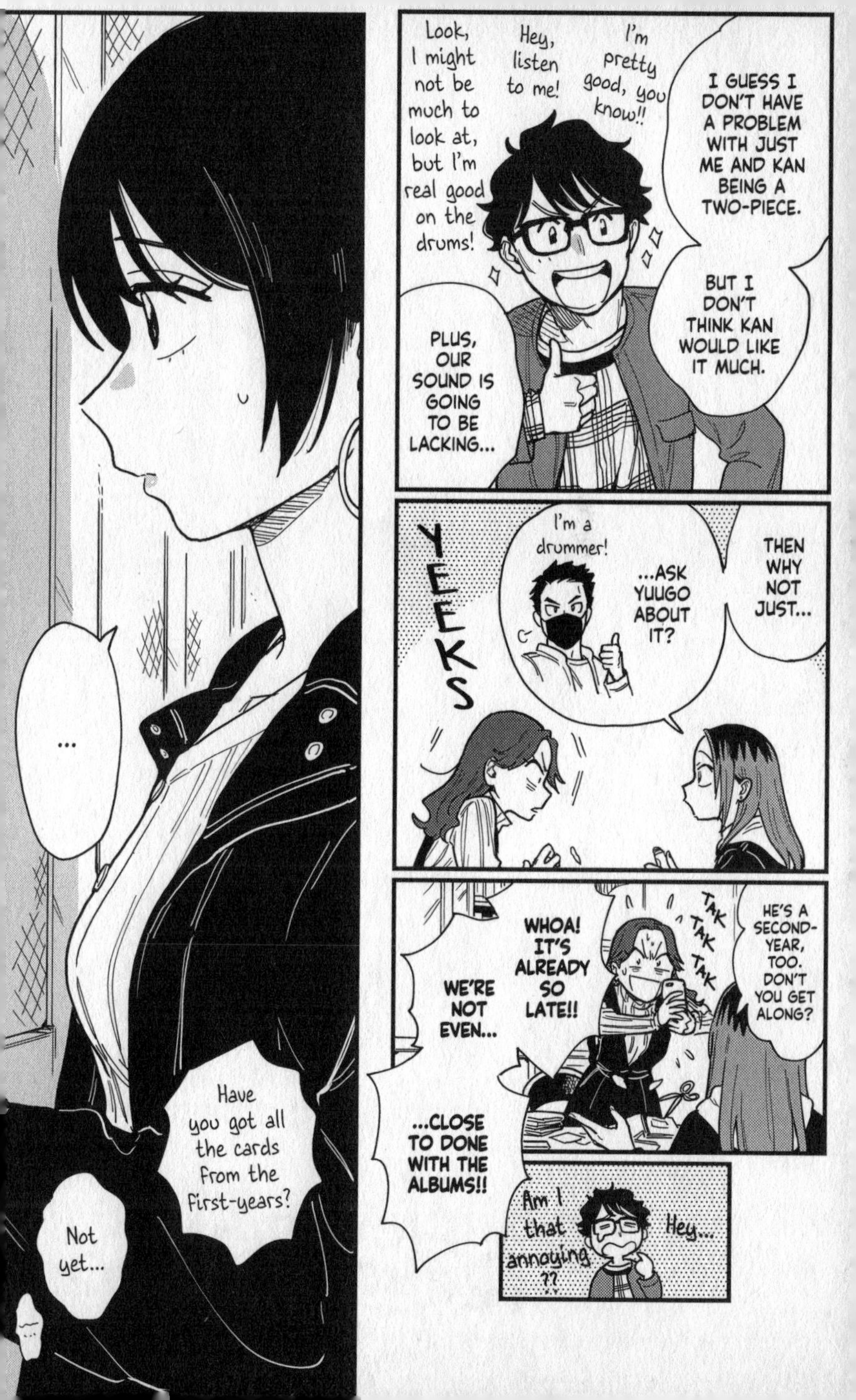

I GUESS I DON'T HAVE A PROBLEM WITH JUST ME AND KAN BEING A TWO-PIECE.
BUT I DON'T THINK KAN WOULD LIKE IT MUCH.
PLUS, OUR SOUND IS GOING TO BE LACKING...
I'm pretty good, you know!!
Hey, listen to me!
Look, I might not be much to look at, but I'm real good on the drums!
THEN WHY NOT JUST...
...ASK YUUGO ABOUT IT?
I'm a drummer!
YEEKS
HE'S A SECOND-YEAR, TOO. DON'T YOU GET ALONG?
TAK TAK TAK
WHOA! IT'S ALREADY SO LATE!!
WE'RE NOT EVEN...
...CLOSE TO DONE WITH THE ALBUMS!!
Hey...
Am I that annoying??
...
Have you got all the cards from the first-years?
Not yet...

HOW DO WE
RELATIONSHIP?

Chapter 35: After the Dream

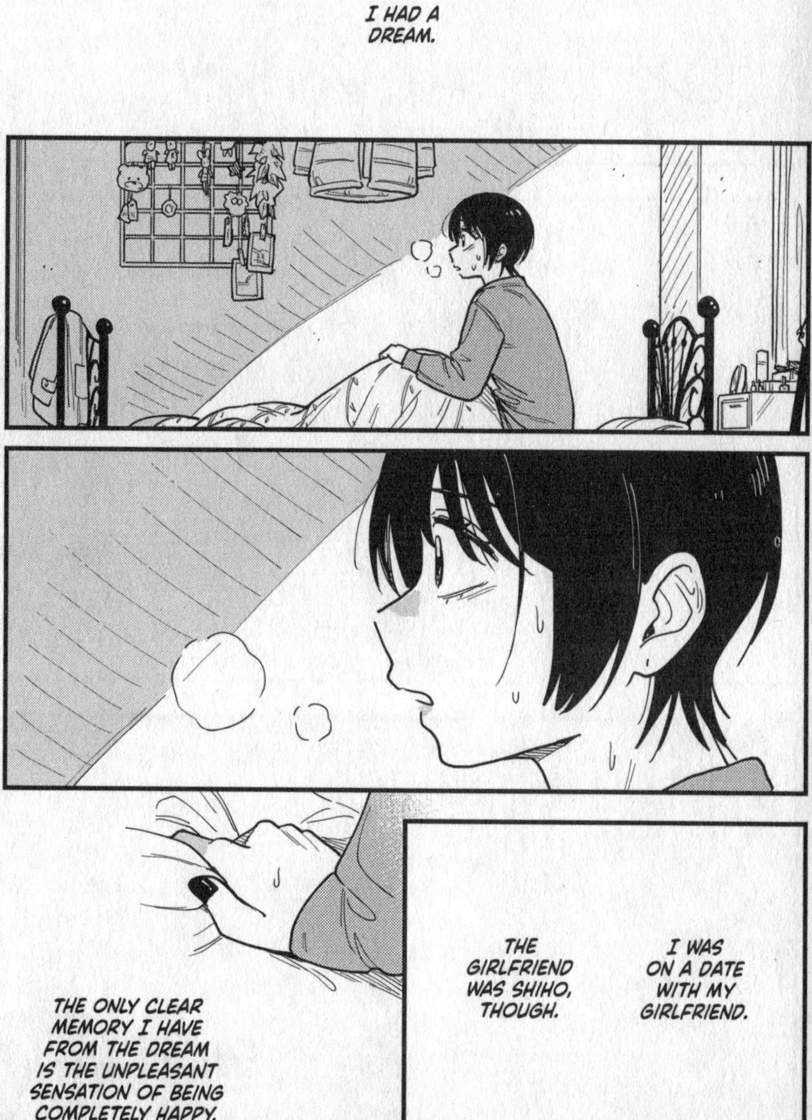
I HAD A DREAM.
I WAS ON A DATE WITH MY GIRLFRIEND.
THE GIRLFRIEND WAS SHIHO, THOUGH.
THE ONLY CLEAR MEMORY I HAVE FROM THE DREAM IS THE UNPLEASANT SENSATION OF BEING COMPLETELY HAPPY.

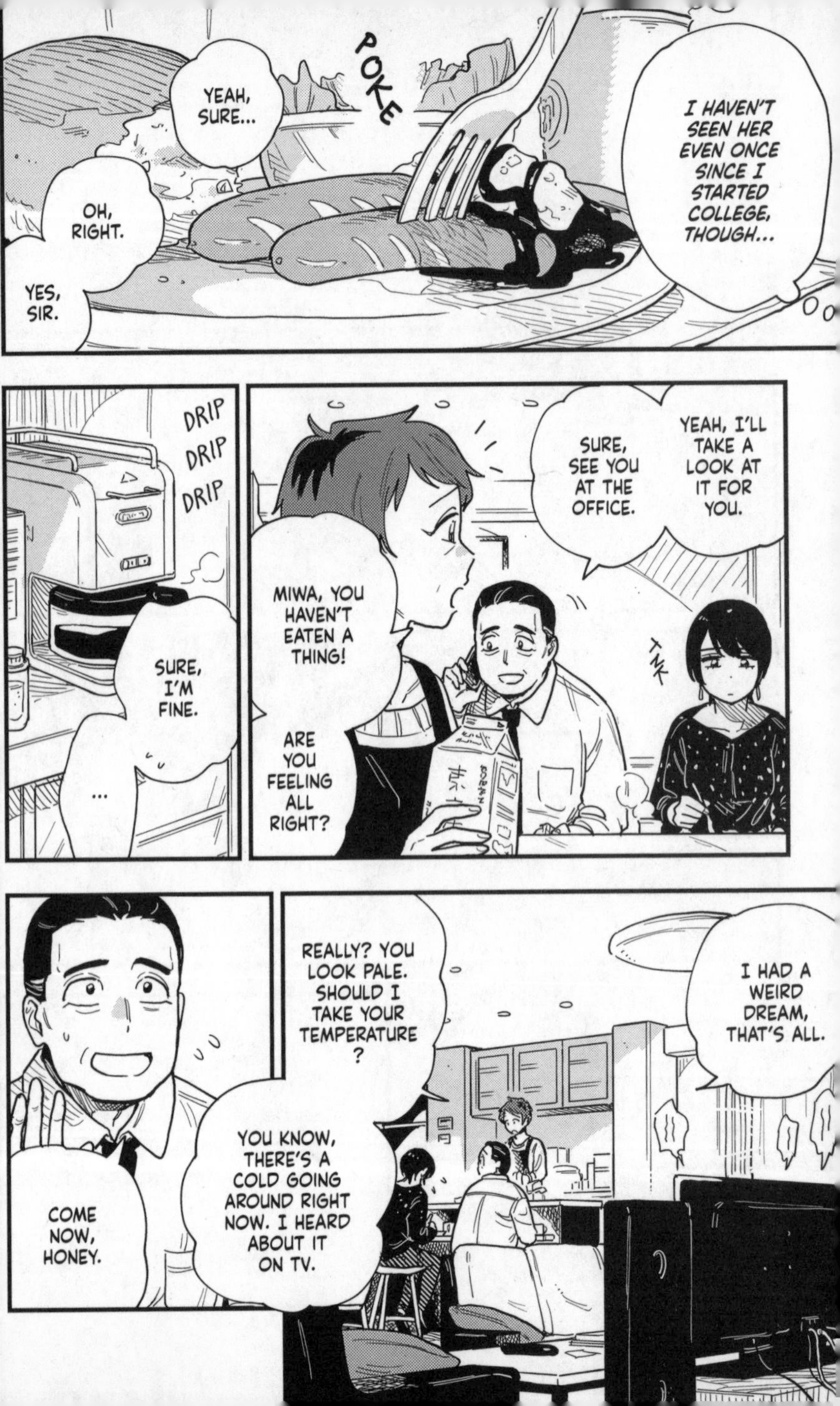
I HAVEN'T SEEN HER EVEN ONCE SINCE I STARTED COLLEGE, THOUGH...
POKE
YEAH, SURE...
OH, RIGHT.
YES, SIR.
YEAH, I'LL TAKE A LOOK AT IT FOR YOU.
SURE, SEE YOU AT THE OFFICE.
TNK
MIWA, YOU HAVEN'T EATEN A THING!
ARE YOU FEELING ALL RIGHT?
DRIP DRIP DRIP
SURE, I'M FINE.
...
I HAD A WEIRD DREAM, THAT'S ALL.
REALLY? YOU LOOK PALE. SHOULD I TAKE YOUR TEMPERATURE?
YOU KNOW, THERE'S A COLD GOING AROUND RIGHT NOW. I HEARD ABOUT IT ON TV.
COME NOW, HONEY.

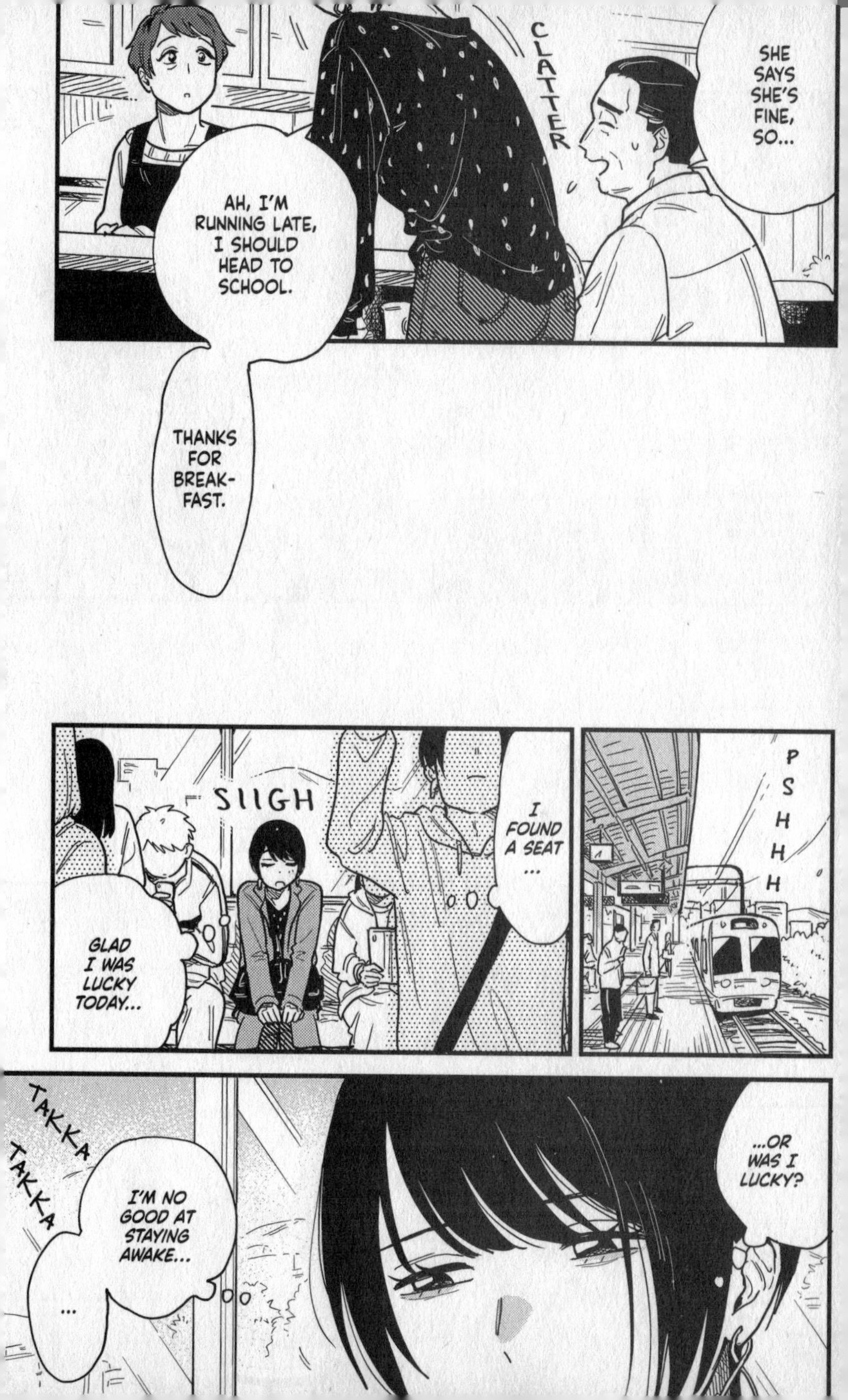
SHE SAYS SHE'S FINE, SO...
CLATTER
AH, I'M RUNNING LATE, I SHOULD HEAD TO SCHOOL.
THANKS FOR BREAK-FAST.
PSHHH
I FOUND A SEAT ...
SIIGH
GLAD I WAS LUCKY TODAY...
...OR WAS I LUCKY?
TAKKA TAKKA
I'M NO GOOD AT STAYING AWAKE...
...

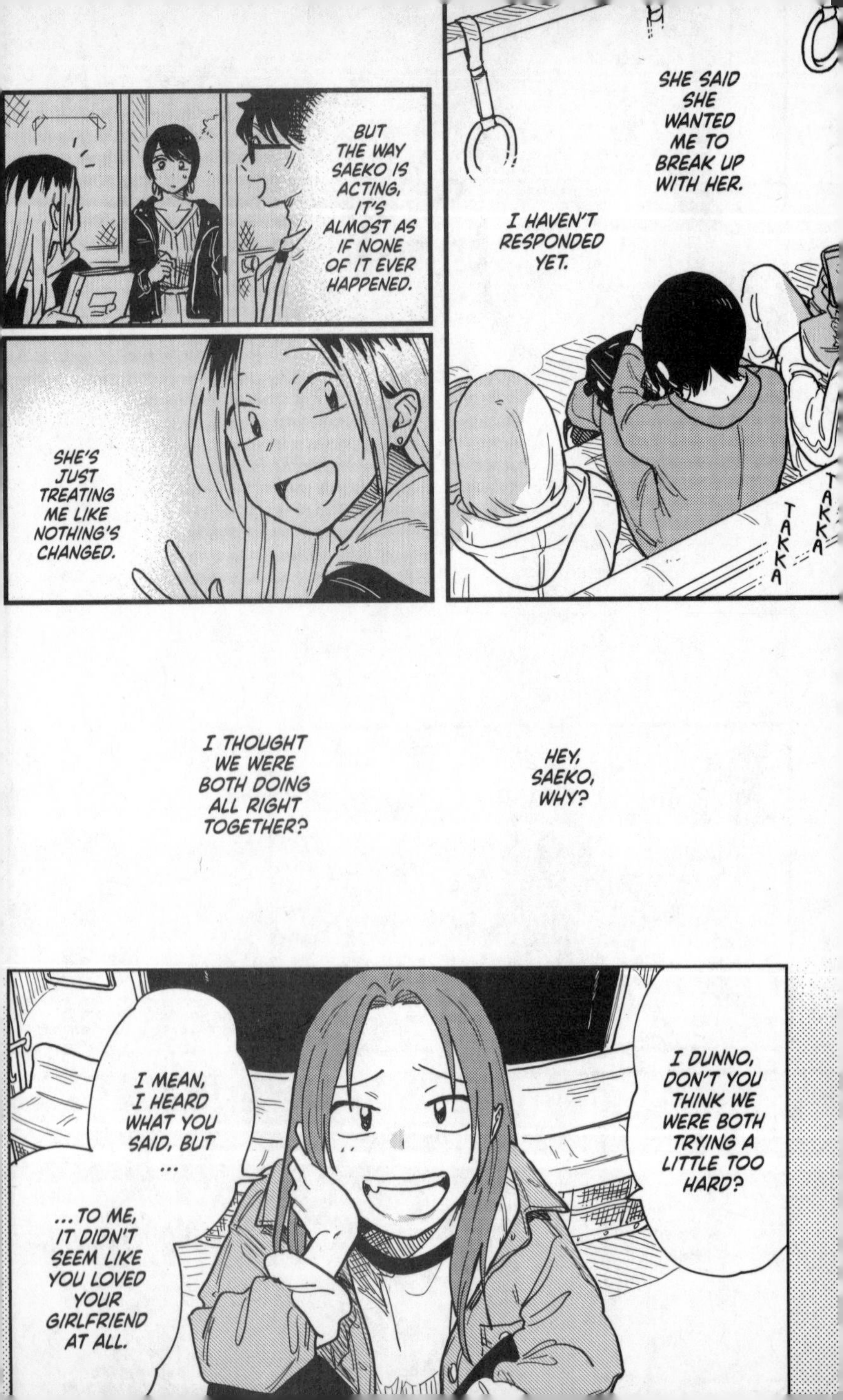
SHE SAID SHE WANTED ME TO BREAK UP WITH HER.
I HAVEN'T RESPONDED YET.
TAKKA
TAKKA
BUT THE WAY SAEKO IS ACTING, IT'S ALMOST AS IF NONE OF IT EVER HAPPENED.
SHE'S JUST TREATING ME LIKE NOTHING'S CHANGED.
HEY, SAEKO, WHY?
I THOUGHT WE WERE BOTH DOING ALL RIGHT TOGETHER?
I DUNNO, DON'T YOU THINK WE WERE BOTH TRYING A LITTLE TOO HARD?
I MEAN, I HEARD WHAT YOU SAID, BUT...
...TO ME, IT DIDN'T SEEM LIKE YOU LOVED YOUR GIRLFRIEND AT ALL.

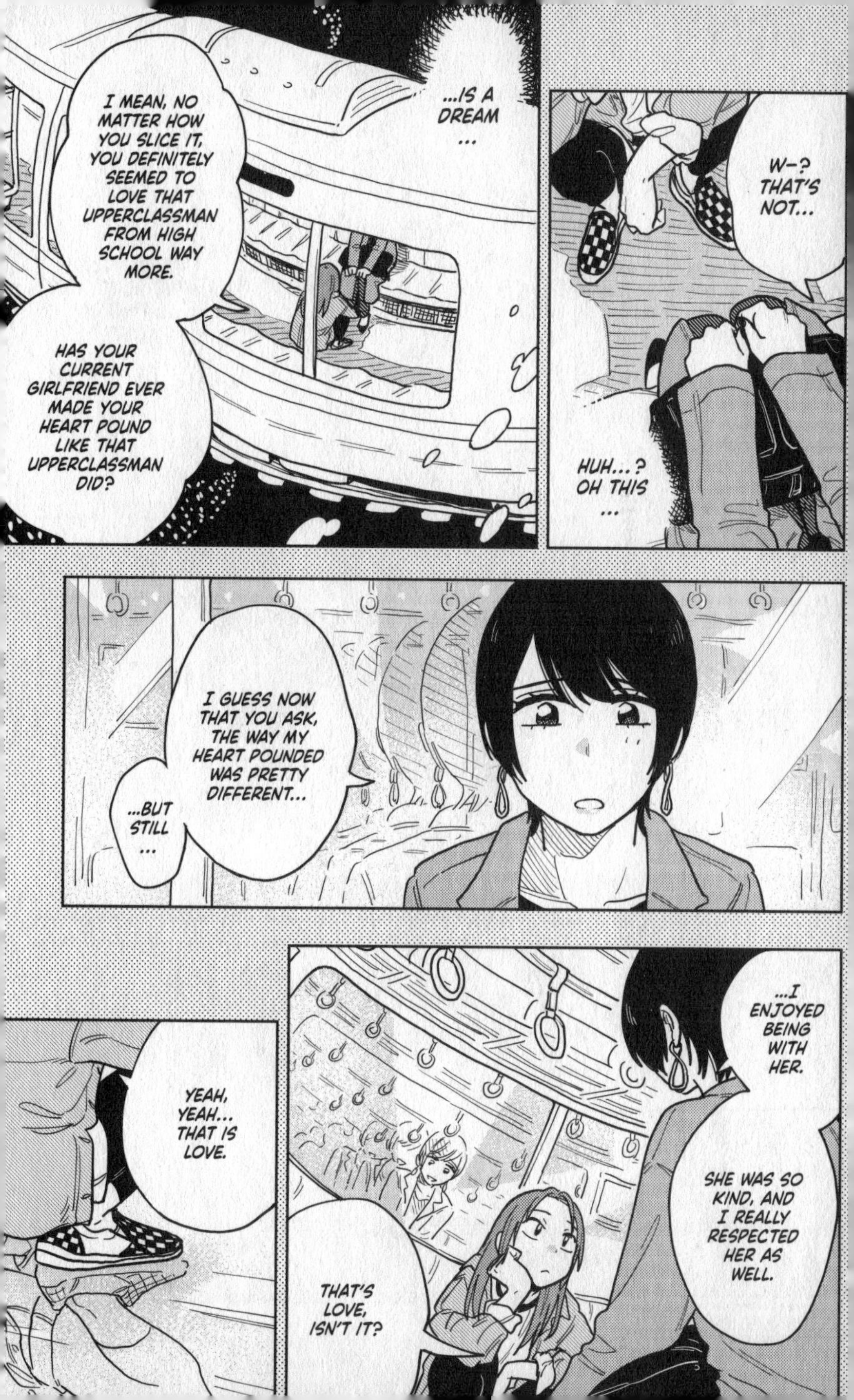
W-? THAT'S NOT...
HUH...? OH THIS ...
...IS A DREAM ...
I MEAN, NO MATTER HOW YOU SLICE IT, YOU DEFINITELY SEEMED TO LOVE THAT UPPERCLASSMAN FROM HIGH SCHOOL WAY MORE.
HAS YOUR CURRENT GIRLFRIEND EVER MADE YOUR HEART POUND LIKE THAT UPPERCLASSMAN DID?
I GUESS NOW THAT YOU ASK, THE WAY MY HEART POUNDED WAS PRETTY DIFFERENT...
...BUT STILL ...
...I ENJOYED BEING WITH HER.
SHE WAS SO KIND, AND I REALLY RESPECTED HER AS WELL.
THAT'S LOVE, ISN'T IT?
YEAH, YEAH... THAT IS LOVE.

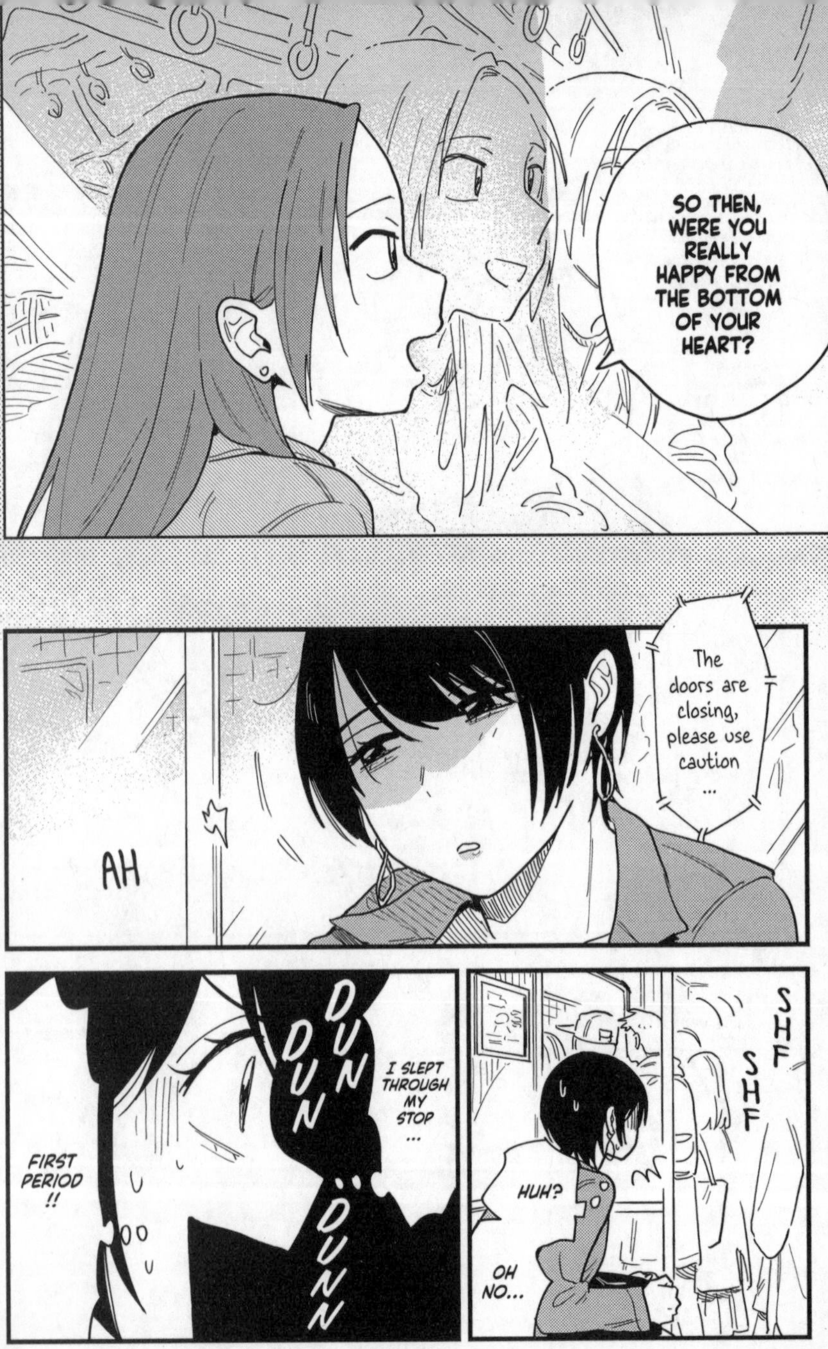
SO THEN, WERE YOU REALLY HAPPY FROM THE BOTTOM OF YOUR HEART?
The doors are closing, please use caution ...
AH
SHF
SHF
...
HUH?
OH NO...
I SLEPT THROUGH MY STOP ...
DUN
DUN
DUNN
FIRST PERIOD !!

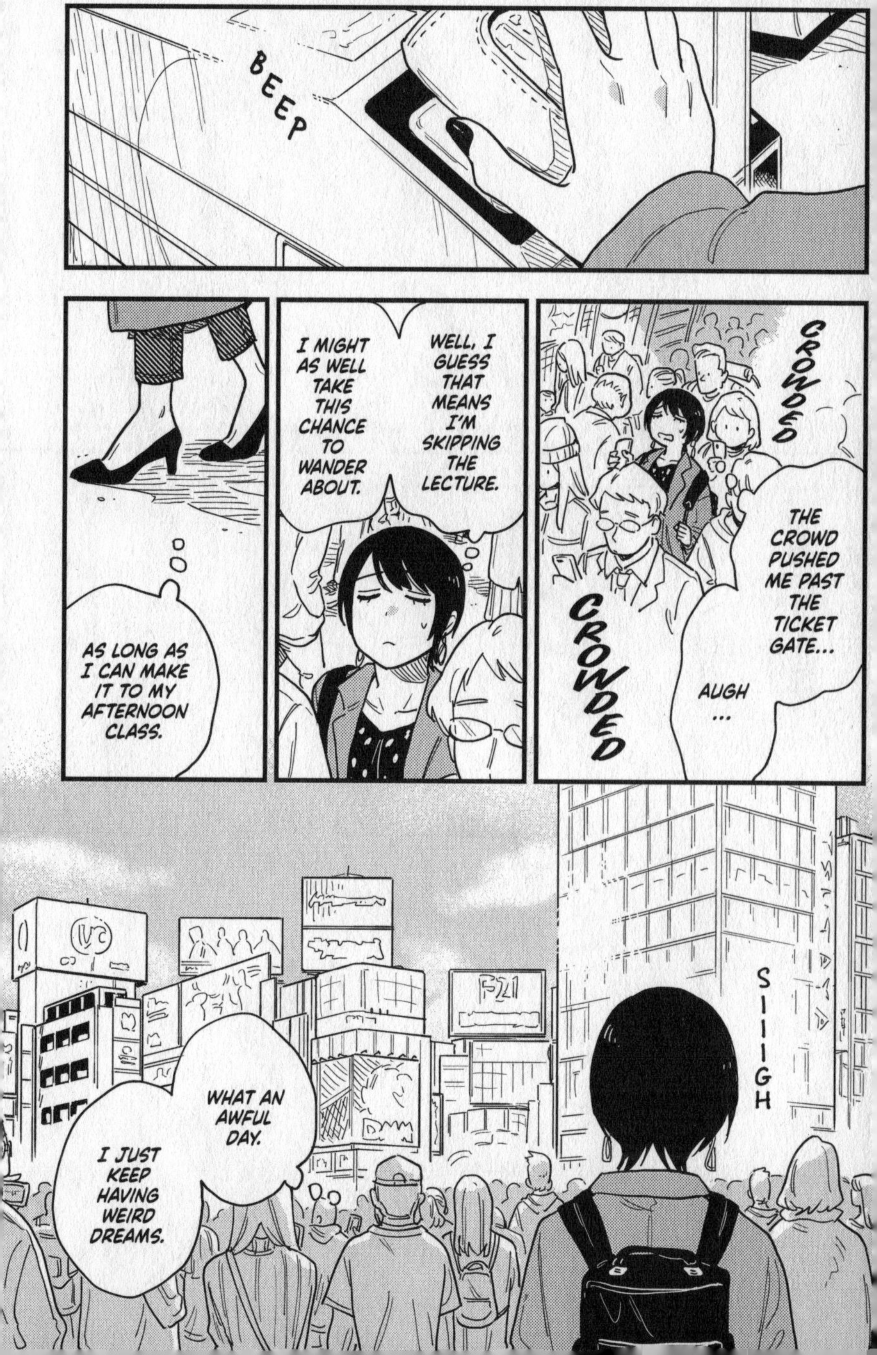
BEEP
CROWDED
THE CROWD PUSHED ME PAST THE TICKET GATE...
CROWDED
AUGH...
WELL, I GUESS THAT MEANS I'M SKIPPING THE LECTURE.
I MIGHT AS WELL TAKE THIS CHANCE TO WANDER ABOUT.
AS LONG AS I CAN MAKE IT TO MY AFTERNOON CLASS.
SIIIGH
WHAT AN AWFUL DAY.
I JUST KEEP HAVING WEIRD DREAMS.

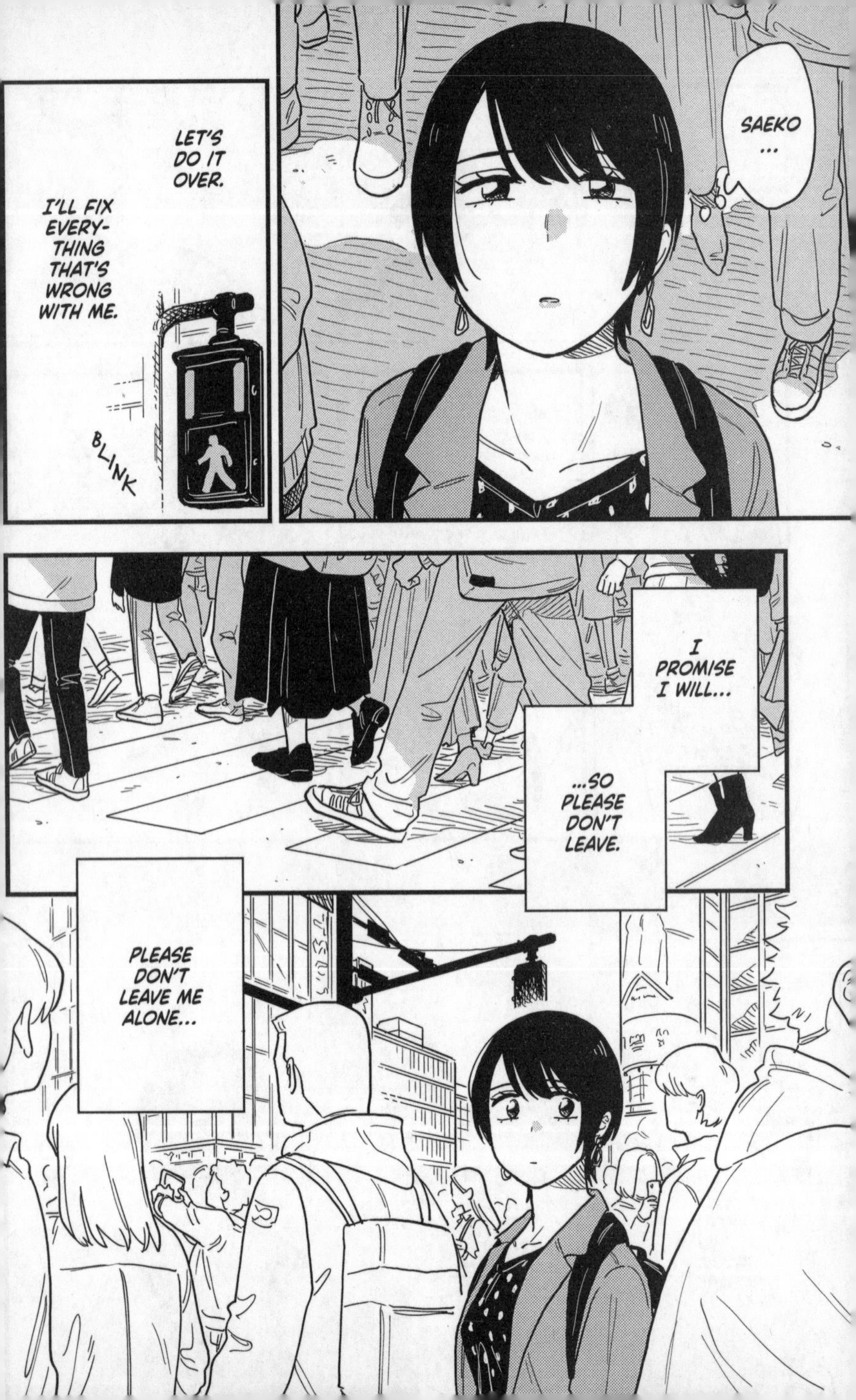
SAEKO ...
LET'S DO IT OVER.
I'LL FIX EVERYTHING THAT'S WRONG WITH ME.
BLINK
I PROMISE I WILL...
...SO PLEASE DON'T LEAVE.
PLEASE DON'T LEAVE ME ALONE...

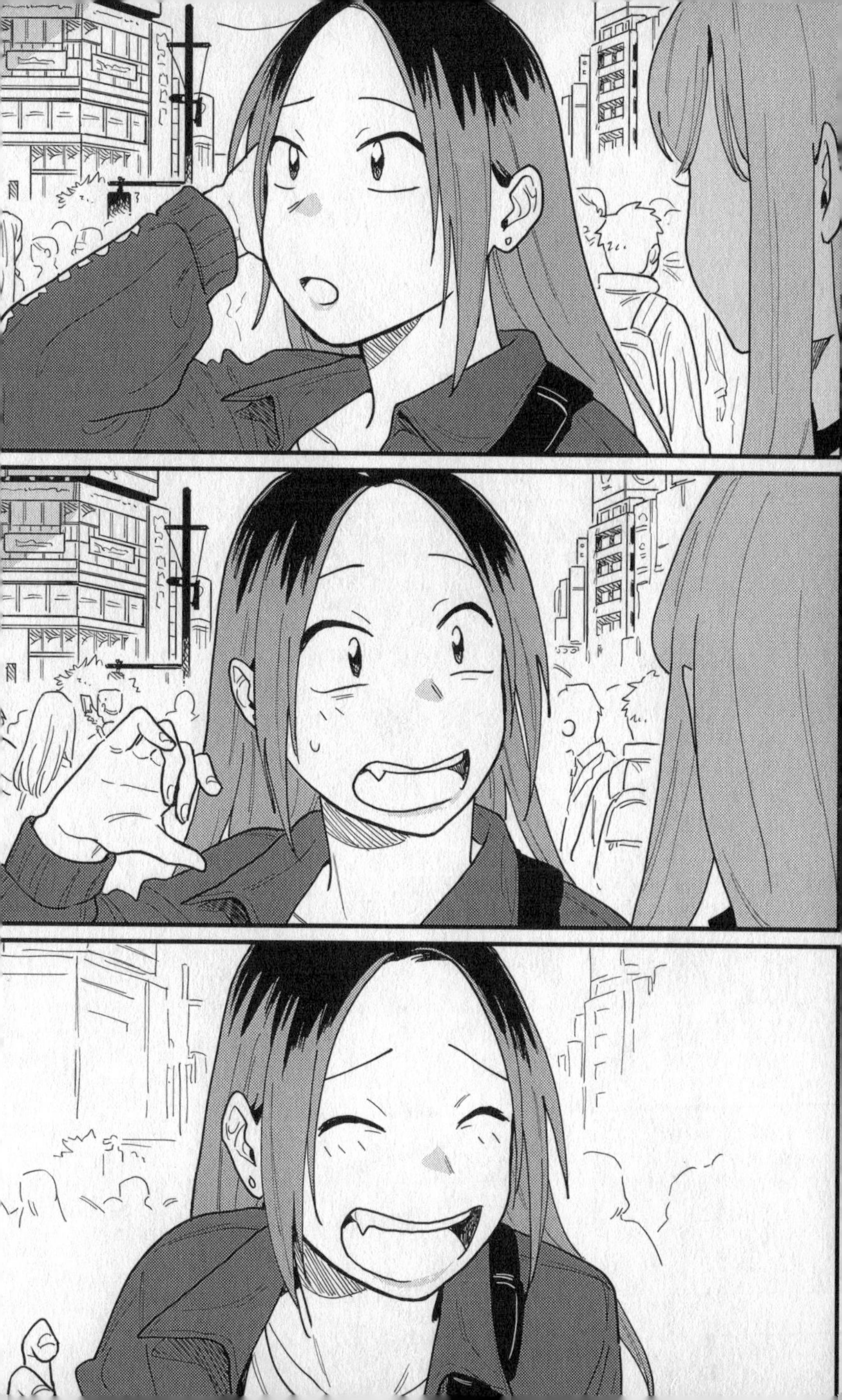

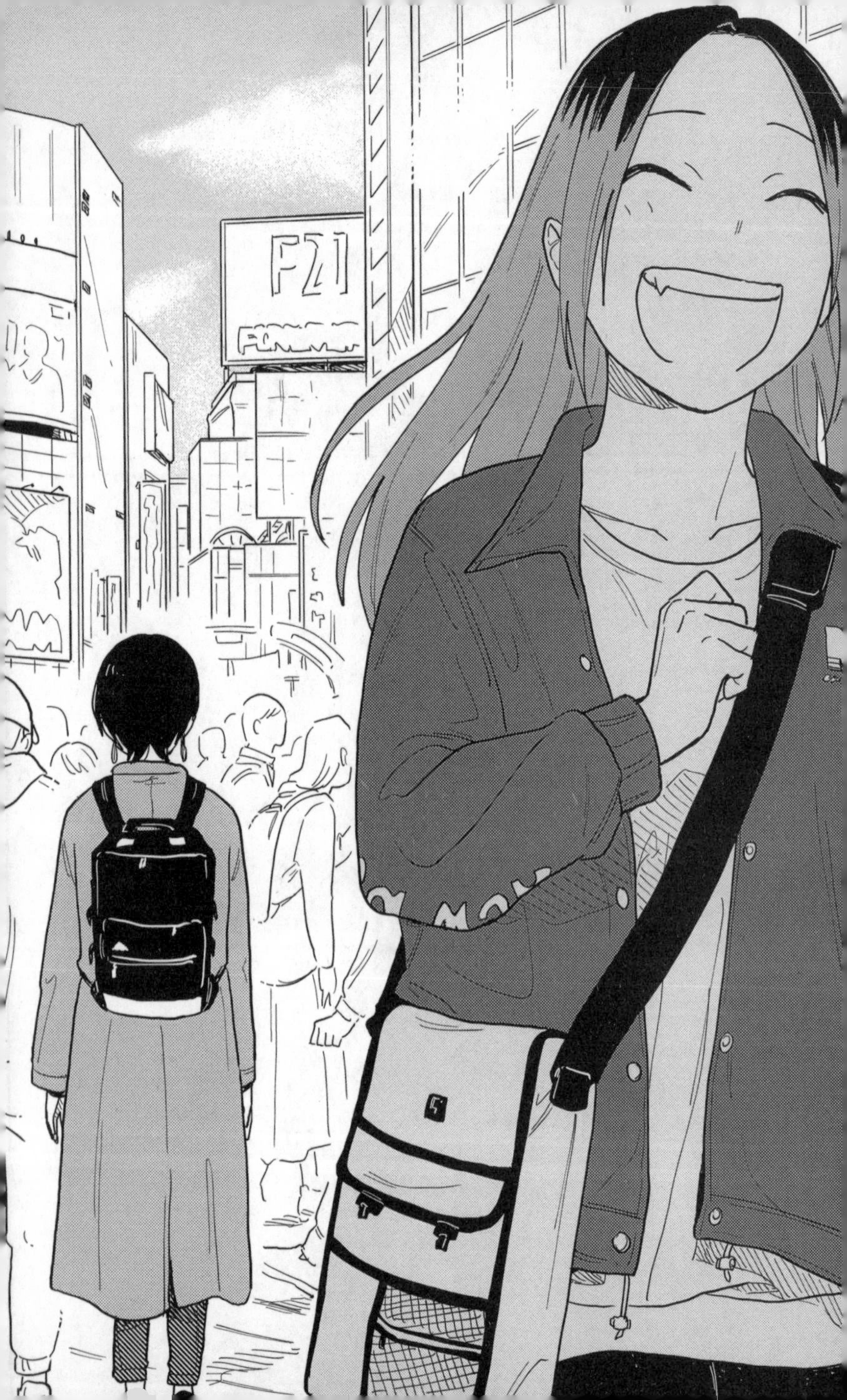
F21

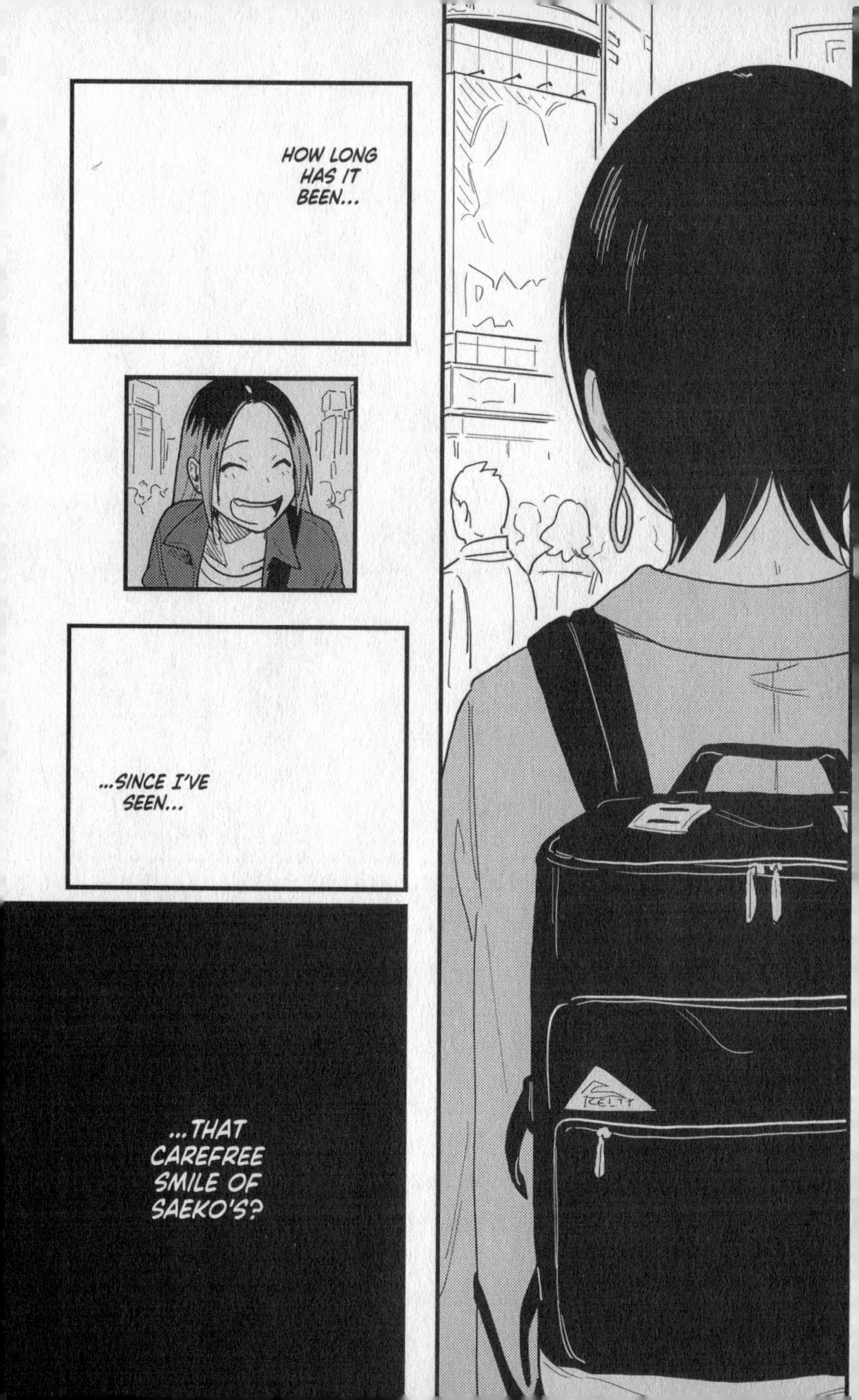
HOW LONG HAS IT BEEN...
...SINCE I'VE SEEN...
...THAT CAREFREE SMILE OF SAEKO'S?

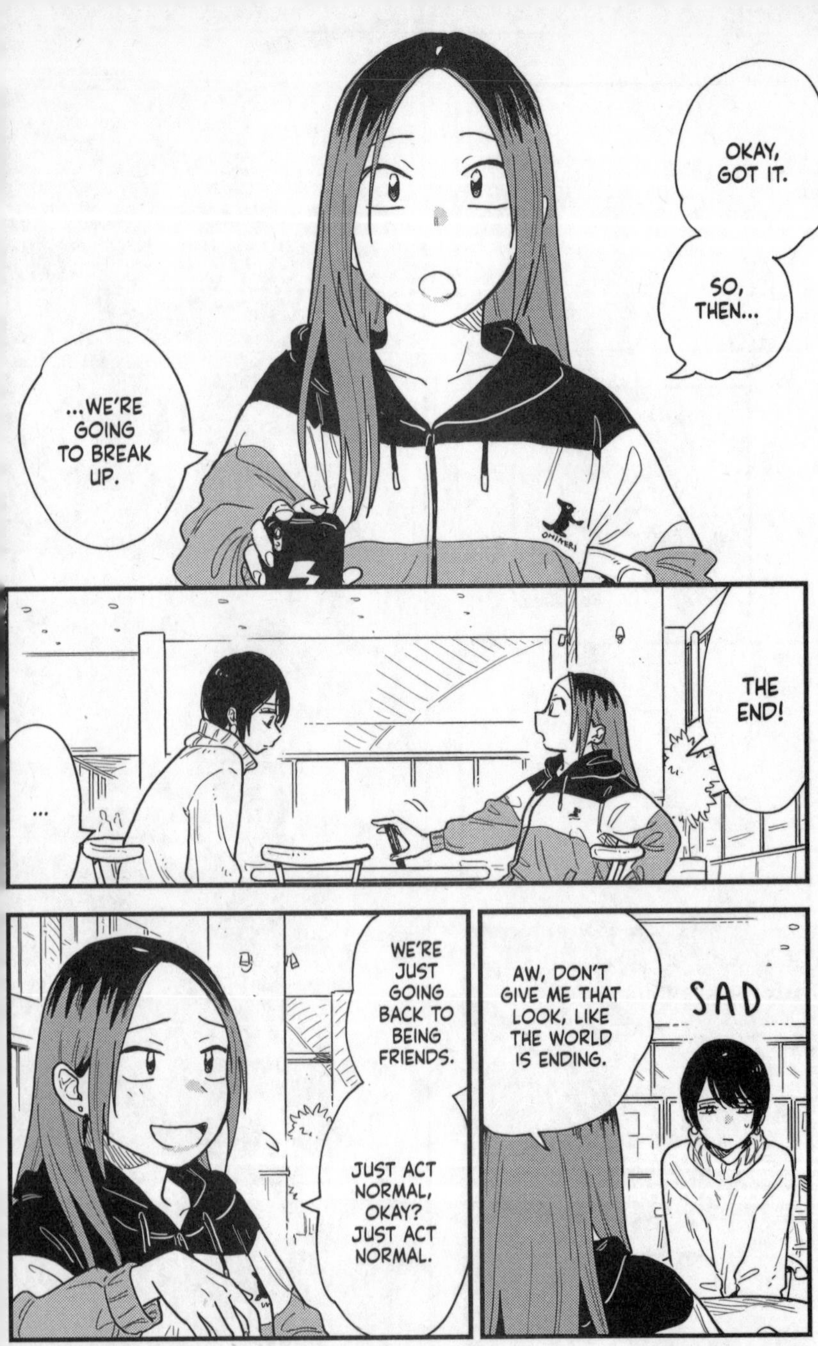
OKAY, GOT IT.
SO, THEN...
...WE'RE GOING TO BREAK UP.
THE END!
...
AW, DON'T GIVE ME THAT LOOK, LIKE THE WORLD IS ENDING.
SAD
WE'RE JUST GOING BACK TO BEING FRIENDS.
JUST ACT NORMAL, OKAY? JUST ACT NORMAL.

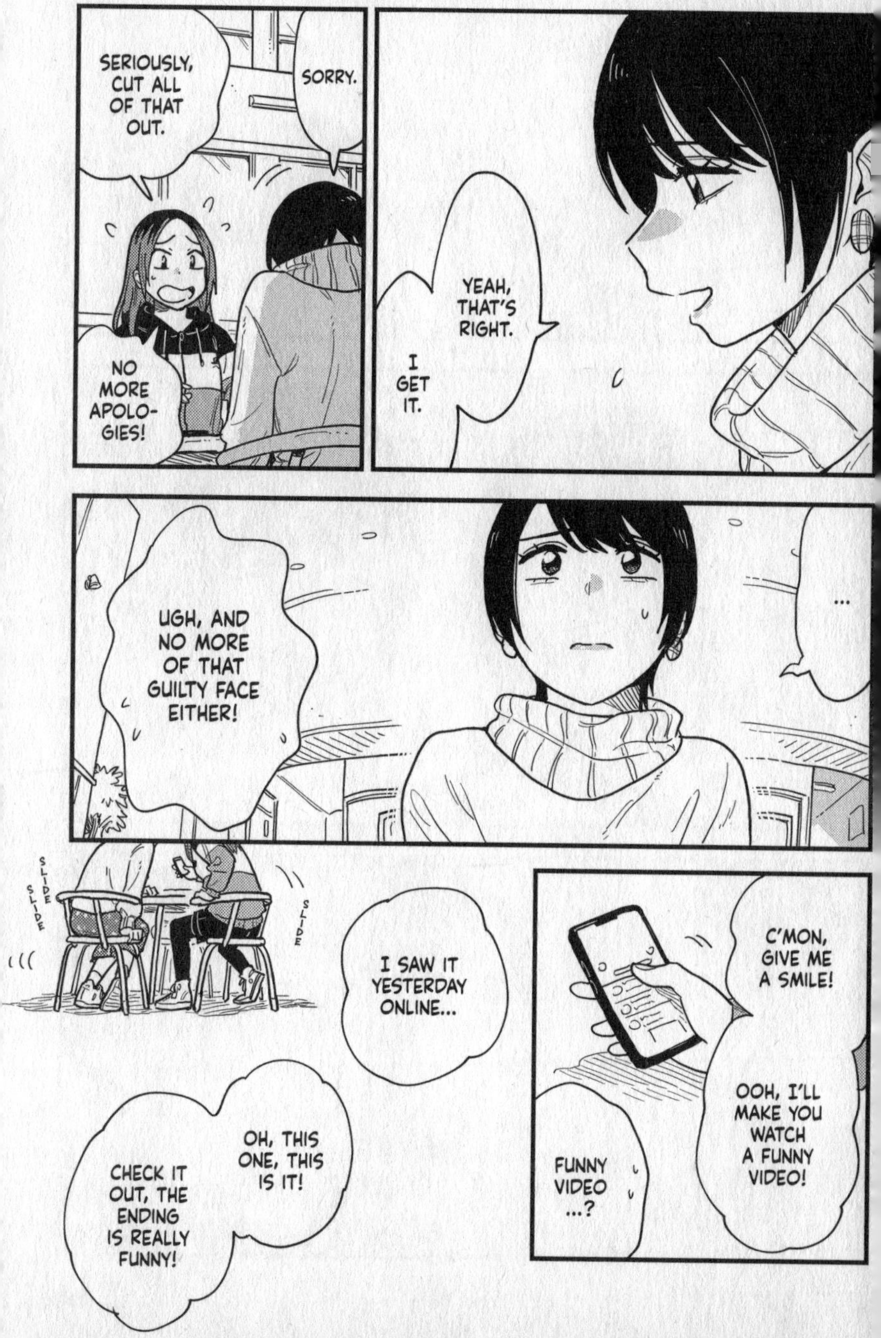
YEAH, THAT'S RIGHT.
I GET IT.
SERIOUSLY, CUT ALL OF THAT OUT.
SORRY.
NO MORE APOLOGIES!
...
UGH, AND NO MORE OF THAT GUILTY FACE EITHER!
C'MON, GIVE ME A SMILE!
OOH, I'LL MAKE YOU WATCH A FUNNY VIDEO!
FUNNY VIDEO ...?
SLIDE
SLIDE SLIDE
I SAW IT YESTERDAY ONLINE...
OH, THIS ONE, THIS IS IT!
CHECK IT OUT, THE ENDING IS REALLY FUNNY!

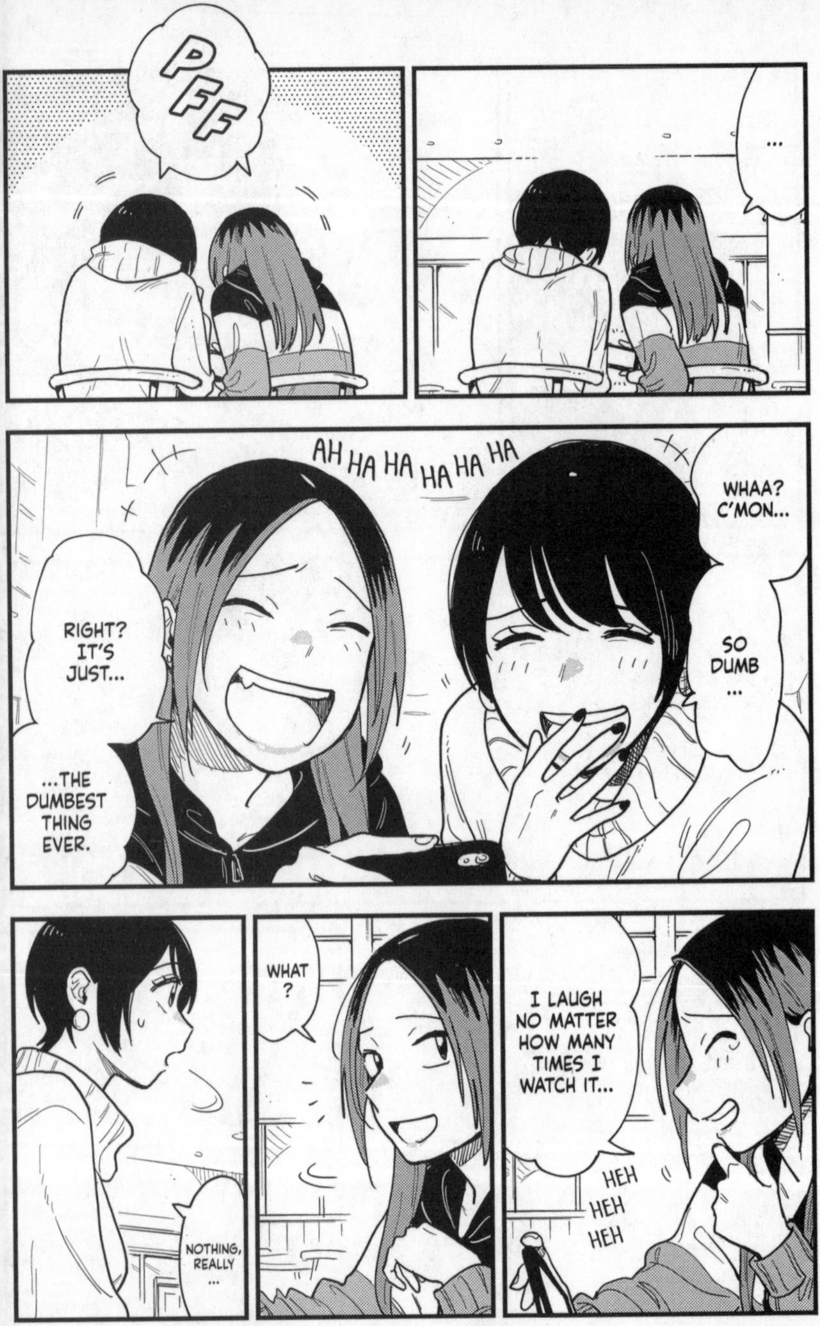
...
PFF
WHAA? C'MON...
AH HA HA HA HA HA
SO DUMB ...
RIGHT? IT'S JUST...
...THE DUMBEST THING EVER.
I LAUGH NO MATTER HOW MANY TIMES I WATCH IT...
HEH HEH HEH
WHAT ?
NOTHING, REALLY ...

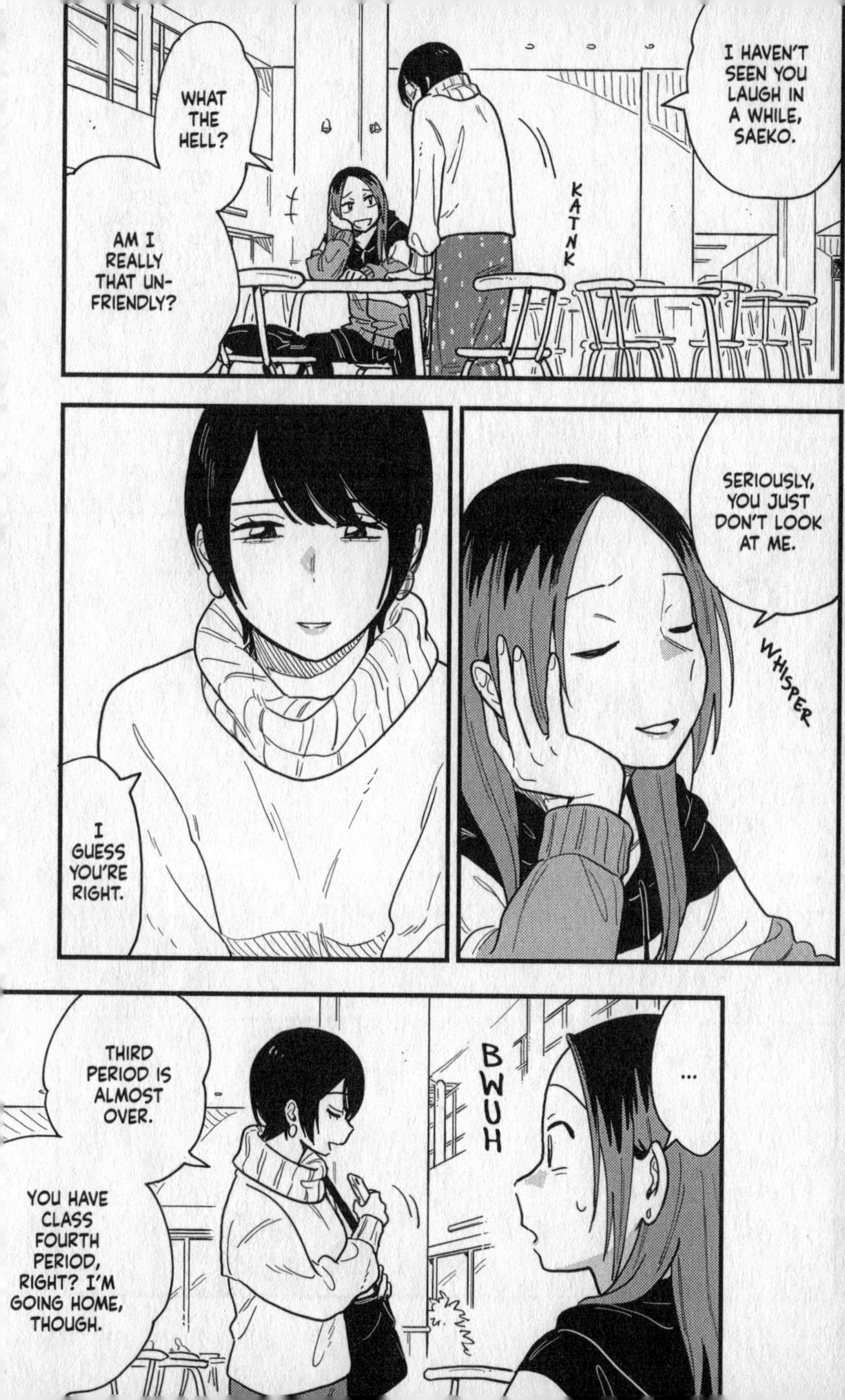
I HAVEN'T SEEN YOU LAUGH IN A WHILE, SAEKO.
KATNK
WHAT THE HELL?
AM I REALLY THAT UN-FRIENDLY?
SERIOUSLY, YOU JUST DON'T LOOK AT ME.
WHISPER
I GUESS YOU'RE RIGHT.
...
BWUH
THIRD PERIOD IS ALMOST OVER.
YOU HAVE CLASS FOURTH PERIOD, RIGHT? I'M GOING HOME, THOUGH.

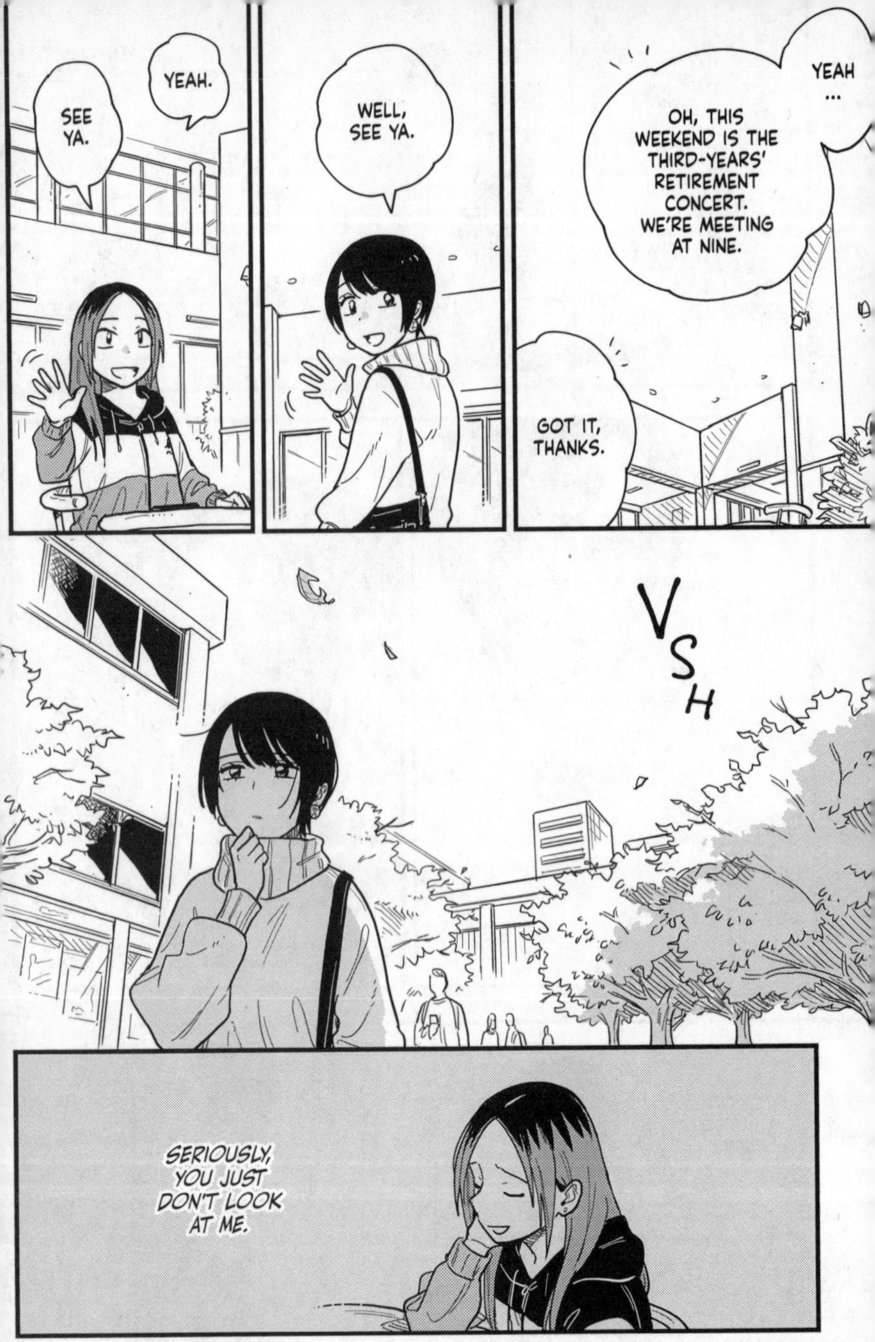
YEAH ...
OH, THIS WEEKEND IS THE THIRD-YEARS' RETIREMENT CONCERT. WE'RE MEETING AT NINE.
GOT IT, THANKS.
WELL, SEE YA.
YEAH.
SEE YA.
VSH
SERIOUSLY, YOU JUST DON'T LOOK AT ME.

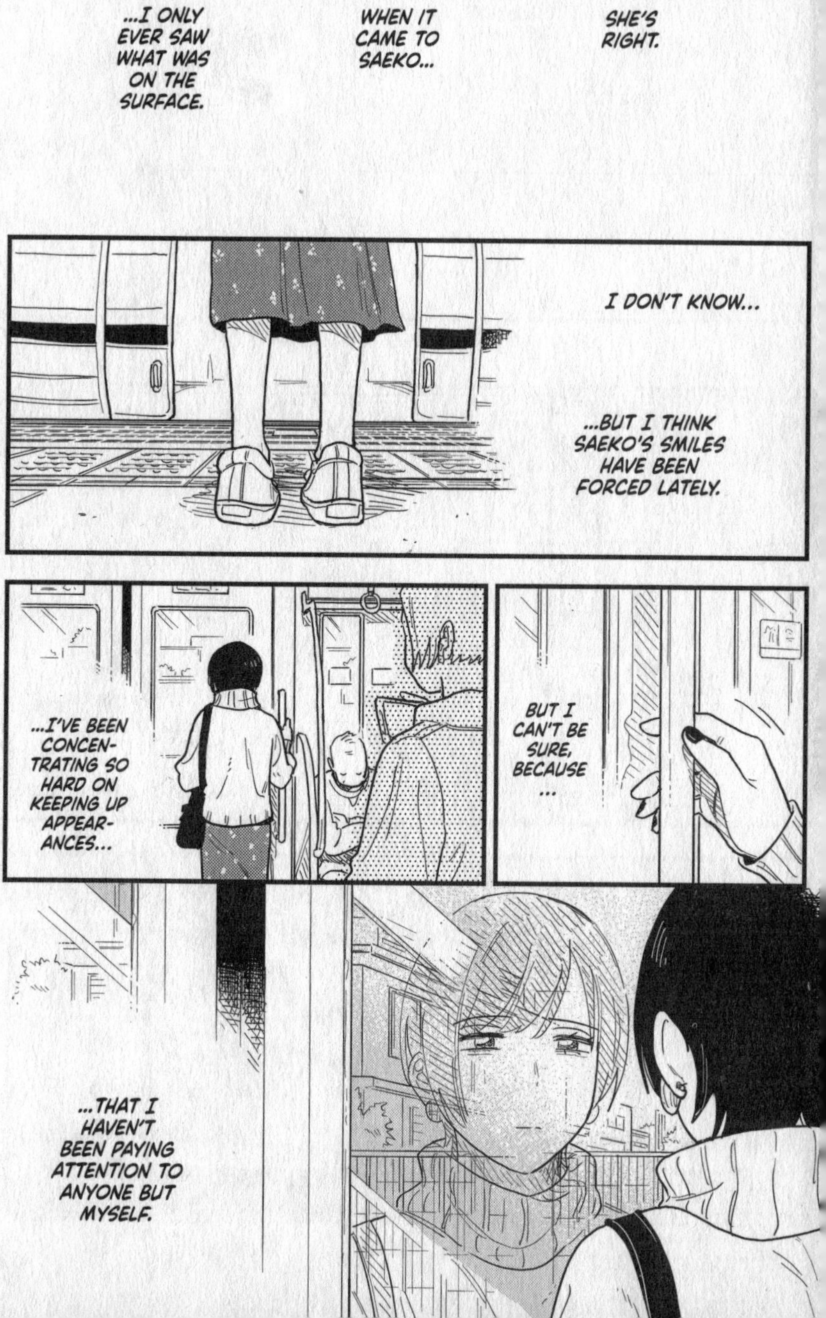
SHE'S RIGHT.
WHEN IT CAME TO SAEKO...
...I ONLY EVER SAW WHAT WAS ON THE SURFACE.
I DON'T KNOW...
...BUT I THINK SAEKO'S SMILES HAVE BEEN FORCED LATELY.
BUT I CAN'T BE SURE, BECAUSE ...
...I'VE BEEN CONCENTRATING SO HARD ON KEEPING UP APPEARANCES...
...THAT I HAVEN'T BEEN PAYING ATTENTION TO ANYONE BUT MYSELF.

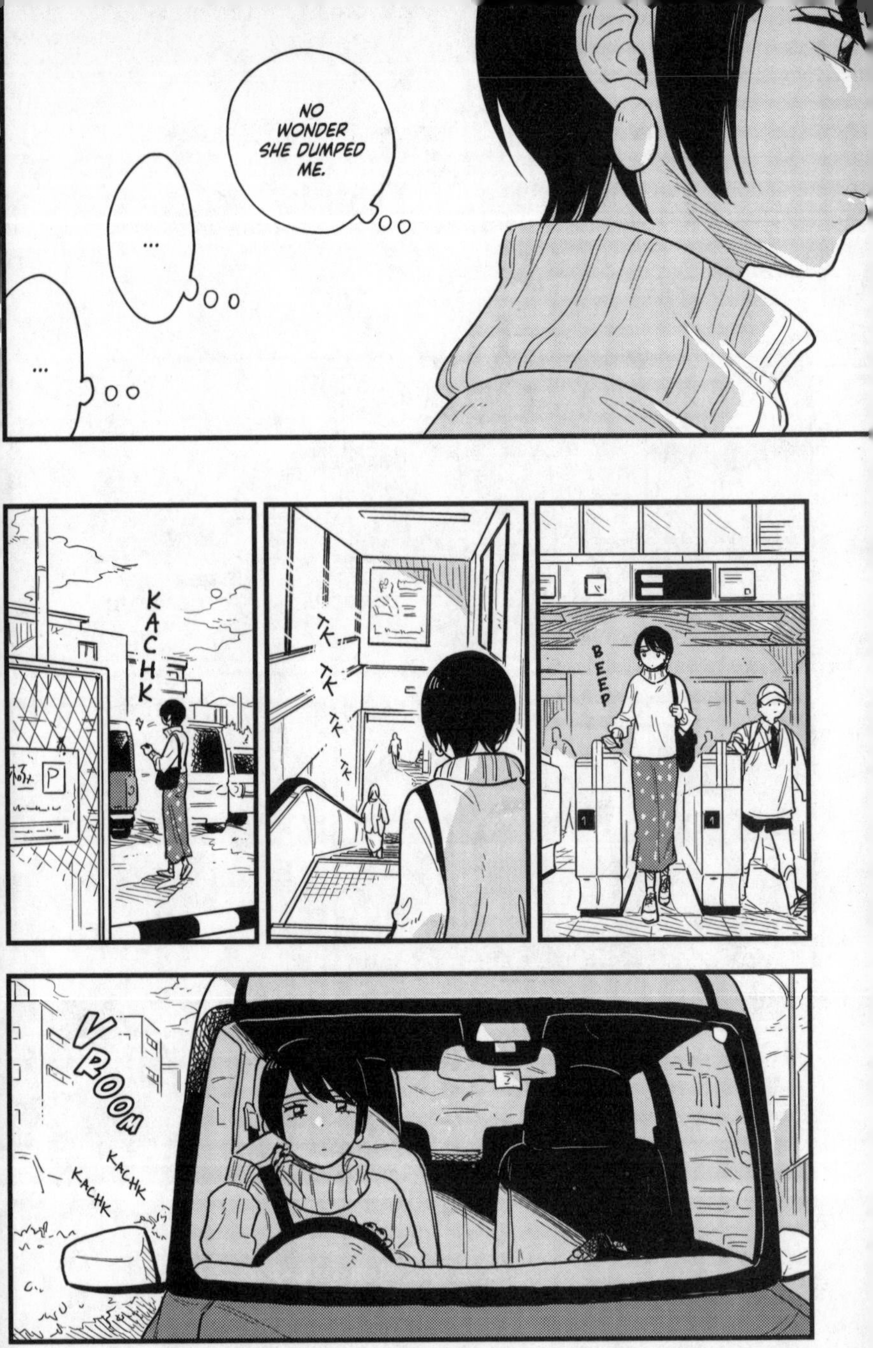
NO WONDER SHE DUMPED ME.
...
...
BEEP
TK TK TK TK
KACHK
VROOM
KACHK KACHK

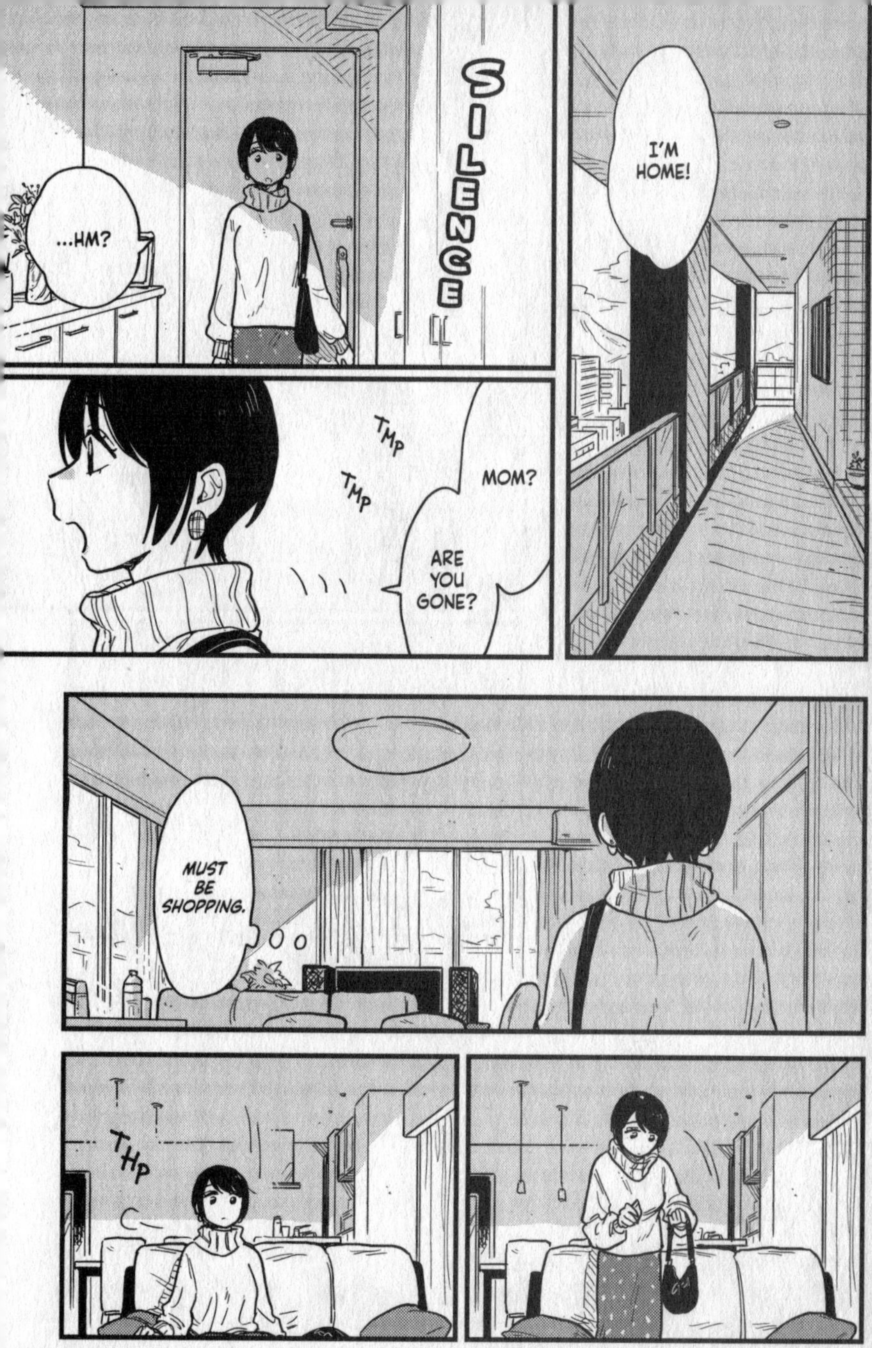
I'M HOME!
SILENCE
...HM?
MOM?
ARE YOU GONE?
TMP
TMP
MUST BE SHOPPING.
THP

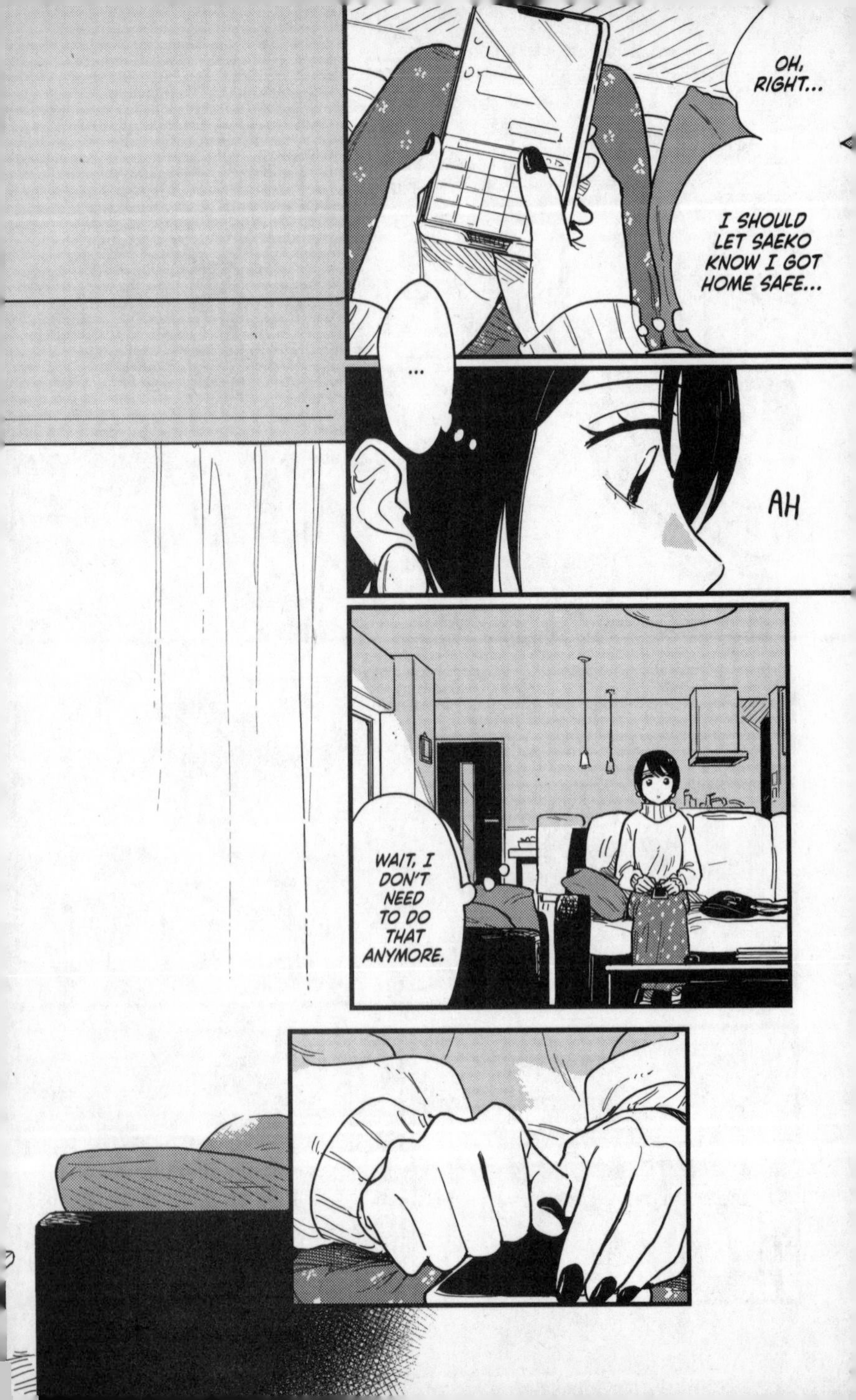
OH, RIGHT...
I SHOULD LET SAEKO KNOW I GOT HOME SAFE...
AH
...
WAIT, I DON'T NEED TO DO THAT ANYMORE.

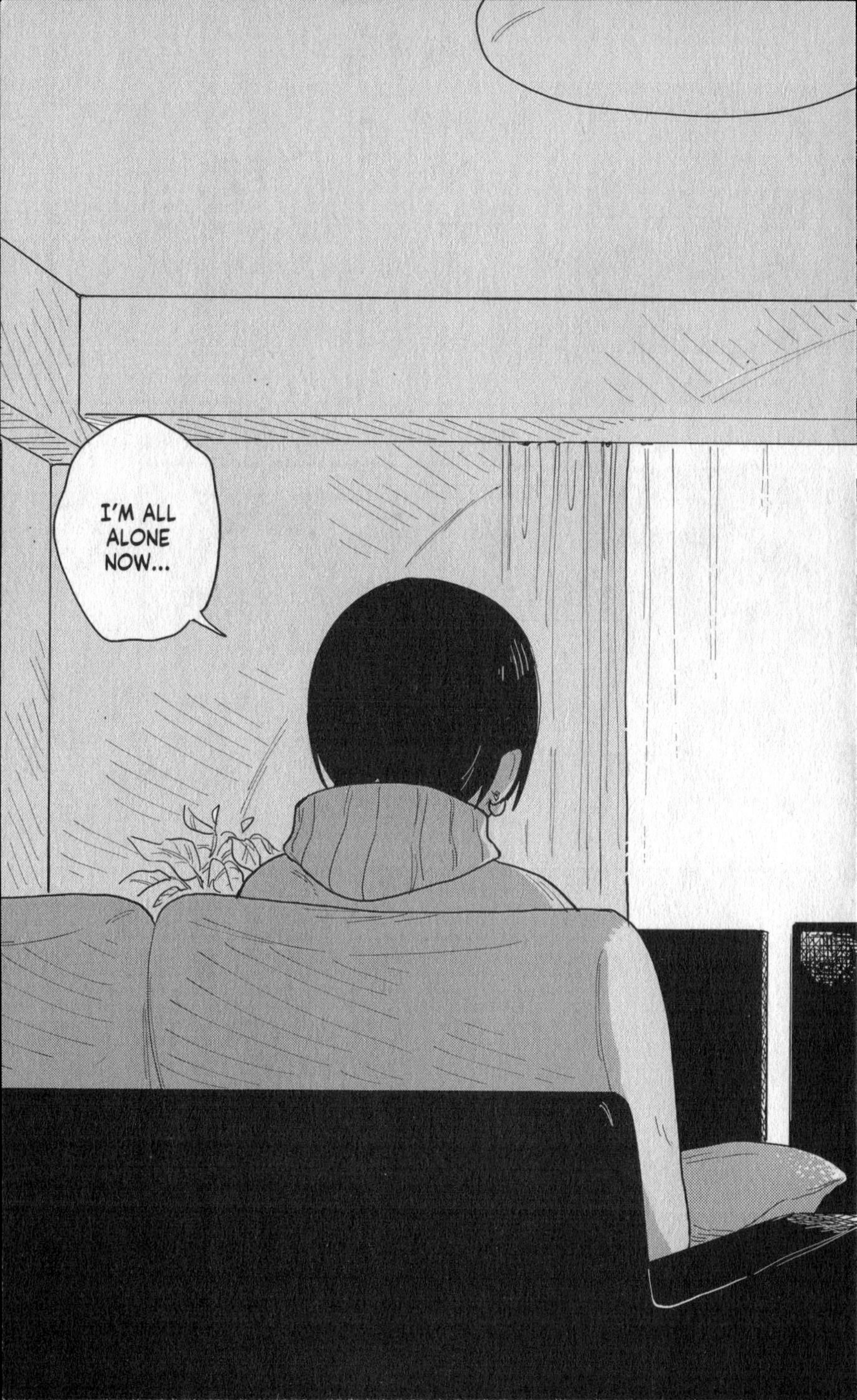
I'M ALL ALONE NOW...

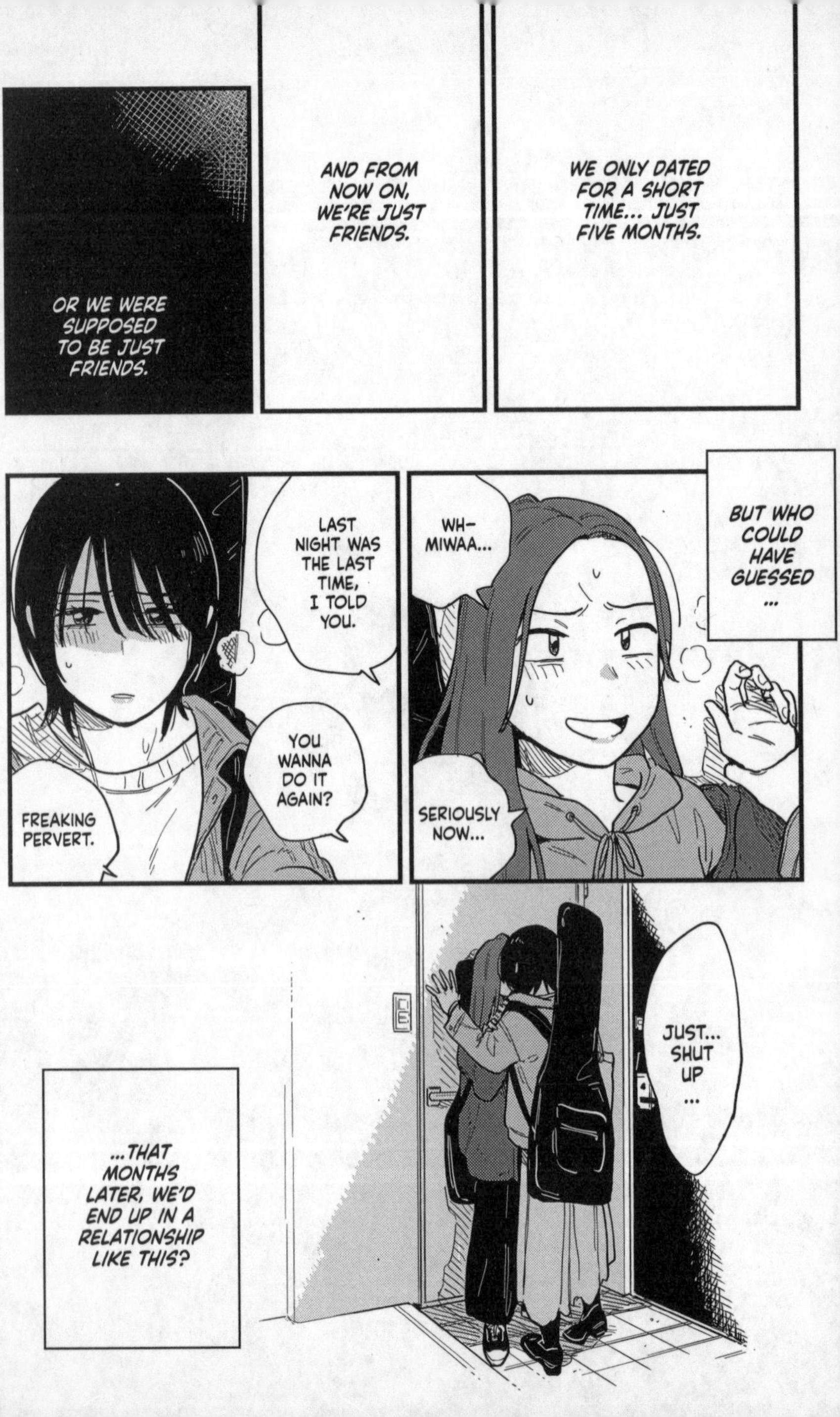
WE ONLY DATED FOR A SHORT TIME... JUST FIVE MONTHS.
AND FROM NOW ON, WE'RE JUST FRIENDS.
OR WE WERE SUPPOSED TO BE JUST FRIENDS.
BUT WHO COULD HAVE GUESSED ...
WH- MIWAA...
SERIOUSLY NOW...
LAST NIGHT WAS THE LAST TIME, I TOLD YOU.
YOU WANNA DO IT AGAIN?
FREAKING PERVERT.
JUST... SHUT UP ...
...THAT MONTHS LATER, WE'D END UP IN A RELATIONSHIP LIKE THIS?

HOW DO WE RELATIONSHIP?

HOW DO WE RELATIONSHIP?

Chapter 36: Time Wouldn't Stop

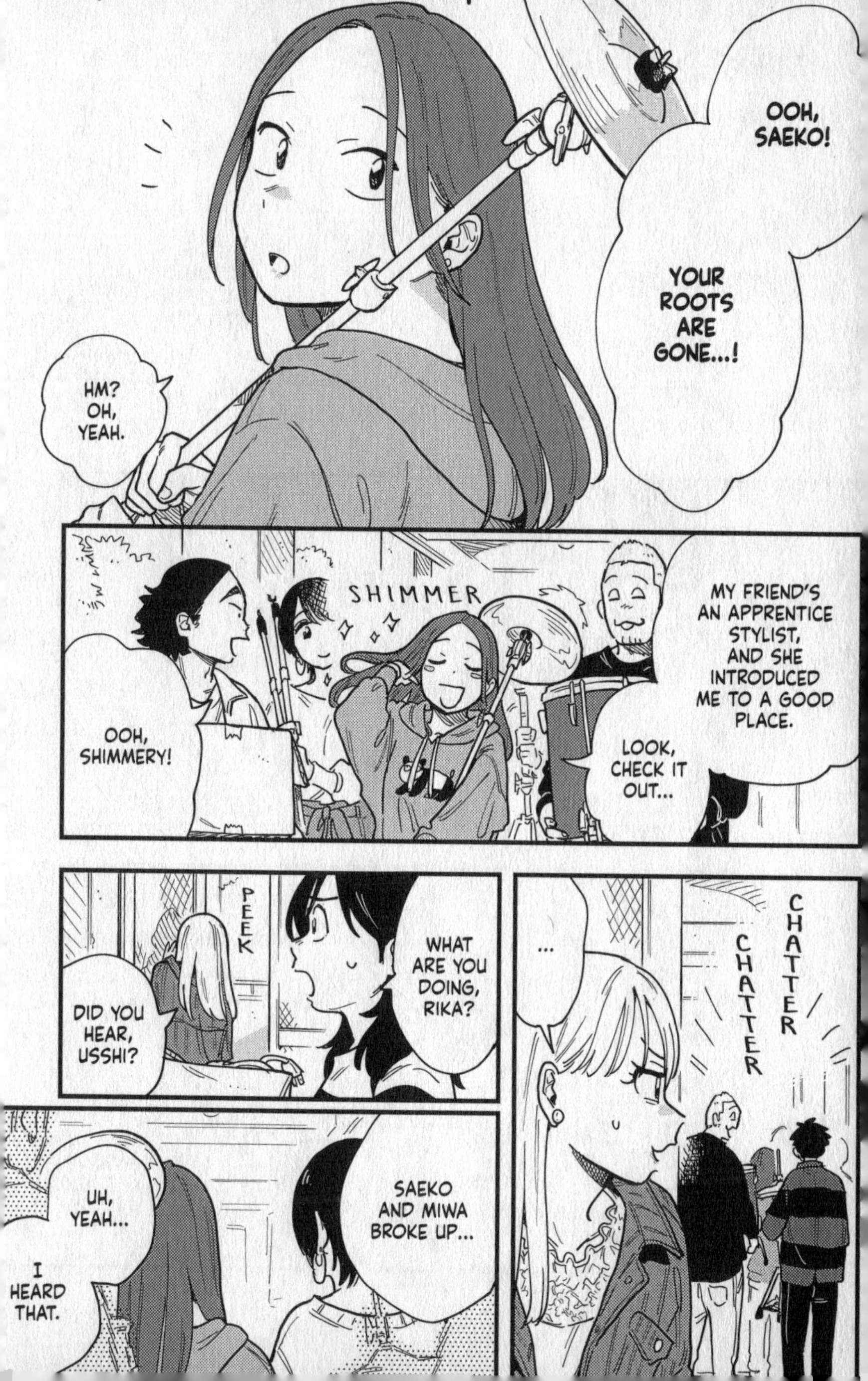
OOH, SAEKO!
YOUR ROOTS ARE GONE...!
HM? OH, YEAH.
MY FRIEND'S AN APPRENTICE STYLIST, AND SHE INTRODUCED ME TO A GOOD PLACE.
LOOK, CHECK IT OUT...
SHIMMER
OOH, SHIMMERY!
CHATTER
CHATTER
...
PEEK
WHAT ARE YOU DOING, RIKA?
DID YOU HEAR, USSHI?
SAEKO AND MIWA BROKE UP...
UH, YEAH...
I HEARD THAT.

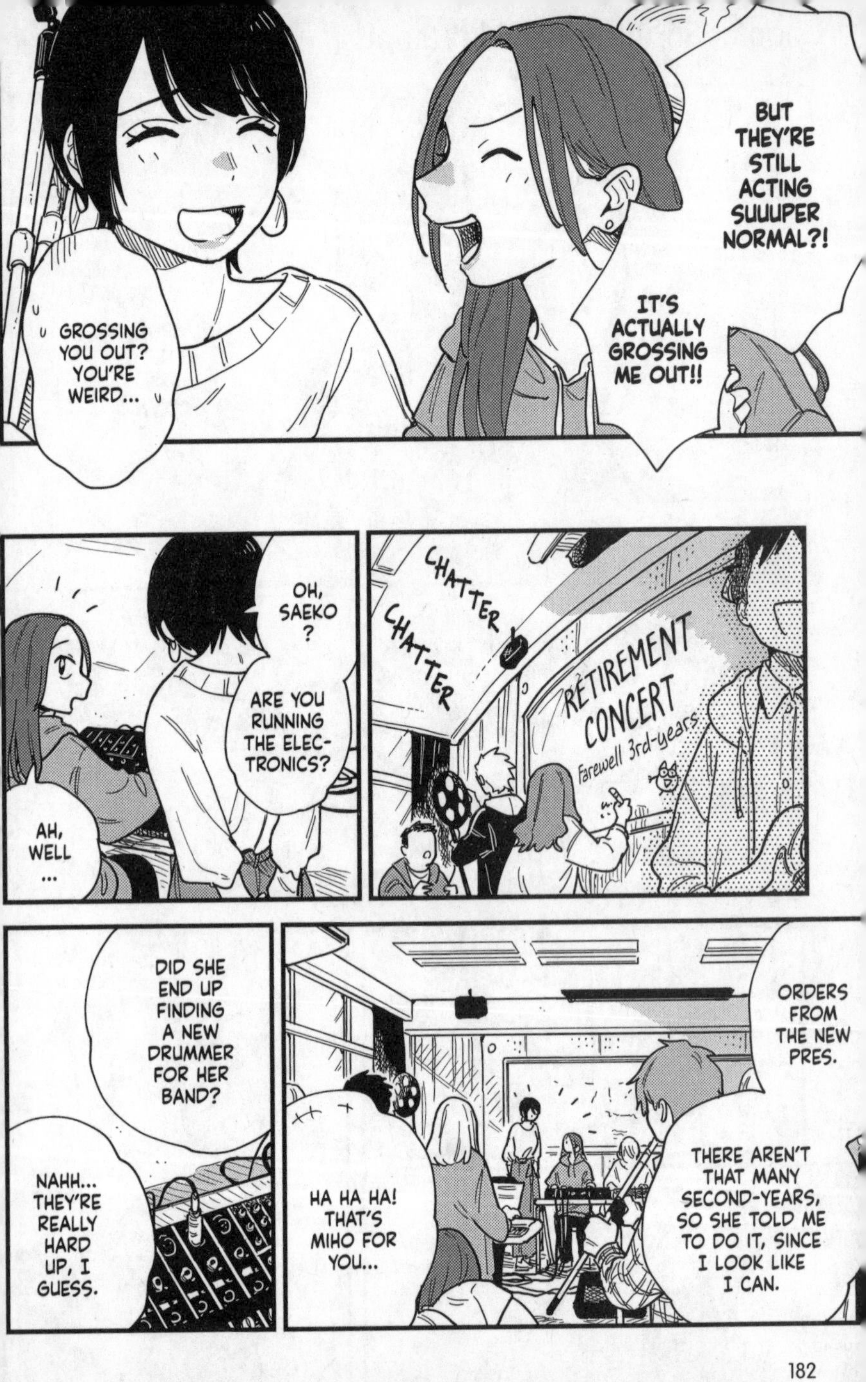
BUT THEY'RE STILL ACTING SUUUPER NORMAL?!
IT'S ACTUALLY GROSSING ME OUT!!
GROSSING YOU OUT? YOU'RE WEIRD...
CHATTER
CHATTER
RETIREMENT CONCERT
Farewell 3rd-years
OH, SAEKO?
ARE YOU RUNNING THE ELEC-TRONICS?
AH, WELL...
ORDERS FROM THE NEW PRES.
THERE AREN'T THAT MANY SECOND-YEARS, SO SHE TOLD ME TO DO IT, SINCE I LOOK LIKE I CAN.
HA HA HA! THAT'S MIHO FOR YOU...
DID SHE END UP FINDING A NEW DRUMMER FOR HER BAND?
NAHH... THEY'RE REALLY HARD UP, I GUESS.

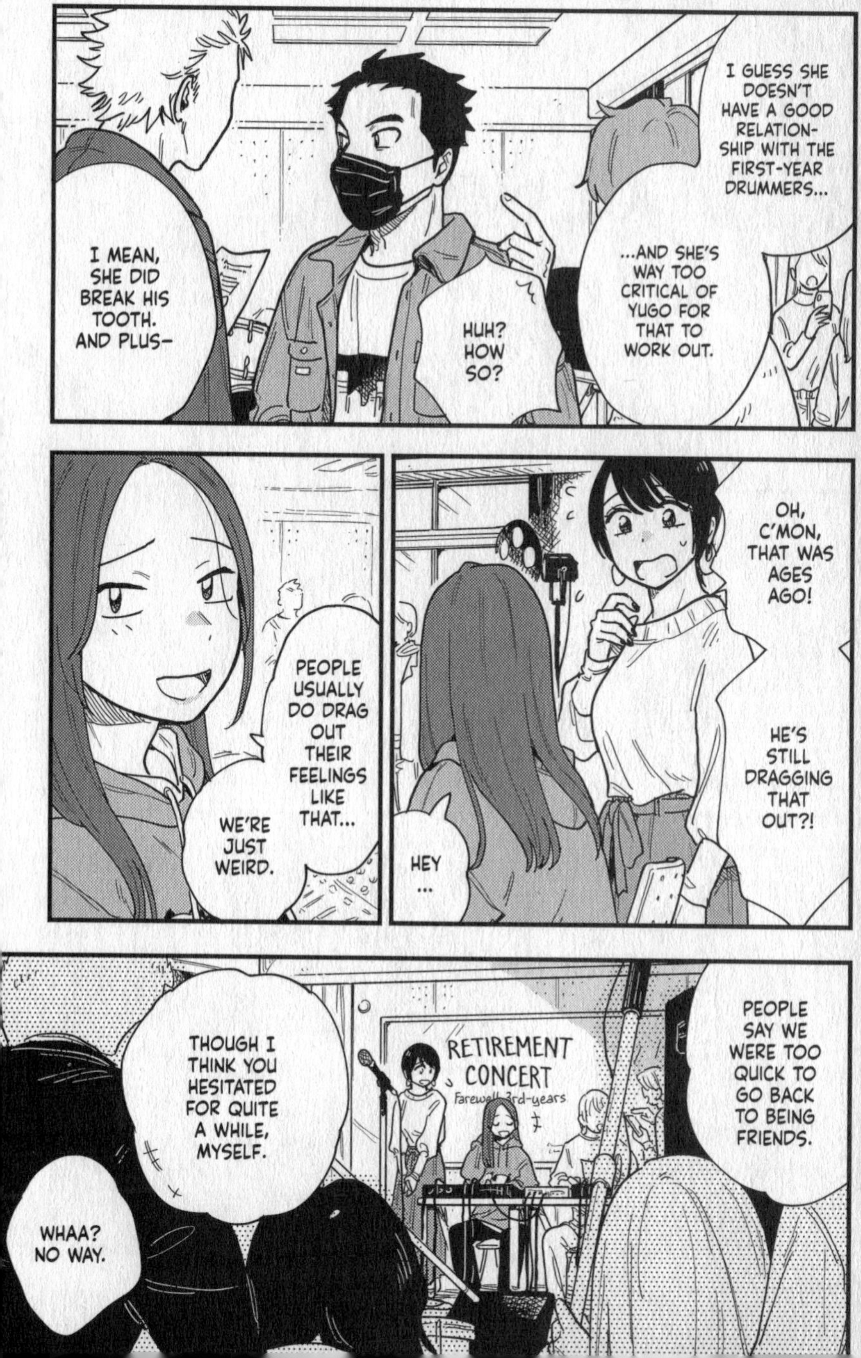
I GUESS SHE DOESN'T HAVE A GOOD RELATIONSHIP WITH THE FIRST-YEAR DRUMMERS...
...AND SHE'S WAY TOO CRITICAL OF YUGO FOR THAT TO WORK OUT.
HUH? HOW SO?
I MEAN, SHE DID BREAK HIS TOOTH. AND PLUS—
OH, C'MON, THAT WAS AGES AGO!
HE'S STILL DRAGGING THAT OUT?!
HEY ...
PEOPLE USUALLY DO DRAG OUT THEIR FEELINGS LIKE THAT...
WE'RE JUST WEIRD.
PEOPLE SAY WE WERE TOO QUICK TO GO BACK TO BEING FRIENDS.
RETIREMENT CONCERT
Farewell 3rd-years
THOUGH I THINK YOU HESITATED FOR QUITE A WHILE, MYSELF.
WHAA? NO WAY.

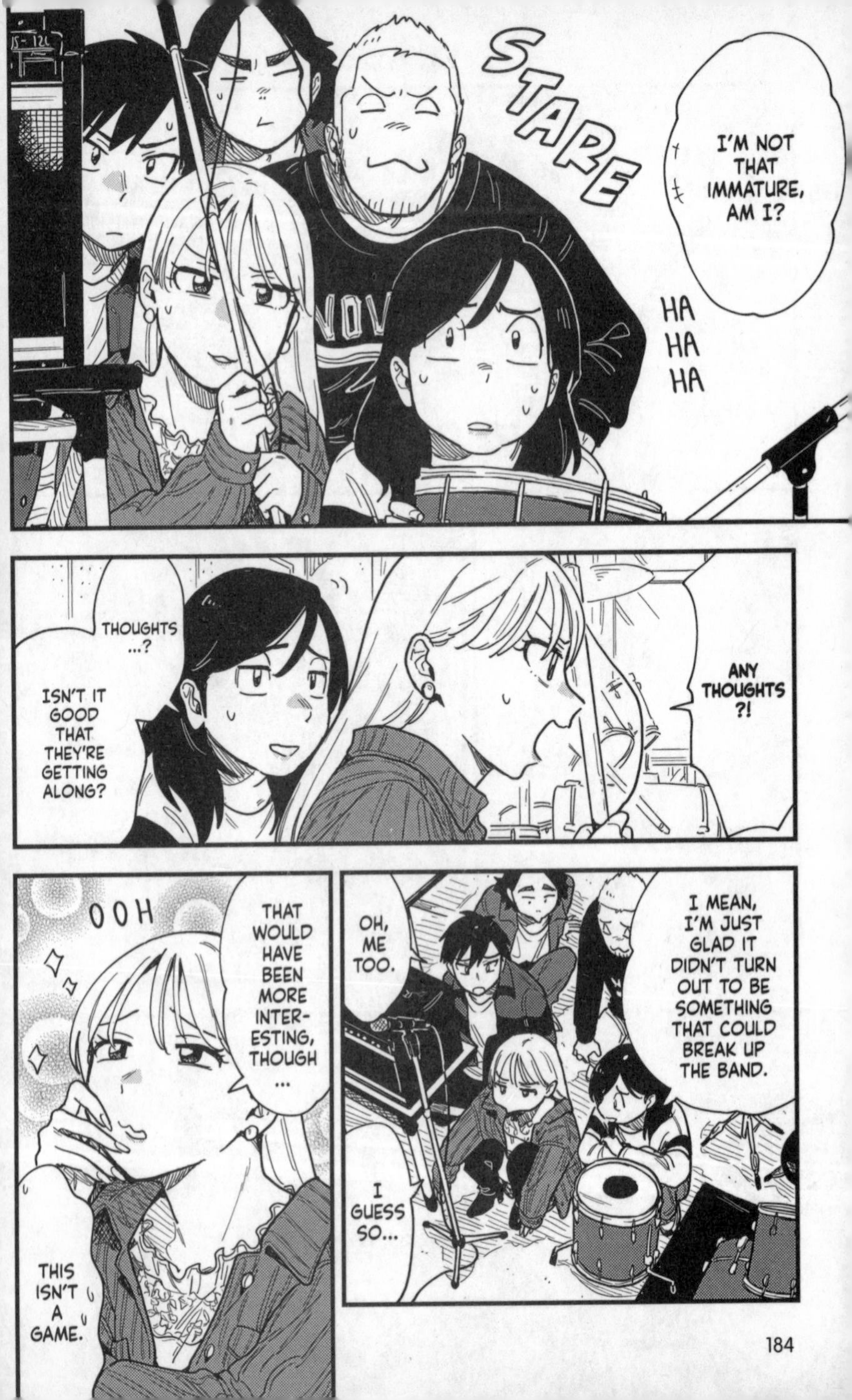
I'M NOT THAT IMMATURE, AM I?
HA HA HA
STARE
ANY THOUGHTS ?!
THOUGHTS ...?
ISN'T IT GOOD THAT THEY'RE GETTING ALONG?
I MEAN, I'M JUST GLAD IT DIDN'T TURN OUT TO BE SOMETHING THAT COULD BREAK UP THE BAND.
OH, ME TOO.
I GUESS SO...
THAT WOULD HAVE BEEN MORE INTER-ESTING, THOUGH ...
OOH
THIS ISN'T A GAME.

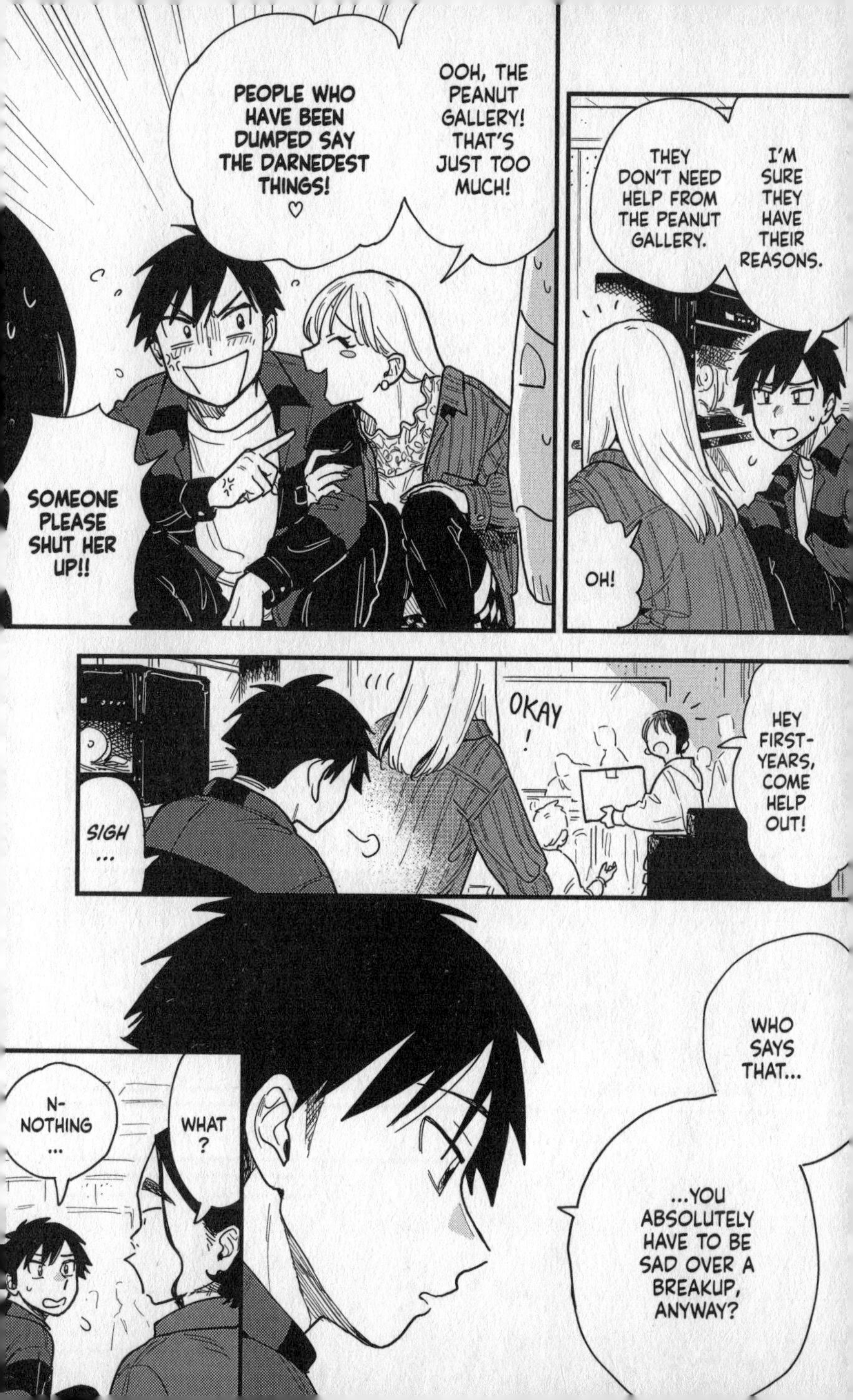
I'M SURE THEY HAVE THEIR REASONS.
THEY DON'T NEED HELP FROM THE PEANUT GALLERY.
OH!
OOH, THE PEANUT GALLERY! THAT'S JUST TOO MUCH!
PEOPLE WHO HAVE BEEN DUMPED SAY THE DARNEDEST THINGS! ♡
SOMEONE PLEASE SHUT HER UP!!
HEY FIRST-YEARS, COME HELP OUT!
OKAY!
SIGH...
WHO SAYS THAT...
...YOU ABSOLUTELY HAVE TO BE SAD OVER A BREAKUP, ANYWAY?
WHAT?
N-NOTHING...

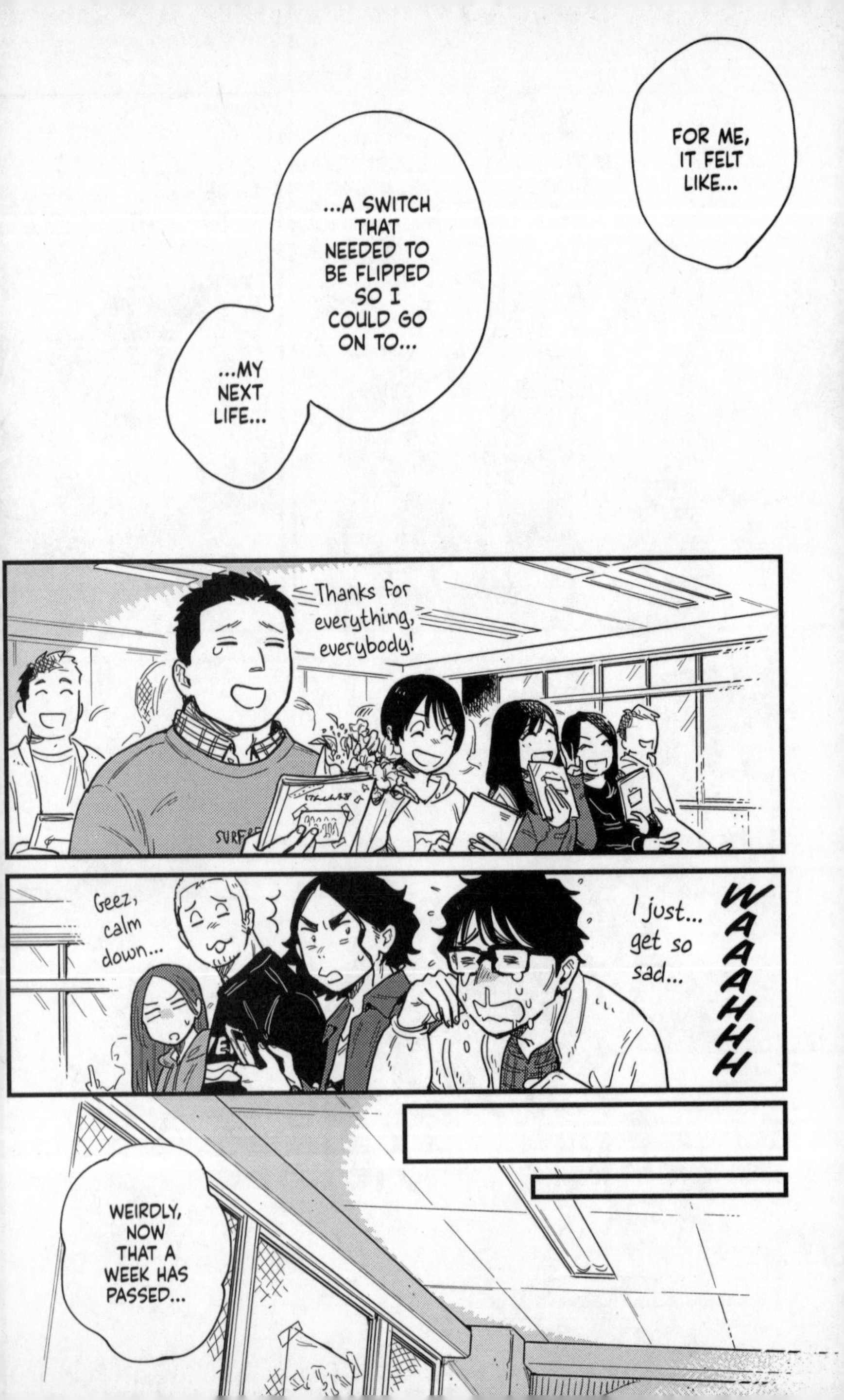
FOR ME, IT FELT LIKE...
...A SWITCH THAT NEEDED TO BE FLIPPED SO I COULD GO ON TO...
...MY NEXT LIFE...
Thanks for everything, everybody!
WAAAAHHH
I just... get so sad...
Geez, calm down...
WEIRDLY, NOW THAT A WEEK HAS PASSED...

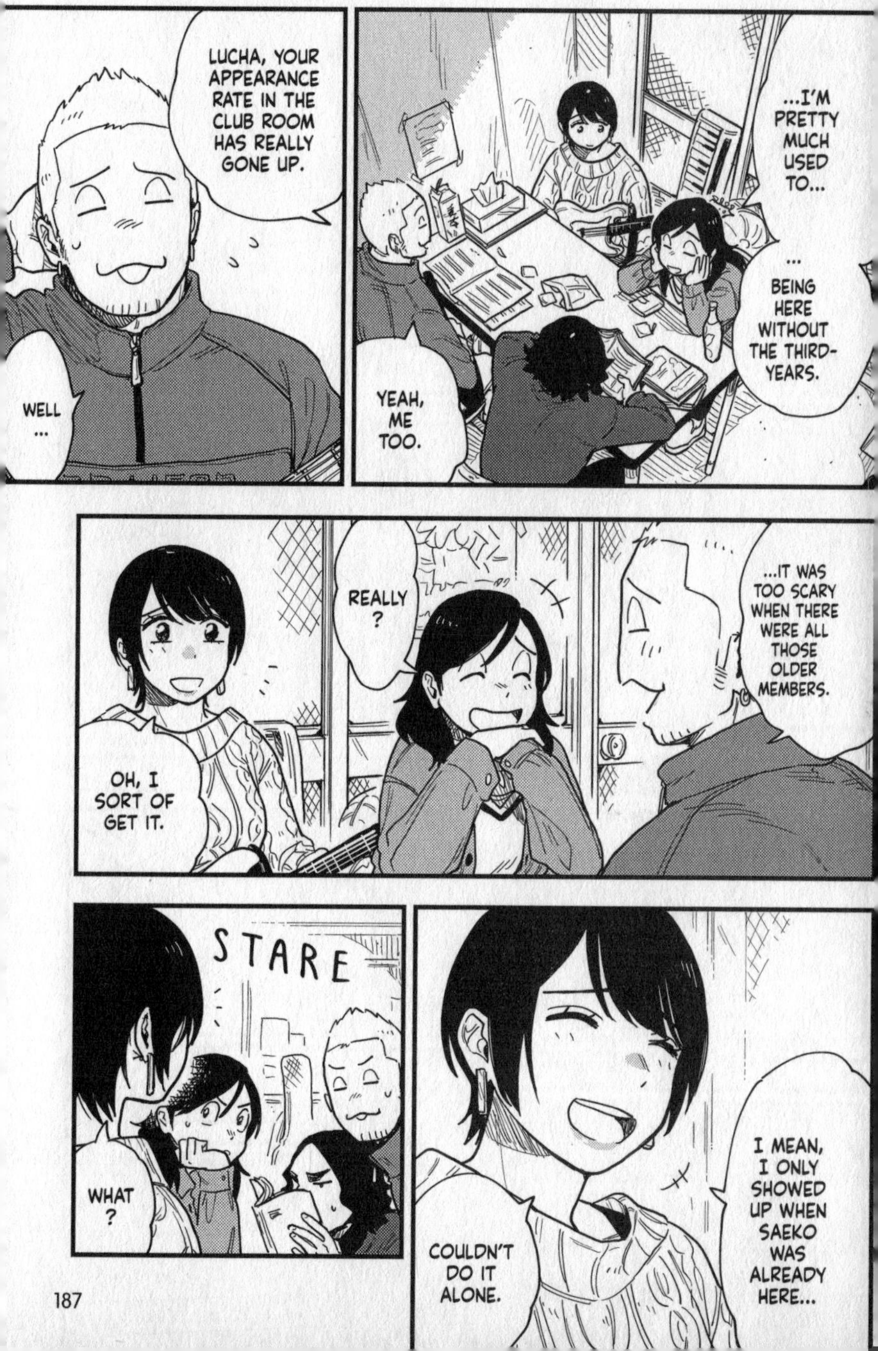
...I'M PRETTY MUCH USED TO...
... BEING HERE WITHOUT THE THIRD-YEARS.
YEAH, ME TOO.
LUCHA, YOUR APPEARANCE RATE IN THE CLUB ROOM HAS REALLY GONE UP.
WELL ...
...IT WAS TOO SCARY WHEN THERE WERE ALL THOSE OLDER MEMBERS.
REALLY ?
OH, I SORT OF GET IT.
I MEAN, I ONLY SHOWED UP WHEN SAEKO WAS ALREADY HERE...
COULDN'T DO IT ALONE.
STARE
WHAT ?

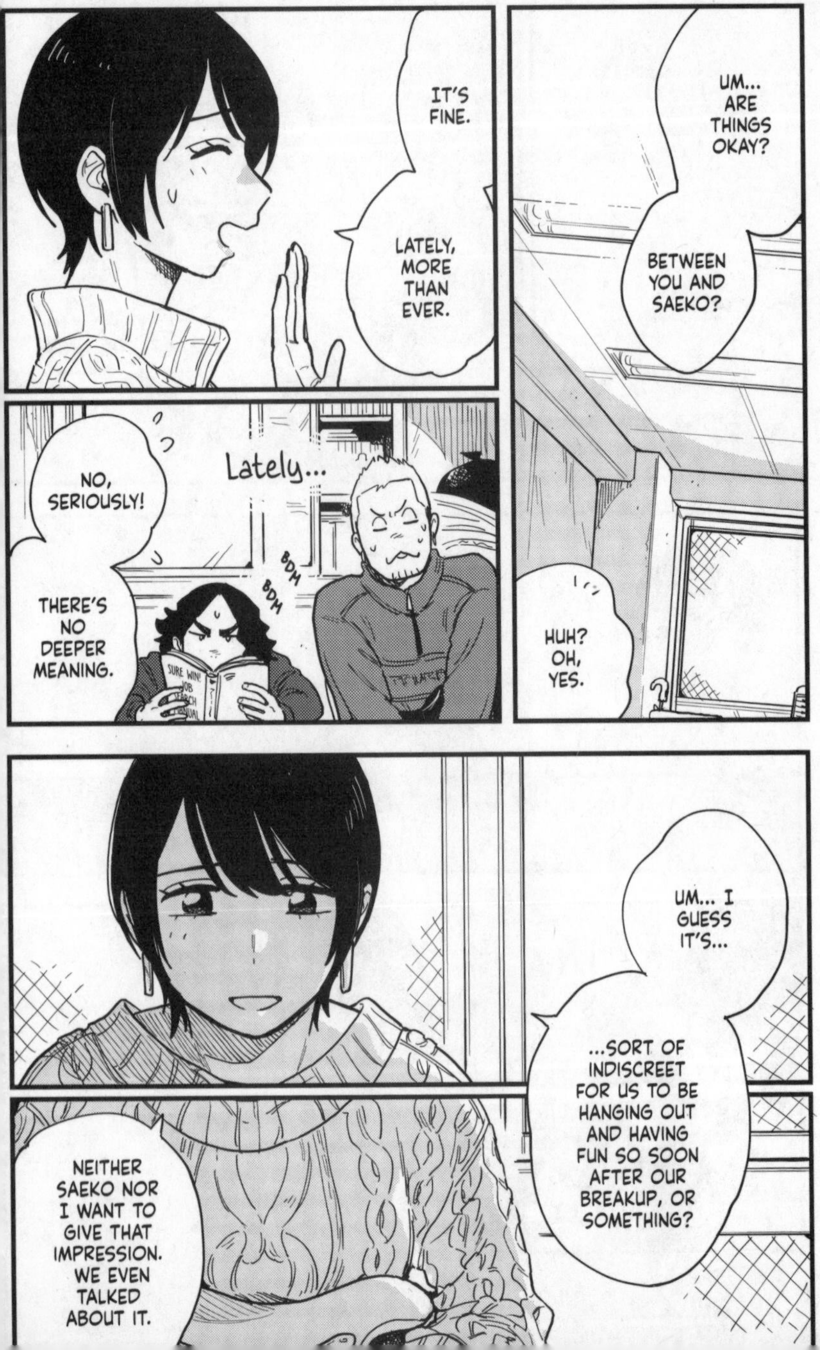
UM... ARE THINGS OKAY?
BETWEEN YOU AND SAEKO?
HUH? OH, YES.
IT'S FINE.
LATELY, MORE THAN EVER.
Lately...
BDM BDM
NO, SERIOUSLY!
THERE'S NO DEEPER MEANING.
SURE WIN! JOB SEARCH MANUAL
UM... I GUESS IT'S...
...SORT OF INDISCREET FOR US TO BE HANGING OUT AND HAVING FUN SO SOON AFTER OUR BREAKUP, OR SOMETHING?
NEITHER SAEKO NOR I WANT TO GIVE THAT IMPRESSION. WE EVEN TALKED ABOUT IT.

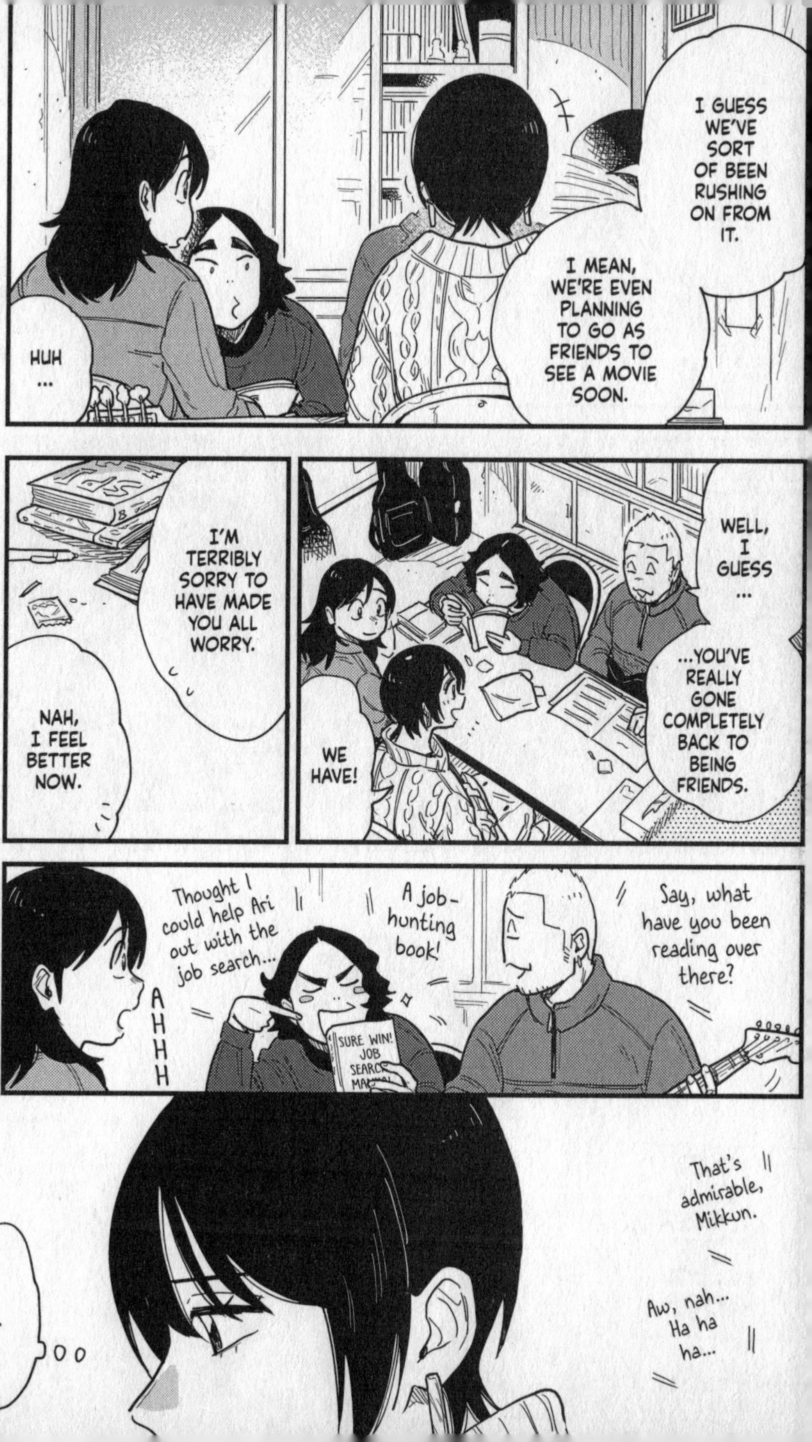
I GUESS WE'VE SORT OF BEEN RUSHING ON FROM IT.
I MEAN, WE'RE EVEN PLANNING TO GO AS FRIENDS TO SEE A MOVIE SOON.
HUH ...
WELL, I GUESS ...
...YOU'VE REALLY GONE COMPLETELY BACK TO BEING FRIENDS.
WE HAVE!
I'M TERRIBLY SORRY TO HAVE MADE YOU ALL WORRY.
NAH, I FEEL BETTER NOW.
Say, what have you been reading over there?
A job-hunting book!
Thought I could help Ari out with the job search...
SURE WIN! JOB
AHHH
That's admirable, Mikkun.
Aw, nah... Ha ha ha...
...

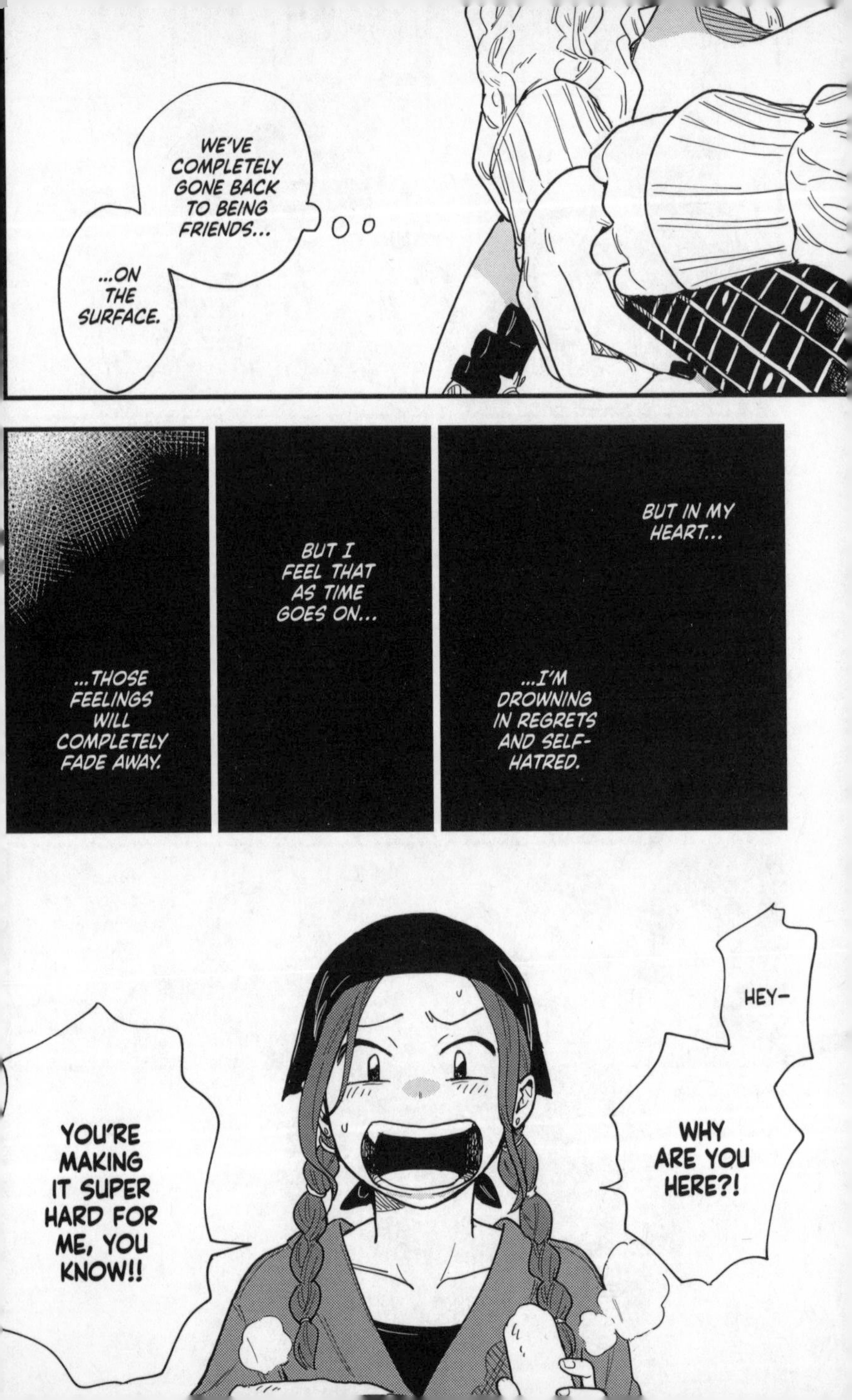
WE'VE COMPLETELY GONE BACK TO BEING FRIENDS...
...ON THE SURFACE.
BUT IN MY HEART...
...I'M DROWNING IN REGRETS AND SELF-HATRED.
BUT I FEEL THAT AS TIME GOES ON...
...THOSE FEELINGS WILL COMPLETELY FADE AWAY.
HEY–
WHY ARE YOU HERE?!
YOU'RE MAKING IT SUPER HARD FOR ME, YOU KNOW!!

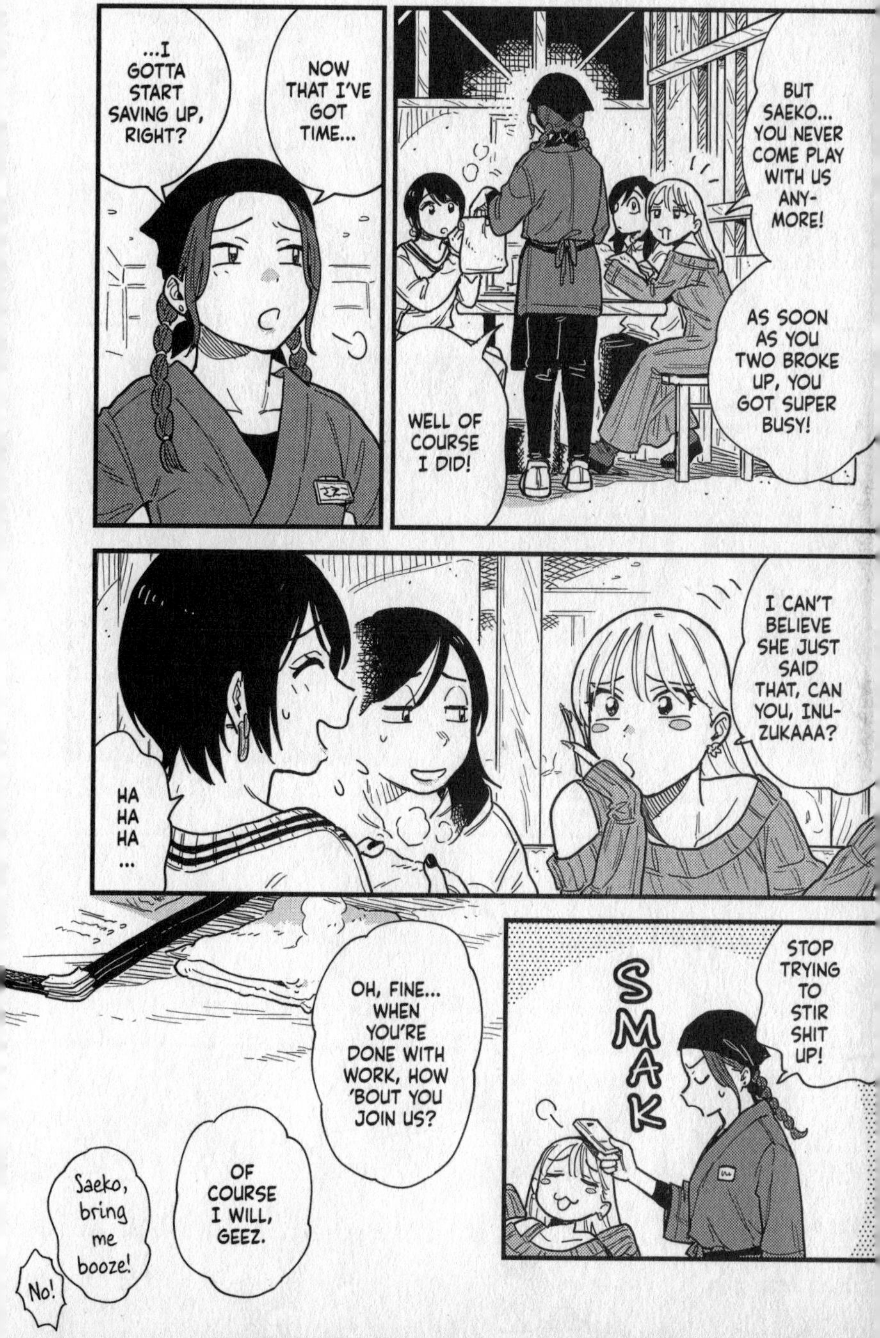
BUT SAEKO... YOU NEVER COME PLAY WITH US ANY-MORE!
AS SOON AS YOU TWO BROKE UP, YOU GOT SUPER BUSY!
WELL OF COURSE I DID!
NOW THAT I'VE GOT TIME...
...I GOTTA START SAVING UP, RIGHT?
I CAN'T BELIEVE SHE JUST SAID THAT, CAN YOU, INU-ZUKAAA?
HA HA HA ...
STOP TRYING TO STIR SHIT UP!
SMAK
OH, FINE... WHEN YOU'RE DONE WITH WORK, HOW 'BOUT YOU JOIN US?
OF COURSE I WILL, GEEZ.
Saeko, bring me booze!
No!

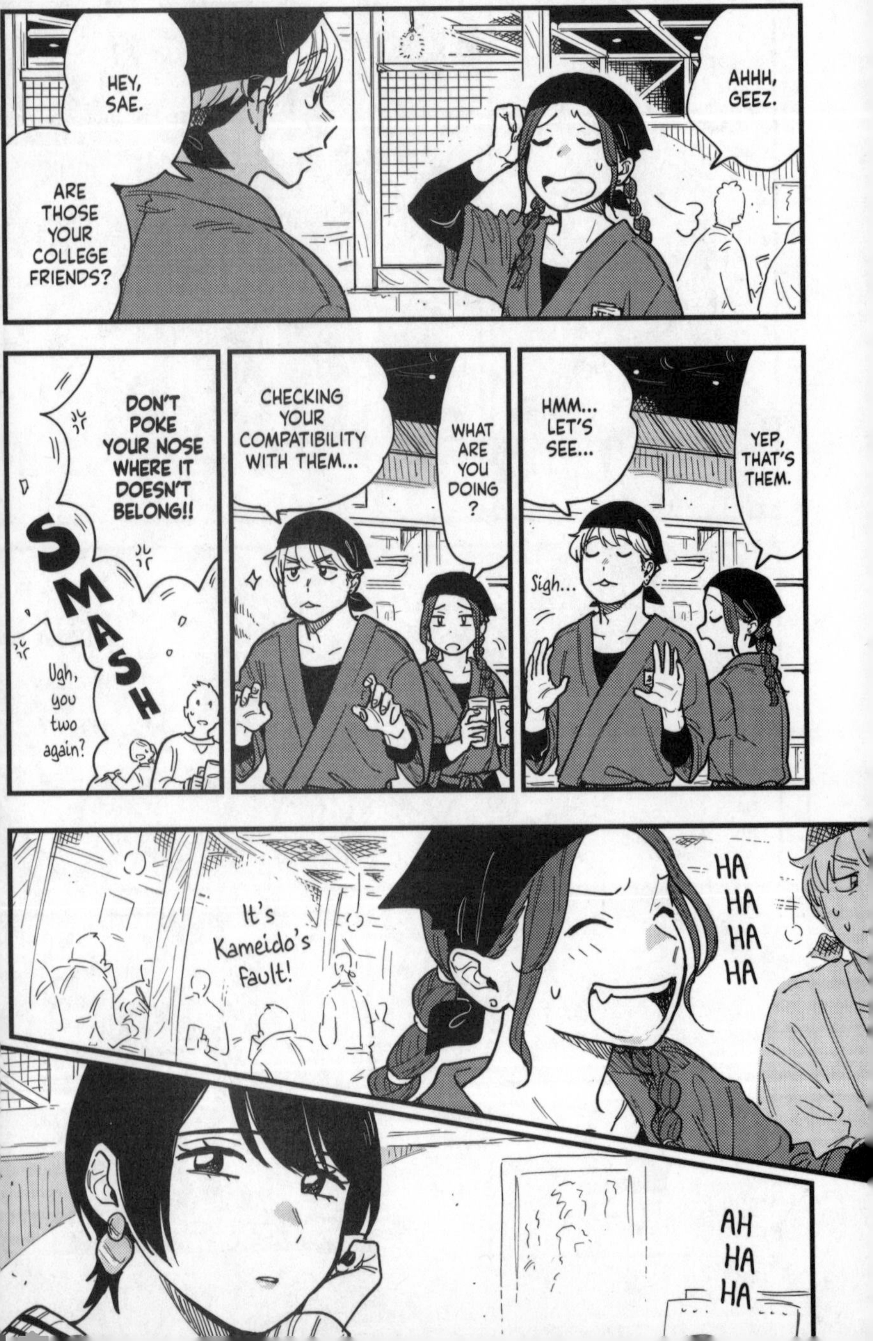
AHHH, GEEZ.
HEY, SAE.
ARE THOSE YOUR COLLEGE FRIENDS?
YEP, THAT'S THEM.
HMM... LET'S SEE...
Sigh...
WHAT ARE YOU DOING?
CHECKING YOUR COMPATIBILITY WITH THEM...
DON'T POKE YOUR NOSE WHERE IT DOESN'T BELONG!!
SMASH
Ugh, you two again?
HA HA HA HA
It's Kameido's fault!
AH HA HA

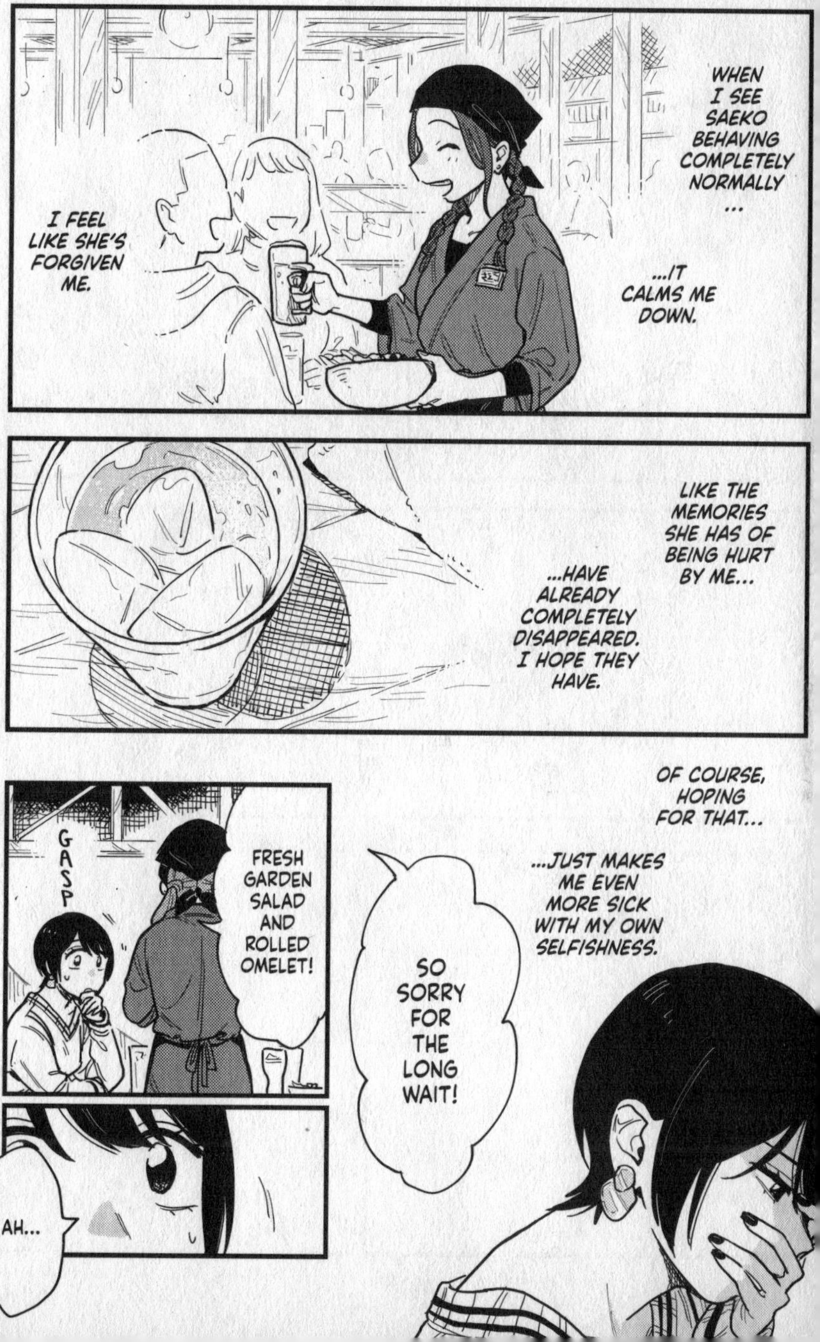
WHEN I SEE SAEKO BEHAVING COMPLETELY NORMALLY ...
...IT CALMS ME DOWN.
I FEEL LIKE SHE'S FORGIVEN ME.
LIKE THE MEMORIES SHE HAS OF BEING HURT BY ME...
...HAVE ALREADY COMPLETELY DISAPPEARED. I HOPE THEY HAVE.
OF COURSE, HOPING FOR THAT...
...JUST MAKES ME EVEN MORE SICK WITH MY OWN SELFISHNESS.
SO SORRY FOR THE LONG WAIT!
FRESH GARDEN SALAD AND ROLLED OMELET!
GASP
AH...

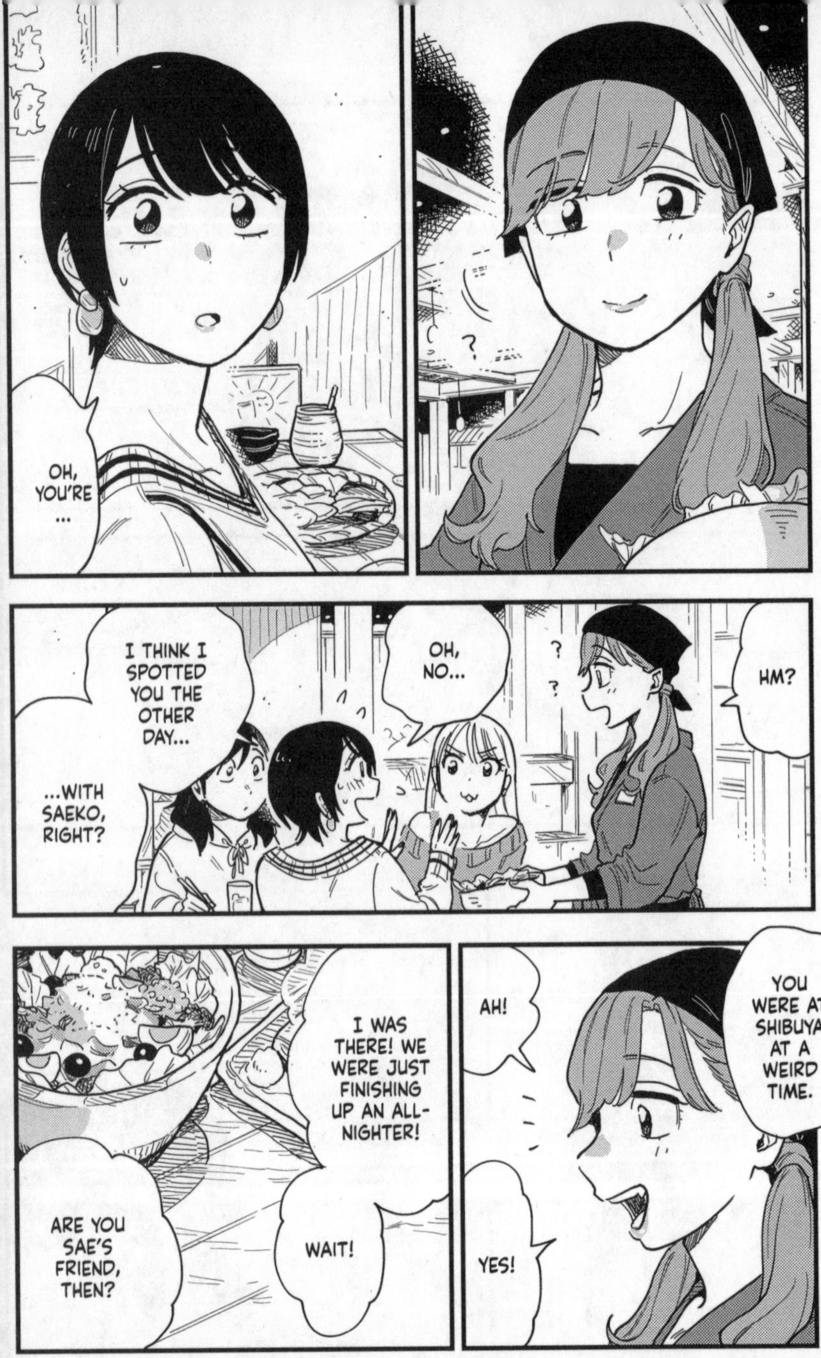
?
OH, YOU'RE ...
HM?
? ?
OH, NO...
I THINK I SPOTTED YOU THE OTHER DAY...
...WITH SAEKO, RIGHT?
YOU WERE AT SHIBUYA AT A WEIRD TIME.
AH!
YES!
I WAS THERE! WE WERE JUST FINISHING UP AN ALL-NIGHTER!
WAIT!
ARE YOU SAE'S FRIEND, THEN?

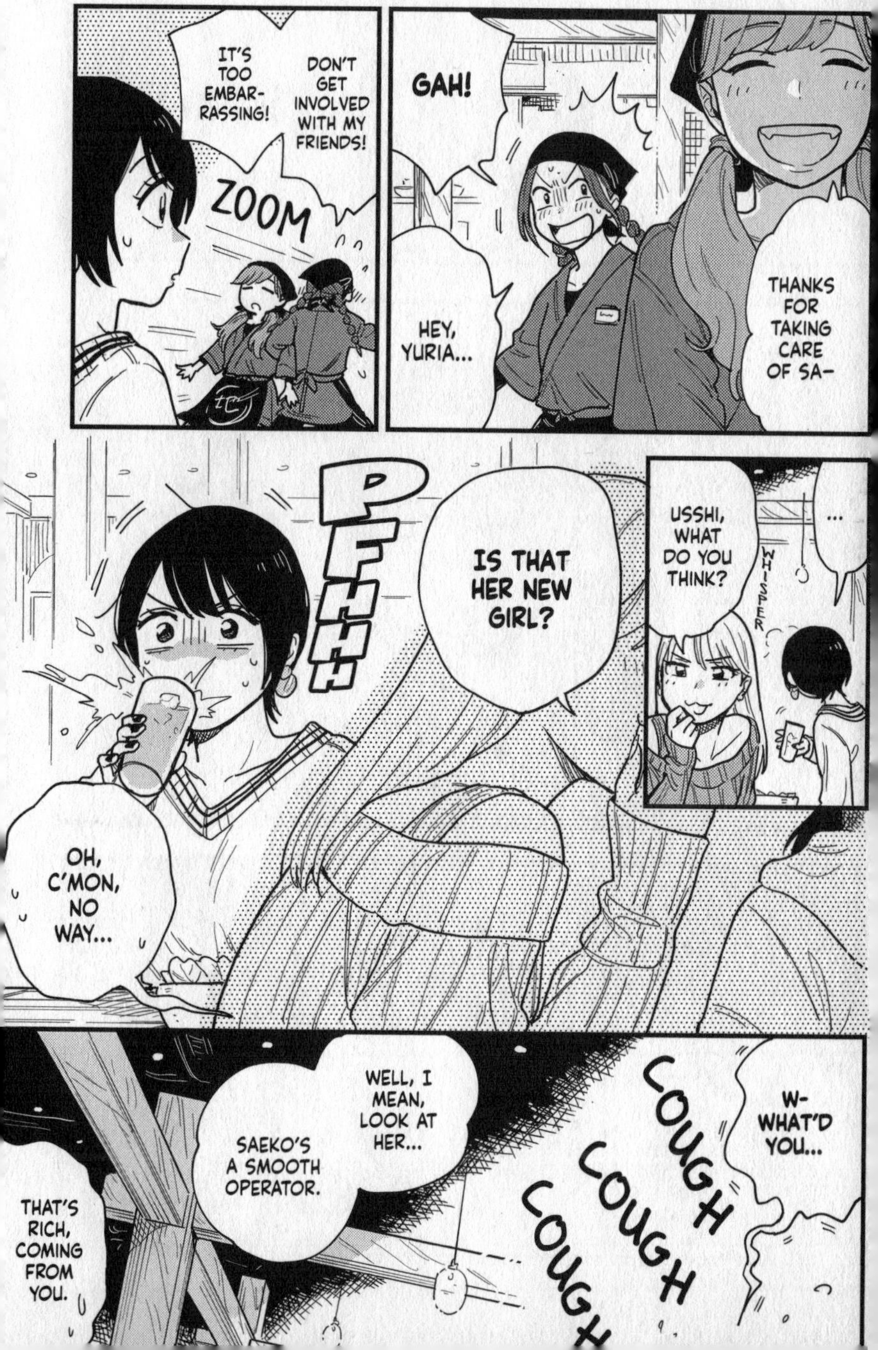
THANKS FOR TAKING CARE OF SA-
HEY, YURIA...
GAH!
DON'T GET INVOLVED WITH MY FRIENDS!
IT'S TOO EMBARRASSING!
ZOOM
...
USSHI, WHAT DO YOU THINK?
WHISPER
IS THAT HER NEW GIRL?
OH, C'MON, NO WAY...
W-WHAT'D YOU...
COUGH
COUGH
COUGH
WELL, I MEAN, LOOK AT HER...
SAEKO'S A SMOOTH OPERATOR.
THAT'S RICH, COMING FROM YOU.

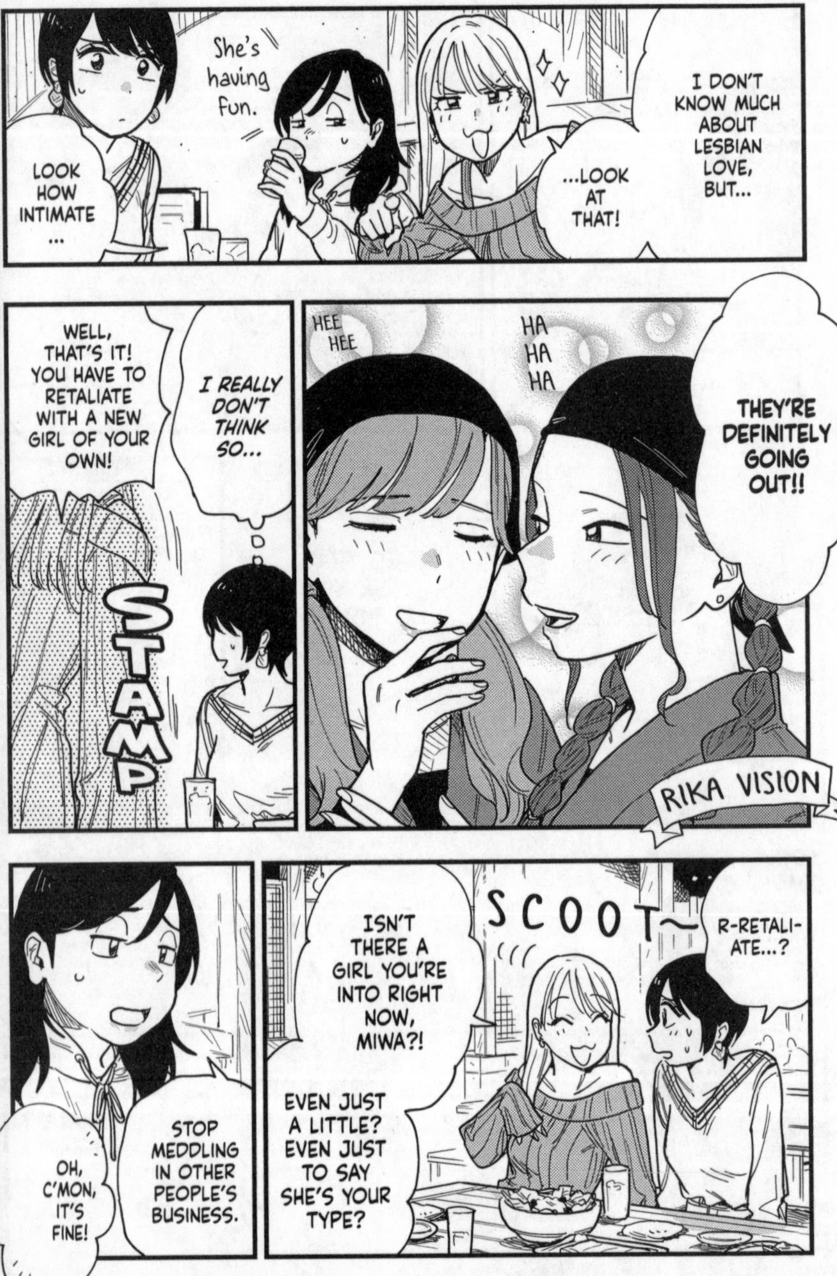
I DON'T KNOW MUCH ABOUT LESBIAN LOVE, BUT...
...LOOK AT THAT!
She's having fun.
LOOK HOW INTIMATE ...
THEY'RE DEFINITELY GOING OUT!!
HA HA HA
HEE HEE
RIKA VISION
I REALLY DON'T THINK SO...
WELL, THAT'S IT! YOU HAVE TO RETALIATE WITH A NEW GIRL OF YOUR OWN!
STAMP
R-RETALIATE...?
SCOOT~
ISN'T THERE A GIRL YOU'RE INTO RIGHT NOW, MIWA?!
EVEN JUST A LITTLE? EVEN JUST TO SAY SHE'S YOUR TYPE?
STOP MEDDLING IN OTHER PEOPLE'S BUSINESS.
OH, C'MON, IT'S FINE!

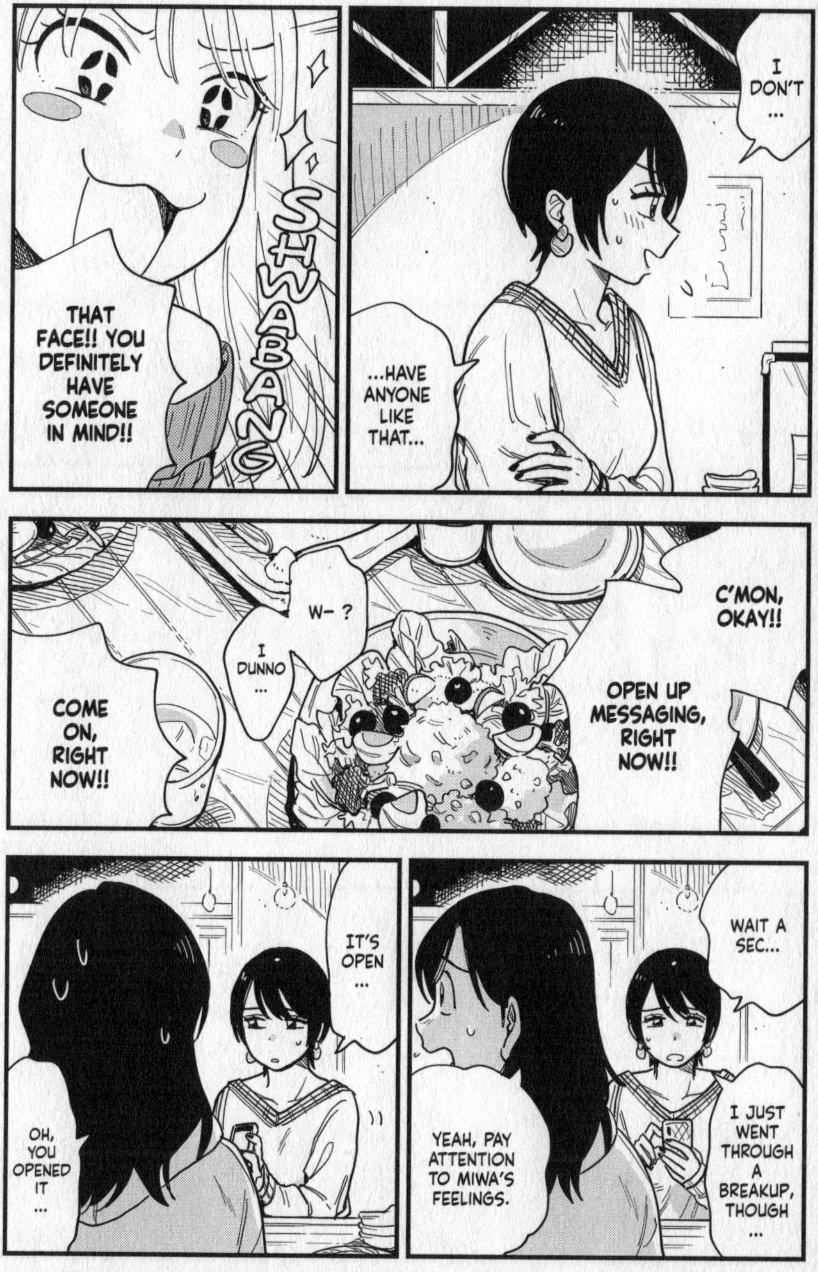
I DON'T ...
...HAVE ANYONE LIKE THAT...
SHWABANG
THAT FACE!! YOU DEFINITELY HAVE SOMEONE IN MIND!!
C'MON, OKAY!!
OPEN UP MESSAGING, RIGHT NOW!!
W- ?
I DUNNO ...
COME ON, RIGHT NOW!!
WAIT A SEC...
I JUST WENT THROUGH A BREAKUP, THOUGH ...
YEAH, PAY ATTENTION TO MIWA'S FEELINGS.
IT'S OPEN ...
OH, YOU OPENED IT ...

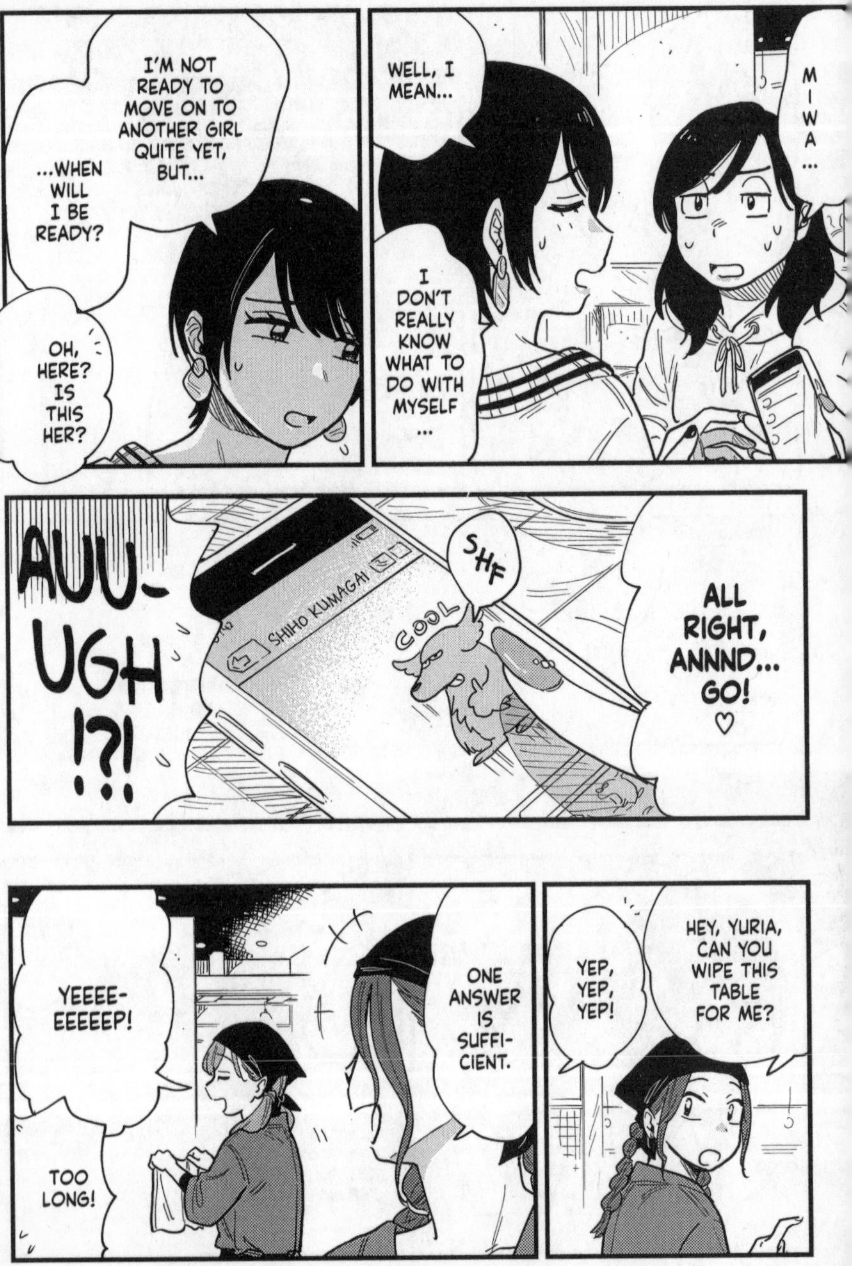
MIWA...
WELL, I MEAN...
I DON'T REALLY KNOW WHAT TO DO WITH MYSELF ...
I'M NOT READY TO MOVE ON TO ANOTHER GIRL QUITE YET, BUT...
...WHEN WILL I BE READY?
OH, HERE? IS THIS HER?
ALL RIGHT, ANNND... GO! ♡
SHF
COOL
SHIHO KUMAGAI
AUU-UGH!?!
HEY, YURIA, CAN YOU WIPE THIS TABLE FOR ME?
YEP, YEP, YEP!
ONE ANSWER IS SUFFICIENT.
YEEEE-EEEEEP!
TOO LONG!

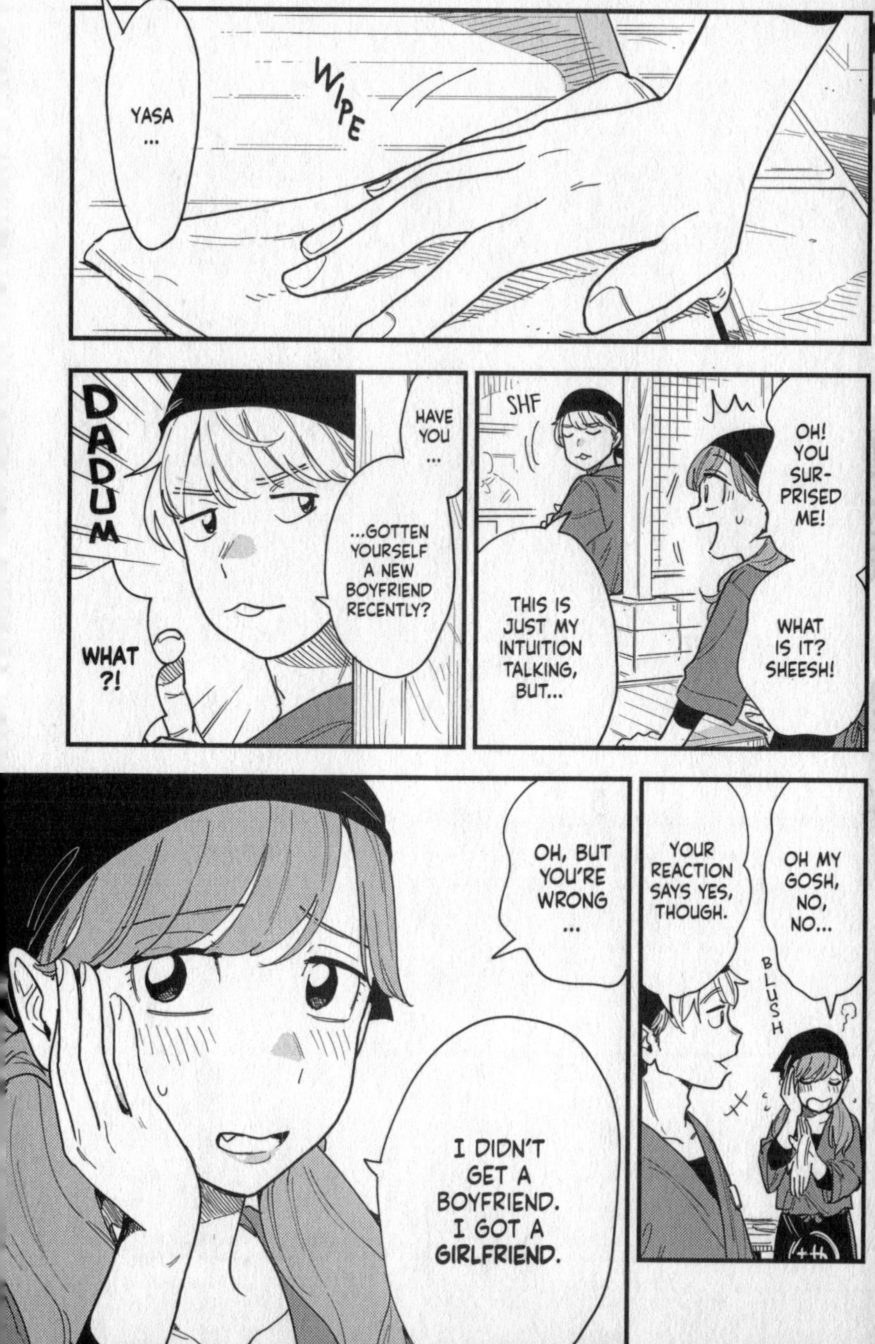
YASA...
WIPE
OH! YOU SURPRISED ME!
WHAT IS IT? SHEESH!
SHF
THIS IS JUST MY INTUITION TALKING, BUT...
HAVE YOU...
...GOTTEN YOURSELF A NEW BOYFRIEND RECENTLY?
DADUM
WHAT?!
OH MY GOSH, NO, NO...
BLUSH
YOUR REACTION SAYS YES, THOUGH.
OH, BUT YOU'RE WRONG...
I DIDN'T GET A BOYFRIEND. I GOT A GIRLFRIEND.

How Do We
Relationship?

Secret Tale: The Formation

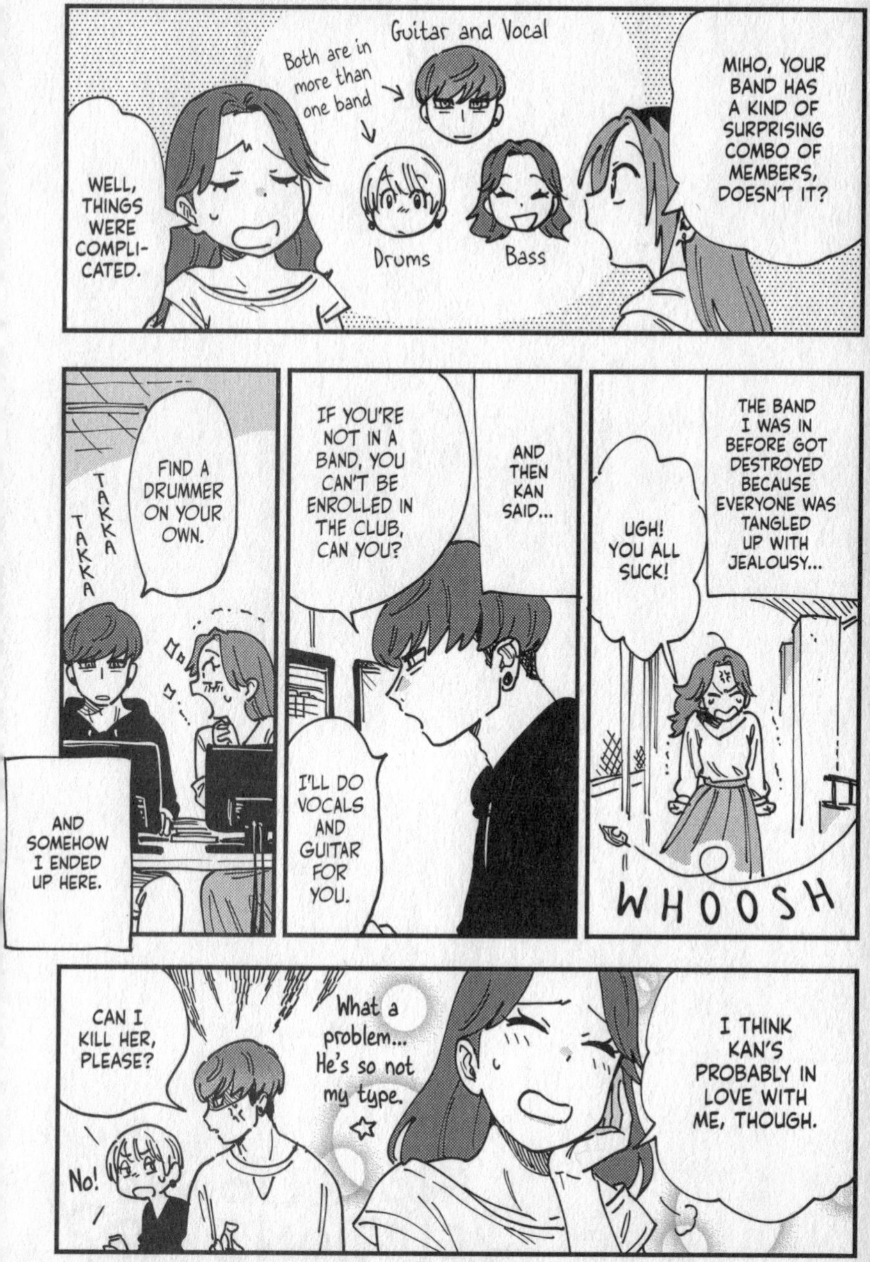
MIHO, YOUR BAND HAS A KIND OF SURPRISING COMBO OF MEMBERS, DOESN'T IT?
Guitar and Vocal
Both are in more than one band
Bass
Drums
WELL, THINGS WERE COMPLI-CATED.
THE BAND I WAS IN BEFORE GOT DESTROYED BECAUSE EVERYONE WAS TANGLED UP WITH JEALOUSY...
UGH! YOU ALL SUCK!
WHOOSH
AND THEN KAN SAID...
IF YOU'RE NOT IN A BAND, YOU CAN'T BE ENROLLED IN THE CLUB, CAN YOU?
I'LL DO VOCALS AND GUITAR FOR YOU.
FIND A DRUMMER ON YOUR OWN.
TAKKA TAKKA
AND SOMEHOW I ENDED UP HERE.
I THINK KAN'S PROBABLY IN LOVE WITH ME, THOUGH.
What a problem... He's so not my type.
CAN I KILL HER, PLEASE?
No!

HOW DO WE
RELATIONSHIP?

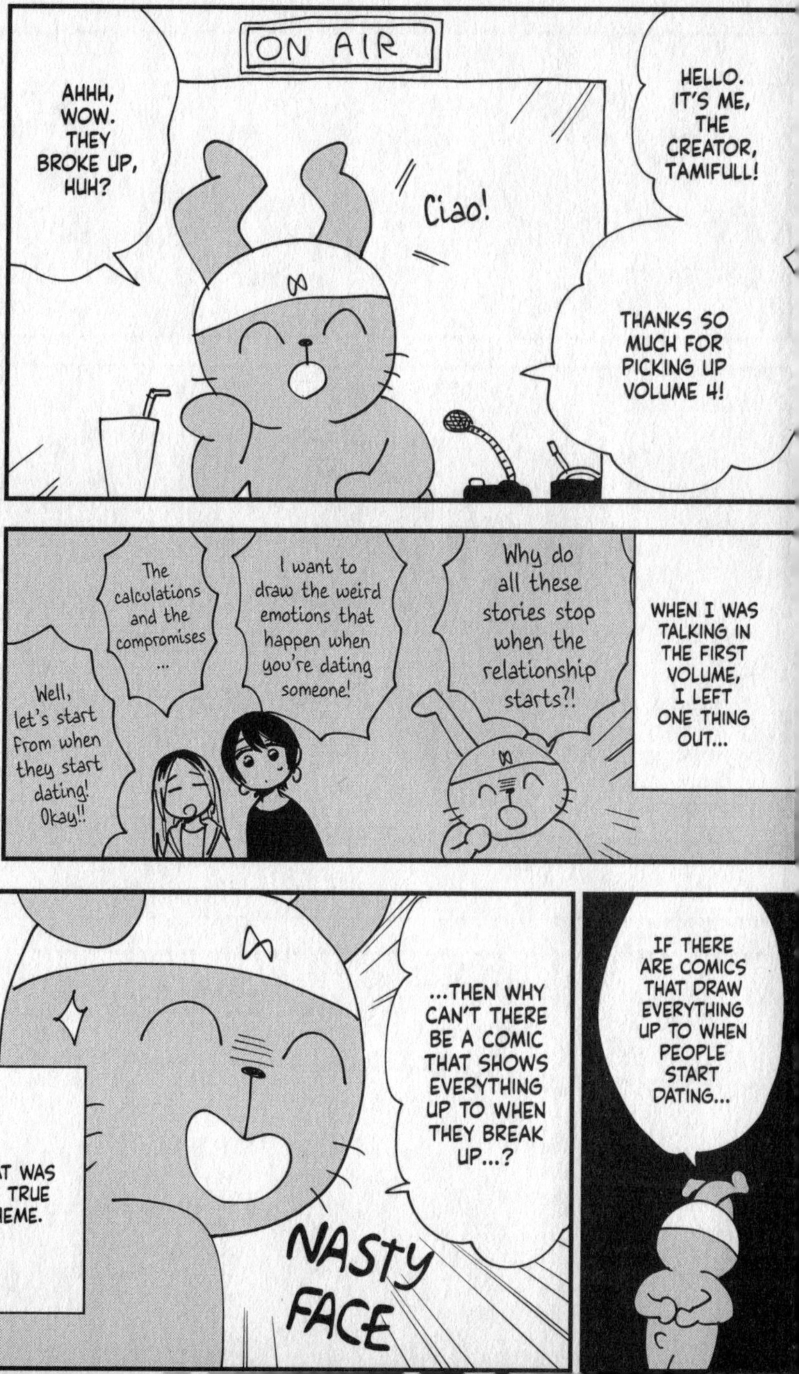
ON AIR
HELLO. IT'S ME, THE CREATOR, TAMIFULL!
Ciao!
THANKS SO MUCH FOR PICKING UP VOLUME 4!
AHHH, WOW. THEY BROKE UP, HUH?
WHEN I WAS TALKING IN THE FIRST VOLUME, I LEFT ONE THING OUT...
Why do all these stories stop when the relationship starts?!
I want to draw the weird emotions that happen when you're dating someone!
The calculations and the compromises ...
Well, let's start from when they start dating! Okay!!
IF THERE ARE COMICS THAT DRAW EVERYTHING UP TO WHEN PEOPLE START DATING...
...THEN WHY CAN'T THERE BE A COMIC THAT SHOWS EVERYTHING UP TO WHEN THEY BREAK UP...?
NASTY FACE
THAT WAS MY TRUE THEME.

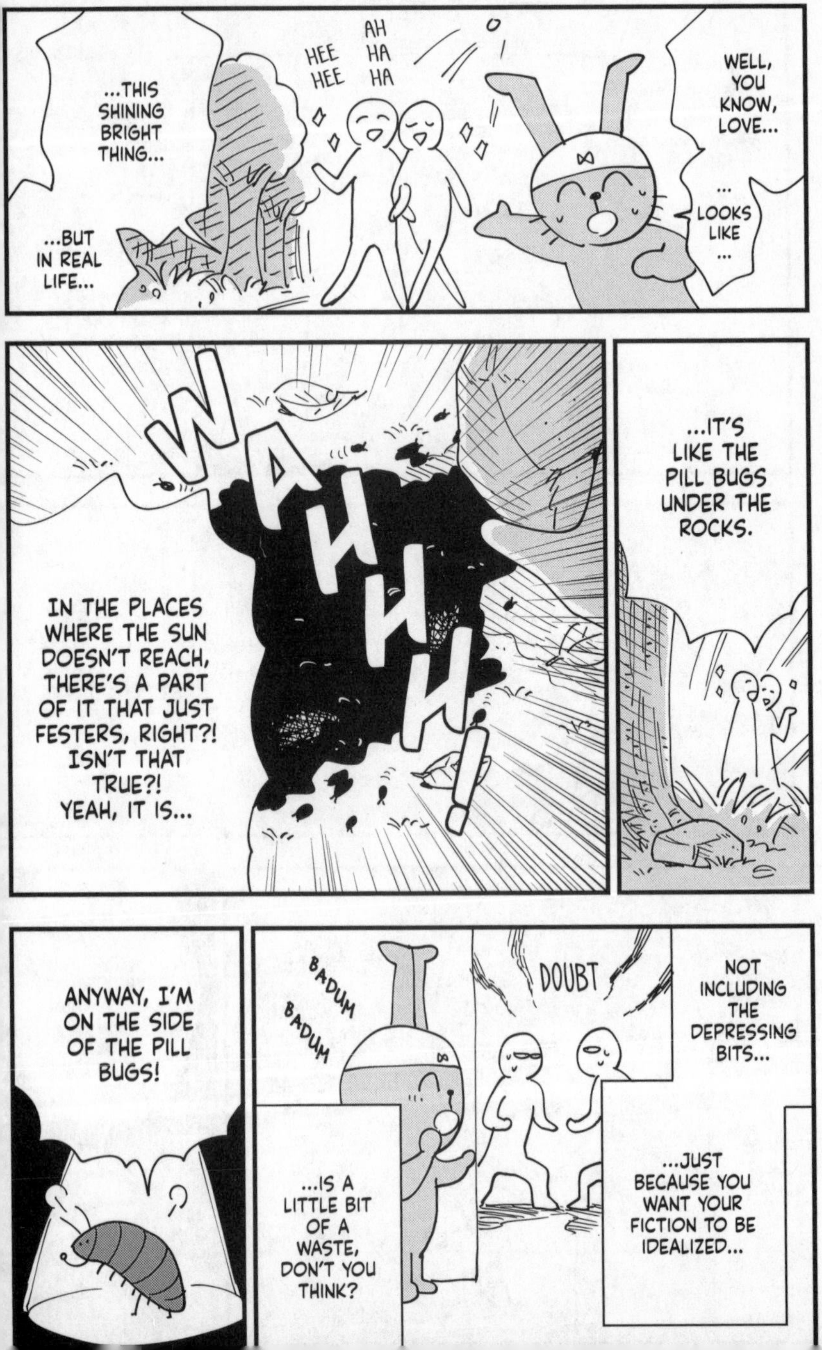
WELL, YOU KNOW, LOVE...
...LOOKS LIKE...
AH HA HA
HEE HEE
...THIS SHINING BRIGHT THING...
...BUT IN REAL LIFE...
...IT'S LIKE THE PILL BUGS UNDER THE ROCKS.
WAHHH!
IN THE PLACES WHERE THE SUN DOESN'T REACH, THERE'S A PART OF IT THAT JUST FESTERS, RIGHT?! ISN'T THAT TRUE?! YEAH, IT IS...
NOT INCLUDING THE DEPRESSING BITS...
DOUBT
...JUST BECAUSE YOU WANT YOUR FICTION TO BE IDEALIZED...
BADUM BADUM
...IS A LITTLE BIT OF A WASTE, DON'T YOU THINK?
ANYWAY, I'M ON THE SIDE OF THE PILL BUGS!

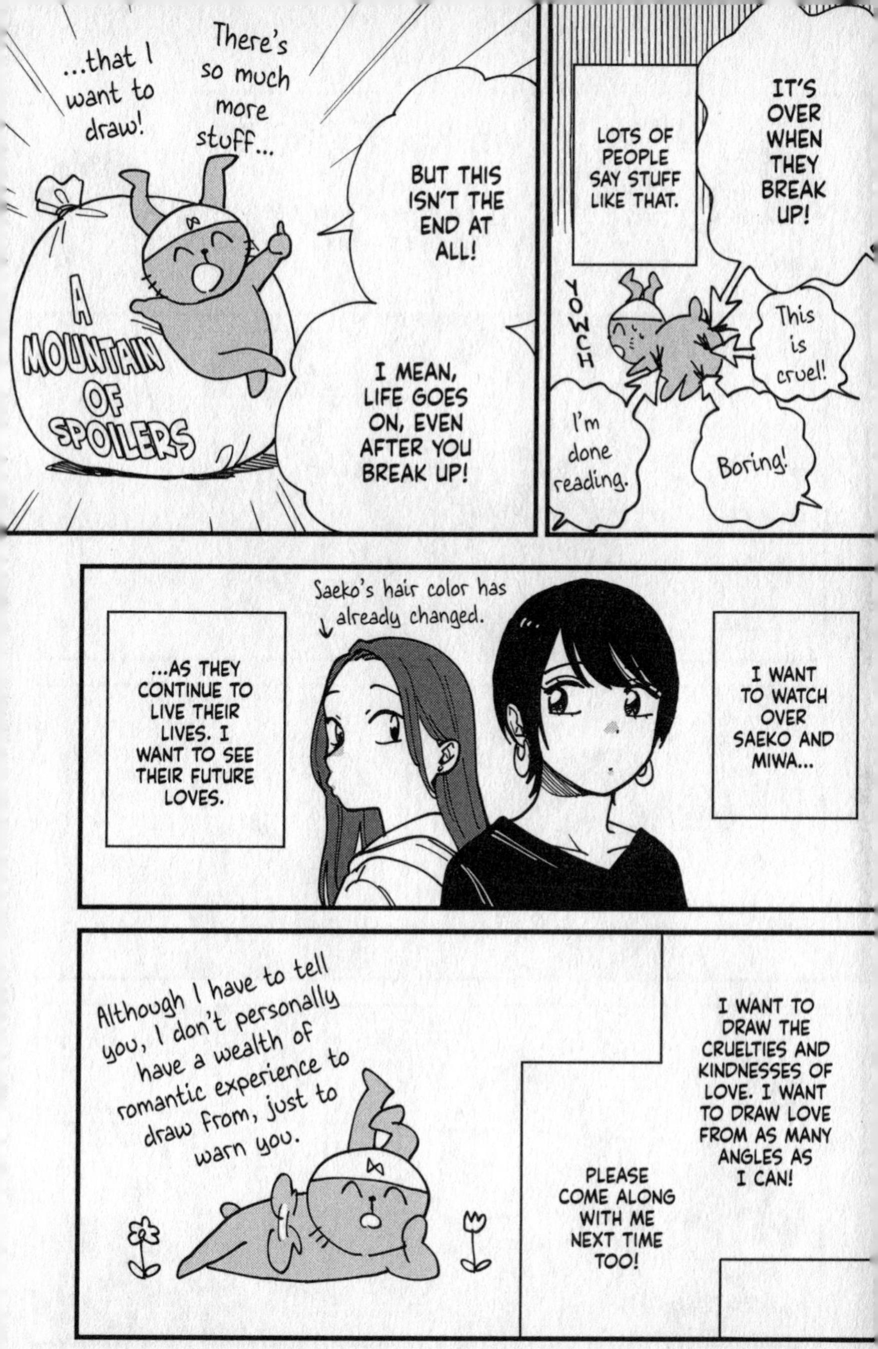
IT'S OVER WHEN THEY BREAK UP!
LOTS OF PEOPLE SAY STUFF LIKE THAT.
YOWCH
This is cruel!
Boring!
I'm done reading.
BUT THIS ISN'T THE END AT ALL!
I MEAN, LIFE GOES ON, EVEN AFTER YOU BREAK UP!
There's so much more stuff...
...that I want to draw!
A MOUNTAIN OF SPOILERS
I WANT TO WATCH OVER SAEKO AND MIWA...
Saeko's hair color has already changed.
...AS THEY CONTINUE TO LIVE THEIR LIVES. I WANT TO SEE THEIR FUTURE LOVES.
I WANT TO DRAW THE CRUELTIES AND KINDNESSES OF LOVE. I WANT TO DRAW LOVE FROM AS MANY ANGLES AS I CAN!
PLEASE COME ALONG WITH ME NEXT TIME TOO!
Although I have to tell you, I don't personally have a wealth of romantic experience to draw from, just to warn you.

HOW DO WE RELATIONSHIP VOLUME 4 COMMENTARY TRACK COMIC

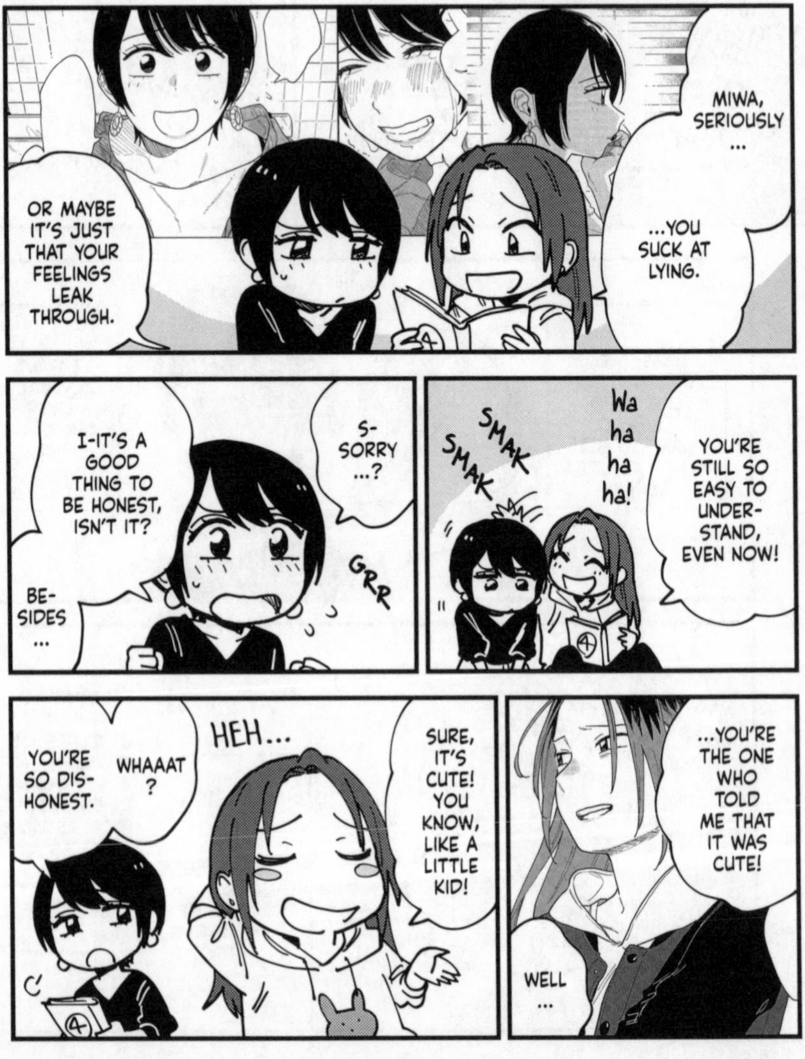
MIWA, SERIOUSLY ...
...YOU SUCK AT LYING.
OR MAYBE IT'S JUST THAT YOUR FEELINGS LEAK THROUGH.
YOU'RE STILL SO EASY TO UNDER-STAND, EVEN NOW!
Wa ha ha ha!
SMAK
SMAK
S-SORRY ...?
GRR
I-IT'S A GOOD THING TO BE HONEST, ISN'T IT?
BE-SIDES ...
...YOU'RE THE ONE WHO TOLD ME THAT IT WAS CUTE!
WELL ...
SURE, IT'S CUTE! YOU KNOW, LIKE A LITTLE KID!
HEH...
WHAAAT?
YOU'RE SO DIS-HONEST.

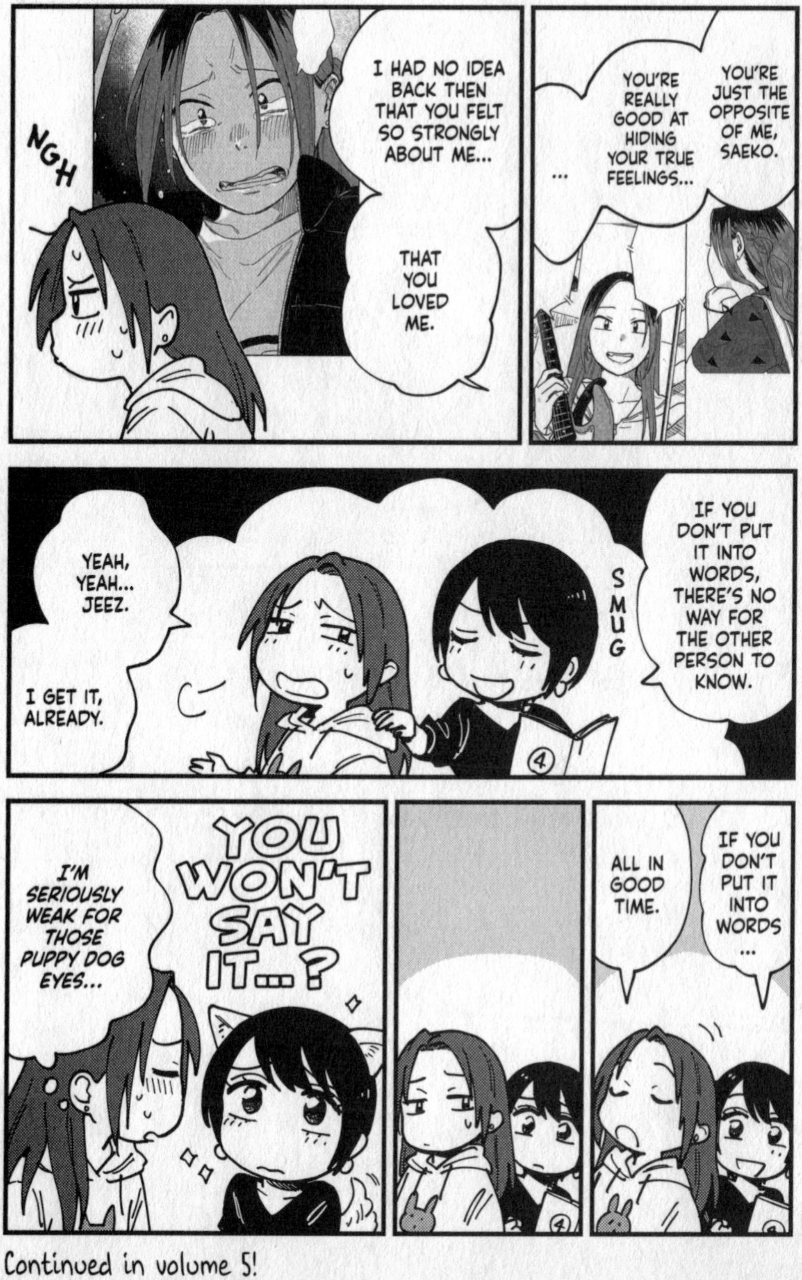
YOU'RE JUST THE OPPOSITE OF ME, SAEKO.
YOU'RE REALLY GOOD AT HIDING YOUR TRUE FEELINGS...
...
I HAD NO IDEA BACK THEN THAT YOU FELT SO STRONGLY ABOUT ME...
THAT YOU LOVED ME.
NGH
IF YOU DON'T PUT IT INTO WORDS, THERE'S NO WAY FOR THE OTHER PERSON TO KNOW.
SMUG
YEAH, YEAH... JEEZ.
I GET IT, ALREADY.
IF YOU DON'T PUT IT INTO WORDS...
ALL IN GOOD TIME.
YOU WON'T SAY IT...?
I'M SERIOUSLY WEAK FOR THOSE PUPPY DOG EYES...

Continued in volume 5!

Tamifull

I want to move, but my current location
is very nice so I'm having a hard time
deciding what I should do. Part of me
wants to live in the heart of a bustling city.

HOW DO WE RELATIONSHIP?

VOLUME 4

VIZ MEDIA EDITION

STORY AND ART BY
Tamifull

ENGLISH TRANSLATION & ADAPTATION
Abby Lehrke

TOUCH-UP ART & LETTERING
Joanna Estep

DESIGN
Alice Lewis

EDITOR
Pancha Diaz

TSUKIATTE AGETEMO IIKANA Vol. 4
by TAMIFULL
© 2019 TAMIFULL
All rights reserved.
Original Japanese edition published by SHOGAKUKAN.
English translation rights in the United States of America, Canada, the United
Kingdom, Ireland, Australia and New Zealand arranged with SHOGAKUKAN.

Published by VIZ Media, LLC
P.O. Box 77010
San Francisco, CA 94107

10 9 8 7 6 5 4 3 2 1
First printing, October 2021

VIZ MEDIA

viz.com

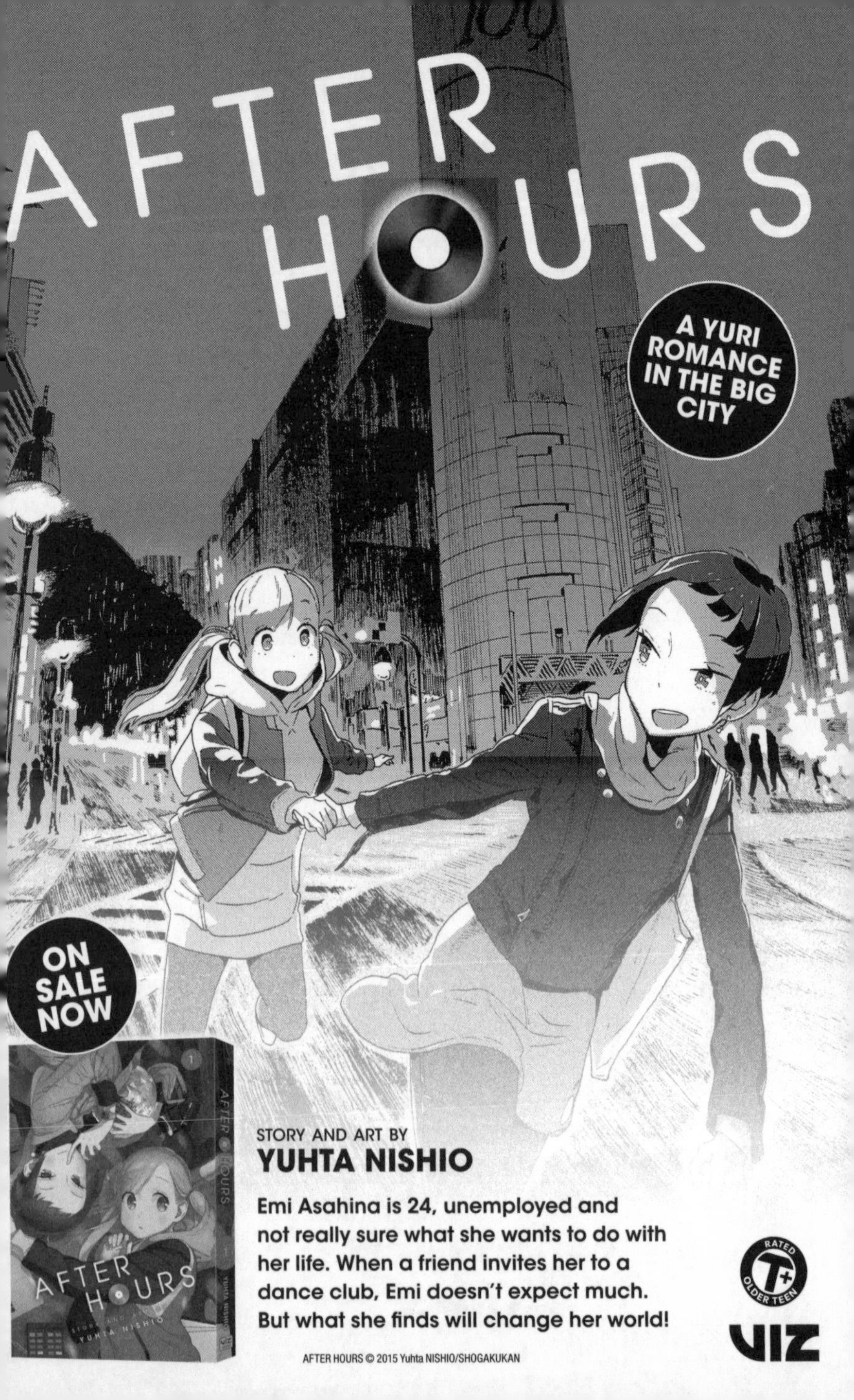
AFTER HOURS
A YURI ROMANCE IN THE BIG CITY
ON SALE NOW
STORY AND ART BY
YUHTA NISHIO
Emi Asahina is 24, unemployed and not really sure what she wants to do with her life. When a friend invites her to a dance club, Emi doesn't expect much. But what she finds will change her world!
RATED T+ OLDER TEEN
VIZ
AFTER HOURS © 2015 Yuhta NISHIO/SHOGAKUKAN

Sweet Blue Flowers

Story and Art by **Takako Shimura**

Akira Okudaira is starting high school and is ready for exciting new experiences. And on the first day of school, she runs into her best friend from kindergarten at the train station! Now Akira and Fumi have the chance to rekindle their friendship, but life has gotten a lot more complicated since they were kids…

Collect the series!

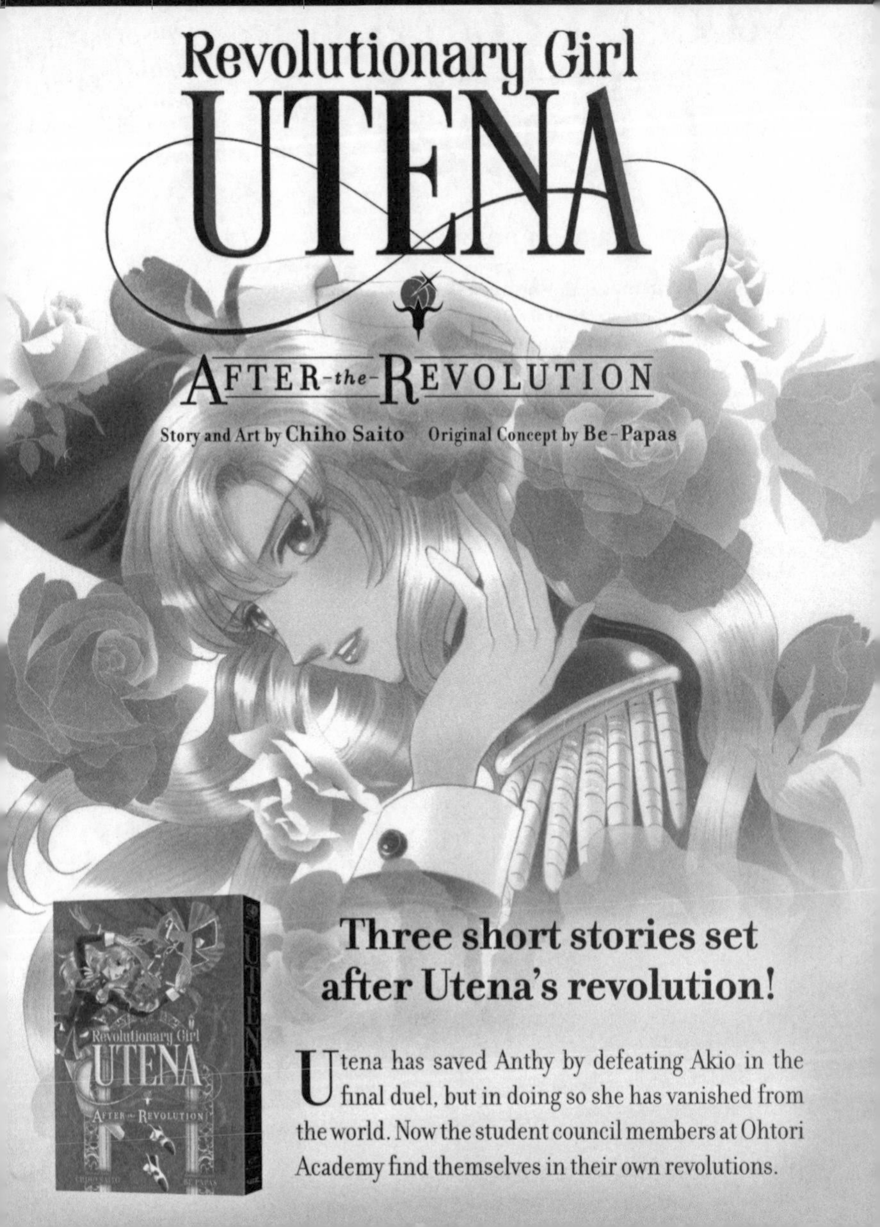
Revolutionary Girl
UTENA
AFTER-the-REVOLUTION
Story and Art by Chiho Saito Original Concept by Be-Papas
Revolutionary Girl
UTENA
AFTER the REVOLUTION
Three short stories set after Utena's revolution!
Utena has saved Anthy by defeating Akio in the final duel, but in doing so she has vanished from the world. Now the student council members at Ohtori Academy find themselves in their own revolutions.

Fushigi Yûgi
BYAKKO SENKI

STORY AND ART BY **YUU WATASE**

The final *Fushigi Yûgi* story in the Universe of the Four Gods begins!

The year is 1923. Suzuno Osugi's father Takao warns her to stay away from *The Universe of the Four Gods*, telling her it's a book that only men can touch. Takao worked with late Einosuke Okuda, who translated its text. He knows that in order to enact its story, the book needs one last heroine: the priestess of Byakko!

VIZ

Queen's Quality

**Story & Art by
Kyousuke Motomi**

Fumi Nishioka lives with Kyutaro Horikita
and his family of "Sweepers," people who
specialize in cleaning the minds of those
overcome by negative energy and harmful
spirits. Fumi has always displayed mysterious
abilities, but will those powers be used for
evil when she begins to truly awaken
as a Queen?

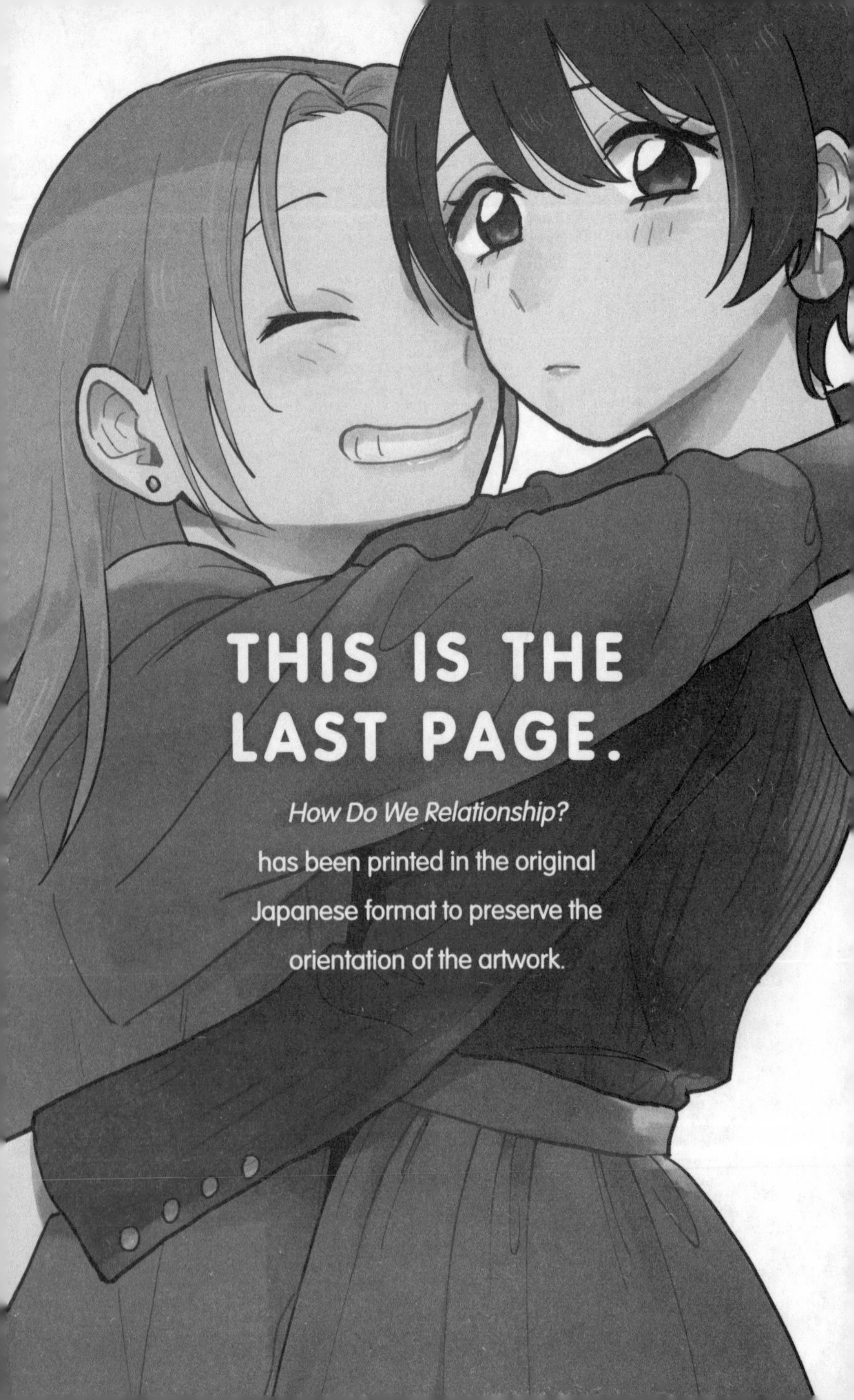

THIS IS THE LAST PAGE.

How Do We Relationship? has been printed in the original Japanese format to preserve the orientation of the artwork.